D1738677

WORD AND IMAGE IN ARTHURIAN LITERATURE

Word and Image in Arthurian Literature

Edited by
Keith Busby

Garland Publishing, Inc.
New York and London
1996

Library of Congress Cataloging-in-Publication Data

Word and image in Arthurian literature / edited by Keith Busby.
    p. cm.
    Includes bibliographical references.
    Contents: A pictorial synopsis of Arthurian episodes for Jacques
d'Armagnac, Duke of Nemours / Susan A. Blackman — Text and image /
Carleton W. Carroll — Imagines historiarum / Carol R. Dover — Seeing the
seer / Donald Hoffman — The implied Arthur / Elizabeth Mazzola — Arthurian
illuminations in Middle Dutch manuscripts / Martine Meuwese — The
discourse of the figural narrative in the illuminated manuscripts of Tristan (c.
1250–1475) / Jacqueline Thibault Schaefer — The illustrations of BN, fr. 95
and Yale 229 / Alison Stones — Discursive illustrations in three Tristan
manuscripts / Stephanie Cain Van D'Elden — The "roi pescheor" and
iconographic implications in the Conte del Graal / Michèle Vauthier —
Wonders and illuminations / Lori Walters.
    ISBN 0-8153-2050-7 (alk. paper)
    1. Arthurian romances—Illustrations. 2. Art. I. Busby, Keith.
N8215.W67 1996
808.8'0351—dc20   96-2769

Contents

Contributors

Susan A. Blackman
720 W. 48th St., #401
Kansas City, MO 64112

Carleton W. Carroll
Dept. of Foreign Languages
Oregon State University
Corvallis, OR 97331

Carol R. Dover
28 Avon Road
Wellesley, MA 02181

Donald L. Hoffman
Dept. of English
Northeastern Illinois
   University
5500 N. St. Louis Ave.
Chicago, IL 60625

Elizabeth Mazzola
4 Park Ave., #4G
New York, NY 10016

Martine Meuwese
NLCM
Rikjsuniversiteit Leiden
Postbus 9515
2300 RA Leiden
The Netherlands

Jacqueline Thibault Schaefer
Comparative Literature
   Program
The University of the South
Sewanee, TN 37383

Alison Stones
3210 Kelton Ave.
Los Angeles, CA 90034

Stephanie Cain Van D'Elden
1920 S. 1st St., #2304
Minneapolis, MN 55454

Michèle Vauthier
226, rue Lecourbe
75015 Paris
France

Lori Walters
Dept. of Foreign Languages
Florida State University
Tallahassee, FL 32306

Keith Busby
Dept. of Modern Languages
University of Oklahoma
Norman, OK 73019

WORD AND IMAGE IN ARTHURIAN LITERATURE

I A PICTORIAL SYNOPSIS OF ARTHURIAN EPISODES FOR JACQUES D'ARMAGNAC, DUKE OF NEMOURS

Susan A. Blackman

It was Cedric Pickford who first observed that Jacques d'Armagnac was a particularly avid reader of Arthurian romances.[1] For not only did he own multiple copies of Arthurian texts, he commissioned many, whereas his contemporaries tended to purchase them. I would like to point to further evidence of the Duke of Nemours's preference for Arthurian subject matter. My study of the duke's unique compilation of Arthurian romances (Paris, BN, fr. 112), with which Pickford was primarily concerned, and his two *Lancelot–Graals* (Paris, BN, fr. 113–116 and 117–120) shows that their miniature cycles were made to interrelate.[2] When taken together, the three cycles result in an exhaustive and largely non-repetitive visual synopsis of Arthurian episodes that emphasizes the completeness of the narrative.

All three manuscripts have the *Lancelot, Queste del Saint Graal,* and *Mort le roi Artu,* romances from the so-called *Vulgate Cycle* or *Lancelot–Graal.*[3] Their miniature cycles additionally have *moduli* that are identical or close variants one of the other. A focus on this specific combination of texts and images has lent itself to an investigation of both iconography and its treatment by Jacques d'Armagnac's artists.

The Duke of Nemours's desire for a synoptic collection of Arthurian images may have evolved from the time he inherited Jean de Berry's *Lancelot–Graal* (fr. 117–120). That manuscript was likely to have been in the same lot with a *Cas des nobles hommes et femmes* (Geneva, BPU, fr. 190), which the Duke of Nemours inherited from this same great-grandfather prior to 1465.[4] It includes the usual five romances of the Vulgate Cycle (i.e., the *Estoire del Saint Graal,* the *Estoire de Merlin,* the *Lancelot du Lac,* which is three times as long as the *Queste del Saint Graal* and the *Mort le roi Artu* combined), plus the *Suite du Merlin.* The *Lancelot* proper is amplified after f. 495 by accounts of Bohort, Lionel, Hector, and Gauvain in search of Lancelot.[5] Textually, it is related to Arsenal 3479–3480, and Pickford thought it might have been copied in the same shop.[6]

The miniatures, secondary decoration, and rubrics had been finished for Jean de Berry, but several miniatures were repainted for Armagnac.[7] In general, the Duke of Nemours's artists left Berry's trees, castles, abstract (and costly) gold, and diapered backgrounds untouched. Out-of-date features, such as old-fashioned armor with square ailettes and women's attire, were also left intact in many cases. What they most frequently retouched were coats of arms, helmets, and hauberts. The flaked paint of the miniature on f. 537 lets one see precisely how Perceval's arms were changed. Originally rose with white St. Andrew's crosses, they were repainted purplish with gold Greek crosses, as is proper for Perceval at this time.[8] In another miniature (f. 534), the trappings of Lancelot's horse were updated from plain orange, to white and silver filigree with orange bends and gold filigree.

On the other hand, changes to Berry's miniatures were not solely made for the purpose of modernizing heraldry, as these examples might suggest. Some repainting deliberately altered subject matter as well. The miniature on f. 536 previously showed a knight with vermilion arms rescuing Perceval in a landscape before a diapered background. Armagnac's artist retained only the landscape and background of this image; he converted the vermilion arms of the knight at left into those of the up-to-date Perceval, and he gave Perceval a troop of opponents to fight. The repainted image now illustrates an earlier moment of the same adventure, which describes Perceval fighting alone before he is aided by the Red Knight (Galahad). The rubrics generally summarize the account and thus would have applied equally well to the former, overpainted image:

> Comment mesire Perceval se combaist contre ung grant tas de chevaliers qui le prindrent et le vouloient tuer mais par la voulante de Dieu feust secouru par ung chevalier aulx armes vermeilles que se ferist a la forest conque Perceval ne le peust a consuivre car a pie estoit, mais lennemi en guise de dame luy amena ung cheval noir et lemporta en une roche ou il moult de choses vit.

In fr. 112 (IV), f. 19v, both Perceval and the Red Knight fight the adversaries, but here the rubrics focus better on the Red Knight's rescue:

> Comment apres que P[er]seval se fut p[ar]ti de la recluse il trouva xx ho[mm]es armes qui leusse[n]t o[cc]is si ne fut le ch[eva]l[ie]r a lescu vermeil q[ui] le descharga [et] lui occire[n]t son cha[va]l do[n]t il eust moult gra[n]t deuil.

Combined, the two miniatures make sequential sense and stress Perceval's combative role.

In another miniature representing the combat of Hector and Persides (f. 252), *pentimenti* show that Armagnac's artist changed the position of Berry's knights, added a new knight (Persides) who strikes the neck of Hector's horse with his sword, and added a horse at the far left of the picture. Armagnac's image is the more active and descriptive of the text, which states that Persides abused Hector's horse in precisely this manner. Particularly exciting accounts, such as that of the battle between Bohort and the giant Maudit (fig. 1.1), could also encourage repainting.

Some changes made to the miniatures were intended to clarify or amplify Berry's iconography. For the miniature depicting Méléagant's stepsister helping Lancelot to escape from his prison (f. 333), Armagnac's artists added a tower, representing Méléagant's prison, as well as Lancelot and Méléagant fighting with swords, details mentioned by the text. In an evident attempt to better localize the battle, similar additions were also made to the miniature showing the combat of Lancelot and Bohort at the Tertre Devée (f. 435).

When he commissioned fr. 113–116, the Duke of Nemours chose a text specimen with a different and longer pictoral cycle than that of fr. 117–120. The iconographical chart at the end of this discussion shows where the two picture cycles agree and deviate from each other. It also shows how fr. 112's cycle complements and amplifies their programs. The interlacing of the three cycles involved no small acquaintance with the texts. The task was obviously orchestrated by someone in a position to supervise the repainting of miniatures in fr. 117–120 and to stipulate any alterations to the miniature cycle of fr. 113–116. If not Armagnac himself, I would suspect this program director was the duke's longtime scribe and compiler, Michel Gonnot.

While it lacks the *Suite du Merlin,* fr. 113–116 does have the same textual additions pertaining to Bohort, Lionel, Hector, and Gauvain, as fr. 117–120.[9] Between its *Queste del Saint Graal* and the *Mort Artu,* there is an account of Tristan's death (ff. 673b–676c) and an episode borrowed from the second version of the Post-Vulgate *Queste* (ff. 676c–677d); both borrowings are unique. In addition, fr. 113–116 uniquely includes excerpts from the *Tristan* in prose: the birth of Tristan (f. 178), the combat of Tristan and the Morholt (f. 206), the combat of Tristan and Lancelot (f. 674), Tristan swearing the oath of the knights of the Round Table (f. 676), and the death of Tristan (f. 676v). The *Estoire del Saint Graal* is closest textually to London, BL, Royal 14 E III and Amsterdam, Bibliotheca Philosophica Hermetica (ms. 1 in three volumes);[10] while the *Estoire de Merlin* is textually most like the Amsterdam copy.[11]

To judge from the some 130 Lancelot miniatures in fr. 113–115, the manuscript model Armagnac provided his workmen was close to the fourteenth-century *Lancelot–Graal* in Amsterdam, and its complementary volumes in Manchester and Oxford.[12] In both copies, the miniatures occur in the same (or very nearly the same) locations, and their subjects are identical roughly three-fourths of the time. There also seems to be an example of contamination. Like the image from the Amsterdam copy (vol. III, f. 1), the corresponding miniature in fr. 114 (f. 327v) mistakenly depicts the Duke of Cambenic's cousin as male instead of female, although the text stipulates a cousin of female gender.

However, the fourteenth-century cycle differs from that of fr. 113–116 in ways that suggest a considerable amount of editorial license on the part of Armagnac or his program director. The two cycles occasionally illustrate different episodes of the same account or chapter. For instance, Armagnac's book shows Lancelot being assaulted at Escalon li Tenebreux rather than Lancelot and Yvain talking to "the sister of the damsel who took Galeshin to Pintadol," a prior episode of the chapter shown in the Amsterdam book (no. 94). One sees Lancelot slaying beasts in the Valley of False Lovers instead of Lancelot and Yvain riding together after this adventure (no. 96), as in the Amsterdam work. And a generic battle scene replaces the combat of Lancelot and Karados at the Dolorous Tower in the Amsterdam manuscript (no. 102).[13]

More subtle differences are found when the cycles illustrate different moments of the same episode. Fr. 115 shows Lancelot simply sitting in the dwarf's cart (no. 117). In the Amsterdam manuscript he is pelted with mud, which happens when the people later see him. Or one might see the cycles conflating or simplifying different miniature subjects. The combat of Gaheriet and Brehus sans Pitié is amplified in Armagnac's manuscript by the addition of Gauvain asking Lancelot not to fight his brothers at the assembly of King d'Outre les Marches (no. 22). Conversely, no. 173 shows Hector riding past a tree having the many shields Terican won from knights in Armagnac's book; the corresponding Rylands image fuses this with the subsequent combat of Hector and Terican.

The last of this group, fr. 112 is a unique compilation of Arthurian texts that contains all the *Lancelot* proper, the prose *Tristan*, three versions of the *Queste del Saint Graal,* the *Mort Artu,* and fragments of the *Huth–Merlin, Palamèdes,* and *Prophéties de Merlin.* [14] It has textual features in common with several manuscripts, including BN, fr. 113–116 and Turin, BN, L. I. 7–9 (*Guiron le Courtois* or *Palamèdes*).[15] G. Hutchings, in fact, suggested that BN, fr. 114–115 was used as a textual model by the scribe/compiler Michel Gonnot because the corresponding *Lancelot* texts resemble each other even to the paragraph divisions. [16]

The resemblance does not apply to the miniature cycle in fr. 112, which differs iconographically from those of fr. 113–116 and fr. 117–120. Except for Book III in fr. 112, which is virtually unillustrated, the compilation amplifies the visual imagery of the other two manuscripts by adding 31 new illustrated subjects to the *Lancelot* proper,[17] 21 new subjects to the *Queste del Saint Graal,*[18] and 17 to the *Mort Artu.* [19] These subjects illustrate various episodes from the text, and often require knowledge of both the text and rubrics. Without such knowledge, the reader would be unable to make sense of the figures who are otherwise unidentified by the image. No. 39 shows a knight in armor, standing between a woman and a seated knight who looks up at him with hands clasped as though in prayer. It is the rubrics that tell us Gauvain and Segurades fought because the latter wished to marry a woman against her will: "Comment messire Gauvain se combatit alencontre de Segurades q[ui] vouloit esposer une da[m]e a force." The text recounts that "Segurades begged Gawain not to force him to pronounce the shameful word, and to intercede for him with the lady." [20] If we are familiar with the story, we can infer that the woman is the Lady of Roestoc. The next image from fr. 112 shows the Lady of Roestoc at Arthur's court inquiring about the identity of her rescuer (no. 40). Arthur and Guenievre are seated on a canopied bed; a woman comes before them to tell them of the encounter of her knight and Segurades. The rubrics describe the image: "Comment la dame de Rohestor vint en la court du roy Artus et luy compta de la bataille de son chevalier et de Segurades." The text explains further that she had gone to Arthur's court because she had allowed Gauvain to slip away before properly thanking him and learning his name.[21] She was "beside herself with grief" and hoped that Arthur could name the knight. These two examples, besides pertaining to the sense of the text, fit chronologically between the illustration of Gauvain and Segurades's combat in fr. 114 (no. 38) and the arrival of the messenger of the Damsel of the Lake and a knight defeated by Gauvain at Arthur's court, which is shown in fr. 118 (no. 41).

The program director paid close attention to the proper temporal sequence of the narrative. During the battle between Arthur against the Saxons and Irish, Lancelot wounds Hargodrabans in the thigh. This subject is illustrated in both fr. 114 and fr. 118 (no. 67). It is appropriately complemented in fr. 112 by a miniature showing Guenievre embracing Lancelot for having freed Arthur and his knights (no. 68). The latter stand outside Camille's prison, where they had been captured and imprisoned during the war. When we come to the account of the false Guenievre and the true queen's reconciliation with Arthur, fr. 114 shows the false Guenievre on her deathbed, being visited by Arthur and Gauvain (no. 80). Fr. 112 follows with an image of the real queen's subsequent return to Arthur from Sorelois, where she had lived while the false Guenievre enjoyed Arthur's company (no. 81). Fr. 118 then has Guenievre talking to Galehaut, Lancelot, and a lady upon her return (no. 82). Fr. 114 ends this group of related illustrations by showing Guenievre kneeling, begging Lancelot to remain at Arthur's court rather than return to Sorelois with Galehaut (no. 83).

Even when the iconography is essentially the same in all three miniature cycles, there could be a suggestion of temporality. No. 95 treats a damsel's attempts to help and subsequently free Gauvain from Karados's prison. In fr. 114 she simply stands outside a prison. In fr. 112, accompanied by a group of women, she speaks to Gauvain through the prison window. Having discovered that Gauvain is in need

ARTHURIAN EPISODES FOR JACQUES D'ARMAGNAC

of pest control, the damsel in the miniature of fr. 118 extends a pole, at the end of which is poisoned bread for the vermin inside.

The Duke of Nemours's interest in the comprehensiveness of his miniature cycles, which function as visual reminders of the narrative, is further indicated by the fact that only 17 miniature subjects (less than 5 percent of Tables 1.2 through 1.4) are duplicated in all three cycles.[22] Five of the duplicated subjects, in turn, have no parallels in the Amsterdam/Rylands/Douce cycle, but they do seem to have been part of fr. 117–120's original cycle. The birth of Lancelot (no. 1), Lancelot retaking the Dolorous Guard (no. 21), the Crucifixion (no. 238), the Holy Grail appearing to knights of the Round Table (no. 244), and the combat of Lancelot and Gauvain (no. 324) would thus seem to have been special requests of the Duke of Nemours for fr. 113–116 and fr. 112.

A Note on the Moduli in BN, Fr. 112–120

There was certainly some form of pattern copying among the artists of Jacques d'Armagnac, since his Arthurian miniatures have similar patterns that are differentiated by variations of hand and occasionally minor details. The Round Table in image no. 251 is a pattern additionally differentiated by scale—it is large in fr. 112 and fr. 120 (fig. 1.2), and small in fr. 116. A closed circle that is opened in the center, this Round Table is an unprecedented type in Arthurian books.[23] Four, apparently traced, patterns are seen in the large quadripartite miniatures of fr. 112 (fig. 1.3) and fr. 116 (fig. 1.4), which preface the *Queste del Saint Graal* (no. 245). Here, fr. 112 rearranges the subjects of fr. 116's composite image. The representation of Lancelot greeting Galahad is placed in the left lower quarter of fr. 112's format; that of Lancelot knighting Galahad has been moved to the right lower quarter. One finds the depiction of Lancelot traveling to the convent where he meets Galahad on the next page in fr. 112 (fig. 1.5). These comparative miniatures show figure groupings that are so close they would seem to have been traced from the same module, and fitted into an image format that is roughly the same size in both manuscripts.[24]

I have briefly described the figure grouping from the 17 miniatures duplicated in all three romances as follows:

TABLE 1.1

Comparative Figure Groupings in BN Fr. 112–120

Fr. 113–116	Fr. 112, Book II	Fr. 117–120
No. 1. Birth of Lancelot (f. 1, top right). Helen in bed, infant held by attendant, 2 more attendants.	(f. 1) Same as 113 but fewer attendants, left	(f. 1) Same as in fr. 114, but more attendants shown
No. 21. Lancelot at the Dolorous Guard (f. 1, bottom right). 2 wildmen raise their swords against Lancelot	(f. 78) L. fights 2 wildmen at right	(f. 200v) L. repainted. He approaches wildmen with raised sword.
No. 27. Galehaut's homage to Arthur (f. 239v). G. kneeling, extending his sword to a mounted king	(f. 96v) Same; no sword	(f. 215v) Entirely repainted and like fr. 114
No. 30. First kiss of Lancelot and Guenievre (f. 244v). Contrary to the text, Lancelot embraces and kisses Guenievre. Galehaut and the Lady of Malohaut flank them. 3 ladies nearby	(f. 101) G. kisses Lancelot in Galehaut's presence; 5 ladies at right	(f. 219v) Heads and foreground repainted. L and G kiss; 3 ladies Galehaut at left
No. 44. Gauvain defeating a knight in a tower (f. 260). Paired mounted knights jousting	(f. 116v) 2 mounted knights fight with swords	(f. 231v) Knights repainted and jousting. Mounted lady holds sword
No. 52. Hector defeating Marganor (f. 272). Two knights with swords	(f. 128v). Paired knights jousting; tower added	(f. 240v) Knights repainted and fighting with swords. Sky added
No. 57. Gauvain killing the seneschal of the duke of Cambenic (280v). Paired mounted knights with swords	(f. 136v) Same	(f. 247) Repainted except for trees. Subject as in fr. 115
No. 89. Lancelot removing Drian from the litter (f. 329). Lady and 2 knights watch	(f. 215) Same. Spectators astonished.	(f. 286) Untouched night scene. A wounded knight slides into the arms of L. and a lady. 2 knights hold torches
No. 95. A lady helping Gauvain to escape from Karados's prison (336v). Lady stands outside a single-naved building. No Gauvain	(f. 223) A group of women talk to Gauvain through a lower window	(f. 288) Untouched. Lady gives Gauvain poison for the vermin bedeviling him in prison

Fr. 113–116	Fr. 112, Book II	Fr. 117–120
No. 96. Lancelot in the Valley of False Lovers (338v). He raises sword against 2 lions and 2 dragons	(f. 224v) L. raises sword against 4 dragons	(f. 296v) Repainted. L. raises sword (?) against 2 dragons before a lady
No. 245. Composite image (f. 607)	(ff. 1 and 2)	(f. 520) Untouched image showing Crucifixion. Similar to fr. 116 with inclusion of Joseph of Arimathea collecting Christ's blood in a chalice
No. 251. The Holy Grail appearing to knights of the Round Table (f. 610v). Round Table with opened center. Names of knights inscribed on their chairs	(f. 5) Same. 2 angels support Grail. Knights identified with much variation from fr. 116 (names transcribed in cat. nos. 72 & 76)	(f. 524v) Entirely repainted. Same table. 2 angels support Grail. Knights not identified
No. 255. Galahad raising the lid of a tomb (f. 615v). Fire, smoke, and devil emerge. Knight in armor inside. 2 white-robed monks watch from building	(f. 10v) Devil emerges. Knight in white shroud. Man astonished. 2 monks in Gothic church	(f. 258) Largely repainted. Smoke and devil emerge. Knight in armor inside tomb. G.'s helmet and shield in foreground. Church
No. 258. Galahad fighting group of knights (618v). All mounted with swords	(f. 13) G. jousting against group before castle	(f. 530) G. jousting with 7 knights, left
No. 262. The Holy Grail curing a sick man (f. 621). Lancelot reclines with elbow on helmet, hand on head. Sick man kneels before an altar with chalice, crucifix, and candlesticks	(f. 15v) L. sits upright and watches. Sick man kneels before altar with chalice and multi-branched candlestick	(fr. 117, f. 1, bottom right) Repainted in part. Same pose for L. as in fr. 116. 2 angels with chalice hovering over tall crucifix
No. 325. Lancelot, Hector, and Bohort rescuing Guenievre (f. 701). The 3 joust with a larger group. Queen kneels, male figure stands behind her, bonfire opposite.	(f. 204v). Mounted knights fighting with swords. Queen and 2 men standing before bonfire. Camelot behind walls.	(f. 581v) Repainted. 2 groups of knights jousting. Queen kneels before bonfire
No. 333. Combat of Lancelot and Gauvain (f. 716). They fight with swords as 2 groups of men and kings watch	(f. 220). Paired knights fighting with swords, afoot	(f. 590v) Repainted, and as in fr. 116, but 2 kings present. City added

Nos. 21, 44, 52, 57, 96, 258, 325, and 333 from table 1.1 employ various patterns of knights who joust or fight with swords.[25] The jousters are typically shown in profile, riding toward each other with lances down. Variants of the pattern show a knight breaking his lance on an opponent's shield, striking his opponent on the chest, which causes him to rear backward in the saddle or be unhorsed (fig. 1.6) and raising the shield better to protect himself from a blow. The knights might also overlap, as in fig. 1.1 (which also shows the breaking of lances). Similar variation applies to the patterns of knights who fight with swords rather than lances. Usually, they approach each other on foot with swords raised and about to deliver blows (figs. 1.7 and 1.8). Variants show them mounted, brandishing the sword after having vanquished an opponent or striking an opponent on the head. Less frequently one finds the knight about to strike a kneeling figure, the latter resulting from a module which is perhaps close to that of Galehaut in no. 27 and Guenievre in no. 325.

The repeated use of patterns obviously results in some visual monotony. But pattern variation and replication enabled the duke's artists to cover economically a great deal of text. They could distinguished the episodes of many like accounts and, with the help of heraldry, identify the figures of the numerous battles portrayed, Indeed, they could precisely illustrate the text. What the Duke of Nemours lost in compositional originality, he therefore made up for in the narrative comprehensiveness of his combined miniature cycles, as Tables 1.2–1.4 show.

Tables 1.2 through 1.4 list all the miniature subjects from the *Lancelot, Queste del Saint Graal,* and *Mort Artu* romances in BN, fr. 112, 113–116, and 117–120. They refer to corresponding text passages in the edition of H. O. Sommer (= S) and to chapters in Alexander Micha's (= M) critical edition of the *Lancelot* romance. They also include references to the fourteenth-century Amsterdam (= A)/Rylands/Douce manuscript.[26] Fuller descriptions of these miniatures will be found in the catalogue to my dissertation.

TABLE 1.2

Comparative Miniature Subjects in the *Lancelot* Proper

Fr. 113	Fr. 112, Book II	Fr. 118
1. Cf. top right image prefacing the *Estoire del Saint Graal*: The birth of Lancelot, 1	Left. The birth of Lancelot 1 (Robert de Borron prologue: *Moult seroit chose des plaisant*...; M 7/1a)	Cf. top left image prefacing the *Estoire del Saint Graal*, fr. 117, 1
2. Lancelot, Bohort, and Lionel with their parents. 150 v (S III 3:1; M 7/1a; A II 37)	—	155 (S III 3:1)
3. Left: Ban, Helen, and Lancelot departing from their castle	Right, 1	—
Right: Ban seeing his castle at Trebes burn and dying of sorrow, 154v (S III 12:29; M 7/3a; A III 41)	2 (S III 12:[29])	—
4. The Damsel of the Lake holding the infant Lancelot, 156v (S III 19:18; M 7/5a; A II 43v)	—	Cf. top right image prefacing the *Estoire del Saint Graal*, fr. 117, 1
5. —	Claudas traveling incognito to Logres, 3 (S III 28; M 7/5a)	—
6. Lancelot about to break a bow on his master for maltreating his greyhound, 162 (S III 33:23; M 7/9a; A II 49)	4	—
7. —	—	Bohort and Dorin fighting; Lionel attempting to help Bohort, 167 v (S III 47:[40]; M 7/12a)
8. Saraide with Bohort and Lionel, disguised as dogs, 167v (S III 47:41; M 7/12a; A II 54v)	5v, artist adds Claudas preparing to strike 2 children	—
9. —	The Damsel of the Lake escorting Lancelot to Arthur's court to be dubbed a knight of the Round Table, 61 (S III 118)	—

Fr. 114	Fr. 112, Book II	Fr. 118
10. —	Lancelot kneeling before King Arthur, 62 (S III 122:5)	—
11. Cf. bottom left image prefacing the *Estoire del Saint Graal:* Arthur knighting Lancelot, fr. 113, 1	Arthur knighting Lancelot, 62v (S III 127)	—
12. —	—	Battle scene; Lancelot and Keu fighting the 2 champions of the king of Northumberland on behalf of the Lady of Nohaut, 186 (S III 138:32; M 7/23a)
13. —	Lancelot defeating knights at the Dolorous Guard, 64v (S III 144; M 7/24a)	188
14. —	—	Lancelot about to enter the castle complex, Saraide holding the magic shield with 3 bends, 189v (S III 149; 38)
15. —	—	Lancelot raising the slab of a tomb at the Dolorous Guard and finding his name written inside, 190v (S III 152·36; M 7/24a; illus.)
16. A knight of the Round Table checking an assault on Arthur by the lord of the Dolorous Guard, 208 (S III 156:35; M 7/26a; A II 98v)	—	—
17. Lancelot routing knights at the Dolorous Guard and capturing its lord, Brandis, 211 (S III 165:10; M 7/30?; A II 102)	—	193c (S III 164:31; M 7/30a?)
18. —	Lancelot defending a knight who had been wrongly accused of dishonoring a woman, 68 (S III 172; M 7/32a)	196 (S III 173:13)

Fr. 114	Fr. 112, Book II	Fr. 118
19. Battle scene; Lancelot wounded at tournament by the king of the Hundred Knights, 216v (S III 179:17; M 7/34a; A II 108)	—	—
20. —	—	Lancelot convalescing at the castle of the Lady of Nohaut and receiving a letter from a damsel, 199 (S III 184:16; M 7/38a?)
21. Cf. bottom right image prefacing the *Estoire del Saint Graal:* Lancelot retaking the castle of the Dolorous Guard, fr. 113, 1	L. ends its enchantments, 78 (S III 191; M 7/40a)	200v (S III 191:7)
21. Accompanied by Gaheriet, Gauvain asks Lancelot not to fight his brothers (Agravain and Guerrehet) at the assembly of King d'Outre les Marches. Gaheriet defeats Brehus Sans Pitie, 221v (S III 194:8; M 7/41a?; A II 114)	—	—
23. Lancelot defeating 2 giants, 225v (S III 206:11; M 7/47a; A II 118v)	—	204v (S III 205)
24. —	—	Lancelot is captured and imprisoned by the Lady of Malehaut, 206v (S III 213; 21; M 7/48a)
25. Battle between forces of Galehaut, lord of the Loingtaine Isles, and Arthur, 234 (S III 242; M 8/49a; A II 129)	92	—
26. —	Same battle on subsequent day, 94 (S III 246)	—
27. Galehaut paying homage to Arthur and surrendering sword, 239v (S III 242; M 8/52aa; A II 135)	96v	215v

Fr. 114	Fr. 112, Book II	Fr. 118
28. —	—	Arthur, Guenievre, and Galehaut visiting Gauvain, who is sick in bed, 217
29. —	—	Lancelot and Guenievre meeting at a grove, 218 v (S II 258; M 8/52aa)
30. Lancelot and Guenievre kiss for the first time, 244v (S III 263; M 8/52aa; A II 140)	101	219v (Micha illustrates)
31. —	Gauvain and 19 companions search for Lancelot, 104 (S III 275; M 8/54a)	—
32. —	Gauvain recognizes Sagremor. With Yvain, Keu, and Girlet they arrive at the Fontaine du pin, 105v (S III 277; M 8/55a)	—
33. —	Sagremor and a knight jousting, 106 (S III 279; M 8/55a)	223 (M 8/55a)
34. —	—	A dwarf arrives to subdue the attacker (Hector des Mares), 223v (S III 280:26; M 8/55a)
35. —	Gauvain finds a beautiful damsel being groomed by attendants, 107 (S III 281; M 8/56a)	—
36. —	—	Hector defeating 2 knights, 225 (S III 286; M 8/56a)
37. —	Hector defeating a knight and 30 supporters on a bridge while Gauvain watches, 109 (S III 287; M 8/56a)	—
38. Gauvain defeating Segurades, 254 (S III 293:20; M 8/56a; A II 150v)	—	—
39. —	Segurades begging Gauvain not to force him to declare himself vanquished, 110 (S III 294)	—

Fr. 114	Fr. 112, Book II	Fr. 118
40. —	The Lady of Roestoc inquiring at Arthur's court about the identity of Gauvain, 113 (S III 300; M 8/56a)	—
41. —	—	A messenger of the Damsel of the Lake and a knight defeated by Gauvain approaching Guenievre and the Lady of Roestoc, 229v (S III 304; M 8/58a)
42. —	Guenievre receives a shield from the damsel's messenger, 114v (S III 304; M 8/58a)	—
43. —	—	The knight surrenders to the Lady of Roestoc, 231 (S III 305; M 8/58a)
44. Gauvain defeating a knight in a tower, 260 (S III 311:8; M 8/60a; A II 157)	116v	231v (S III 311:13)
45. —	—	Gauvain, a lady, and knights around the bed of a wounded knight (Agravain), 232 (S III 313:8; M 8/60)
46. —	Gauvain recognizing and greeting Agravain, 118 (S III 316; M 8/60a)	—
47. —	—	Hector and a dwarf discovering a lady and wounded knight, 234 (S III 322:14; M 8/61a)
48. —	Hector piercing Guinas's shield with his lance, 121 (S III 324)	—
49. Hector about to strike Guinas, 265 (S III 325:28; M 8/61a; A II 162)	—	—

Fr. 114	Fr. 112, Book II	Fr. 118
50. —	—	Hector approaching the castle of the Estroite Marche, 237v (S III 334; M 8/61a illus.)
51. —	—	Hector defeating Marganor at the castle of the Estroite Marche, 239 (S III 340:24)
52. Hector defeating Marganor, 272 (S III 346:10; M 8/61a; A II 170)	128v	240v (S III 340:24)
53. —	—	A dwarf telling Hector that he killed Maltaillié, 242 (S III 353:11; M 8/61a)
54. —	—	Maltaillié's pallbearers with his coffin, 243 (M 8/61a)
55. —	Battle scene: sympathizers of Maltaillié attacking Hector, 131 (S III 353:42; M 8/61a)	—
56. —	Battle scene: Gauvain fighting on the side of the duke of Cambenic against the king of Norgales, 134v (S III 363; M 8/63a)	245
57. Gauvain killing the seneschal of the duke of Cambenic, 280v (S III 371:34; M 8/63a; A II[?])	136v	247 (S III 371:15)
58. —	—	Gauvain lying with the daughter of the king of Norgales, 250 (S III 383; M 8/64a)
59. —	Combat of Hector and Persides 143 (S III 392; M 8/65a)	252
60. —	—	Battle scene: Gauvain fighting knights on the Pont Norgalois 253v (S III 396; M 8/67a)

Fr. 114	Fr. 112, Book II	Fr. 118
61. Hector and Gawain fighting incognito on the Pont Norgales, 289 (S III 398:22; M 8/68a; A II[?])	145	—
62. —	—	Hector and Gauvain fighting 2 of Galehaut's men outside the castle of the Ile Perdue, 254v (S III 401:33; M 8/70a)
63. —	Hector fighting the king of the Hundred Knights. Gauvain fighting Lancelot on the Ile Perdue, 146 (S III 402; M 8/70a)	—
64. —	Battle between Arthur and the Saxons, 148 (S III 408; M 8/70a)	—
65. —	—	Guenievre distraught upon seeing Lancelot in a demented state before her hostel, 258 (S III 415:5; M 8/71a)
66. —	Battle between King Arthur, the Saxons, and Irish recommences, 151 (S III 420)	—
67. Lancelot wounding Hargodrabrans in the thigh, 295v (S III 422; M 8/71a; A II 196)	—	L.'s general combat, 260
68. —	Guenievre embracing Lancelot for having freed Arthur and his men from Camille's prison, 152v (S III 426; M 8/71a)	—
69. Lancelot and Galehaut journeying to Sorelois, 297v (S IV 3:1; M 8/71a; A II 199)	—	—
70. The cousin of the false Guenievre at Camelot before Arthur's court, 300 (S IV 10:14; M 1/2?; A II 202)	—	Accompanied by Bertelet le Vieu, the cousin gives a letter to Arthur, 264 (S IV 11:13; M 1/3, illustrated)

Fr. 114	Fr. 112, Book II	Fr. 118
71. —	—	Bertelet le Vie is presented to Arthur, 265 (S IV 13:12; M 1/4)
72. —	Galehaut talking to wise clerks, 158v (M 1/15)	269v-a, Helyes of Toulouse expounding Galehaut's dream (S IV 32:30)
73. —	—	269v-b, Helyes and Galehaut in a chapel seeing an arm holding a bloody sword (S IV 33:26)
74. —	A knight standing between the "Pont d'espée" and "Pont dessous eau" 164 (S IV 40; M 1/6)	—
75. Arthur listening to the false Guenievre from a prison cell 313v (S IV 49:25; M 1/6; A Ii 218)	—	—
76. —	Arthur handing a letter to a messenger, 167 (S IV 51?; M 1/6)	—
77. Arthur's barons electing Gauvain king of England, 314 (S IV 51:15?; M 1/8; A II 219)		
78. —	The barons of Carmelide rejecting Guenievre as Arthur's lawful wife, 171 (S IV 56)	Bertelet le Vieu swearing on behalf of the false Guenievre, 275v (S IV 56:3)
79. —	Lancelot defeating knights for Guenievre, 172 (S IV 63; M 1/8)	277v
80. The false Guenievre on her deathbed, visited by Arthur and Gauvain, 321v (S IV 72:9; M 1/9; A II 227v)	—	—
81. —	Guenievre returning to Arthur from Sorelois, 211v (S IV 82)	—

Fr. 114	Fr. 112, Book II	Fr. 118
82. —	—	Lancelot, Galehaut, Guenievre, and a lady talking, 283 (S IV 83:19?)
83. Guenievre kneeling, begging Lancelot to remain at Arthur's court, 325v (S IV 84:12; M 1/9; A II 232)	—	—
84. —	Lionel knighted at King Arthur's court in London, 212v (S IV 86; M 1/10?)	—
85. —	Gauvain being seized by Karados of the Dolorous Tower 213 (S IV 88; M 1/10)	283v
86. The Duke of Clarence arriving at the White Castle, 327v (S IV 89:5; M 1/11; A III 1)	—	—
87. Yvain encountering a wounded knight, accompanied by a lady and knights, 328v (S IV 92:21; M 1/12; A III 2)	—	285a, Yvain omitted
88. —	Yvain attempting to remove the knight from the litter, 285b (S IV 93:8)	
89. Lancelot removing the knight, Drain "li gais," from the litter, 329 (S IV 93:22; M 1/13; A III 2v)	215	286 (S IV 94:11)
90. Yvain delivering a castle and lady from thieves, 330 (S IV 96:30; M 1/17; A III 4)	216v	—
91. Lancelot coming to the aid of Yvain in combat, 331v (S IV 100:10; M 1/19; A III 5v)	217	—
92. Galehaut and Lionel riding, 332 (S IV 101:19; M 1/15; A III 6)	—	—

Fr. 114	Fr. 112, Book II	Fr. 118
93. —	The duke of Clarence in combat with 3 knights at the castle of Pintadol, 219 (S IV 106:5; M 1/16)	—
94. Lancelot assaulted at Escalon li Tenebreux, 335 (S IV 109:16; M 1/20; A III 9)	220v	—
95. A lady helping Gauvain in Karados's prison, 336v (S IV 112:35; M 1/14; A III 10v	223	288
96. Lancelot slaying dragons in the Valley of False Lovers, 338v (S IV 118:24; M /21; A III 13)	224v	296v (M illus.)
97. Lancelot in Morgain's prison, 341v (S IV 126:34; M 1/24; A III 16v)	—	—
98. —	Morgain's damsel testing Lancelot's fidelity to Guenievre, 226 (S IV 127)	299v (S IV 127:38)
99. —	Lancelot and Morgain's damsel en route to the Dolorous Tower 227 (S IV 127; M 1/26)	—
100. Yvain being rushed by 10 knights of the Dolorous Tower, 343 (S IV 130; M 1/27; A II 18v)	—	—
101. —	Yvain and the duke of Clarence being led into the Dolorous Tower as prisoners, 228 (S IV 131)	—
102. Battle at the Dolorous Tower, 343v (S IV 132:1; M 1/28; A III 18v)	—	—
103. —	Lancelot and 3 knights defeating Karados's forces, 229 (S IV 133)	—

Fr. 114	Fr. 112, Book II	Fr. 118
104. —	Lancelot preparing to decapitate Karados, 230v (S IV 137)	—
105. —	Lancelot returning to Morgain's prison, 231v (S IV 139)	—
106. Having drugged Lancelot, Morgain exchanges her ring for his, 346v (S IV 139:37; M 1/29; A III 22)	—	—
107. —	Morgain's damsel displaying Lancelot's ring before Arthur's court in London, 232 (S IV 140; M 1/29)	—
108. Galehaut with Lancelot's shield, 348 (S IV 143:32; M 1/30; A III 24)	—	—
109. —	Galehaut fighting knights who see him with Lancelot's shield, 233 (S IV 144)	—
110. Gauvain fighting a knight, 349 (S IV 146:31; M 1/32; A III 25)	—	—
111. Lionel visiting Galehaut who is seriously wounded, 349v (S IV 148:22; M 1/32; A III 26)	—	—
112. Yvain rescuing Gauvain, 351 (S IV 147:26; M 1/33; A III 27v)	—	—

Fr. 114	Fr. 112, Book II	Fr. 119
113. —	Lancelot breaking the bars of Morgain's prison, 234 (cf. S IV 152; M 1/3). This image follows the text, which does not allow Morgain to release Lancelot; cf. no. 202	—

Fr. 114	Fr. 112, Book II	Fr. 119
114. —	Gauvain and Yvain finding Lancelot lamenting in a woods, 236 (S IV 153)	—
115. —	Death of Galehaut, 248 (S IV 155; M 1/35)	—
116. The Damsel of the Lake finding Lancelot roaming in a forest, 352 (S IV 155:19; M 1/34?; A III 29)	—	—
117. Gauvain and a squire seeing Lancelot in a cart pulled by a dwarf, 355v (S IV 162:39; M 2/36 illus.; A III 31v)	—	312v
118. Lancelot defeats 2 knights who guard a forest pass, 360 (S IV 171?; M 2/37; A III 37v)	—	—
119. A damsel directing Gauvain to the Pont Perdu, 361v (S IV 182:34; M 2/37?; A III 39)	—	—
120. Lancelot challenged by a knight, 366 (S IV 195:31; M 2/38; A III 43v)	—	—
121. Lancelot crossing the sword bridge, 367v (S IV 200:19; M 2/38 illus.; A III 45)	—	321v
Fr. 115	Fr. 112, Book III	Fr. 119
122. —	Battle scene; Lancelot fights Méléagant, 3 (S IV [203:26]; M 2/39). Ink sketch	—
123. Lancelot and Guenievre reconciled, 370v (S IV 208:37; M 2/39; A III 48)	—	327

Fr. 115	Fr. 112, Book III	Fr. 119
124. Lancelot's squire informing Gauvain and others that Lancelot left with a dwarf and never returned, 372 (S IV 213:18; M 2/39; A III 50)	—	—
125. Lancelot at the tournament of Pomeglai, 374 (S IV 218:40; M 2/41; A III 52)	—	—
126. Méléagant's sister helping Lancelot to escape from prison, 375v (S IV 222:22; M 2/42; A III 53v)	—	333 (S IV 222:22)
127. Lancelot about to decapitate Méléagant, 376v (S IV 225:1; M 2/42; A III 54v)	—	—
128. Margondes kneeling before Guenievre, 380v (S IV 236:20; M 2/43; A III 58v)	—	—
129. Bohort defeating Galindes, 383v (S IV 244:37; M 2/44; A III 61v)	—	—
130. Galindes kneeling before the Lady of Hongrefort, 386v (S IV 254:3; M 2/44; A III 65)	—	—
131. Messenger of the Damsel of the Lake inviting Bohort to the forest of Roevent, 387 (S IV 254:28; M 2/45; A III 65v)	—	—
132. Bohort rescuing the Damsel of Glocedon from knights en route to drown her, 393 (S IV 271; M 2/47; A III 72)	—	—
133. Lancelot greeting the knights who guard Galehaut's tomb, 394v (S IV 275:37; M 2/49; A III 73)	—	Lancelot meeting a damsel who leads him to Galehaut's tomb, 344 (S IV 275; M 2/49)
134. —	—	Arramant seizing a square, 346 (S IV 283:6; M 2/50)

Fr. 115	Fr. 112, Book III	Fr. 119
135. Lancelot and Argondas grappling, 400v (S IV 292:16; M 2/50; A III 79v)	—	—
136. Bohort rescuing Lambesgue, 402 (S IV 296:19; M 2/51; A III 81)	—	350
137. —	Patrides killing the count of Flanders, 223 (Sommer ref.?; M 2/52) (Note: Nos. 138 through 244 are not illustrated in fr. 112, Book III)	—
138. —	—	Lancelot defeating Patrides, 351v (S IV 294; M 2/52)
139. Patrides kneeling before Baudemagus, 403v (S IV 300:18; M 2/52; A III 82v)	—	—
140. Lancelot defeating a knight (Bohort) who seized Guenievre, 404 (S IV 301:11; M 2/53; A III 83)	—	—
141. —	—	Sagremore defeating a knight before Dodinel, 352v (S IV 302:24; M 2/54)
142. A damsel beating a dwarf who kissed her. Dodinel fighting the dwarf's knight, 408 (S IV 313:38; M 2/55; A III 87v)	—	354v
143. Lancelot and an old damsel encountering Griffon del Mal Pas, who displays a decapitated head, 409 (S IV 316:1; M 2/56; A III 88)		
144. —	—	Guenievre and her ladies crying upon seeing Griffon at the Fontaine aux Fees with both the head and Lancelot's shield, 355v (S IV 317)

145. Griffon kidnapping Keu, 409v (S IV 317:17; M 2/56; A III 88v) — —

146. Lancelot encountering a woman on a white mule, 410a (S IV 317:40; M 2/58; A II 89a) — —

147. Dodinel pursuing a lady on the plank of the Château de Langue, 410b (S IV 318:24; M 2/59; A III 89b) — —

148. Guenievre fretting in Lancelot's room, 410v (S IV 319:21; M 2/60; A III 89v) — —

149. Gauvain and companions at the Black Cross, agreeing to search separately for Lancelot, 411v (S IV 323:1; M 2/60; A III 91) — —

150. Agloval defeating Griffon and freeing Keu, 413v (S IV 329:5; M 2/62; A III 93) — —

151. Gauvain and Mathainas grappling, 414v (S IV 331:7; M 2/63; A III 93v) — —

152. Squires on their knees thanking Hector, who had defeated a despised knight, 415 (S IV 332:23; M 2/64; A III 94) — —

153. Lady approaching Gauvain, who is drinking at a fountain, 416 (S IV 334:36; M 2/65; A III 95) — —

154. — — Gauvain and Hector seeing the burning tombs, 363 (S IV 339; M 2/65)

155. Gauvain departing from Corbenic in a cart, 420 (S IV 347:25; M 2/66; A III 99) — —

Fr. 115	Fr. 112, Book III	Fr. 119
156. Hector defeating the knight on the bridge, 420v (S IV 349:22; M 2/67; A III 99v)	—	—
157. —	—	Hector killing 2 lions and delivering a lady from the cave they guard, 366v (S IV 352; M 2/67)
158. Yvain defeating a knight who wanted his horse, 422v (S IV 355:5; M 2/68; A III 102)	—	—
159. Mordred seizing the hair of the dwarf who shot and killed his horse with an arrow, 424 (S IV 358:14; M 2/69; A III 103)	—	—
160. Agravain seeing monks mourn the death of a knight killed by Drias le Felon. Agravain decapitating Drias, 425v (S V 3:1; M 4/70 illus.; Douce 215, f. 1)	—	Omits second part, 369v
161. Gueheriet delivering an old knight from an attack by several others, 428 (S V 10:[11]; M 4/71; Douce 215, f. 3v)	—	—
162. —	—	Gueheriet defeating a knight who won a damsel he coveted, 374 (S V 29–30; M 4/71)
163. —	—	Gueheriet defeating a knight of the count of Guinas as Sagremor watches, 376 (S V 27; M 4/71)
164. Gaheriet defeating Guinas, 436v (S V 37:[28]; M 4/72; not illus. Douce 215 or Rylands ms. 1)	—	—
165. —	—	Gaheriet defeating a knight and rescuing Brandelis, 379v (S V 39; M 4/72)

Fr. 115	Fr. 112, Book III	Fr. 119
166. —	—	Gaheriet defeating Guidan, 381 (S V 45; M 4/72)
167. —	—	Gaheriet, Gueheriet, and Agravain fighting in a battle against the duke of Kales's son, 384v (S V 54; M 4/72)
168. Lionel returning to Arthur's court, 444v (S V 59:15; M 4/73; Rylands ms. 1, f. 1)	—	—
169. Guenievre's dream: Lancelot finding a beautiful damsel asleep in bed, 446 (S V 63:[20]; M 4/74; Rylands ms. 1, f. 15)	—	—
170. Lancelot encountering a sad damsel whose sister was dishonored, 447v (S V 67:[14]; M 4/75; Rylands ms. 1, f. 16v?)	—	—
171. Lancelot arriving at the poisonous fountain where he finds two couples eating, 449 (S V 71:[6]; M 4/76; not illus. Rylands)	—	—
172. Lancelot sleeping. Lionel awake in a landscape, 455 (S V 88:[38]; M 4/76; Rylands ms. 1, f. 24)	—	—
173. Hector riding past a tree where he sees the many shields that Terican has won from knights, 455v (S V 89; M 4/77; Rylands ms. 1., f. 24v	—	—
174. —	—	Combat of Hector and Terican, 393v (S V 90:25)
175. Still asleep, Lancelot is carried away by 3 enchantresses (Queen Sorestan, Morgain, and Sebile), 456 (S V 91:[23]; M 4/78; Rylands ms. 1, f. 25v)	—	—

Fr. 115	Fr. 112, Book III	Fr. 119
176. —	—	Tournament: Lancelot fighting on behalf of King Baudemagus, 396 (S V 101; M 4/78)
177. —	—	Lancelot slaying a fire-breathing dragon at Corbenic, 397v (S V 106:25; M 4/78)
178. —	—	Lancelot under Brisane's spell and about to sleep with King Pelles's daughter, 398v (S V 110:21; M 4/78)
179. Lancelot threatening Pelles's daughter with sword in hand, 463v (S V 111:[23]; M 4/79; Rylands ms. 1., f. 33v)	—	—
180. —	—	A squire and Lancelot at the cross of the Forêt Perdue, 401v (S V 121:2; M 4/79)
181. Combat of Yvain and Bohort (incognito) over a dog, 468 (S V 124:[35]; M 4/80; Rylands ms. 1, f. 38v)	—	403 (S V 125:3)
182. —	—	An old woman and Yvain approaching a pavilion where they find a helmet and sword, 403v (S V 127:19)
183. —	—	Yvain defeating Triadan du Plaissié, 405v (S V 133:38; M 4/80)
184. Bohort visiting the Lady of Gallevoye, 473 (S V 138:[36]; M 4/81; Rylands ms. 1, f. 44)	—	—
185. Gauvain taking leave of a lady and squire, 476a (S V 147:[37]; M 4/82; not illustrated in Rylands ms. 1)	—	—

Fr. 115	Fr. 112, Book III	Fr. 119
186. Ladies and knights dancing to the magic carol, whose enchantments Lancelot ends, 476b (S V 148:28; M 4/83 illus.; Rylands ms. 1, f. 46)	—	—
187. Lancelot being attacked by a troop of knights, who kill his horse, 478 (S V 154:[39]; M 4/83; Rylands ms. 1, f. 48v)	—	410v (S V 154:41)
188. —	—	A damsel pulling Lancelot from a well infested with snakes, 411v (S V 157:36; M 4/83)
189. —	—	Lancelot seeing a knight with the severed head of a woman, 412v (S V 160:28; M 4/83)
190. —	—	Lancelot rescuing the damsel of no. 188 from the stake, 413v (S V 163:7; M 4/83
191. The knight of no. 189 surrendering his sword to Guenievre at Camelot, 482v (S V 167:[17]; M 4/83; Rylands ms. 1, f. 53v)	—	—
192. —	—	Lancelot retrieving Guenievre's letter from the Giant's Cross and being greeted by the queen's damsel, 416 (S V 171:13; M 4/84)
193. Guenievre receiving a letter from Lancelot, 483 (S V 171:36; M 4/84; Rylands ms. 1, f. 54)	—	—
194. —	—	Knights of the Round Table fighting in the tournament at Camelot, 417 (S V 176:20; M 4/84)

Fr. 115	Fr. 112, Book III	Fr. 119
195. —	—	Lancelot at the tournament 3 days later, 421 (S V 187; M 4/84)
196. —	—	Bohort, Gaheriet, Baudemagus, and Lancelot finding Mordred stripped and assaulted by the people of Matain le Félon, 423 (S V 197:3; M 5/85)
197. —	—	Combat of Bohort and Maudit, 424v (S V 202; M 5/85)
198. —	—	Same subject as no. 197 with slight variation, 426 (S V 202:37; M 5/85)
199. A lady informing Lancelot that Lionel is in Teriquan's prison, 494v (S V 204:27; M 5/85; Rylands ms. 1, f. 66v)	—	—
200. Lancelot fighting a robber-knight who took a damsel's palfry, 496v (S V 211; M 5/86; Rylands ms. 1, f. 69)	—	—
201. Gauvain visiting Baudemagus, who is convalescing in an abbey, 499v (S V 219; M 5/87; Rylands ms. 1, f. 72)	—	—
202. Lancelot breaking the bars of Morgain's prison to pluck a rose that reminds him of Guenievre, and escaping, 500v (S V 222–223; M 5/88; Rylands f. 73v)	—	—
203. Lancelot greeting a wounded knight, 501v (S V 224; M 5/88; unillus. in Rylands)	—	Lancelot asleep on the grass and approached by the wounded knight in a cart, 431 (S V 224:19; M 5/88)

204. —	—	Lancelot defeating Marrabron at the Ile Estrange, 432v (S V 230; M 5/88)
205. A monk giving alms to a starving king (Heliser), 504 (S V 231; M 5/89; unillus. in Rylands)	—	—
206. Lancelot and Lionel arriving at the abbey of the Petite Aumône, 505v (S V 235:8; M 5/89; unillus. in Rylands)	—	—
207. —	—	Lancelot arriving at a cross near Tertre Devée whose sign states that no one has ascended the hill without dying, 434v (S V 237:3; M 5/91)
208. —	—	Lancelot and Bohort (incognito) fighting at Tertre Devée, 435 (S V 238–239; M 5/91)
209. —	—	Having learned the name of his opponent, Lancelot shakes hands with Bohort, 435v (S V 239; M 5/91)
210. —	—	Bohort kneeling before a wounded knight of the Round Table and surrendering his sword, 439v (S V 242:16; M 5/91)
211. Lancelot slaying the lions that guard the tomb of his grandfather in the perilous forest, 507v (S V 244:5; M 5/93; Rylands ms. 1, f. 76v)	—	440v
212. Guenievre's messenger being interrogated about Lancelot by Claudas, 512 (S V 256:28; M 5/94; Rylands ms. 1, f. 81v)	—	—

Fr. 115	Fr. 112, Book III	Fr. 119
213. —	—	Guenievre secretly sending Claudas a threatening letter, 445 (S V 261; M 5/94)
214. Combat of Lancelot and Belyas le Noir, 514v (S V 263:36; M 5/95; Rylands ms. 1, f. 84v)	—	446v
215. —	—	Gauvain and companions defending Agloval against Galehodin's men, 449 (S V 272:29; M 5/95)
216. Lancelot and Mordred seeing a white stag and 4 lions, 519v (S V 277:37; M 5/96; Rylands ms. 1, f. 90)	—	—
217. —	—	Lancelot and Mordred arrive at a fountain; Mordred prepares to drink from it, 461v (S V 281:7; M 5/96)
218. —	—	Mordred about to kill the hermit who revealed his future, 462v (S V 285:6; M 5/96
219. Hector and Lionel searching the field at Galehodin's tournament for Bohort, 524v (S V 290:16; M 5/97; Rylands ms. 1, f. 95). Rubrics erroneously state that Bohort and Lionel find Mordred.	—	—
220. Bohort rescuing Landoine and Marant from thieves, 525v (S V 292:21; M 5/98; Rylands ms. 1, f. 96)	—	—
221. —	—	Bohort at Corbenic being introduced to Galahad, 466v (S V 296:40; M 5/98 illus.)

Fr. 115	Fr. 112, Book III	Fr. 119
222. Lancelot talking to a jealous husband and his brother before tents, 531v (S V 304:16; M 5/99; Rylands f. 101v)	—	—
223. Lancelot (with Keu's shield?) defeating Gauvain, Yvain, Hector, and Sagremor, 535v (S V 312:13; M 5/99; Rylands, ms. 1, f. 105v)	—	470 (S V 309:14)
224. —	—	A large group of knights jousting and Lancelot unhorsed by Gauvain, 474 (S V 317:19; M 6/100)

Fr. 115	Fr. 112, Book III	Fr. 120
225. Brumant l'Orgueilleux preparing to sit in the perilous seat, 539v (S V 320:21; M 6/100; Rylands ms. 1, f. 109v)	—	Brumant is consumed by the flames, 474 (S V 320:9; f. 474 is misnumbered and should be 475)
226. —	—	Having seized Gauvain, Arthur lifts him onto his horse, 475 (S V 326:1; M 6/101)
227. Lancelot recounting his adventures at Arthur's court, 544v (S V 332:8; M 6/101; Rylands ms. 1, f. 114v)	—	—
228. Battle scene: Forces of Arthur and the Romans in Flanders, 548 (S V 337:2; M 6/102; Rylands ms. 1, f. 118)	—	—
229. Claudas incarcerating British knights at Gaunes, 551 (S V 342:11; M 6/103; Rylands ms. 1, f. 121)	—	—
230. Battle before the castle of Tor, 552 (S V 344:4; M 6/104; Rylands ms. 1, f. 122)	—	481v (S V 342:11)

Fr. 115	Fr. 112, Book III	Fr. 120
231. Lancelot's messenger briefing Arthur at Camelot about the campaign in Gaul, 562v (S V 369:21; M 6/105; Rylands, ms. 1, f. 133)	—	—
232. —	—	Arthur defeating Frolle, 490v (S V 373; M 6/105)
233. Guenievre confronting Lancelot after he had been deceived a second time by Pelles's daughter, 568v (S V 381:11; M 6/105; Rylands ms. 1, f. 139)	—	493v (S V 380:15; M 6/105)
234. 2 mounted knights arriving at a castle where they are greeted by 2 men, 596v (Special addition, S V 413:1; Rylands ms. 1, f. 140v)	—	—
235. Bohort ascending a hill on which stands a hermit, 572 (Special addition, S V 419:28; Rylands ms. 1, f. 143v)	—	—

Fr. 116	Fr. 112, Book III	Fr. 120
236. Hector listening to the complaint of an old widow, 577 (Special addition, S V 432:21; Rylands ms. 1, f. 149)	—	—
237. —	—	Hector defeating Hernieux de Malagait (Hervi), 501 (Special addition, S V 439:13)
238. Gauvain arriving at the fountain that changes color five times a day, 586 (Special addition, S V 455:20; Rylands ms. 1, f. 158v)	—	505 (S V 455:30)
239. —	—	Gauvain fighting a knight on behalf of a disingenuous lady(?), 509 (Special addition, S V 457)

Fr. 116	Fr. 112, Book III	Fr. 120
240. Agloval visiting his mother and meeting Perceval, his young brother, 593v (S V 383:8; M 6/106 illus.; Rylands ms. 1. f. 167)	—	—
241. —	—	Top left: Perceval preparing to cut the chains from Patrides and defeating a knight, 512v (S V 388; M 6/106)
242. —	—	Combat of Perceval and Hector, 519 (S V 389:39; M 6/106)
243. Lancelot wandering into Bliant's pavilion, 598v (S V 393:39; M 6/107; Ryland ms. 1, f. 172)	—	—
244. A lady with a falcon telling Hector and Perceval where to find Lancelot, 604v (S V 404; M 6/108; Rylands ms. 1, f. 179v)	—	—

TABLE 1.3

Comparative Miniature Subjects in the *Queste del Saint Graal*

Fr. 116	Fr. 112, Book II	Fr. 117–120
245. Top left: Crucifixion with the Virgin Mary and St. John	Top left, 1	520
Top right: Arthur presenting Lancelot to a lady	Top right, 1	—
Bottom left: Lancelot escorting the lady to a convent	2 (S VI 4:35)	—
Bottom right: Lancelot greeting Galahad, 607 (S VI 3:1)	Bottom left, 1	—
246. —	Bottom right: Lancelot knighting Galahad, 1	522v (S VI 3:1)

37

Fr. 116	Fr. 112, Book II	Fr. 117–120
247. Lancelot taking leave of Galahad at the abbey, 607v (S VI 4:31)	—	—
248. Gauvain trying to remove the sword from the stone, 608v (S VI 7:6)	3	See no. 251
249. An old man assisting Galahad at the perilous seat, 609 (S VI 8:13)	3 v	—
250. A damsel on the grounds of Camelot informing Lancelot that he is no longer the best knight in the world, 610 (S VI 11:6)	—	—
251. The Holy Grail appearing to the knights of the Round Table, 610v (S VI 13:13)	5 (S VI 13:11)	524v (S VI 11:1); and left, Galahad pulling sword from stone
252. —	Galahad taking the oath to search for the Holy Grail, 6 (S VI 14)	526
253. A knight with white arms defeating Baudemagus for taking the shield reserved for Galahad, 614 (S VI 22:18; Rylands, ms. 1, f. 188)	8 v	—
254. Galahad, his squire, and the White Knight riding together, 614v (S VI 24:18)	9	—
255. Galahad raising the cover of a sarcophagus and seeing a knight in full armor, 615v (S VI 27:28; Rylands, ms. 1, f. 190)	10v	528
256. Having bid Galahad farewell, Melians takes the road to the left, 617 (S VI 31:1)	—	—
257. —	Melians defeated by a knight 11v (S VI 31:1)	—

Fr. 116	Fr. 112, Book II	Fr. 117–120
258. Galahad routing 7 knights at the Castle of the Maidens, 618v (S VI 35:18; Rylands ms. 1, f. 192v)	13	And he is given the keys to the castle, 530
259. —	Combat of Gauvain, Gaheriet, and Yvain against the 7 brothers, 14 (S VI 38:28)	—
260. Gauvain finding Melians convalescing at an abbey, 619 (S VI 37:27)	—	—
261. Galahad defeating Lancelot in combat. Perceval waits his turn, 620 (S VI 40:26)	15	—
262. The Holy Grail curing a sick knight as Lancelot watches, unable to move, 621 (S VI 42:35; Rylands, f. 195v)	15v	Cf. bottom right image prefacing the *Estoire del Saint Graal*, fr. 117, 1
263. Perceval asking a recluse (nun) for news of the knight with the white shield (Galahad), 623v (S VI 52:3)	18v (adds a knight)	—
264. —	Perceval and Galahad fight 20 opponents, 19v (S VI 63)	Perceval fighting alone, 536
265. —	Perceval slaying a dragon as a hermit and lion watch. An enchantress in a boat, 23 (S VI 68 & 75)	No hermit or enchantress, 537
266. —	Perceval talking to a hermit (monk), 27 (S VI 80)	—
267. A hermit admonishing Lancelot before a chapel, 634 (S VI 83:1; Douce 215, f. 14)	—	—
268. —	Lancelot kneeling before the hermit, confessing his sins, 129 (S VI 83)	—
269. —	—	Combat of Lancelot and a knight, 543 (S VI 94)

Fr. 116	Fr. 112, Book II	Fr. 117–120
270. —	—	Lancelot fighting at a tourney, 544 (S VI 100)
271. —	Gauvain and Hector seated in a chapel, 135v (S VI 106)	
272. Gauvain and Hector dreaming, 642 (S VI 106)	—	546; includes a disembodied floating arm in an orange sleeve, its hand holding a candle
273. —	Gauvain and Hector arriving at hermitage, 136v (S VI 108)	—
274. A kneeling knight (Yvain?) receiving Communion as another (Gauvain?) watches, 643v (S VI 110:30)	—	—
275. Bohort visits an old friar, 645v (S VI 116:17)	—	—
276. —	Combat of Bohort and Priadan, 155 (S VI 124)	549v
277. —	Combat of Bohort and a knight who seized a damsel, 155v (S VI 126)	—
278. —	Lionel about to strike the hermit protecting Bohort, 159v (S VI 136)	Lionel slaughters the hermit, 552, (S VI 136:31)
279. —	Galahad fighting marvelously at a tournament, 163b (S V 140)	—
280. Galahad defeating Gauvain at the tournament, 654 (S VI 141:1)	—	—
281. —	Galahad talking to a hermit at Corbenic. Lady present, 163v, (S VI 142)	—

Fr. 116	Fr. 112, Book II	Fr. 117–120
282. Galahad, his squire(?), and Perceval's sister standing in a ship at sea, 654v (S VI 142:[14])	—	—
283. —	Galahad, Bohort, Perceval, and P.'s sister on a ship, 3 trees on shore, 167 (S VI 143)	—
284. —	King Solomon and his queen on a ship. Solomon holding and pointing to David's sword, 169 (S VI 145)	—
285. Adam and Eve eating the forbidden fruit, 657v (S VI 151:11; Douce 215, f. 31v)	—	—
286. God commending Eve to Adam, 658v (S VI 153:12; Douce 215, f. 32)	—	—
287. Galahad, Bohort, and Perceval in Solomon's ship with David's sword and three spindles; they read a letter, 661 (S VI 161:23; Douce 215, f. 35)	170. Rubrics substitute Hector for Bohort	—
288. —	Galahad, Bohort, and Perceval fighting knights at Cartelois, 170v. Rubrics again name Hector instead of Bohort (S VI 163–164)	—
289. —	Galahad, Bohort, and Perceval fighting knights who want a dishful of blood from Perceval's sister, 172 (S VI 169)	—
290. Galahad and Perceval standing before the burning castle of the leprous lady, 665 (S VI 173:9; Douce 215, f. 39v)	—	—
291. —	Lancelot surrounded by forest, sea, and rocks at Marchoise, 174 (S VI 174)	—

Fr. 116	Fr. 112, Book II	Fr. 117–120
292. Having found the corpse of P.'s sister in a boat, Lancelot reads the letter that Perceval wrote about her, 665v (S VI 174:10)	—	—
293. —	Lancelot finds Galahad, 175 (S VI 177)	—
294. Having been charged by the White Knight to achieve the adventures of Logres, Galahad takes leave of Lancelot, 667 (S VI 178:1)	—	—
295. —	Lancelot struck down by a fiery wind at Corbenic, 176 (S VI 180)	—
296. King Mordrain collapsing into the arms of Galahad and dying, 669 (S VI 184:28)	177v	—
297. —	Galahad rejoins the broken sword, 178 (S VI 188)	—
298. —	Galahad, Bohort, and Perceval at Corbenic kneeling before an altar supporting the Holy Grail, 179v (S VI 190)	—
299. —	Galahad, Bohort, and Perceval arriving at Sarras, 180 (S VI 193)	—
300. Galahad, Bohort, and Perceval carrying the Holy Grail into Sarras. A beggar with crutches watches, 672 (S VI 195:4)	—	—
301. —	The beggar rises to help Galahad carry the Grail, 181 (S VI 195)	—
302. —	Galahad dying before the Holy Grail. Bohort and Perceval support him, 181v (S VI 197)	—

TABLE 1.4

Comparative Miniature Subjects in the *Mort le roi Artu*

Fr. 116	Fr. 112, Book IV	Fr. 120
303. Cf. top left image of Walter Map presenting his translation of the grail quest to King Henry, fr. 113, 1 (S VI 203:1)	—	—
304. Left: Bohort recounting the deaths of Galahad and Perceval at Arthur's court. Right: Gauvain admitting to having killed 18 questers, 678 (S VI 203:1)	Image shows a knight at Arthur's court, 182 (S VI 203:1)	—
305. —	Agravain telling Arthur about the love between Lancelot and Guenievre, 183 (S VI 205)	—
306. —	Arthur and his nephews watching the tournament at Winchester, 184v (S VI 210–211)	—
307. Gauvain and Gaheriet riding in search of Lancelot, 681v (S VI 241:1)	—	—
308. —	They meet 2 squires carrying a dead knight on a stretcher, 185v (S VI 214)	—
309. —	Gauvain telling Guenievre and Arthur that Lancelot wore a red sleeve and won the tournament at Winchester, 188v (S VI 220)	—
310. The Damsel of Escalot visiting Lancelot, who is convalescing from a serious wound, 685v (S VI 225:21)	She gives him a ring, 189v	—
311. —	Arthur and his company entering Morgain's castle, 192 (S VI 236)	—

Fr. 116	Fr. 112, Book IV	Fr. 120
312. Morgain showing Arthur the wall paintings that treat the history of Lancelot, including his love of Guenievre, 688v (S VI 237:25)	Arthur views them alone, 193v	—
313. Lancelot taking leave of the Damsel of Escalot, who is shown sick in bed, 690v (S VI 242:4)	—	—
314. —	Lancelot, Bohort, Gauvain, and the 2 brothers of Escalot riding, 194v (S VI 243). The rubrics substitute Hector for Bohort	—
315. —	Bohort telling Lancelot of the queen's ire against him, 195v (S VI 246)	—
316. —	Avarlon giving a poisoned apple to Guenievre, 196v (S VI 248)	—
317. Gaheries de Kareheu dying after having eaten the poisoned apple, 692v (S VI 248:[9])	—	—
318. Lancelot accidentally shot in the thigh by one of Arthur's huntsmen, 693v (S VI 250:9)	197	—
319. Battle scene: Bohort winning the prize at the tournament at Camelot, 695 (S VI 252:9)	197v. Rubrics substitute Hector for Bohort	—
320. Arthur and Gauvain looking into a barge that carries the dead maiden of Escalot, 695v (S VI 258:25)	They await the barge on shore, 199	—
321. Hector and Bohort at Arthur's court, 697v (S VI 263:4)	—	—
322. After having defeated Mador, Lancelot receives his sword, 698v (S VI 268;[16])	202	—

Fr. 116	Fr. 112, Book IV	Fr. 120
323. —	Agravain and knights surprising Lancelot at Guenievre's room, 203v (S VI 275)	—
324. —	Arthur's barons sentence the queen to death by fire, 204 (S VI 278–279). Rubrics misstate that Mordred sentenced Guenievre to death by fire	—
325. Lancelot, Hector, and Bohort defeating Arthur's knights and rescuing Guenievre, 701 (S VI 278:[36])	204v	581v
326. Arthur, Gauvain, and barons mourning the death of Gaheriet and the other knights killed by Lancelot and his kin, 702 (S VI 284:[6])	206	—
327. Arthur administering the oath of the Round Table to 72 new knights, 704v (S VI 293)	207v	—
328. —	Battle scene: the forces of Arthur and Lancelot fighting at the Joyous Guard, 209v (S VI 299)	—
329. —	Same battle on a subsequent day, 211 (S VI 304–307) (Folios 213–217 are missing here)	—
330. Lancelot's forces set sail for Benoyc, 711v (S VI 314:14)	—	—
331. Arthur's forces pursue Lancelot, 712 (S VI 316:29)	—	—
332. Mordred having a forged letter from Arthur read to the barons and Guenievre, 713v (S VI 321:11)	—	—

Fr. 116	Fr. 112, Book IV	Fr. 120
333. Combat of Lancelot and Gauvain at Gaunes, 716 (S VI 328:18)	220	590v (S VI 328:18)
334. —	Battle scene: Arthur's forces fighting the Romans, 221v (S VI 347)	—
335. Mordred besieging Guenievre in the tower at Logres, 722v (S VI 351:22)	—	—
336. Guenievre arriving at a convent, where she asks to take the veil, 723v (S VI 353:6)	—	—
337. Arthur and barons at Dover, mourning Gauvain's death, 724 (S VI 355:14)	223v	—
338. The lord of Beloe killing his wife on account of her love for Gauvain, 724v (S VI 358:[3])	224	—
339. Arthur's dream: Gauvain warns him not to fight Mordred without Lancelot, 725v (S VI 360:1)	—	—
340. —	Battle scene: Arthur's forces fighting Mordred and his allies at Salisbury, 226 (S VI 365)	—
341. —	Arthur mortally wounding Mordred with lance, 228v (S VI 376)	—
342. —	Girflet preparing to throw Excalibur into the lake, 229v (S VI 380)	—
343. —	Battle scene: Lancelot's forces fighting the sons of Mordred and their allies at Winchester, 231 (S VI 384)	—

Fr. 116	Fr. 112, Book IV	Fr. 120
344. Lancelot goes to a hermitage, where he lives with the archbishop of Canterbury and Blioberis and where he dies. Angels bear his soul to Heaven, 734 (S VI 387:24)	—	—
345. —	Blioberis and the archbishop placing Lancelot's body into Galehaut's tomb, 232v (S VI 388–389). Rubrics substitute Hector for Bohort and say that Hector caused Lancelot's body to be taken to the Joyous Guard	—

NOTES

1. Cedric Pickford, *L'Evolution de roman arthurien en prose vers la fin du moyen âge, d'après le manuscrit 112 du fonds français de la Bibliothèque nationale* (Paris: Nizet, 1959), pp. 278–290, esp. p. 289.

2. I draw on material from my University of Pittsburgh dissertation, *The Manuscripts and Patronage of Jacques d'Armagnac, Duke of Nemours (1433–1477)* (Ann Arbor, Mich.: University Microfilms, 1994), pp. 182–245.

3. Alexandre Micha, *Lancelot, roman en prose du XIIIe siècle*, 9 vols. (Geneva: Droz, 1979–83); Albert Pauphilet, *La Queste du Saint Graal: translaté des manuscrits du XIIIe siècle* (Paris: La Sirène, 1921), and *Etudes sur la Queste del Saint Graal* (Paris: Champion, 1921; Jean Frappier, *La Mort le roi Artu, roman du XIIIe siècle* (Paris: Droz, 1936). See also H. Oskar Sommer, *The Vulgate Version of the Arthurian Romances*, 8 vols. (Washington, D.C.: The Carnegie Institution, 1908–1916).

4. Blackman, *The Manuscripts of Jacques d'Armagnac*, pp. 73–76.

5. Alexandre Micha, "Les Manuscrits du Lancelot en prose," *Romania*, 81 (1960), p. 158.

6. Pickford, *L'Evolution du roman arthurien*, p. 280.

7. This was not an uncommon practice according to Jonathan Alexander, *Medieval Illuminators and Their Methods of Work* (New Haven and London: Yale Univ. Press, 1992), p. 47.

8. Michel Pastoureau, *Armorial des chevaliers de la table ronde* (Paris: Le Léopard d'Or, 1983), p. 95, no. 149.

9. Beginning on f. 569. For these text additions, see Micha, "Les manuscrits du *Lancelot* en prose," pp. 154–156; and Jean-Paul Ponceau, "Etude de la tradition manuscrite de *L'Estoire del Saint Graal*, roman du XIIIe

siècle" (Ph.D. diss. Univ. de Paris IV—Sorbonne, 1983; rev. 1986), pp. 142–147. Ponceau indicates that the additions are found equally in BN, fr. 342; Arsenal 3479–3480; London, BL, Harley 6342; and Manchester, Rylands Library, fr. 1.

10. Ponceau, op cit., 147.

11. Alexandre Micha, *Merlin, roman du XIIIe siècle* (Geneva: Droz, 1980). Fr. 113 is Micha's I.

12. For a recent discussion of these manuscripts, see Alison Stones, "Another Short Note on Rylands French I," in *Romanesque and Gothic: Essays for George Zarnecki*, ed. Neil Stratford (Bury St. Edmunds: Boydell and Brewer, 1987), 185–191. The complementary manuscripts are Manchester, Rylands Library, fr. 1, and Oxford, Bodleian Library, Douce 215. The three-volume Amsterdam manuscript is described and partly illustrated in *Cimelia. A Catalogue of Important Illuminated and Textual Manuscripts Published in Commemoration of the Sale of the Ludwig Collection. Catalogue 165* (New York: Kraus, 1983), pp. 12–15.

13. Cf. also (no. 2) Ban's castle being assaulted, below Ban, Helen and Lancelot leave the castle; (no. 83) Arthur greeting Lancelot; (no. 100) Yvain and the Duke of Clarence about to be imprisoned; (no. 108) Gauvain and companions in search of Lancelot; (no. 111) Lionel killing a knight; (no. 123) Lancelot attempting suicide; (no. 133) Lancelot rescuing a damsel; (no. 135) Lancelot beheading Argondas; (no. 140) Guenievre being detained while traveling; (no. 148) Lancelot on a litter; (no. 155) Gauvain speaking to a hermit; (no. 156) Hector greeting a lady before a castle; (no. 158) Yvain and a lady talking; (no. 159) Mordred and a dwarf talking; (no. 184) Bohort about to strike Mariales, who has fallen; (no. 211) Lancelot carrying his grandfather's head to a hermitage for burial.

The Amsterdam manuscript in no. 3 shows only Ban's castle burning; no. 4 adds Ban dying; no. 169 adds Guenievre and Lancelot riding together; and no. 172 includes Lionel's combat with a knight.

14. Pickford, *L'Evolution du roman arthurien*, p. 293 and Appendix I, pp. 297–319.

15. Ibid., pp. 26, 34, and 82–83. According to Fanni Bogdanow, the Turin work antedates fr. 112 because the "account of the Bon Chevalier sans Peur's delivery from the Val du Servage begins in both T and 112 with a reference to his imprisonment in the Second Livre, . . . and this only makes sense in the context of the Turin manuscript, which relates the Bon Chevalier Sans Peur's imprisonment in Part II of the romance." See "Part III of the Turin Version of *Guiron le Courtois*: a Hitherto Unknown Source of Ms. B.N. fr. 112," in *Medieval Miscellany Presented to Eugène Vinaver by Pupils, Colleagues and Friends*, ed. F. Whitehead, A.H. Diverres and F.E. Sutcliffe (New York: Barnes and Noble, 1965), p. 58.

16. G. Hutchings, *Le Roman en prose de Lancelot du Lac, Le Conte de la Charrette* (Paris: Droz, 1938), p. xlii, as quoted by Pickford, *L'Evolution du roman arthurien*, p. 35, n. 49.

17. Cf. nos, 5, 9–10, 31–32, 35, 37, 39–40, 42, 46, 55, 63–64, 66, 68,

74, 76, 79, 81, 84, 93, 99, 101, 103–105, 107, 109, 113, and 115.

18. Nos. 252, 257, 259, 266, 273, 276–277, 279, 281, 283–284, 288–289, 291, 293, 295, 297–299, 301–302.

19. Nos. 305–306, 308–309, 311, 314–316, 323–324, 328 (329 has same subject), 334, 340–343, and 345.

20. The quoted passage is Sommer's, *The Vulgate Version*, III, 295: 33.

21. Ibid., III, 295–300.

22. In the *Lancelot* proper the duplicated subjects are as follows: nos. 1, 21, 27, 30, 44, 52, 57, 89, 95, and 96. *Queste del Saint Graal:* nos. 245, 251, 255, 258, and 262. *Mort Artu:* nos. 325 and 333. Nos. 1, 21, 245, and 262 are each part of composite images.

23. Emmanuèle Baumgartner, "La Couronne et le cercle: Arthur et la Table Ronde dans les manuscrits du *Lancelot-Graal,*" in *Texte et image, actes du colloque internationale de Chantilly* (Paris, 1982), pp. 197–198.

24. This does not preclude the possibility that fr. 112's artist collaborated with the fr. 116 artist or that he saw fr. 116 itself. Since he begins to use the fr. 116 artist's palette (especially red) to good effect in the rest of Book IV, it implies that his working situation involved more than coloring patterns drawn by someone else.

25. As an indication of their frequency, jousting knights are seen 45 times in fr. 112, Book II: ff. 18, 18v, 30, 34v, 48, 54v, 57v, 68, 76, 106, 128v, 145, 146, 175v, 177v, 180v, 184, 189v, 206v, 237v, 245v; Book IV: 8v, 11v, 14, 15, 28v, 29v, 30, 32v, 33, 36v, 38, 56v, 72, 86, 106, 118v, 142, 142v, 155v, 160v, 172v, 184v, 211, 228v.

Knights in combat with swords are found 52 times in the same manuscript. They are depicted standing in combat on the following folios in Book II: 9, 50v, 52v, 60, 64v, 73, 116v, 1143, 172, 194v, 201, 204, 219, 237, 243v, 247v; Book III: 218v; Book IV: 29, 30, 35, 38, 38v, 77v, 92v, 104, 110, 119v, 148, 161. They are mounted here, Book II: 31, 136v, 217, 229, 233, 236v, 240v; Book IV: 13, 19v, 44, 49v, 58v, 89, 121v, 126, 138v, 163, 170v, 204v, 209v, 211, 226, 231.

26. See note 12 above.

Fig. 1.1. Detail of the miniature of the battle between Bohort and the giant Maudit. Paris, BN, fr. 119, f. 424v. Reproduced by permission.

Fig. 1.2. Detail of miniature of the Round Table. Paris, BN, fr. 120, f. 524v. Reproduced by permission.

Fig. 1.3. Paris, BN, fr. 112 (Book IV), f. 1.
Reproduced by permission.

Fig. 1.4. Detail of miniature. Paris, BN, fr. 116, f. 607.
Reproduced by permission.

Fig. 1.5. Detail of miniature. Paris, BN, fr. 112 (Book IV), f. 2.
Reproduced by permission.

Fig. 1.6. Detail of miniature. Paris, BN, fr. 118, f. 189v.
Reproduced by permission.

Fig. 1.7. Detail of miniature. Paris, BN, fr. 116, f. 674.
Reproduced by permission.

Fig. 1.8. Detail of miniature. Paris, BN, fr. 120, f. 590v.
Reproduced by permission.

2 TEXT AND IMAGE

THE CASE OF *EREC ET ENIDE*

Carleton W. Carroll

Though rather sparsely illustrated, the surviving manuscripts of Chrétien's first Arthurian romance present us with iconographic materials that are interesting both in their execution and in their relationship to the text they accompany. I propose to examine the relationship between text and image in the two illustrated manuscripts of *Erec et Enide*—Paris, BN, fr. 1376, which presents a historiated initial, and Paris, BN, fr. 24403, which contains three miniatures. Henceforth they will be referred to by the sigla first assigned by Foerster in his 1890 edition: B for 1376 and V for 24403.[1]

Both manuscripts begin with an illustration of the central element of the romance's first movement, the well-known hunt of the white stag (figs. 2.1, *B*, and 2.2, *V*). It will be recalled that, immediately after his prologue, Chrétien sets the action at Cardigan Castle. Speaking of King Arthur's court there, the author tells us that

> Einz si riche ne fu veüe,
> que molt i ot boens chevaliers,
> hardiz et conbatanz et fiers,
> et riches dames et puceles,
> filles de rois, gentes et beles. . . . (ll. 30–34)[2]

This fine setting is not without its problems, however, and Chrétien immediately announces what is to be a central dramatic element of the first part of the romance: "mes einçois que la corz fausist, / li rois a ses chevaliers dist / qu'il voloit le blanc cerf chacier / por la costume ressaucier" (ll. 35–38).

We see that from the outset this hunt is presented as Arthur's initiative. His nephew, the wise Gawain, opposes the king's plan, citing the presence of no fewer than *cinc cenz* (l. 50) of the *filles de rois* mentioned in the narration, each with an *ami* / *chevalier vaillant et hardi* (ll. 53–54) ready to contend that SHE deserves the kiss traditionally given to the fairest by the winner of the hunt: "'qui le blanc cerf ocirre puet / par reson beisier li estuet / des puceles de vostre cort [says Gawain to Arthur] / la plus bele, a que que il tort'" (ll. 45–48).

Despite Gawain's misgivings, the king insists on going ahead with his plan, and the next day, at first light (69) everyone sets off for the hunt. Or, rather, *almost* everyone. Chrétien gives us a very clear picture: the king and the knights ride into the forest; "Aprés aus monte la reïne, / ansanble o li une meschine" (ll. 77–78) and "Aprés les siust a esperon / uns chevaliers, Erec a non" (ll. 81–82). The fact that Erec deliberately follows the queen and her *meschine*, rather than the king and his knights, is unambiguously established by Erec himself in his very first speech: "'Dame,' fet il, 'a vos seroie, / s'il vos pleisoit, an ceste voie. / Je ne ving ça por autre afere / fors por vos conpaignie fere'" (107–10).

Although the text is very clear on this point, various scholars have stated that it is Erec who is seen hunting the white stag in the images we find at the beginning of the romance, in the two illustrated manuscripts. The Loomises may have been the first to put forth this identification, stating that the illustration "shows the hero blowing his horn and chasing a leaping stag."[3] Micha followed soon thereafter, with what was perhaps an independent error since his study appeared the following year: "Au début d'*Erec* [in manuscript *B*] l'initiale L est assez joliment historiée . . . : Erec à cheval, portant un arc et suivi d'un chien, poursuit un cerf."[4] And speaking of manuscript *V*, Micha identified the first miniature as "Erec à la chasse" (*Tradition manuscrite*, p. 50).

In fact, it is not only the text that indicates that this is Arthur and not Erec: the main figure in the two illustrations is wearing a crown. We may wonder about the verisimilitude of this detail, and Chrétien says only that the king put on *une corte cote* (l. 72). We must therefore ascribe the detail of the crown to the painter or to the person under whose orders he was working. The fact remains that, in the painter's mind, the figure was indeed a king, and who other than King Arthur?

Given the small number of images that accompany this romance, at least in the surviving manuscripts, it is in a sense regrettable that two of them illustrate exactly the same scene.

However, this duplication allows us to compare and contrast the work of two miniaturists faced with the same task, as well as to consider these two images within the tradition of miniatures illustrating the hunting of the stag.[5]

As stated earlier, these images occur at exactly the same point, at the very beginning of the text. In *B* we have a historiated letter, the initial *L* of *Li vilains dit an son respit*. This letter occupies roughly two thirds of the width of the column; to the right of it, on eight lines, we find the first four lines of the text. A similar arrangement of text and image was probably intended in *V*, for we find only the letter *i* of the first word *Li*, the miniature replacing the capital *L*. This impression is supported by the fact that, as in the case of *B*, the miniature does not occupy the whole width of the column, the right-most portion presenting the first two lines of text, spread over ten manuscript lines of one or two words each. But there is no sign of a letter in this image; it is, in fact, a miniature. Let us mention in passing that this image has been reproduced on several occasions: in black and white in the Loomises' study (fig. 258), and on the cover of Jean Frappier's *Chrétien de Troyes: l'homme et l'œuvre* (Paris: Hatier, 1957; 1968); in color on the cover of Jean-Marie Fritz's edition (see note 2) and on that of Dorothy Gilbert's translation (Berkeley: University of California Press, 1992).[6] Both hunting scenes, as well as the other two miniatures from manuscript *V*, are reproduced in black and white in my edition (see note 2).

The extensive similarities between the two scenes are readily apparent. Both show King Arthur on horseback, a bow in his hand, accompanied by two companions; he arrives from the left, and the stag, pursued by two dogs, bounds toward the right. In both cases the figure of the king partially conceals those of his two companions. We see very little of the second figure in *B*, only the face and a bit of the body; the third figure in *B* is easily overlooked, as only the top of the head and part of the hair are visible. The second figure in *V* is more clearly visible, holding a weapon in his right hand, perhaps a club; the third figure is hidden except for the top of his head and the upper part of his face. In *B* we see the mane, ears, and one of the front feet of a second horse, whereas in *V* only the king's own mount is visible. Conversely, we can see part of the cantle of the second figure. In *B* both dogs are leaping in the same direction as the stag; in *V* the right-hand dog has turned about and is attacking the stag from the side.

The king carries the bow in his left hand in *B* and in his right hand in *V*, where the left hand holds the traditional hunting-horn. The bow may be at variance with the hunting practice of the time: Roger Middleton affirms that "archers in stag hunts were normally on foot" ("Coloured Capitals," p. 156, note 13). We may be surprised to note that, in *V*, the king has no free hand with which to guide his horse. Among the numerous manuscript illustrations of stag hunts, apparently a very popular genre, one can nevertheless find other examples where the hunter, on horseback, uses both hands for other tasks besides the guiding of his horse, e.g., Oxford, Bodleian, Ashmole 828, f. 45v (fig. 2.3), where the hunter fits an arrow to his bow.[7] The image in *B* also has the king riding without holding the reins, making what Roger Middleton calls "a rather inappropriate rhetorical gesture" with his right hand ("Coloured Capitals," p. 156, note 13).

In *V* we have a square image (50 × 50 mm),[8] arbitrarily limited by a frame that cuts off a portion of one of the figures and the hind quarters of the horse on the left and the front feet of the stag on the right. In *B*, on the other hand, the feet of the stag cover a portion of the frame, enhancing the dynamic feel of the image. The slope of the foot of the letter *L* gives further emphasis to the movement of the scene, which is upward and to the right.

As to the painters' choice of colors, both images are set against a plain gilded background. In both cases the king's tunic is deep blue with a red lining, and the sleeves of his undergarment are also red, as is his crown. The tree in *B* is a rather pale green, whereas the principal tree of *V* is a surprising, vivid red. Despite the use of black lines in both images to indicate the individual leaves, the treatment of the trees is strikingly different, those of *V* being much more stylized—one is tempted to say "primitive"—than the one in *B*. Similarly, the stag in *V* seems less well observed, and even slightly anthropomorphic, whereas *B*'s is spotted rather than being completely white, and thus farther from the ideal of the text. Finally, the treatment of the human faces shows more finesse in *B* than in *V*.

We should probably not conclude, on the basis of the similarities in these two illustrations, that the two manuscripts are closely related, "for the scene itself is so commonplace that the same pattern could have been widely circulated amongst the artists of the time" ("Coloured Capitals," p. 156). The Loomises assert that illuminators used "a host of generalized subjects . . . of a sort that could be and were endlessly reproduced in all sorts of texts" [9] and they place the first miniature of *V* (they do not mention *B*'s historiated initial) in a long line of hunting scenes where the quarry is specifically a stag. [10]

This series of similar hunting scenes begins with that of the stag leading the hunters to the tomb of Saints Denis, Rustique, and Eleuthère (fig. 2.4), from a manuscript executed in 1250 (BN, n.a. fr. 1098, f. 51v). [11] The prose romance formerly known as the *Huth Merlin*, now London, BL. Add. 38117, contains a historiated initial presenting a scene identified as Arthur hunting. [12]

One of the best-known sources of hunting illustrations is the *Livre de chasse* of Gaston Phébus, composed in the latter part of the fourteenth century (the author died in 1391). This work survives in over forty manuscripts, many of them richly illustrated. [13] One of these is M. 1044 of the Pierpont Morgan Library in New York, dating from c. 1410 (fig. 2.5), illustrated in full color; [14] another is fr. 619 of the Bibliothèque Nationale, executed around 1440 and illustrated in grisaille (fig. 2.6). [15] As Roger Middleton observes, "These later illustrations have more detail than the *Erec* miniatures, but the essential similarity of the design is not in doubt" ("Coloured Capitals," p. 126, note 13).

This similarity can even be found in the marginal drawings of a large number of manuscripts, where the images do not appear to illustrate the accompanying text. Such is the case, among many others, in BN, lat. 14284, f. 16v., lower margin (a late twelfth-century book of hours). It is worth noting that almost all these stag-hunting scenes have several elements in common: on the left, one or two mounted hunters (sometimes more), generally with one or more hunting horns; hunting dogs, sometimes only two but occasionally as many as nine; and, at the right of the composition, the bounding stag. The movement, in the vast majority of cases I have examined, is from left to right. The opposite movement is occasionally found, however, as in fig. 2.7, a marginal illustration from the *Roman d'Alexandre* (Oxford, Bodleian Library, Bodley 264, f. 122v), illuminated by Jehan de Brise, Bruges, 1338–1344. [16] It would be tempting to conclude that it is because the hunter is a woman that the composition runs counter to the apparent norm, but this would be inaccurate, given the existence of at least one image showing a man pursuing the stag from right to left. [17]

Let us turn now to the second miniature of manuscript V (fig. 2.8), which occurs slightly before the mid-point of the text, fol. 142r.[18] This miniature seems thus far to have inspired very little commentary. The Loomises do not mention it; Micha notes its presence but says nothing of its contents; Foerster and Roques do not mention it. In my edition I briefly described it in the following terms: "combat between two mounted knights, one of whom (presumably Erec) runs the other through with his lance, as a lady (Enide?) observes" (p. xxvi).

The text surrounding this miniature, corresponding to lines 2744–95 of my edition (Foerster 2782–833; Roques 2778–829; Fritz 2778–829) comes soon after the couple sets out *en avanture*, following the famous crisis precipitated by Enide's words "*Amis, con mar fus!*" (C2469). On the verso of the preceding folio, facing the text and miniature, we find the lines in which Erec orders his wife to ride speedily ahead of him and to say nothing unless he first speaks to her. Folio 142 then begins with Enide's lament, followed by

> Que qu'ele se demente ainsi,
> Uns chevaliers del bos issi
> —Deus conpaignons od lui avoit—
> Qui de roberie vivoit,
> Et s'estoient armé tot troi. (ll. 2757–61, Carroll ed.)[19]

This presentation of the three robber-knights continues for about thirty lines, in the course of which the first of the robbers announces his intention of taking the lady's palfrey and leaving the rest to his companions. The two others agree to this, he rushes to attack Erec, and Chrétien comments that at that time it was a recognized custom that two knights should not attack a single knight and that to do so would be considered an act of treachery (C2788–92). Beside the miniature we find the lines "Enide vit les robeours; / Molt l'en est prise grant paors," followed by the beginning of the internal monologue in which Enide debates whether to remain silent or to disregard Erec's orders and warn him of the imminent danger.

This image is thus placed at a dramatic turning point in the romance. It should be noted that this same line, *Enide vit les robeours*, is marked by a large colored capital letter in all the other manuscripts that preserve this portion of the text.[20] But the colored capitals, occupying just two lines in each case, are much less imposing than V's miniature.[21]

As in the case of the first miniature in V, the image extends over ten lines and fills nearly the entire column, leaving just enough space for a few letters, so that the word *robeours* is divided between two lines. This arrangement would once again be more appropriate for a historiated initial than for a miniature, but in this case the first word, Enide's name, is written out in full, and the initial *e* is the same size as the final one.

The colors are basically the same as those we have already seen: red for Enide's tunic (Erec tells her to put on her most beautiful dress, C2543, but Chrétien does not tell us the color) and for the robber-knight's helmet; blue for Erec's shield and the other knight's surcoat; a sort of pinkish grey for Erec's surcoat and the trappings of his horse— a black horse, another detail not specified by Chrétien. Here, too, the scene is set against a gilded background. We have a nearly square image (48 × 49 mm), for the most part limited by its frame, but with a slight exception on the right-hand side: the point of the lance and the flank of the horse extend about one millimeter beyond the inner edge of the decorative frame. We find the same sort of stylized tree as in the first miniature in V; here the paint has partially flaked off, so that there are almost no lines representing the leaves.

The jousting scene between two knights must surely have been one of the stock images for the illustration of both romance and epic, what Stephanie Cain Van D'Elden calls a "generic" image (see note 9). Nonetheless, this does not preclude some degree of adaptation. What sets this scene apart and links it more closely to the accompanying text is the presence of the lady, whom we may identify as Enide. One can see that she too is on horseback, although her horse is not illustrated: she is at essentially the same level as the two knights, and we can see the cantle of her saddle. In point of fact, she seems too near the combat. The illuminator could have placed her farther from it, in the background, but he seems to have wanted to give her a pictorial importance equal to that of Erec. Another detail that ties the image more specifically to the text in this case is the fact that, despite the mention of three robber-knights and the presence of the plural *les robeours* in the lines immediately beside the miniature, the scene depicts a single combat. And as we have seen, Chrétien insists on the fact that it is just one of the robber-knights who attacks Erec.

We may note a few "realistic" embellishments: an irregular brown band stippled with short black strokes, across the lower edge of the scene, representing the ground and grass;[22] the tree, stylized like the first one, but this time pale green with small red touches; traces of red representing blood, where Erec's lance strikes his opponent. Chrétien specifically relates (C2828–33) that Erec's lance first splits the knight's shield, then strikes him in the middle of the chest. The painter represents the scene a bit differently: we do not see the split shield and the lance penetrates the other knight's shoulder.

Another manuscript illustration that may be compared to this miniature is a jousting scene from the *Roman de Fauvel* (fig. 2.9). Henry Martin states that this manuscript, BN, fr. 146, f. 40v, "paraît avoir été copié sous le règne de Charles [IV] le Bel (1322–1328)" (*Joyaux*, p. 42; reproduced, fig. XLIV). Unlike Enide, the lady observing the scene is pictorially separated from the action, protected by a stone structure—as is the man on the other side. Similarly, in a number of illustrations reproduced in *Arthurian Legends,* when one or more ladies observe a joust or a tourney, they do so from a gallery, the ramparts of a castle, or some other structure.[23] Additional examples of this motif can be found in ms. Douce 308 in the Bodleian Library and in mss. 805–806 in the Pierpont Morgan Library, among numerous others.[24]

The third miniature in *V* (fig. 2.10) is to be found on f. 155r, about two-thirds of the way through the text in terms of the folio structure of this manuscript. Like the second, this image seems to have inspired very little critical commentary: the Loomises, Foerster, and Roques do not mention it; Micha merely indicates its presence, without attempting to identify it. My own description (p. xxvi) was both hesitant and, I now believe, inaccurate.

The text accompanying this miniature, corresponding to lines 4287–338 of my edition (Foerster 4333–84; Roques 4307–58; Fritz 4329–80), occupies a place in the narration analogous to that of the text of the second miniature. There it was the first adventure encountered by the couple following their departure; here the minia-ture is positioned shortly after what may be called their second departure. In the course of their wanderings, Erec and Enide briefly come back into contact with the world of the court, not in one of Arthur's towns or castles, but in the forest, where the king has gone to hunt. They spend one night in the royal camp, but Erec adamantly refuses to stay longer. Scarcely have they set out when they hear the cries of a damsel in distress, and Erec rides to her rescue. She tells him that two giants have taken her beloved; Erec sets out in pursuit. Like the second miniature in V, this one is placed near the bottom of the right-hand column. The surrounding text includes the end of the description of the damsel, the explanation she gives Erec, the conversation that ensues, and Erec's departure to rescue the knight.

As in the case of the first miniature in V, this one takes the place of a historiated initial and replaces the initial E of Erec's name in *Erec s'an vet tote la trace* (C4333). This same line is marked by a two-line colored capital letter in all the other manuscripts that contain this portion of the text.[25]

The palette is essentially the same as for the other miniatures in this manuscript. There is only a trace of green remaining on one of the helmets on the right; this color seems generally to have survived less well than the others. The dominant colors are bright red (a few helmets but particularly the shield and the horse-trappings of the principal knight), deep blue (helmets and a surcoat on each side), and pinkish grey (the surcoats of the principal knight and of one of his opponents and the trappings of one of the horses on the right). The image is again square, or very nearly so (46 × 48 mm), basically limited by its frame, but this time the image protrudes a bit more: the hand of one of the figures on the right and the lower portion of his club extend enough to cover part of the frame at the upper right. The scenery is reduced to a minimum: the illustrator has included only an irregular brown band, at the very bottom, representing the ground. We do not even see the stylized type of tree observed earlier. Once again the scene is set against a featureless gilded background.

On the left we see five knights, but the main one masks the others to a great extent, just as the figure of the king conceals those of his companions: here, the presence of two of the knights can be guessed only from the tops of their helmets. The black horse of the main knight is clearly visible, but nothing shows of the other horses, neither feet nor ears, and nothing suggests their presence. The shield of the main knight is decorated, perhaps with a large bird, but this is not the same decoration as in the second miniature. In fact, Erec's shield is never described by Chrétien.

On the right we see a group of giants—but how many? The fact that they are indeed giants is evidenced less by their size, which is scarcely greater than that of the knights, but by their weapons: they fight with clubs, a detail which faithfully reflects the text, where Chrétien specifically states that "Li jaiant n'avoient espiez / escuz, n'espees esmolues, / ne lances; einz orent maçues; / escorgiees andui tenoient" (C4342–45).[26] The *maçues* are clearly visible (though not the *escorgiees*); on the other hand, we see the shield of one of the giants, which goes against Chrétien's text. The fact that the gesture of one of the giants covers a portion of the frame reinforces the idea of the character's exceptional size, suggesting that the frame is insufficient to hold him. The lance of the main knight pierces the helmet of one of the giants, on which a few traces of red indicate blood. The text reads "[Erec] fiert le premerain an l'uel / si par mi outre le cervel / que d'autre part le haterel / li sans et la cervele an saut" (C4398–401). The giants are on horseback, another detail that conforms to the text.

But what of the number of combatants on each side? In the text, as is appropriate, Erec defeats the two giants with no help from anyone else. Might the miniaturist have painted five knights in order to represent the successive actions of Erec? The presence of three different colors of helmet would seem to weigh against this hypotheses. And how many giants are depicted? At first glance there seem to be two (two clubs, two surcoats of different colors, the cantles of two saddles), but the actual number is higher. A third helmet, deep blue in color, can be seen above the lighter-colored one that is pierced by the lance; the tops of two other helmets are found at the upper limit of the picture; finally, a sixth is partially hidden by the two clubs. The relationship of these various helmets to the arms wielding the clubs is not completely clear. One would expect to see the feet of at least one of the giants' horses, but, although there is plenty of room for the artist to show them, we find no trace of them.

In this case a comparable image can be taken from the works of Chrétien himself: the combat between Yvain and the giant Harpin de la Montagne, in *Le Chevalier au lion*, as that romance is preserved in Princeton University's manuscript Garrett 125 (fig. 2.11).[27] There too we find some discrepancies between text and image, but for the most part the latter faithfully reflects the former: Yvain is on horseback; the giant is on foot (strongly suggested by Chrétien's saying that "li jaianz li vint le cors" (Kibler 4200; Roques 4192),[28] and he wears no armor (K4210–12; R4202–04); Yvain strikes the giant on the cheek with his sword (K4213–17; R4205–09); the lion is not only present, but he attacks the giant on the haunch, precisely as specified by Chrétien (K4227; R4219). On the other hand, the giant's club is not exactly as described in the text ("grant et quarré, agu devant," K4095; R4087), but rather slender and pointed at the end; instead of the bearskin mentioned in K4199 and 4225 (R4191 and 4217), the giant wears a red tunic, which appears quite intact, whereas Yvain had already struck him a first blow to the chest with his lance (K4202–05; R4194–97).

We can only deplore the fact that we do not have the rest of this manuscript, which may well have contained the collected works of Chrétien de Troyes, and we are left to wonder how that miniaturist may have treated *Erec et Enide*. But perhaps the rest of the Garrett manuscript will one day be found, bringing us an important complement to the illustration of Chrétien's first Arthurian romance.

But to return from the realm of speculation, and limiting ourselves to the known images at hand, what can we say of the illustrations that accompany this text? That they represent a curious mixture of fidelity and independence, sometimes precisely mirroring the letter of the text, and elsewhere inexplicably departing from it. Other studies will perhaps help us to see whether this inconsistency in the text-image relationship is a usual feature in the domain of Arthurian texts or whether, on the contrary, this romance constitutes an exception.

NOTES

    1. Christian von Troyes, *Sämtliche Werke, nach allen bekannten Handschriften herausgegeben von Wendelin Foerster, III, Erec und Enide* (Halle: Niemeyer, 1890; rpt. Amsterdam: Rodopi, 1965).

    2. Unless otherwise noted, all quotations from *Erec et Enide* are from my own edition: Chrétien de Troyes, *Erec and Enide*, ed. Carleton W. Carroll, with an introduction by William W. Kibler (New York and London: Garland, 1987). Where line numbers differ in other editions, they will be indicated: Foerster 1890 (see note 1); *Les Romans de Chrétien de Troyes édités d'après la copie de Guiot (Bibl. nat., fr. 794), I, Erec et Enide*, ed. Mario Roques (Paris: Champion, 1952; rpt. 1955, etc.); *Erec et Enide: Edition critique d'après le manuscrit B.N. fr. 1376*, ed. Jean-Marie Fritz (Paris: Librairie Générale Française, 1992).

    3. Roger Sherman Loomis and Laura Hibbard Loomis, *Arthurian Legends in Medieval Art* (New York: MLA, 1938; rpt. New York: Kraus, 1966), p. 100.

4. Alexandre Micha, *La Tradition manuscrite des romans de Chrétien de Troyes* (Geneva: Droz, 1939; rpt. 1966), p. 43.

5. I wish to express my profound gratitude to my colleague Roger Middleton, of the University of Nottingham, who generously allowed me to consult a pre-publication copy of his article, "Coloured Capitals in the Manuscripts of *Erec et Enide*," subsequently published in *The Manuscripts of Chrétien de Troyes*, ed. Keith Busby et al. (Amsterdam: Rodopi, 1993), I, pp. 149–93, which contains several excellent observations on these two hunting scenes.

6. The miniature is also reproduced in black and white facing the title page. It should be noted that the source of the illustration is incorrectly identified as "B.N. 1376, fol. 107" rather than BN 24403, f. 119. The colors are more accurately reproduced on the cover of the Fritz edition.

7. Another example may be seen in Paris, BN, lat. 16260, f. 5v, where the hunter has a spear or lance in his right hand and a hunting horn in his left.

8. Dimensions are those of the image itself, inside the decorative frame. The image inside the initial *L* of *B* measures approximately 28 × 37 mm.

9. *Arthurian Legends*, p. 91; the notion of generic versus specific images has been studied more recently by Stephanie Cain Van D'Elden, "Specific and Generic Scenes: A Model for Analyzing Medieval Illustrated Texts Based on the Example of *Yvain/Iwein*," *Bibliographical Bulletin of the International Arthurian Society*, 44 (1992), 255–69.

10. For the purposes of this discussion, I make no distinction between "stag," Old French and Modern French *cerf*, and other similar animals, in particular the *daim* ("fallow deer") and the *chevrel* ("roebuck").

11. Reproduced in Henry Martin, *Les Joyaux de l'enluminure à la Bibliothèque nationale* (Paris and Brussels: Van Oest, 1928), fig. XXXV.

12. Reproduced in *Arthurian Legends*, fig. 257; the authors date the manuscript c. 1300–1325 and call this "a typical French scene of the chase" (p. 100).

13. A complete list, 44 medieval manuscripts, can be found in Gaston Phébus, *Livre de chasse*, ed. Gunnar Tilander (Karlshamn: Johanssons, 1971), pp. 24–27.

14. The date is that given by the Pierpont Morgan Library. Several miniatures from this manuscript have been reproduced in color: Lori Pepe, "Medieval Dogs Brought to Light," *Pure-Bred Dogs/American Kennel Gazette*, 109.9 (September 1992), 66–71; the scene from f. 76 is on p. 69, " *Cy deuise comment le bon veneur doit chascier et prendre le daim a force*." I am grateful to my colleague Sheila Cordray, of the Department of Sociology, Oregon State University, for bringing this article to my attention.

15. The date is that proposed by Charles Samaran (Tilander, p. 35). The stag hunt from f. 75 was earlier reproduced in Henry Martin, *La Miniature française du XIIIe au XVe siècle*, 2d ed. (Paris et Bruxelles: Van Oest, 1924), fig. CVIII. Martin places this copy earlier, in the last years of the fourteenth century or the first of the fifteenth (*Joyaux*, 54). For black and white reproductions of stag hunts from another luxuriously decorated manuscript of

the *Livre de chasse*, BN, fr. 616, see Tilander's edition, pp. 193, 212, 213, and 216; for color reproductions, see *Illuminated Manuscripts: Medieval Hunting Scenes ("The Hunting Book" by Gaston Phœbus)*, with text by Gabriel Bise after Gaston Phoebus, trans. J. Peter Tallon (n.p.: Miller Graphics, n.d. [designed and produced by Productions Liber SA, copyright Productions Liber SA and Editions Minerva SA, Fribourg-Geneva, 1978]), particularly pp. 60–61, 64–67, and 70.

16. Reproduced in part (the stag and the tree are not shown) in Lilian M. C. Randall, *Images in the Margins of Gothic Manuscripts* (Berkeley and Los Angeles: University of California Press, 1966), fig. 715.

17. Of 18 manuscript illustrations examined in the preparation of this study (miniatures, historiated initials, and marginal drawings) depicting at least one mounted figure hunting a stag, 16 (88.9 percent) involve a movement from left to right, and just 2 present a movement from right to left (the other shows a knight: Oxford, Bodleian Library, Douce 118, ff. 47v-48r). This sample is small but essentially random, and may therefore be representative. It is probable that Morgan M. 1044 and BN, fr. 619 contain additional miniatures that could be added to this count. The illustrations involving left-to-right movement are as follows:

London, BL, Add. 38117, f. 193r (*Merlin*)

New York, Pierpont Morgan Library M. 820, f. 12 (*Le Livre du roy Modus et de la royne Racio*)

New York, Pierpont Morgan Library M. 1044, f. 76r (*Le Livre de la chasse*)

Oxford, Bodleian Library, Ashmole 828, f. 45v (*Lancelot*)

Paris, B.N., fr. 616 [four miniatures, folio numbers unknown; reproduced in Tilander, ed., *Le Livre de chasse*, pp. 193, 212, 213, 216]

Paris, BN, fr. 619, f. 75r (*Le Livre de la chasse*)

Paris, BN, fr. 776, f. 1r (*Le Roman de Tristan*)

Paris, BN, fr. 1376, f. 95r (*Erec et Enide*)

Paris, BN, fr. 24403, f. 119r (*Erec et Enide*)

Paris, BN, fr. 25526, f. 42v (*Le Roman de la rose*)

Paris, BN, lat. 14284, f. 16v (book of hours)

Paris, BN, lat. 16260, f. 5v (Bible)

Paris, BN, n.a. lat. 1098, f. 51v (*Vie et histoire de saint Denis*)

18. This is two-fifths of the way through the text, in terms of the folio structure of this manuscript.

19. Spelling as in *V*, punctuation added; the third and fourth lines are interverted with respect to the editions: Foerster 2797–98, Roques 2793–94, Carroll 2759–60, Fritz 2794–95.

20. *Erec et Enide* is preserved in essentially complete form in seven manuscripts. Six are in the Bibliothèque Nationale, fonds français: in addition to *B* and *V*, they are traditionally designated by the sigla *C* (794), *E* (1420), *H* (1450), and *P* (375). The seventh is in Chantilly, Musée Condé, ms. 472 (*A*). There are also four relatively short fragments, none of which contains the passages illustrated by the miniatures in *V*.

21. According to Roger Middleton's Table 3, "Alphabetical list of words with coloured capitals in each manuscript" ("Coloured Capitals," pp. 189–92), in three manuscripts this is the only point in which Enide's name is made to stand out in this way; in the three others, her name is so decorated only twice (manuscripts *H* and *E*) or three times (manuscript *A*).

22. This detail can also be observed in the first miniature in *V*.

23. See figs. 219, 306, 311, 323, 345, 346, and 354. Fig. 346 is reproduced in color in Elizabeth Jenkins, *The Mystery of King Arthur* (New York: Coward, McCann & Geoghegan, 1975), p. 96; a color photograph of the miniature of fig. 354 appears in Richard Barber, *The Arthurian Legends: An Illustrated Anthology* (Totowa, N.J.: Littlefield Adams, 1979), between pp. 70 and 71. Fig. 306 constitutes a partial exception in that some of the women observing the tourney seem to be standing at the edge of the field on which the knights are jousting. I have found no other illustrations showing a lady on horseback observing a combat between mounted knights.

24. Morgan 805–806, f. 262, reproduced in color in Barber, *Arthurian Legends* (see note 23), illustrations between pp. 70 and 71; Douce l. 308, f. 117r, reproduced in Stephanie Cain Van D'Elden, "In a 'Blazon' of Glory: Three Tournament and Siege Poems," *The Coat of Arms*, n.s. 3.105 (spring 1978), p. 3. I am grateful to Professor Van D'Elden for bringing these illustrations to my attention. Other examples of ladies watching combats or tournaments from an elevated structure can be found in Chantilly, Musée Condé 315–17; Oxford, Douce 383, f. 16; Paris, Arsenal 3479, f. 1 (all reproduced among the color photographs in Barber).

25. Manuscript *E* omits a block of text corresponding to Carroll 4285–4344 (Foerster 4331–90, Roques 4305–64, Fritz 4327–86). *C*, *H*, *B*, *P*, and *A* (see note 21) have two-line colored initials.

26. The text of the third line is slightly different in *V*: "Fors que tot seulement machues" (fol 155va, l. 6).

27. This miniature has been reproduced, in black and white, along with the others from the same manuscript, in Robert L. McGrath, "A Newly Discovered Illustrated Manuscript of Chrétien de Troyes' *Yvain* and *Lancelot* in the Princeton University Library," *Speculum*, 38 (1963), 583–94: in *The Knight with the Lion, or Yvain (Le Chevalier au Lion)*, ed. William W. Kibler (New York and London: Garland, 1985), p. [xliv] (unnumbered); and in *The Arthurian Encyclopedia*, ed. Norris J. Lacy et al. (New York and London: Garland, 1986), plate 41 (between pp. 360 and 361). It is reproduced in color as the cover illustration to Chrétien de Troyes, *Arthurian Romances*, tr. by William W. Kibler and Carleton W. Carroll (London: Penguin, 1991).

28. Line references are to the Kibler edition (see previous note) and to *Les Romans de Chrétien de Troyes édités d'après la copie de Guiot (Bibl. nat., fr. 794)*, ed. Mario Roques (Paris: Champion, 1960; rpt. 1963, etc.).

Top left. Fig. 2.1. Paris, BN, fr. 1376 (B), f. 95r.

Top right. Fig. 2.2. Paris, BN, fr. 24403 (V), f. 119r.

Bottom. Fig. 2.3. Detail of miniature. Oxford,
Bodleian Library, Ashmole 828, f. 45v.

Reproduced by permission.

Fig. 2.4. Paris, BN, n.a. fr. 1098, f. 51v.
Reproduced by permission.

Fig. 2.5. New York, the Pierpont Morgan Library, M. 1044, f. 76r.
Reproduced by permission.

Fig. 2.6. Paris, BN, fr. 619, f. 75r.
Reproduced by permission.

Fig. 2.7. Detail of lower margin. Oxford, the Bodleian Library, Bodley 264, f. 122v. Reproduced by permission.

Fig. 2.8. Paris, BN, fr. 24403 (V), f. 142r.
Reproduced by permission.

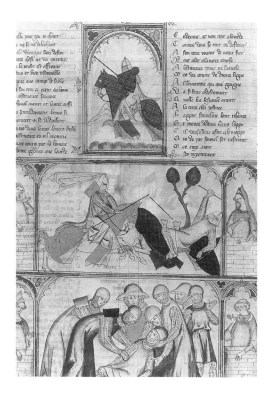

Fig. 2.9. Paris, BN, fr. 146, f. 40v.
Reproduced by permission.

Fig. 2.10. Paris, BN, fr. 24403 (V), f. 155r.
Reproduced by permission.

Fig. 2.11. Princeton, Princeton University Library, Garrett 125, f. 56v.
Reproduced by permission.

3   "IMAGINES HISTORIARUM"

TEXT AND IMAGE IN THE FRENCH PROSE *LANCELOT*

Carol R. Dover

Cassiodorus considered it the duty of the chronicler to record the "imagines historiarum" (images of the stories) in order to tell the truth.[1] "Imagines" and "historiae" together are the two basic, defining elements of the illustrated manuscript: handwritten narratives accompanied by images called pictures. Both of them are presented in visual form because words as well as pictures are visual signs. The pictures are signs of "painture," while the words are signs of "parole," to use the distinction spelled out by Richart de Fournival in his thirteenth-century *Bestiaire*. He explains that they correspond to two modes of reception:

> Car quant on voit painte une estoire, ou de Troies ou d'autre, on voit les fais des preudommes ki cha en ariere furent, ausi com s'il fussent present. Et tout ensi est il de parole. Car quant on ot .i. romans lire, on entent les aventures, ausi com on les veïst en present.[2]

Both hearing and seeing a story depicted: these are the conditions of reception of a medieval illustrated manuscript, and they rely essentially on the creation of visual images within the audience's mind,[3] images that are so vivid as to "make present" the events they serve to recall. The audience remembers them because it has been put psychologically in the situation of an eyewitness, albeit at second hand. Richart's explanation is a simple yet powerful statement of the process by which the medieval illuminated manuscript was created, responded to and remembered, how it communicated its meanings to its audience and made them meaningful by "re-presentation."[4] The re-presentation relied on visual images in the form of pictures from spoken words (what Dante called "visible speech") and words from pictures, the one received by the ear and the other by the eye, the two gates of memory.[5]

Cassiodorus wanted his chronicle to tell the truth, but what does the thirteenth-century prose *Lancelot* have to do with truth?[6] It is, after all, a romance. I do not intend to claim that the *Lancelot* is a chronicle in the sense that Cassidorus understood the term, although romance may at times co-opt some of the aspirations and affinities of that form. Romance is by definition a fabulous, reputedly "unreliable" form that arrives at its own kind of truth by a more cleverly crafted art than that of the chronicler. In this paper I aim first to show what that truth is in the *Lancelot*—its "veritas historiarum"—and then to explore how the pictorial images ("imagines") on the one hand and the verbal images on the other (the "historiae") combine strategically to convey that particular vision of truth to the audience of the illustrated manuscript.

THE WRITTEN, VERBAL TEXT

The *Lancelot*'s aspiration to truth in its storytelling comes from its status as rewriting; by this I mean that it creates for its times a retelling of Lancelot's adventures *as already known from other romances*, with additions and an assemblage technique we call interlace. The work takes on conventional adventures of Arthurian romance and gives them a new context. The resulting "ré-écriture," rich in intertextual echoes, creates a grid of "repetition with variation" in which the variation presents a critical stance.[7] The author's retelling requires reinterpretation by the audience. He achieves this by two devices: structurally, through the organization of the interlace, and rhetorically, through the narrative voices. The ordering of the interlace juxtaposes adventures that parallel one another in content, and contrast with one another in their outcome and consequences,[8] thereby creating an internal critical perspective on events and characters that invites the audience to a comparative evaluation of characters "by deed." At the same time, the audience is invited to reevaluate the primary characters, notably the hero, "by word," from the evidence of voices within the narrative. This takes the form of commenting voices in the narrative action itself—comments from characters—and commenting narratorial voice(s).

These two strategic devices enact an aspiration to "tell the truth" in the romance, by telling what had previously been ignored as matter for story-telling or had been glossed over. I suspect that if the author of the *Lancelot* were alive today, he would find earlier Arthurian romance guilty of "lying by omission." As Emmanuèle Baumgartner recently observed, in Arthurian verse romance "tout peut être dit sauf les aventures sentimentales."[9] They are alluded to rather than narrated. The author of the *Lancelot* intends to rectify just such an omission. Yet his narrative techniques are those of romance, not those of a treatise or a chronicle, so he embeds his significance in conventional elements of romance. The most vivid example of this technique occurs at a culminating point in the tale, where Lancelot has established himself as the greatest of Arthur's knights, inspired by his love for Arthur's queen. It presents one of the founding conventions of Arthurian romance. In a ritualistic gesture that justifies the very existence of historically valid accounts of the greatness of Arthur's reign, the king assembles his clerks to record in writing, in chronicle fashion, the exploits of his knights:

> et furent mandé li clerc qui metoient en escript lez proeches des compaignons de la maison le roy Artu. Si en y avoit. IIII., si en ot non li uns Arodiens de Coloigne et li secons Tantalides de Vergeaus et li tiers Thumas de Toulete et li quars Sapiens de Baudas. Cil quatre metoient en escript tout chou que li compaignon le roy Artu faisoient d'armes, ne ia lor grant feit ne fusent autrement seu. (LM VIII:488; LK 571)

It is important to note here the authority status given to the four clerks by virtue of their being named; they were not simply any old clerks, but reputable men with reputations that could be evoked in the naming.[10] In this way, the narrator builds around them an aura of authority and reliability that allows certain claims to be made implicitly by the narrator: (1) the accounts kept by Arthur's clerks were the sole historical document ("ne ia lor grant feit ne fusent autrement seu"); (2) the written record was limited to military accomplishments ("Tout chou que li compaignon le roy Artu faisoient d'armes"); (3) the record was complete and laudatory and written down by the clerks themselves ("metoient en escript lez proeches"; "metoient en escript *tout* che que li compaignon le roy Artu faisoient d'armes" [my emphasis]).[11]

The fact that the record was kept by men endowed with authority, who themselves wrote it down is clearly of prime importance in establishing the reliability and historical validity of the accounts for posterity. Yet we cannot escape the fact that one of the communicating parties to this transaction is missing: the source who conveyed the information to the clerks, and the credibility of that source. We know from Arthurian romance convention that it was the knights who related their deeds to the clerks. These same knights are representatives of the king who enforce justice in the land in Arthur's name. Their judiciary function surely imposes on them a commitment to truth and to telling the truth. We assume, of course, that they did tell the truth and did faithfully recount to the clerks what we have just been reading in the tale itself. But sad to say, they did not, and the *Lancelot* author wants his audience to understand this fact. At one point Arthur orders Lancelot to recount his adventures to the clerks:

> li commande desor son sairement qu'il die, voiant les compaignons de laiens, les aventures que li estoient avenues puis qu'il se parti de la cort, et il l'en conta pluisors et pluisors l'en cela. (LM II:110–11)

If we place this conventional event side by side with the one noted earlier, we can see that the author has varied his motif to produce important differences. In the first account, the record consists of military deeds ("lez proeches," "tout che que li compaignon . . . faisoient d'armes"); in the second one, Arthur stipulates that Lancelot is to relate not his military exploits but his "aventures," which is a broader category of activity than the "faits d'armes" that the earlier reference established as the matter of conventional records. Thus the contrast implies that the first record is incomplete because it is limited to laudatory military activity only. The narrator's variations also concern the mode of communication. Whereas the first record was a "reliable" written one, the second is an oral account that restores the source of the information and has Arthur's other knights as witnesses; there is no mention of the clerks, although we might assume they were present as tradition has led us to expect. If this account was not written down, it is unrecorded, off the record, which suggests once again that the official record is incomplete. On the other hand if it was recorded, the suggestion is that it constituted an "unofficial" record. Lastly, the account is given by the knight who was not only the author but also the principal actor of the adventures; the product is therefore autobiographical, with all the limitations of perspective and distortion that first-person narratives imply. As if to emphasize these limitations, the narrator goes one step further. He goes to the trouble of pointing out that Lancelot told some of his adventures and concealed others, leaving the romance audience to speculate on which ones, so that all we have to do is read for ourselves and draw our own conclusions as to which ones he omitted and, maybe, which ones *we* would omit if we were in his shoes. The conclusions to be drawn from the variations are far-reaching. Firstly, since the historical record consisted of military exploits alone and this was the stuff of the historical record handed down from Arthur's reign for romancers and historians alike, the historical record was incomplete and needs to be reconstituted. Secondly, since the knights' adventures (unexpected encounters that were considered worth recounting) provided a broader and more accurate account of the range of their achievements, these should be given credence as legitimate matter for the historical record. The implication is that we need to rethink the terms by which we believe and judge written records, that is, their veracity and function as a mirror of a particular class and civilization, because the record was incomplete. Thirdly, since the record was a first-person narrative of self, it is therefore open to the distortions of subjectivity rather than to the certification of the eyewitness. But the critical factor in this first-person narration is that the knights (in this case Lancelot) had total control over their narrative, to the extent that they could choose what to tell and what not to tell. Lancelot chooses, in fact, to conceal some of his autobiographical adventures, and therefore the historical record is incomplete on a different, more personal, more reprehensible score. The official court documents handed down to chroniclers, historians, and romancers are not only an incomplete and inaccurate record of events but mendacious too. In modern parlance we would call Lancelot's act, "lying by omission" and "lying under oath."

But the concealed adventures are ones that we as readers have been privileged to read. The prose *Lancelot*, then, aims to set the record straight by narrating not only the military but also the sentimental life of its hero; not only the official "estoire" recorded for posterity by the clerks, with its supposed historical veracity, but also this "conte" of Lancelot that contributes the hidden underside of recorded history. This, I think, is the nature of the "truth" to be told.

The Verbal Image

I have chosen one narrative event—the split-shield episode—to illustrate the author's technique of creating a picture in words to convey this hidden "truth."[12] He uses the rhetorical device of "descriptio," which describes in order to elucidate the narrative.[13] "Descriptio" marks this narrative moment by making it stand out descriptively, which means creating a visually memorable description in the text and hence in the audience's mind. "Descriptio" produces visual images. This special rhetorical treatment is the cognitive and imaginative link between the verbal text and the pictorial text it generates, between what I have called pictures from words and words from pictures.

The split-shield is one of the most curious shields in all of romance literature. It is brought to court as a gift for Queen Guenievre from the Dame du Lac. It arrives while Lancelot is residing with his friend Galehaut in Sorelois, where separation from the queen brings on lovesickness. The shield is delivered by a damsel accompanied by an injured knight. The damsel presents the shield to the queen as a gift from the wisest and most beautiful maiden who ever lived and instructs the queen to keep it for the sake of him she loves best (note the guarded, enigmatic language). She explains to Guenievre that the shield has a purpose: "'se vous cest escu gardés, il vous garira de la grignor dolor que vous eussiés onques et metera en la grignor joie ou vous onques fussiés'" (LM VIII:207; LK 402). Guenievre is delighted. This is clearly no ordinary shield, as is borne out by its description: it is split vertically, and the two halves are connected only at the center point, the "bras de la borcle" (LM VIII:206; LK 402). The split, wide enough for two hands, separates the images of a beautiful lady and a knight who is richly armed except for the head. The two figures are barely separated at the top and would be embracing were it not for the split, "s'entrebaisoient se ne fust la fendeure de l'escu, mais par desous estoient si loign li uns de l'autre com plus pooient" (LM VIII:206; LK 402–03). The damsel explains its "senefiance": the knight is the finest who ever lived within or without Arthur's court, who by his love and prowess has been awarded the lady's love but so far has received nothing more than embraces. When their love is consummated ("enterine"), the two halves of the shield will join and Guenievre will be released from her suffering and find joy; this will not happen, however, until this finest of all knights has become a member of Arthur's household.[14]

In this verbal narrative a specific object has been introduced into the action and has created an element of mystery and anticipation. Why would the Dame du Lac send the shield? Who are the lady and knight in question? Why are they depicted on the shield? Why is the shield split? Too many questions have been raised by this object for it to be ignored by the reader, and the specificity of its description—its status as ekphrasis within the verbal text—makes it difficult to forget as a visual object.

The visual stimuli for remembering the split-shield are provided by the object itself, whose ekphrastic status is conveyed rhetorically by the "descriptio." Earlier episodes of this romance have typed the shield in general as a device that protects in battle and identifies its bearer through its decorative insignia, and in one instance as a source of supernatural strength for its wearer.[15] The split-shield, however, is useless for physical protection because of its dilapidated state. The prediction that the split will disappear and the two halves of the shield will be joined, in fact comes true when the two lovers are physically united on their first night of love (LM VIII:444; LK 547). If we regard the description of the shield itself as a painting in words that must be converted into a visual picture in order to speak, we find that this prediction was inscribed in the description. The narrator points out that the beautiful lady and finest knight "would be embracing were it not for the split," which is to say that because they were physically separated they were not embracing. There is, however, one point where the two halves of the shield—hence the two images—are joined: at the "bras de la borcle." This is the reinforcing bar that passed across the width of the shield horizontally; it held the vertical wooden strips of the shield together and was the fastening point for the straps by which the shield was carried. The *Lancelot's* narrator specifies it is still in place on the shield. In visualizing the description, I assumed that the two figures were spaced harmoniously on the shield, with due regard to proportion, with head near top, feet near the base.[16] If this is so, the picture in fact describes considerably more than a would-be embrace, especially if we remember that the two figures face one another: the "bras de la borcle" joins the two figures at what might be called a compromising point of the body and in a compromising situation (fig.

3.1). The inescapable conclusion is that the description of the split-shield gives a powerful visual image of the sexual union of the knight and the lady. It "tells it like it is," leaving no doubt about the erotic nature of the forthcoming Lancelot-Guenievre union, provided that the audience listens attentively and uses its imagination to make a pictorial image of the verbal description. If we align the shield with the heraldic divisions of an armorial shield (fig. 3.2), the "bras de la borcle" corresponds to the "fesse" area, an appropriate term to which I will return.

It would be presumptuous to equate the sexual explicitness of the description with a critical authorial viewpoint. At this stage in the tale we already know that the narrative extols greatness of the hero, but we have not yet arrived at the point where he deliberately withholds information from Arthur's clerks. So we are not yet aware of the author-narrator's moral judgment of his hero's conduct. What is certainly not presumptuous is our recognition of the anticipatory value of this particular verbal image, for the shield description appears over 150 pages in advance of the sexual act it emblematizes, so it provides visual prediction within the verbal text.

The author's invention assigns to the split-shield the commonplace semiotic function of revealing the wearer's identity, yet the function has been remotivated and redefined. It indicates not only an identity but also the source and nature of the identity, which the split-shield itself will confirm not only through its power as image but also through its narrative power. Specifically, when Lancelot goes mad through deprivation of love, it is the restored split-shield, literally and physically forced upon him by the Dame du Lac, which restores to him the sanity and wholeness that are essential to his fulfillment of chivalric duties (LM VIII:445–62; LK 553–58). His subsequent resumption of these duties is surely infused with irony, for he will execute an heroic rescue of the imprisoned Arthur and an equally heroic defense of the king's kingdom against the Saxon enemy. In this dazzling performance Lancelot will ride into battle protecting himself with this same shield and will "fight like a lion" now that consummated love with the king's wife has made him and the shield whole again. [17] The restored split-shield serves, then, as an emblem of both the force of love and the exemplary centrality of the inspiration of love that identify the knight in his efforts to be the greatest knight ever. His military identity as inscribed on the split-shield is one of sexual union with the queen of the king he is rescuing, and the rescue is conditional upon the union. [18] The fact that the author depicts Lancelot and Guenievre as separated but united on the shield provides a more reflective, critical context for the union. As I have suggested elsewhere, the author uses knowledge of heraldic devices in creating the description and the narrative power of the split-shield. [19] In heraldry a shield was split vertically by a process called "dimidiation" to indicate a matrimonial alliance. [20] The arms of the husband were assigned to the left side and the arms of the wife to the right side. The husband-wife alliance is certainly pertinent to the Lancelot-Guenievre situation, for Arthur is the queen's lawful husband. The author appears to be taking a conventional dynastic symbol of wedlock and applying it to the romance convention of love between lady and knight. For what purpose? Is he emphasizing the triangular nature of the relationship by superimposing one pairing on another pairing? Is he suggesting that the lady-knight relationship is analogous to that of husband and wife? That the two relationships, and the two men, are equivalent? Is he suggesting that Lancelot is a usurper of Arthur's bed? Or, if prowess alone is used as the basis for parallels, does Lancelot protect where Arthur fails to protect?[21] The author's structuring of his tale within the interlace in fact makes all of these interpretations admissible, for while Lancelot spends the night in Guenievre's bed, Arthur spends the night in the arms of Camille, an "enchantress" from the Saxon enemy camp. Which of the two men commits the greater folly? We might conclude that the author is following Chrétien's lead and preserving the ambiguity of Lancelot's relations with Arthur, were it not for additional visual evidence from the split-shield. Medieval lawbooks used a split-shield—literally a shield splitting or already split down the middle—to indicate pictorially divorce of husband and wife. [22]

The Pictorial Image

The *Lancelot* exists in over 90 manuscripts.[23] There is as yet no comprehensive study listing or describing the illustrations of all the illuminated manuscripts, My current recension lists 53 of them as having pictures, with or without illumination.[24] The split-shield episode appears to be a relatively frequent subject for illustration. I have examined the episode as illustrated in four manuscripts from the late thirteenth to the late fourteenth centuries, the high period of Gothic illumination. Given the highly visual quality of the split-shield in the verbal text, I wanted to find out if this emphasis was carried over by the illustrator. I have considered the illustrations simply as pictorial narrative equivalents of the written narrative, which have been included in the artifact we call an illustrated manuscript because they play a role in the reception of the tale.

Miniatures and historiated initials are commonly used as space-markers that help the reader to find the relevant place in the manuscript, but they also divide the verbal text for other purposes. In the case of the *Lancelot,* the narrative is broken into segments that constitute the interlace. The manuscripts cater for this mechanism visually through a systematic use of decorated initials and miniatures that mark off "chapters," and sometimes "paragraphs."[25] Oxford, Bodleian Library, MS Ashmole 828 is typical in that its miniatures are placed at the end of each "chapter," sealing it off from the next chapter. This is significant in the case of the arrival of the split-shield, which is a brief narrative and occupies only a portion of the space and events of the chapter in which it occurs. The fact that it is illustrated by the miniature seems to single it out for attention as *the* most significant moment of the chapter.

The miniature in Ashmole 828 f. 98v. (fig. 3.3) marks the end of the chapter in which the split-shield is delivered to court. There are no rubrics, so we do not know what the illuminator's instructions were, if any. The shield seems to stand out from an external wall, rather like a shop sign, with towers indicating the court; the verbal text states that the queen hung the shield on her wall. The illuminator presents a composite picture of the arrival of the shield at court, combining its descriptive value and its anticipatory value. The shield is divided down the middle and is decorated with images of a knight (left) and lady (right). There are no visible traces of the "bras de la borcle," as the halves of the shield are in fact joined, but a thick black vertical line indicates the place of the split. Three figures are present—the damsel, the queen, the injured knight—all of whom look up at the shield; the queen's hands direct attention to the shield.[26] The illuminator seems not to have taken account of the dynamics of embracing, since he depicts the pictorial knight and lady in a three-quarters frontal pose, but this is in fact the conventional facial angle.[27] The figures' gestures and the compositional division into a left grouping (people) and right grouping (split-shield) gives the impression that the audience in the picture are being asked to remember the shield and the split itself, while the closed split anticipates the union of knight and lady without indicating the erotic nature of the union.

The miniature in London, British Library, Add. 10293, f. 90v. (fig. 3.4) appears not at the end of a chapter but at the exact point in the text where the damsel from the lake arrives and greets the queen. The damsel, in handing over the shield to the queen, holds it up while she and the queen look at it. The knight (right) and lady (left) on the shield are indeed embracing but separated by the split, and they face one another in profile. The split is clearly visible; indeed, its existence is given emphasis as a wide split from top to bottom, with no join at the top. There is clearly a join at the "bras de la borcle," as visualized in the verbal text, and another at a higher point where the embracing arms would meet.[28] The illuminator seems to know the story well as a verbal text and as a visual text. He has insisted on the two halves of the shield being connected, and he emphasizes this by two joins, both of them strategically placed. The upper one is justified by the knight's right hand being clearly curled round the shoulder of the lady, showing an actual embrace that is split rather than a potential one. Moreover, he seems to have used the hands of the damsel and the queen to draw attention to the lower join at the "bras de la borcle," for whereas Guenievre's left hand supports the base of the shield, the damsel's left hand is open, indicating direction, and its fingertips point to the join specified by the verbal text.[29]

In Paris, BN, fr. 344, f. 251v. (fig. 3.5), the split-shield is illustrated in an historiated initial that opens the chapter containing the episode. The shield is shown hanging on the wall, and the queen points to it; her back-turned head indicates that she is drawing it to the attention of a female figure with whom she is conversing. The headgear of the interlocutor identifies her as the damsel from the lake. The shield is clearly split and is painted with images of a lady (right) and knight (left). They are indeed facing one another, arms extended, as one does for an embrace. The knight is shown in a three-quarters facial pose, while the lady's features are too blurred to distinguish the facial pose.[30] The illuminator appears to know the details of the verbal text, for the shield is joined at the top, the split widens as it nears the base, and the arms of the figures suggest an embrace. The split appears to be joined in the same two places as in Add. 10293, which coincide with the arms of the figures. The upper point of linkage is the "half" of the embrace effected by the two hands furthest from the eye of the viewer. The front hand of knight and lady reach the edge of the shield at the point of the "bras de la borcle" that links the two halves of the shield in the verbal text. The hands and arms reinforce, in other words, the shield's two points of linkage: the embrace named by the verbal text and the crucial point of linkage that is suggested but not named.

The miniature in Paris, BN, MS. fr. 16999, f. 102r (fig. 3.6) depicts the split-shield being handed over to Guenievre by the damsel from the lake, in the presence of the Dame de Malohaut and the injured knight. Their gestures indicate discussion of the shield. Unlike the other three depictions, this shield is richly decorated in gold, but there are no images on it. This manuscript has other helpful information, however, in the form of rubrics: "Comment une demoisele porte a son cou un ecu dessus dessous et l'ecu est fendu de long et sure l'une partie il y a un chevalier peint et sur l'autre partie une dame et lui tient le bras sur l'espaule."[31] Did the illuminator somehow forget the two images on the shield? Did he find them distasteful? Did someone paint over them? The miniature itself appears not to provide any visual clues to the significance of the split-shield.

While illustration helped the medieval reader to locate specific parts of the verbal text, its implications are important for the audience's reception of a story read out loud. The audience's initial reception is aural, not visual. In the case of the split-shield episode the reader would have read aloud certain key words which, in the verbal text and the miniatures, encapsulate the episode: "l'ecu fendu," for example. Any word or group of words has the power to generate new meanings, and never more so than when it is isolated from its original setting. The possibilities are particularly fertile in aural reception because the words are spoken out loud, not read, and once freed from the constraints of their visual form we call writing, they are more open to homophony.[32] The split-shield claims a homophone of its own for the reader willing to repeat the phrase out loud: "l'escu fendu," "les culs fendus." Ashmole 828 only reveals its homophony if we see and hear its entire folio (fig. 3.7). Its artful design consists of the miniature and a "bas de page." In the "bas de page," an ape bends over on all fours, baring his hind quarters and looking back to his posterior and the archer. On the left side, a clothed male figure prepares to shoot an arrow at the ape, and his target is clearly "le cul," which is also a homonym of "fesse" (as found in "fesse point" on the heraldic shield).

Arrows, like pointing fingers, were a common visual marginal mechanism for drawing attention to places in the manuscript. The illuminator of Ashmole 828 seems to have transformed this technical convention into a pictorial narrative in the "bas de page," where the arrow literally points to the "fesse" of the ape, to create a hunting scene. It is an invention that reminds us of the dynastic dimensions of the heraldic shield (see fig. 3.2), in which the location of the "bras de la borcle" corresponded to the "fesse." Etymology plays its part here, for the semantic common ground of "le cul" and "la fesse" is a visual image rooted in etymology: OF "fesse" = buttock < VL "fissa" = crack, split. The fissure that defines "le cul" as a semantic equivalent of "la fesse" also defines the split-shield.

The bared "fesse" depicted in the "bas de page" belongs to an ape. Apes are by far the most prolific creatures in Gothic marginal illustrations.[33] The ape appears in all types of Gothic manuscripts, sacred as well as profane, verse and prose, Latin and vernacular, and all genres. The figures in the margins of manuscripts have been shown to serve an elucidative, moralizing purpose and to be derived from exempla and fables already known to the audience.[34] The figures in the margins would recall for the audience the moral lesson of the exemplum or fable. So the marginalia would be pictorial shortcuts to meaning that would be enshrined in a proverbial phrase such as "the early bird catches the worm." Certain animals in margins represented certain social groups.[35] However, as Michael Camille shows, apes in margins fill a much more complex function.[36] The frequency of the ape in the margin is the result of his socio-cultural history, which is just as marginal as his position in the manuscripts. Given the vogue in the 1200s and 1300s of imputing probative value to the original meaning of a word, we need look no further than the ape's etymology, found in the encyclopedic writers. Apes belong to the class called "simia." Isidore of Seville, in fact, gives five types of ape under this nomenclature, but the only one known to Western Europe in the thirteenth and fourteenth centuries was the tailless Barbary ape, as seen in the margin of Ashmole 828.[37] "Simia" was believed to derive from the Latin adjective "similis" = similar, like—"simia quam similis" as Ennius says.[38] The ape was thus by name and by nature a visual figure of similitude, "similitudo hominis" in real life, since he tries to ape man, to pass himself off as man, but cannot be more than a likeness because his true nature given at creation is that of a beast. For the moralist his bestial nature both separates him from and joins him to mankind—to mankind in his fallen state, fallen by disobedience to God expressed as the sexual act. The particular hubris implied in such disobedience makes the ape an image of the sinner. By the mid-thirteenth century, when Gothic marginal art began to flourish, the ape therefore had a reputation for "'unclean' sensuality" and "could be conceived as the antitype and enemy of knighthood."[39] This unflattering relationship to knighthood took on parodic tones in Gothic marginalia; the ape was cast in the role of the chivalrous knight himself because of the reputation for worldliness, hypocrisy, and mock chastity acquired by the chivalrous knight in the moralist's eyes.[40] "Vice parading as virtue" is how Alexander Neckham moralistically describes the ape, echoing the tension between reality and appearances, between the inner and outer self built into the creature's natural identity, but identifying it even more forcefully with male sexual rapacity that leads to adultery.[41]

What are we to make of the ape in the margin of Ashmole 828, f. 98v? What is its relevance to the marginal scene, to the miniature, and to the verbal text with its visual image in words? The "bas de page" shows a man and an ape. The ape's "cul" is clearly visible, clearly "fendu" by nature.[42] In the case of the ape, this fact of nature is unmistakable because the animal has no tail and no clothing, and the gaping of the animal's rear is literally mirrored on f. 98v in the male face with gaping mouth that flourishes at the tip of the foliage.[43] The full face of the ape, as he glances back toward his other "face," doubles the illustrator's focus on the simian body rather than on the simian mind.[44] With hindsight, the ape is going to "get it in the arse," to use the popular language of consequences.[45]

The "bas de page" depicts a hunting scene, "la chasse," with all its perennial martial and sexual associations. Despite their visual differences, the man and the ape are alike in one respect. Both have a "cul fendu" and both therefore have the propensity for the kind of love represented by "l'escu fendu," which is adulterous; whereas the ape's "cul fendu" is visible for all to see, that of the clothed figure is concealed beneath the clothing. This makes the two figures, ape and man, reverse images of each other: the ape here reveals his "cul fendu," his "unclean sensuality," his mock chastity, while the man conceals his. The man thus doubles the ape image of fallen man through his own concealed unclean sensuality and mock chastity, both of which make him a potential adulterer.

The "parole" has been given two painted forms ("painture") in Ashmole 828, first in the miniature and second in the lower margin. The miniature limits its pictorial record to the surface of the verbal narrative of the split-shield episode by drawing attention to an event without directing attention to the significance, moral or otherwise, of the event. The marginal illustration in the "bas de page," however, breaks through the surface of this visual narrative. The human figure is about to engage in a hostile act that emphasizes the split as the butt of his attack and the locus of penetration. His attack is aimed at the "cul fendu" itself, which belongs to a figure of the worldly sinner. The two contrasting figures and their contrasting actions seem to echo the contrast between the two narrative systems of miniature and marginalia, in which the ape's similitudinous identity posits the marginal scene as "like" the miniature. Yet the man is not any man, for his garment identifies him as a clerk (is he a writer?), and his arrow in the margin has marginal precedents elsewhere, where it is used to indicate strong disagreement with the text it targets.[46] The ape's function as a figure of similitude extends equally to the text itself, for "the ape came to signify the dubious status of representation itself, *le singe* being an anagram for *le signe*—the sign."[47] The ape and his "cul fendu" symbolize, then, the episode as written and pictorialized in the miniature, while the clerk indicates a stance (could it be hypocritical?) to be taken towards it. The "bas de page" thus incorporates both interpretation and moral disapproval of the episode depicted in the miniature. I think we can safely say that what the miniature with its proper, conventional pictorial imaging cannot signify, the marginal figures do express (albeit indirectly). Their signifying practice is not that of the courtly mode of the miniature, not a courtly code of concealment, but a code that lets the audience see for themselves, by reading visually between the lines, that the split-shield illustrates and anticipates an erotic encounter that ought not to occur. The illuminator of Ashmole 828 seems to have wanted his audience to "see through it" and stand against it.

If we needed further confirmation of the concealed erotic overtones in Ashmole 828's miniature of the split-shield episode, together with a moral point of view of its significance, it can be found in BN, fr. 16999 (fig. 3.6). Its illuminator left the split-shield as a plain gold shield, without the images of knight and lady specified by the verbal text. The depiction of the shield also differs from the others being considered here in that it is being carried upside down, "dessus dessous," as the rubric specifies. An upside-down shield signifies shame, the "bête noire" of chivalry and the dishonor most closely associated with the identity of Chrétien de Troyes's Lancelot.[48] In this manuscript, the Prose *Lancelot*'s split-shield is a shield of shame, for those who understand the chivalric code. This illuminator does not use apes and arrows down below to drive home his point; instead, he reveals the source of the shame from the margin above. Leaning down from the top left corner of the miniature is a marginal figure playing the bagpipe. In a festive, communal context the bagpipe connotes festivity. On its own, however, it represents the male sexual organs. This explains why the player points his instrument down toward the miniature and looks toward the other illustration of the "ecu fendu" as he plays its tune. The artist has used the heraldic convention of dimidiation to denote the split in the shield and a second heraldic convention (the upside-down shield) to convey its contravention of courtly ethics, yet he has also emblazoned it with gold to suggest the ambiguous splendor of Lancelot's conduct. The marginal figure looks in from the outside and presents a body-based version ("the same old song?") of the significance of the shield to let the audience know the source of the shame. Here, as in Ashmole 828 (fig. 3.7), the miniature focuses on the split shield without reference to the sexual connotations of the split. While the miniature itself conveys a moral stance expressed in terms of chivalric standards, the sexual reference comes from a different register found in the margin: the source of the shame is Lancelot's sexual encounter with the queen. Once again, the margin expresses that which the miniature cannot visualize, and in doing so it reinterprets the miniature for the onlooker.

The four examples of manuscript illumination used in this paper present two groupings, those with marginalia and those without, which resolve the question of pictorial meaning in two ways. Ashmole 828 and BN, fr. 16999 rely on the external voice of their marginal gloss to cut through the nicety of the courtly miniatures in order to translate, in a different pictorial (and perhaps social or political) register, the "truth" of the split-shield that is hidden in the verbal narrative. Add. 10293 and BN, fr. 344, on the other hand, incorporate the problematic "truth" within the boundaries of the miniature/historiated initial itself.

They adhere closely to the wording of the written narrative, translating it visually through the shield itself, so that the audience can see the nature of the bodily link between the knight and the lady without resorting to a different register. These are two approaches to reading its consequences, with a foresight that searches for a "truth" that cuts through the conventions of Arthurian knighthood, which are conventions of concealment. Lancelot's relationship with Queen Guenievre will be a source of shame and will contribute to the downfall of Arthur's kingdom.

By way of conclusion, it is useful to remember that reading from an illustrated manuscript was an interactive, multimedia affair. As the reader did the reading, the group of listeners were gathered round close enough to be able to see for themselves the illustrations in these very large manuscripts, and they would point, laugh, giggle, sigh at what they saw and heard with ear and eye. What they saw and heard was an interweaving of word ("parole") and image ("painture"), in which the visual imagination and the sound of the spoken word each have their own prominence. The significance is interwoven by visually and aurally powerful words and pictures and in two instances by two types of pictures that in two cases correspond to two voices. Weaving has been the commonest metaphor used to describe the composition of the *Lancelot* text since Lot first coined it, but I will conclude by suggesting that the work's illustrated manuscripts exemplify the weaving process more powerfully than the non-illustrated manuscripts because they show us that the prose *Lancelot* is a complex text. A text is defined first and foremost by its etymological Latin root, "tegere" = "to weave." The *Lancelot* illuminated manuscripts embody this process in an interweaving not only of narrative segments, but also in a weaving together of image and word, of miniature and margin, of audience and manuscript designer in a common promotion of imagination and understanding of something we could loosely call "truth," but which needs our ears and our eyes to make it meaningful.

NOTES

1. Cassiodorus Senator, *Institutiones*, ed. R.A.B. Mynors (London: Oxford Univ. Press, 1937); trans. Leslie W. Jones as *An Introduction to Divine and Human Readings* (New York: Columbia Univ. Press, 1946), p. 116.

2. *Li Bestiaire d'Amour*, ed. Cesare Segre (Milan: Riccardi, 1957), p. 5.

3. Mary J. Carruthers, *The Book of Memory: A Study of Memory in Medieval Culture* (Cambridge: Cambridge Univ. Press, 1990), p. 222.

4. Carruthers, *Book of Memory*, pp. 222–23, and the entire chapter seven.

5. For the role of ear and eye in memory, with reference to Richart de Fournival, see Carruthers, *Book of Memory*, p. 224; also V.A. Kolve, *Chaucer and the Imagery of Narrative: The First Five Canterbury Tales* (Stanford: Stanford Univ. Press, 1984), p. 20–32.

6. Following A. Micha's example, I use the title *Lancelot* to mean the central section (formerly called "Lancelot propre") of the *Lancelot-Grail* cycle. All textual references are from *Lancelot: Roman en prose du XIIIe siecle*, ed. A. Micha, 9 vols. (Paris-Geneva: Droz, 1978–83) and indicate (LM) volume and page numbers. Where applicable they are cross referenced to *Lancelot do Lac: The Non-cyclic Old French Prose Romance*, ed. E. Kennedy (Oxford: Oxford Univ. Press, 1980), using (LK) page numbers.

7. See Gilles Deleuze, *Différence et Répétition* (Paris: Presses Universitaires de France, 1968), and Peter Haidu, "Repetition: Modern Reflections on Medieval Aesthetics," *Modern Language Notes*, 92 (1977), 875–87.

8. See Amelia Rutledge's structuralist analysis of part of the *Lancelot*'s interlace in her unpublished dissertation, "Narrative Structures in the Old French Prose *Lancelot*" (Diss., Yale, 1974), and Elspeth Kennedy's explication of the process in *Lancelot and the Grail: A Study of the Prose Lancelot* (Oxford: Clarendon, 1986), pp. 156–235.

9. In a discussion session at the Colloquium on Narrative Cycles in the Chansons de Geste and Romances of the Middle Ages, organized by the Royal Dutch Academy of Arts and Sciences, Amsterdam, 17–18 December, 1992.

10. For a discussion of the notion of authority and authoring/authority, see Marie-Dominique Chenu, "'Auctor,' 'actor,' 'autor,'" *Bulletin du Cange, 3* (1927), 81–86; Alastair J. Minnis, *Medieval Theory of Authorship* (London: Scolar Press, 1984).

11. For an account of this incident in the context of romance tradition, see Jean M. Dornbush, *Pygmalion's Figure: Reading Old French Romance*, (Lexington, Ky.: French Forum, 1990), pp. 100–02. Dornbush uses the typical configuration of "clergie" vs. "chevalerie" to demonstrate the specificity of the authority of the *Lancelot*'s narrator in relation to one earlier and one later verse romance. She does not consider the implications of the autobiographical nature of the record-keeping, which are the focus of my interest.

12. The episode occurs in three parts: (1) the shield arrives at court (LM VIII:204–08; LK 401–03), (2) the halves of the shield come together as predicted (LM VIII:444; LK 546), and (3) the shield is used to restore Lancelot to sanity (LM VIII:453–64; LK 552–58).

13. On "descriptio," see Douglas Kelly, *The Art of Medieval French Romance*, (Madison: Univ. of Wisconsin Press, 1992), pp. 12–13, 51–58, 98–99, 147, 160–66, 229, 231–40, 292–304.

14. This paragraph and the following two repeat material from Carol R. Dover, "The Split-Shield Motif in the Old French Prose *Lancelot*," *The Arthurian Yearbook*, 1 (1991), 43–61; here, 48–49.

15. In the Doloreuse Garde episode, for example.

16. This is the case with Arthur's shield, Pridwen, which carries the image of the Virgin Mary in Geoffrey of Monmouth's *Historia Regum Britanniae*; the illustration of it in Peter Langtoft's *Chronicle of England* (London, BL, Royal 20 A II, f. 4) shows this concern for proportion. The illustration is reproduced in Muriel Whitaker, *The Legends of King Arthur in Art* (Cambridge: Brewer, 1990) pp. 3–4. For an historical discussion, see Helmut Nickel, "About Arms and Armor in the Age of Arthur," in *Avalon to Camelot*, 1 (1983), 19–21.

17. The choice of the word "lion" is important because, in the prophetic language that intervenes from time to time in the *Lancelot*, the lion is the symbolic figure of King Arthur.

18. Intertextually, this narrative function of the split-shield is a rewriting of the events that caused the hero's attempted suicide in Chrétien de Troyes's Lancelot romance, producing a similar conclusion: that Lancelot's ability to protect Arthur's kingdom (and this includes Arthur himself) is conditional upon his love for Arthur's queen, which is a sexual union.

19. "The Split-Shield Motif," pp. 51–52, summarized in the rest of this paragraph.

20. Dimidiation was already practiced in the late twelfth and early thirteenth centuries; see Thomas Woodcock and John M. Robinson, *The Oxford Guide to Heraldry* (Oxford: Oxford Univ. Press, 1988), pp. 118–19.

21. As in Chrétien's *Chevalier de la charrette*, where Lancelot's rescue of the queen is motivated, on one level, by Arthur's failure to protect her from Meleagant.

22. The early thirteenth-century *Spiegel der Sassen*, an extremely well-known and widely used book of law, presents the main points of law in words and in pictures. The section on family law ("Familienrecht" and "Erbrecht") uses a split-shield to indicate the splitting of the inheritance when the wife dies: "Der gespaltene Schild, den der hinterbliebene Mann und die Kinder der Verstorbenen anfassen, bedeutet die Erbteilung," *Der Sachsenspiegel in Bildern aus der Heidelberger Bilderhandschrift*, ed. Walter Koschorreck (Frankfurt-am-Main: Insel, 1976), p. 105, fig. 107. I thank Martine Meuwese for bringing this text and its example to my attention.

23. For a listing see Brian Woledge and H.P. Clive, *Répertoire des plus anciens textes en prose française depuis 842 jusqu'aux premières années du XIIIe siècle* (Geneva: Droz, 1964), and *Supplément*. For a description of all the known manuscripts, see Alexandre Micha, "Les manuscrits du *Lancelot en prose*: I," *Romania*, 81 (1960), 28–60; "Les manuscrits du *Lancelot en prose*: II," *Romania*, 81 (1960), 145–87; "La tradition manuscrite du *Lancelot* en prose," *Romania*, 85 (1964), 293–318; "La tradition manuscrite du *Lancelot* en prose," *Romania*, 85 (1964), 478–517. *Lancelot do Lac* I, pp. 1–9.

24. This is my own current, provisional count, using the manuscripts themselves and the data provided by A. Micha in his series of *Romania* articles, by B. Woledge, *Bibliographie des romans et nouvelles en prose française antérieurs à 1500*. (Geneva: Droz, 1954); *Supplement 1954–1973* (Geneva:

Droz, 1875), and by Kennedy, 1, pp. 1–11. For recent work on Vulgate Cycle manuscript illustrations, see Alison Stones' extensive work in "Images of Temptation, Seduction and Discovery in the *Prose Lancelot*," *Wiener Jahrbuch für Kunstgeschichte* 46/47 (1993/1994), 725–35 and 885–88; "Arthurian Art Since Loomis," in *Arturus Rex II: Acta Conventus Lovaniensis 1987*, ed. W. van Hoecke, G. Tournoy, and W. Verbeke (Leuven: Leuven Univ. Press, 1991), 21–78; "Some Aspects of Arthur's Death in Medieval Illumination." in *The Passing of Arthur: New Essays in Arthurian Tradition*, ed. C. Baswell and W. Sharpe (New York: Garland, 1988), 52–101; "Sacred and Profane Art: Secular and Liturgical Book Illumination in the Thirteenth Century," in *The Epic in Medieval Society: Aesthetic and Moral Values*, ed. Harald Scholler (Tubingen: Niemeyer, 1977), 100–12; "The Earliest Illustrated Prose *Lancelot* Manuscript?" *Reading Medieval Studies*, III (1975–76), 3–44; and her unpublished doctoral dissertation, "The Illustrations of the French Prose *Lancelot* in Flanders, Belgium, and Paris: 1250–1340," 2 vols. (Diss., Univ. of London, 1970 [1971]). See also Susan Blackman's comparative table of illustrations in three of the *Lancelot* manuscripts in the present volume.

25. In his edition of the *Vulgate Version of the Arthurian Romances*, H.O. Sommer provided footnotes with descriptions of each miniature and the accompanying rubrics at the points where they occurred in his base manuscript(s). See also Micha's descriptions of the *Lancelot* manuscripts in his series of articles in *Romania*.

26. For hand gestures and their various meanings, see François Garnier, *Le Langage de l'image au moyen âge. Signification et symbolique* (Paris: Le Léopard d'Or, 1982), pp. 159–233.

27. Garnier, *Le Langage*, "En règle générale, aucun personnage de qualité n'est représenté de profil. Les exceptions, relativement rares s'expliquent facilement par les nécessités de l'action. La position de profil est en effet le signe d'une infériorité" (p. 142).

28. The illustrator also shows the straps by which the damsel carries the shield. They pass from her neck to the back of the shield. It is possible to construe the two connectors as being the two straps, particularly since they are of a similar beige color as the straps. This possibility lends ambiguity to the image, without lessening the fact that the halves of the shield are linked.

29. The contrast between the hands of the damsel and the queen is considerable. Guenievre's lower hand is half hidden, as it supports the base of the shield and is clearly a grasp. The damsel's hand could have been similarly placed to indicate support of the object.

30. Curiously, the facial features of the female figure on the shield are similarly blurred.

31. The rubric is at the bottom of f. 101v.

32. I have assumed that the manuscripts were read aloud to a small-group audience, but homophony applies equally to private reading, particularly in light of the many medieval attestations we have to so-called silent reading being audible reading.

33. See Lilian M.C. Randall, *Images in the Margins of Gothic Manuscripts* (Berkeley and Los Angeles: Univ. of California Press, 1966), pp. 16, 18, 56–65; H.W. Janson, *Apes and Ape Lore in the Middle Ages and the Renaissance* (London: Warburg Institute, 1952), esp. chs. I-VII, IX; Janson observes (p. 164) that "apes play a more conspicuous part in marginal grotesques than any other animal. In certain Flemish manuscripts of the late thirteenth and early fourteenth centuries, they are so numerous as to crowd the rest of the animal kingdom off the page." More recently, see Michael Camille, *Image on the Edge: The Margins of Medieval Art*, (Cambridge: Harvard Univ. Press, 1992).

34. Randall, "Exempla as a Source of Gothic Marginal Illumination, " *Art Bulletin*, XXXIX (1957), 97–107.

35. L. Randall, "The Snail in Gothic Marginal Warfare," *Speculum*, XXVII (1962), 358.

36. See Camille, *Image on the Edge* , "The ape came to signify the dubious status of representation itself, *le singe* being an anagram for *le signe*— the sign" (p. 13).

37. Janson, *Apes*, p. 16.

38. Janson, *Apes*, p. 19.

39. Janson, *Apes*, p. 167.

40. Thus the thirteenth-century mystic Mechthild of Magdeburg refers to "the ape of worldliness" ("den Affen der Welt"), see Janson, *Apes*, pp. 51 and 113.

41. Janson, *Apes*, pp. 30, 34, 207–08, 229.

42. Littré, *Dictionnaire de la Langue Francaise*, points out that in the fourteenth century "fesse" referred to the split itself rather than the buttock.

43. The ape's taillessness was explained by Isidore (*Etymologiae*) and hence by Christian moralists as proof of its inability to choose between good and evil; since this choice was available only to the tailless creature called man, the ape's taillessness is proof of his hubris in wanting to raise himself to man's level (Janson, *Apes*, pp. 18–19).

44. The ape's stance clearly excludes any confusion with the "intellectual" apes that engaged in reading or writing in Gothic margins; see Janson, *Apes*, p. 167.

45. Compare the modern French expression "en avoir dans les fesses."

46. See Peter Lombard's gloss on the Psalms, Trinity College, Cambridge, B.V.5 f. 33v, where Saint Augustine prods the text laterally from the margin with a large, spearlike arrow to signify that he is attacking it because he disagrees with what it says. Camille provides an illustration in *Image on the Edge*, p. 21.

47. Camille, *Image on the Edge*, p. 13.

48. I am grateful to Martine Meuwese for suggesting this connection. My thanks also to Janet F. van der Meulen for sharing with me her ongoing examination of a thirteenth-century "dit," "Le triomphe des Carmes," in which the "varlets" who ride in their late lord's funeral procession carry their shields upside down.

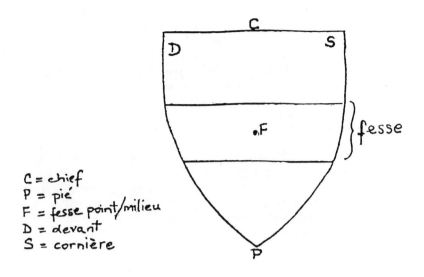

C = chief
P = pié
F = fesse point/milieu
D = devant
S = cornière

Top. Fig. 3.1. Heraldic divisions of an armorial shield.

Bottom. Fig. 3.2. Split-shield.

Fig. 3.3. Oxford, Bodleian Library, Ashmole 828, f. 98v (detail).
Reproduced by permission.

Fig. 3.4. London, BL, Add. 10293, f. 90v (detail).
Reproduced by permission.

Fig. 3.5. Paris, BN, fr. 344, f. 251v.
Reproduced by permission.

Fig. 3.6. Paris, BN, fr. 16999, f. 102 (detail).
Reproduced by permission.

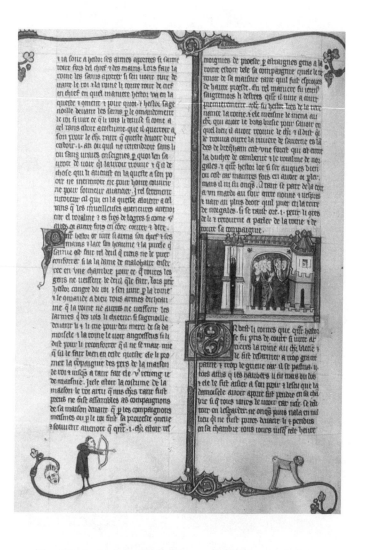

Fig. 3.7. Oxford, Bodleian Library, Ashmole 828, f. 98v.
Reproduced by permission.

4 SEEING THE SEER

IMAGES OF MERLIN IN THE MIDDLE AGES AND BEYOND

Donald L. Hoffman

By 1874, when Julia Margaret Cameron photographed Vivian trapping him in a hollow tree, Merlin was seen as an elderly wizard. Drawing upon her impressions of Tennyson's *Idylls of the King*, and the good will of various friends, neighbors, and servitors (Arthur, for example, was portrayed by William Warder, a porter from Yarmouth), Mrs. Cameron undertook to illustrate Tennyson photographically (figs. 4.1 and 4.2).[1] Vivian was portrayed by an anonymous visitor (possibly the "Lady Amateur" who provided a "Reminiscence of Mrs. Cameron" for the *Photographic News* in 1886), while the doddering Merlin was portrayed by Charles Hay Cameron (Cameron's husband), whose giggling made the entombing tree quiver mysteriously, creating an effect that, for the "Lady Amateur" was "more than mortal could stand."[2] The ancient, ethereal, wizened, if whimsical, wizard captured on film by Julia Cameron in 1874 is, essentially, the Merlin that has been etched in the mind of Arthurians for nearly 120 years.

This quasi-Jungian archetype of Merlin as the Wise Old Man is, however, at odds with the image of Merlin presented in more ancient manuscripts. The purpose of this paper is (1) to present a sort of picto-biography of Merlin from the lavishly illustrated fourteenth-century manuscript, BL, Add. 10292,[3] and (2) to show how the images of Merlin, under pressure from the forces of the Counter-Reformation in Italy and the Puritans in England, begin to alter to create a Merlin whose visage reflects the artist's position in the religio-political conflicts of his age.

Merlin iconography begins with his conception. The frontispiece of *Le premiere volume de Merlin*[4] presents a particularly striking image of the engendering of Merlin (fig. 4.3). After the satanic counsel has determined to create a demonic child as a counterblast to Christ, the devils begin to implement their plan by slaying the cattle belonging to a rich bourgeois, whose family they have planned to reduce to such despair that they will be able to corrupt the virgin daughter, who will become the mortal mother of the demon seed. Like Satan in the Book of Job, whose opening is echoed in the demonic counsel, the devils begin by attacking the rich man's property, then move in on his family. The cattle gone, the bourgeois is impoverished and destroyed, and his younger daughters fall into lechery and prostitution. Reduced to nearly total despair, the eldest daughter skips her bedtime prayers, and that little lapse is enough to give the devil his opening.

The pastures on the right show the devils beginning to implement their plan of torture, while the architecture on the left, the rich bedroom and the roomy bed, contains the archetypal Beauty and the Beast. The extraordinary illustration of the intercourse of the horned and hairy demon with the whitest woman in the Western world records not only a plot episode but a major theme of the *Merlin* as well. This literal *conjunctio oppositorum* defines Merlin as the site of an uneasy reconciliation. He bears his father's powers and his mother's goodness, but this union is rarely an easy one. Neither entirely mortal, nor entirely supernatural, he is continually perceived as a potentially destabilizing force. Both the biographies of Merlin derived from Robert de Boron and the complicated agglutination of episodes recorded in the Franco-Italian *Prophecies de Merlin* record occasions when he is challenged by the established church and forced to demonstrate his orthodoxy.[5] The clash of virtue and violence, prophecy and patience imaged in this dramatic vision of his conception establishes the psychic and ideological tension that vibrates at the heart of nearly every treatment of Merlin from Geoffrey of Monmouth to Malory to T.H. White and Mary Stewart.

After this late-fifteenth-century incunable, the fourteenth-century manuscript, BL, Add. 10292, is considerably less impressive. Its illustration of the engendering Merlin (77) (fig. 4.4) is smaller in size and scope than the frontispiece of Vérard's edition and poorly preserved, but this manuscript's blurry devil may be even more grotesque and vicious than the relatively complacent beast in Verard's edition. The same pattern of bedded bodies recurs later in the conception of Arthur (96) (fig. 4.5).[6] The repeated configuration of intercourse suggests that Uther's adultery with Ygerne replicates the devil's rape of Merlin's mother, so that he essentially imitates a demonic initiative. Placing Uther *in loco demonis* underscores a truth unstated in the text that Arthur's conception partakes of the same moral ambiguity as the conception of Merlin. In both cases, the son's power (imperial in one case, prophetic in the other) is derived from the father, but his potential to wield that power justly is derived from the ravished mother. While it is probably true that the artist did not have a wide choice of models to choose from when he was obliged to draw a man and a woman in bed, the limited number of exemplars accents the moral implications. Simply by coming first, the intercourse of the demon and the virgin establishes the model, so that all subsequent heterosexual intercourse becomes by definition the replication of a demonic rape.[7]

Between these acts of sexual intercourse, the manuscript illustrates another form of intercourse, that between Merlin and Blaise (80) (fig. 4.6). The double meaning of *intercourse* subtends this illustration, which is surprisingly similar to the poses taken by Plato and Socrates depicted in the Bodleian manuscript of Matthew Paris made famous by Derrida in *The Postcard*. Both illustrations of a scribal relation feature a curious phallic projection that unites and separates the author and his scribe (a feature upon which Derrida spends several pages).[8] Both illustrations also raise the significant issue of authority and priority. As the one shows Plato dictating to Socrates, so here Merlin dictates to his master Blaise. Signifcantly, this scene of dictating is the feature most often illustrated, and it is an encounter that generates a prolific succession of scribes culminating in the six amanuenses of *Les Prophecies de Merlin*.

In this series of miniatures the scribes prefigure contemporary fascination with the *mise en abîme*, as a long chain of signifying scribes traces its lineage back to the originating moment when the master inscribes a knot of origin in the scribal version of the riddle of the chicken and the egg: which did come first, the written or the spoken word? The knot of voice and writing is tied even tighter if it is accepted that Blaise is derived from Bleheris, the legendary Breton *conteur*.[9] Inscribing the original master/scribe, the illuminator/scribe inscribes the origin of his own authority by concretizing in the image the origin of the text in Merlin's words to Blaise and the simultaneous monumentalizing of voice and letter. In this miniature metanarrative questions are resolved to establish the authority of the text as the visible record of the silent speech of Merlin, whose voice remains entombed until captured and recuperated by the scribe's.

After this encounter with Blaise, the next major event illustrated in the manuscript is Merlin's revelation to Vortigern of the secret of the collapsing tower (84) (fig. 4.7). This is, of course, the moment when the fatherless boy reveals his prophetic powers by announcing the presence of the subterranean dragons. Like most medieval dragons, these creatures are more like puppies than monsters and are in fact less horrific than Merlin's father. But it is this appearance before Vortigern, not the seduction by Vivian that so captivated Mrs. Cameron, that defines Merlin; the beginning, not the end, of Merlin's career defines him and establishes his image. For the Middle Ages, he is the boy prophesying to Vortigern, the *Wunderkind*, neither the Wise Old Man, nor the vixen's victim. At the court of Vortigern, he defines himself as a politician, advisor, and prophet—and, however wondrous, as a boy.

Although it does not have the authority of the *Historia*, the famous prophecy of the triple death became one of the most frequently illustrated events in Merlin's life (89) (fig. 4.8). In an attempt to expose the prophet as a fraud, a man in three different disguises three times asks Merlin how he will die; on each occasion, Merlin gives the man a different version of his death. He is told he will be killed in a riding accident; he is told he will be hanged; he is told he will be drowned. This evident contradiction appears to prove that Merlin is a liar, until the news arrives that the young man was riding his horse across a river when the animal stumbled, and as the horse fell, his rider became trapped in the branches of a tree, so that he was suspended upside down in the river and drowned. The cleverness of this anecdote makes it an easy demonstration of Merlin's power. Memorable as it is, however, it would seem a pretty tricky one to illustrate. Given the complexities of the content and the limitations of the space, the illustrator of Add. 10292 has done a remarkably ingenious job of getting the horse, the rider, the tree, and the river all sufficiently entangled in each other to make the point and sufficiently distinct for the drawing to be legible.

The remaining examples from the manuscript illustrate rather simpler episodes, simpler, at least, from the point of view of the miniaturist. The first encounter of Arthur and Merlin (105) (fig. 4.9) adds little to our image of Merlin. Although one should note the increase in size, denoting Merlin's development from a boy to a young man, his image remains a youthful one. Boy or youth, however, his pinkish-orange gown remains his almost invariable costume throughout the manuscript, except for the charming instance when Merlin confers with the three kings (123) (fig. 4.10) and is dressed in blue to distinguish him from the three monarchs, who are clothed in gowns of reddish hues with their crowns and little feet breaking into the frame to disrupt the excess of closure and suggest that kings, unlike prophets, are too important to be constrained by ordinary boundaries. This rupture of the frame contradicts the impression of equality conveyed by their relative similarity to Merlin. It is clear that kings are willing to listen to him, but that they are not compelled to obey him.

In the last example from the manuscript, Merlin is not only once again dressed in his customary red, and is not only once again conferring with Arthur, but is, in fact, just as he was in the beginning, except, perhaps, just a bit taller (213) (fig. 4.11). Because to an unusual degree this manuscript attempts to match the variety of episodes with a variety of illuminations, this relatively rare repetition of an image serves to remind us of how typical this image of Merlin is meant to be and reinforces our recognition of Merlin as a young man.

In the second miniature on this page (see fig. 4.11, right), Arthur is achieving victory over an enemy on a lovely pink horse. Lest our attention be riveted by this festive equine, we should note that the manuscript does go on to the end of Merlin's life and touches on his seduction by Vivian and his eventual claustration, but these definitive moments are not illustrated for us.[10] What seems most remarkable about this illustrative program is the predominance of attempts to picture speech. Dictating to Blaise, advising Arthur, or conferring with the kings, we see Merlin speaking. This attempt to make speech visible is indeed the medieval equivalent of "talking pictures"; the text is the voice given to the illustration's mute speakers.

The illustrative program of Antoine Vérard's 1498 incunable is both more and less ambitious than that of the earlier manuscript. The illustrations are ambitious because they are well and carefully drawn and colored. The scene of Merlin's engendering (see fig. 4.3) establishes that, but it is also nearly the last illustration that takes particular care to integrate the text and the image. The traditional iconography of Merlin is maintained as in, for example, the illustration of Merlin and the three kings (f. 46a) (fig. 4.12). The drawing is crisp, clear, and well-preserved, but there is, if anything, even less individuality in the faces of the kings than in the manuscript. As something of a change of pace, the care and consistent interest in scenes of nature can be illustrated by the drawing on f. 23b. While the illustrator is competent and his pictures vibrant, his love of nature becomes almost a quirky obsession with the color green. His trees and bushes serve to balance his compostions or fill in the blanks in his repetitive battle scenes. While the artist seems happier with battles and horses, he does occasionally animate his greenery with the sorts of creatures likely to inhabit it. Thus, the illustration of the stag (fig. 4.13) is a typical example of these talents. It has, however, an additional interest for this too is an image of Merlin. This illustration, more carefully linked to the text than many in this volume, depicts Merlin's transformation into a stag. While this is, of course, a unique and temporary metamorphosis, it provides one example of a rarely depicted aspect of Merlin, his trickster-transformations, and offers a variant on his typical medieval image as a young man.

The iconography of Merlin undergoes a subtle change in the 1505 edition printed by Michel le Noir.[11] While the volume is considerably less attractive than Vérard's elegant, colorful text, it does acquire a certain posthumous glamor, for it was once owned by the notorious Mme de Pompadour. While the glamour of its eighteenth-century owner cannot compensate for the decidedly unimpressive appearance of the text, the colophon to Volume One provides a new perspective on the image of Merlin (fig. 4.14). Up to this point, Merlin had been depicted as a young man, whose youth is fixed by his arrival at Vortigern's court and his initiating interpretive prophecy of the dragons. With this woodcut, we can see the degree to which prophecy (and Merlin) are now more seriously implicated in the occult. While earlier texts had been concerned to distinguish between the son of the virgin and the son of the devil and to establish Merlin's orthodoxy, the later illustrations (sometimes in conflict with the text itself, which retains its concern with orthodoxy) reflect the early Renaissance interest in speculative alchemy (as in the rise of the Faust legend, for example). Here the image of Merlin as a sorcerer surrounded by devils and angels suggests something of the conflict of good and evil that was established in the 1498 frontispiece, but now the focus has shifted from the forces that vie for mastery over Merlin at his birth to the forces over which Merlin has mastery in his maturity. This bearded Merlin signals a crucial stage in the metamorphosis of his image from boy wonder to bearded sorcerer, master of demons and angels. While this occult power is inscribed more deeply in the illustration than in the text, one wonders if this promised power, Merlin's ability not only to foresee but also to forestall the forces of destiny and history may not have been among the secrets Mme de Pompadour hoped would be revealed when she added this text to her collection.

Five years after Michel le Noir published his edition, the widow of Jehan le Trepperel published hers.[12] While Jehan's widow is surely (probably?) not thinking of feminist issues, she provides us with one of the first dramatic images of Merlin and his seducer, Vivian (facing f. 1a) (fig. 4.15). The exemplar for this illustration seems to be Adam and Eve, now dressed in the modern fashion rather than in fig leaves. While it is entirely possible that the similarity between Adam and Eve and Merlin and Vivian is the result of the artist's lack of imagination and a rapid search for the most readily available semi-appropriate model, it is an accident that does, in fact, enrich the context of Merlin's seduction. The demonic rape that initiated the illustrative program of BL, Add. 10292 is replaced by the model of man seduced by woman. While the entrepreneurial widow probably merely anticipated the motto of her modern sisters, such as Danielle Steele and Jackie Collins: "sex sells," she also reflects the medieval anti-feminist tradition with the iconographical twist that women are now more dangerous than demons. On the other hand, it is just possible that the widow Trepperel may have chosen this unique image as the preface to her *Merlin* not as a tribute to woman's evil but as an icon of woman's power.

Moving from France to Italy, the title page of the 1539 edition of *La Vita di Merlino* published by Rossinelli[13] shows the aftereffects of the encounter with Vivian, the *sepoltura di Merlino*, as well as the succession of scribes invented in the late thirteenth-century *Les Prophecies de Merlin* (fig. 4.16). In this text, the scribes who take over from Merlin's master, Blaise, who is now identified as a hermit, are named and a line of descent established. The dictating child we have seen in Add. 10292 is the origin of the line that defines a "genealogy" of scribes establishing the continuity of Merlin's prophecy and invents a voice that, at least in *Les Prophecies de Merlin*, speaks beyond death and constrains and is constrained by the Lady of the Lake, to whom he has promised that, although his flesh will rot away within the month, his spirit will continue to speak.[14] True to his word, a month later, when the Lady of the Lake asks, "se sa char estoit porrie," he replies "oïl" (I, p. 172). In the end, Merlin's voice seems authorized by his putrefying flesh, as if death unwinds the veil of flesh to reveal the truth through his disembodied voice. As his penultimate scribe, the Lady of the Lake becomes the recorder of that voice, maintaining power over the publication of the word, while she is nevertheless powerless without the authority of his enabling speech. Thus, as the chain of signification begins with the loop in which the master becomes the student's scribe, so the final loop links the claustrating woman to the claustrated voice of the mastered man.[15]

The seclusion of Merlin in his tomb is refigured in the elaborate folio edition of Giulio Strozzi's *Venetia Edificata* published in 1624.[16] This remarkable text, which has much more to do with the history of Venice than with the history of Merlin, nevertheless provides evidence of a significant moment in the transformation of the image of Merlin (fig. 4.17). During a siege of Venice, Gelderico approaches Merlino from whom among other things he receives a telescope, which he puts away for a later age. But the figure of Merlin here is extraordinary. Like the familiar figure trapped by Viviana, Merlino still dwells in a cave, but in this case, he is not trapped by the sorceress. Rather he is enclosed by choice. While earlier images had associated the lecherous Merlin with the fallen Adam, now he seems to have been elided with the image of St. Jerome, the patristic cave dweller. Although this demi-Jerome lacks his lion, that role may be taken by the hero of this epic, the city of San Marco, Venice herself. This eremitical Merlin, however, merges the orthodoxy of his habit (note the prominence of the rosary) with the beard associated with Michel le Noir's sorcerer. Thus, the roots of our modern images of Merlin seem to lie in a peculiar marriage of the occult and the Counter-Reformation.

A few decades after Strozzi incorporated Merlin into the mythology of Venice, the frontispiece to Thomas Heywood's remarkable *Life of Merlin*[17] returns the seer to his native island with some extraordinary differences (fig. 4.18). Published in 1641, Merlin's final prophecy ironically predicts a long and glorious reign for Charles I. In this context, Merlin's monkish garb implies a political as well as a religious interpretation. Although beardless, the monastic Merlin seems derived from a clerical and Catholic tradition allied with the image of Merlin in the Italian *Les Prophecies* and *Vita di Merlino*. As in those texts also, the emphasis is on Merlin as scribe.

The tree against which Merlin reclines may echo the Eden allusions of the early printed books, but the absence of Vivian evokes a contemplative's paradise where woman does not disturb the revery of the monk and lust does not disrupt the accuracy of revelation. The absence of Vivian, however, is no less remarkable than the absence of Blaise. Merlin is now no longer the speaker of prophecy, but the writer of his own text. Thus, the arrogant humility of the earlier scribes who reflected themselves in the figure of Blaise, authorizing their texts through the chain of transmission initiated by the "pictured voice" of the dictating Merlin, is replaced by the literate illusion of unmediated authority. We are persuaded to believe not that we have a scribal copy, but that we have the last copy in a monogenetic series whose authority derives from the imagined Merlin holograph. The public is beginning to be trained to accept the accuracy of the printed text, an accuracy in this case ironically undermined by Heywood's dramatic error: Merlin's inability to see, less than a decade in the future, the decapitation of Charles I.

The last image of Merlin to be discussed occurs in a single folio dated 1709 (fig. 4.19), which presents a portrait of Merlinus Verax in contemporary dress.[18] The work claims to be a 200–year-old translation of a 1000–year-old prophecy found in an edition of Merlin's prophecies printed in 1530. The work is, in fact, a further entry in Jonathan Swift's propaganda war waged under the pseudonym, Isaac Bickerstaff. In "Predictions for the Year 1708," Swift parodied the contemporary fondness for astrology and predicted the death of John Partridge, whose annual almanac was published under the title "Merlinus Liberatus."[19] In *Merlinus Verax*, Swift, a shape-shifter to rival Merlin himself, becomes T.N. Philomath to defend the reliability of prophecy in general and Merlin in particular.

Behind both productions lurk hints of Swift's gradual move toward becoming the "defender and spokesman of the Tory ministry's campaign to terminate the War of the Spanish Succession,"[20] and his loathing of the Dutch policy of religious toleration.[21] *Merlinus* concerns itself with the rival claims of the kings of Spain with particular praise for the country's recent liberation from the Hapsburgs, the claimant supported by the Tories but tacitly abandoned in favor of the Bourbon claimant in the Tory pursuit of peace.[22] The disagreements between Tories and Whigs are the consequence of the "Glorious Revolution" and the coronation of William of Orange and the subsequent problem of English succession after the death of Queen Anne, the last of the Stuart monarchs. Behind the Swiftian role-playing, *Merlinus Verax* seems to support the Whig cause and to embed Merlin in the problem of royal authority. With this prophecy, however, Merlin swerves from his traditional royalist posture, and his quirky intervention as a Whig marks one of his last appearances as an active player in political controversies.

Critically, in this text, Merlin's authority is seriously undermined. The need, however satirical in intent, to distinguish between *Merlinus Verax* and the implicit *Merlinus Mendax* already casts doubt on the possibility of a reliable prophetic vision issuing from a verifiable ancient source. Furthermore, the text goes on to undermine its authority by questioning its own origins in the confession that it may not actually issue from Merlin himself, although it is at least 170 years old. Indeed, even the presumably solid foundation of the definable *personæ* of Swift wearing the mask of Bickerstaff wearing the mask of Philomath crumbles when we read in the introduction to the 1711 edition (an anthology of surreptitiously published short pieces) that "the supposed Author is at Liberty to Disown as much as he thinks fit of what is here published." [23] Thus, *Merlinus Verax* portrays not only a unique image of the seer but the crumbling authority of Merlin himself, establishing this piece as something of an iconographic and prophetic dead end. It is quite possibly the last Merlin to be imagined as a beardless contemporary and the last Merlin to intervene directly in contemporary politics. [24]

When the nineteenth century reinvents Merlin, it is as the prophet of the past rather than the future, the dodderer imagined by Tennyson, imitated and parodied by Mark Twain, and photographed by Julia Cameron, all of whom would have rejected the occult (as in Michel le Noir) and Roman Catholic (as in Strozzi) origins of their image of the seer. He becomes the fading voice of a lost age that is held up as a mirror for modern times either to imitate (Tennyson) or criticize (Twain). As Camelot dwindles into a dream of a lost childhood, rather than a recuperable ideal, its prophet ages into a infatuated dodderer, a dithering incompetent as in Disney's *The Sword in the Stone*, or a pitchman for mufflers or mint teas.

The decline of Merlin signals a secular age no longer comfortable with prophets, but it also signals an age reluctant to find meaning in history or to acknowledge any narratological basis to history apart from the story of positivist progress towards a technological utopia. This progressivist myth can hardly accommodate an ancient wizard with the power to read the future as already past, as recyclable repetition. A New Historicist *avant la lettre*, Merlin demystifies history, presenting it as a question of narrative rather than pure truth, of engaged polemic rather than detached objectivity, a discourse of power rather than a transparent record of documented achievement. Merlin, then, loses his effectiveness when Western Civilization replaces the fiction of prophetic authority with the fiction of academic objectivity, and he "is disappeared" not when truth replaces fiction but when history's fictive roots are occluded and the ivory tower supplants the crystal cave.

APPENDIX

Register of Merlin Miniatures in BL, Add. 10292
[Note: The titles are transcribed from *Le Roman de Merlin; or, The Early History of King Arthur*, ed. H. Oskar Sommer (London, 1894). The numbering follows the sequence in Sommer's edition.]

2. Ensi comme le dyables engenra merlin (77)
3. Ensi que la mere tient son enfant (Merlin) en la tour ou elle est en prison (78)
4. Ensi que merlins parole au juge por delivrer sa mere (79)
5. Ensi que merlins fait ecrire .j. liure de merueilles a blase sen clerc (80)
8. Ensi que li iiij messagers emmeinent merlin & .j. vilains aloit deuant qui porta son quir sor .j. baton (83)
9. Ensi que merlins divise au roy uerteger commant se tour porra tenir (84)
10. Ensi que merlins monstra au roy uerteger les meruailles de deus serpens (85)
11. Untitled [Merlin dictates to Blaise] (85)
13. Ensi que merlins en gise dun garcon porta .j. lettre au roy pandragon & a ut[er] sen frere (87)
14. Ensi que uns ons se fet malades et merlins li deuise sa mort par deuant le roy (88)
15. Ensi que .j. ons pent en leuwe et si noie et si brise le col (89)
17. Ensi que gens sient au diner & merlins apela & Roi si lui monstra le lieu wit (91)
22. Ensi com .j. Roys gist au lit del mort. Et merlins parla a lui par deuant ses barons (98)
28. Ensi que li roi artu ist hors dun castel & desconfit .j. bataille par le conseil de merlin (102)

1. Julia Margaret Cameron, *Idylls of the King and Other Poems Photographically Illustrated by Julia Margaret Cameron, Text by Alfred Lord Tennyson* (New York: Janet Lehr, 1985).

2. Quoted in Constance C. Relihan, "Vivian, Elaine, and the Model's Gaze: Cameron's Reading of The Idylls of the King," in *Popular Arthurian Traditions*, ed. Sally K. Slocum (New York: Bowling Green State Univ. Press, 1992), p. 118.

3. For a description of the manuscript and its contents, see H.L.D. Ward, *Catalogue of Romances in the Department of Manuscripts in the British Museum*, 3 vols. (London, 1883–1910), II, pp. 343–44. A complete list of the miniatures is provided in the notes to *Le Roman de Merlin; or, The Early History of King Arthur*, ed. H. Oskar Sommer (London, 1894).

4. *Le premiere* (second) *volume de Merlin*. 3 vols. (Paris: Antoine Vérard, 1498).

5. This is particularly true in *Les Prophecies de Merlin*, where, since Merlin is used to provide a critique of clerical abuses, it is crucial to establish that he is not the agent of a demonic plot.

6. The actual inscription for the miniature reads, "Ensi que .j. Roy et une royne paraulent ensamble en leur lit." The intriguing verb ("paraulent") may be an attempt to bowdlerize regal intercourse, but links this act of conception with the frequent "parlance" of Merlin with Blaise and various kings.

7. A detailed model of and justification for reading generic illustrations with specific relevance is provided in Stephanie Cain van d'Elden, "Specific and Generic Scenes: A Model for Analyzing Medieval Illustrated Texts Based on the Example of Yvain/Iwein," *BBSIA* 44 (1992), 255–69.

8. Jacques Derrida, *The Postcard: From Socrates to Freud and Beyond*, trans. Alan Bass (Chicago: Univ. of Chicago Press, 1987), pp. 25, 64.

9. Roger Sherman Loomis, "The Oral Diffusion of the Arthurian Legend," in *Arthurian Literature in the Middle Ages: A Collaborative History*, ed. Roger Sherman Loomis et al. (Oxford: Clarendon Press, 1959), p. 57.

10. Miniature #74 (f. 138) seems meant to depict the first meeting of Merlin and Viviane, but it is in too poor a condition to reproduce. Apart from this, there is no attempt to illustrate the romantic aspects of Merlin's life.

11. *Le premiere* (second) *volume de Merlin*, 3 vols. (Paris: Michel le Noir, 1505).

12. *Le premiere* (second) *volume de Merlin*, 3 vols. (Paris: Imprimé par le veufve du feu Jehan trepperel et Jehan jehannot, 1510).

13. *La Vita di Merlino con le sue profetie nouamente ristampata & con somma diligentia corrette & istoriate, Le quali trattano de le cose che hanno a venire* (Venice, 1539).

14. *Les Prophecies de Merlin*, ed. Lucy Allen Paton. 2 vols. (New York: Heath, 1926–1927), I, p. 270.

15. Meliadus, the last scribe, covers the historical space from the living Merlin to the anonymous scribes of *Les Prophecies*. The Lady of the Lake

remains, then, the last scribe to take dictation from the living Merlin, and presides over, indeed causes, his transition from living prophet to post-mortal disembodied voice.

16. Giulio Strozzi, *La Venetia Edificata, poema eroica* (Venice, 1624).

17. T. Heywood, *The Life of Merlin, sirnamed Ambrosius. His prophecies and predictions, interpreted; and their truth made good by our English Annalls* ([London], 1641).

18. See BL, Ashley 5250. *A Famous Prediction of MERLIN the British Wizard; / written above a Thousand Years ago, and relating to this / perfect Year // With Explanatory Notes by T.N. Philomath* (London, 1709).

19. Jonathan Swift, *The Writings of Jonathan Swift: Authoritative Texts, Backgrounds, Criticism,* ed. Robert A. Greenberg and William Bowman Piper (New York: Norton, 1973), p. 426.

20. Richard I. Cook, *Jonathan Swift as a Tory Pamphleteer* (Seattle: Univ. of Washington Press, 1967), p. xvi.

21. Greenberg and Pyser, p. 128.

22. F.P. Lock, *Swift's Tory Politics* (Newark: Univ. of Delaware Press, 1983), p. 41.

23. [Jonathan Swift], *Miscellanies in Verse and Prose* (London: John Morphew, 1711), sig. A3.

The disavowals of the 1711 edition raise the intriguing possibility that the *Merlinus* may not, in fact, have been written by anyone at all. The authorship of the text is further mystified, however, by the curious fact that the surviving folio, preserved in Ashley 5250, is bound with the bookplate of Thomas J. Wise, the notorious forger and cataloguer of the Ashley Library. While the 1711 edition does seem sufficient proof of the date, if not the authorship, of *Merlinus,* it is intriguing to note that the first line of the prophecy which establishes the date of 1709 ("Seven and ten added to nyne") could yield, with no less an exercise of ingenuity, the date 1907, the midpoint, in effect, of Wise's work on the Ashley catalogue published 1905–1908. See Thomas J. Wise, *The Ashley Library: A Catalogue of Printed Books, Manuscripts, and Autograph Letters,* 2 vols. (London: Printed for Private Circulation Only, 1905–1908). Curiously, *Merlinus Verax,* although it bears his bookplate, does not appear in Wise's catalogue of the Ashley Library. (For accounts of Wise's success as a forger, see, for example, William B. Todd, *Suppressed Commentaries on The Wisean Forgeries: Addendum to an Enquiry* [Austin: Univ. of Texas Press, 1969] and Katharine Greenleaf Pedley, *Moriarty in the Stacks: The Nefarious Adventures of Thomas J. Wise* [Berkeley, CA: Peacock Press, 1966].)

24. A peculiar exception to this rule is to be found in Merlin's involvement in the controversy over the construction of Richmond Park as a private playground for Queen Caroline. "LITTLE MERLIN'S CAVE / As it was lately discouer'd by a Gentleman's Gardener,/ in Maidenhead-Thicket / To which is added, / A RIDDLE:/ or, a / Paradoxical Character / of an / Hairy Monster / Often found under Holland" published in 1787 is a unique relic of

Merlinian pornography. (See "Little Merlin's Cave" [London: T. Read, in Dogwell-Court, White-Fryers, 1787]).

Fig. 4.1. Merlin and Vivian as photographed by Julia Margaret Cameron. Reproduced by permission of Janet Lehr, Inc.

Fig. 4.2. Merlin and Vivian as photographed by Julia Margaret Cameron. Reproduced by permission of Janet Lehr, Inc.

Fig. 4.3. The conception of Merlin from the 1498 edition of Antoine Verard.
London, the British Library. Reproduced by permission.

 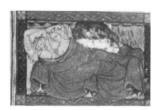

Top left. Fig. 4.4. The conception of Merlin.

Top right. Fig. 4.5. The conception of Arthur.

Bottom left. Fig. 4.6. Merlin and Blaise.

Bottom right. Fig. 4.7. Vortigern's tower.

All from London, BL, Add. 10292.

Reproduced by permission.

Top left. Fig. 4.8. The triple death.
Top right. Fig. 4.9. Arthur and Merlin.
Bottom left. Fig. 4.10. Merlin and the three kings.
Bottom right. Fig. 4.11. Merlin and Arthur.

All from London, BL, Add. 10292.

Reproduced by permission.

Fig. 4.12. Merlin and the three kings from the 1498 edition of Antoine Verard. London, the British Library. Reproduced by permission.

Fig. 4.13. Merlin disguised as a stag from the 1498 edition of Antoine Verard. London, the British Library. Reproduced by permission.

Fig. 4.14. Merlin the sorcerer from the 1505 edition
of Michel le Noir. London, the British Library.
Reproduced by permission.

Senluyt cy aps le secōt
volume de Merlin/qui parle des merueillē
es auẽtures du monde. Et en la fin commen
Uiuiane lenferma en bne tour fermee de lau
u ledit merlin est encoꝛe de pꝛesent enferme.

Merlin

Diuiane

Fig. 4.15. Merlin and Vivian from the 1510 edition by the
widow Jehan le Trepperel. London, the British Library.
Reproduced by permission.

Fig. 4.16. Merlin and his scribes from the
1539 *Vita*. London, the British Library.
Reproduced by permission.

Fig. 4.17. Merlin as a hermit from Giulio Strozzi's
Venetia Edificata. London, the British Library.
Reproduced by permission.

Fig. 4.18. The frontispiece from Thomas Heywood's
Life of Merlin. London, the British Library.
Reproduced by permission.

Fig. 4.19. The portrait of Merlin from the 1709 edition
of *Merlinus Verax*. London, the British Library.
Reproduced by permission.

5 THE IMPLIED ARTHUR

MASS PUBLICS AND SPLINTERED SUBJECTS IN SPENSER'S *FAERIE QUEENE*, BOOK II[1]

Elizabeth Mazzola

INTRODUCTION

Gloriana's court is renowned throughout faery land, and the reputation of her knights often precedes them. Even the clownish Braggadocchio, completely cut off from court, appears to have been exposed to its discourse of publicity, a vocabulary of royal legitimation and knightly reward, which instructs a public how to behave, whom it might recognize, and what it should know about itself. Despite his vulgar errors and boorish presumptions, Braggadocchio is an important spokesman for courtly values in fact, taking the court to be the only site of consensus and stable meaning. And he provides an example the public can read exactly because his relation to it is never in question. When Belphoebe first approaches him and Trompart in the forest, he fearfully hides away and it is his servant who, previously failing to detect Braggadocchio's posturing, now instinctively perceives his embarrassment and preserves his inflated ego.[2] When Braggadocchio finally emerges from the bushes to admire Belphoebe, he recommends she get herself a place at court—the same place from which he has been excluded because of his lowly status—and he tells her: "There maist thou best be seene, and best may see" (3 st. 39.8).[3] Braggadocchio derides his own ability simply to look by defining publicity as the only form of mutuality between separate people.

Belphoebe argues the point, however. Like Shakespeare's Hal, whose famous soliloquy exposes a plan to remain guarded, she wishes to closet herself because she views the court as actually a place of oblivion:

Who so in pompe of proud estate (quoth she)
Does swim, and bathes himselfe in courtly blis,
Does waste his dayes in darke obscuritee,
And in obliuion euer buried is. (3 st. 40.1–4)

Although Belphoebe disowns courtly publicity, readers are able to idolize her anyway. The poet recalls us to Gloriana's court by waylaying the inexplicable action of canto 3—what Harry Berger calls a "conspicuous irrelevance"—taking ten stanzas to adoringly describe her. [4]

Ironically, the oblivion Belphoebe describes is epitomized by Spenser's Arthur and Gloriana, both of whom are similarly inaccessible to the allegorical world of the poem. It is for this reason, according to James Nohrnberg, that Arthur and Gloriana embody the organizing principles of *The Faerie Queene*: "like the magnified but unfulfilled Arthur, the queen is allegorically concealed in the present poem, and allegorically revealed in it. Arthur and Gloriana belong to the poem's framework and partly express the poem's theory" (p. 55). [5] But Arthur and Gloriana express the poem's theory in two entirely different ways. What we know of Gloriana is achieved through publicity, the discourse with which even Braggadocchio is familiar, whose primary function is to explain why he cannot see her. What we know of Arthur is, in contrast, mostly derived from gaps in this public discourse and his general isolation from the ongoing conversation of publicity. That Arthur is completely cut off from public knowledge is indicated by the fact that he lacks the name of his mother, something Spenser tells the rest of us in his letter to Ralegh. [6] Nor does Arthur have the access to the identity provided by the archaeological evidence of his sword or shield, currently available for our inspection (see I.8 st.36). If Gloriana is absent because she is the source of public knowledge, Arthur is absent because he has none.

Especially for those readers who thus view Arthur as either an initial model later abandoned by the poet or ideal formulated after the basic structure of the poem was laid down, it is almost as easy to view Braggadocchio's portrait as a digression and read the tale of a foolish knave parading atop Guyon's stolen horse as a temporary withdrawal of interest from the allegorical legend of Guyon's temperance. Yet Arthur is extrinsic in many similar ways, and although the connections between Arthur and Braggadocchio have remained unnoticed by most critics, the two figures can be closely linked. In their common isolation both figures serve as rhetorical devices communicating more to readers of the poem than to any inhabitant within. As I discuss in this essay, they signify what it means to view them, incorporating a new form of publicity employed not to represent authority, but to show the relation of Spenser's readers to each other.

This means that while Arthur and Braggadocchio are part of the continued allegory of the poem, they are not part of its meaning. Instead, their status signals what Spenser understands about his readers. For instance, Braggadocchio's separation from Guyon defines allegory for us as a publicly exclusive language, just as Gloriana's court supplies meaning for some knightly quests and denies it to others. But allegory is only one of many such languages. Elizabeth's court provided a primary means of intelligibility in Tudor culture, but as Louis Montrose claims, its methods, pageantry, icons, and tournaments might also supply vehicles for her spectators to reconstitute her. Allegory similarly gives way to other forms of publicity in *The Faerie Queene*, when, in the process of insisting upon the importance of the public realm, Spenser records a new form of public knowledge. In his capacity as New Poet he now presides over a reading public to whom are revealed situations and characters—like Arthur or Braggadocchio—normally unavailable or uninteresting to it.

Sociologists have recently begun to chronicle the birth of the "public sphere," an arena in which people recognize each other as fellow members or parts of a group rather than "scattered individuals," who speak to each other not through "expansive dialogue" but through a discourse specifically addressed to "no one in particular."[7] The most prominent of these theorists, Jürgen Habermas, emphasizes the democratic nature of this public sphere, claiming its origins are located in eighteenth-century coffeehouses and salons open to wealthy and poor shopkeepers alike; even organizations formed by princes during this time "avoided social exclusiveness," and "later attempts to transform them into knightly orders failed."[8] The public life Habermas describes is not to be identified with "collective life" or "popular culture" because it is not experienced over and against the prevailing official order. Rather the public sphere provides the most successful vehicle for making the official order intelligible and more accessible.[9] But I would contend that the origins of a public sphere are found almost two centuries earlier. Alongside the "self-fashioning" Stephen J.

Greenblatt described more than a decade ago occurs the creation of a Renaissance "public sphere" required to acknowledge and respond to the roles individuals adopted. Increased self-consciousness about the fashioning of human identity would likely coincide with a greater awareness of the environment and its "systems of public signification," which had to be negotiated if self-fashioning was to take place; such an arena, however unsheltered or unregulated, would necessarily comprehend and protect the "less tangible achievements" Greenblatt describes, like the formation of "a distinctive personality, a characteristic address to the world, a consistent mode of perceiving and behaving" (p. 5, p. 2).[10] According to Greenblatt's model, only certain selves would become available as texts because of the public's limited development and restricted access: only certain selves could be viewed, and therefore only selected selves fashioned. But self-fashioning might prompt a chain reaction or mirroring effect since, as I suggest in this essay, a public sphere would provide a place where one might view others viewing.

We could then locate the beginnings of a public sphere in Tudor England, when Henry's Arthurian lineage is collectively researched and appreciated, or in the massive public relations campaign which accompanies his divorce and explains why the marriage to his brother's wife was misguided from the outset, so that Rome was at fault in permitting it. The "refeudalization" of Elizabeth's court described by Roy Strong is another example of a sophisticated courtly apparatus designed to create public opinion. Yet the ballets, banquets, and tournaments she sponsored were not only "ideal vehicles for exponents of absolutism," as Strong maintains, but opportunities for each person to sense his or her membership in a larger group of spectators and observe what they saw together.[11] Once more, this public discourse was not simply collective or popular; it did not represent how common people thought or what they wanted; it did not supply better models of virtue or democratic values; it just enlarged the spectacle and increased its visibility. Elizabeth's refeudalization did not promote a knightly order since tournaments basically pitted knights against each other.[12] Similarly, Spenser chooses Arthur to serve not as a model, but as assumption, and his figuration functions in *The Faerie Queene* not as a role, but a site for role-playing.

Introduced only at intervals when the titular hero of a book as fallen, Arthur's own position within *The Faerie Queene* is curiously disoriented. Robert J. Mueller states that Arthur's distance from and relation to Gloriana, for instance, "significantly departs from that of the poem's other heroes" (p. 751).[13] Clearly, since he is a main topic of publicity, or the discourse by which a public knows itself, Arthur possesses both a different identity and a different relation to it. Exploring Arthur's estrangement from the discourse which describes him, Mueller notes the extent to which Arthur and Guyon, discussing the image of the faery queen on Guyon's shield in canto 9, "remain unaligned in the poem's allegorical roster." Their colloquy, he claims, "poses for us as readers of Spenserian allegory the issue of how far allegory communicates a satisfying model of conduct at one level, and, at another, a coherent picture of the individual's place in the political and universal orders." Mueller concludes:

> It is with desire and its effects that Arthur's position is especially critical, where the envisioned object seems to mark an extreme limit. Arthur's quest, in other words, comments on the very nature of allegory. Guyon, on the other hand, remains at a much less remote level of experience. He describes for Arthur's sake a condition of desire from which [Guyon] finds himself effectively immune. (p. 748)

This verdict implies that Arthur's status is more figurative than Guyon's, and reading Arthur's isolation from the ongoing concerns of the poem, Mueller evaluates his quest as Platonic. But this interpretation ignores Spenser's method of isolation as uninteresting. In other words, Mueller basically reads allegory allegorically.

It is not that Arthur transcends a remote, material world; instead, he finds its conditions singularly problematic. The underside of Arthur's visionary quest for the faery queen is his often intractable experience in faery land. Arthur's body continues in the poem to be an obstacle, his dreams a mystery, his self-knowledge mistaken. For these reasons too he can be aligned with Braggadocchio, when we approach him not in terms of his "universalizing transcendence" but because of his inability to mobilize himself (see Warner, p. 377). In a way, their joint status presents a thorny methodological problem for new historicist critics because Arthur and Braggadocchio possess subjectivities whose experiences or "experiments" in ambition and power are unsuccessful and yet apparently motivated by the same impulses for honor, fame, and glory that govern successful achievements. In other words, the selves they fashion are rejected or incomplete; they nevertheless offer a register of the pressures exerted by their environment and, ultimately, an accounting of power.

Usually Spenser's representations of class and social status are dislocated by larger allegorical structures which analyze weakness and strength, or action and passivity, or virtue and sin. But unlike Timias's portrait, where the depiction of a servant's amorous frustrations serves both to explain and excuse Ralegh's offenses, Braggadocchio's portrait is completely circumscribed by his class. In contrast to the doubling of Florimell, to whom Braggadocchio is often compared, it is Braggadocchio's failure to imitate the codes of chivalry that defines him for us. As we learn in Book V.3, Florimell is simply not allowed to function as a double, for when she and her original coincide, the false Florimell disappears. If the second Florimell is false because she is an image or copy, Braggadocchio is false because he is not one. He is recognizable as a character who has no place in the poem.

This is clear from the first moment readers are introduced to him. At the beginning of the third canto of Book II, while Guyon is struggling to determine how to wash Ruddymane's stained hands, readers are told that "a losell wandring by the way, / One that to bountie neuer cast his mind, / Ne thought of honour euer did assay / His baser brest," steals Guyon's steed and spear and rides away (st. 4.1–4). The orphaned Ruddymane presents Guyon and the palmer with a full-fledged allegorical dilemma in canto 2 when Christian and classical frameworks obstruct each other and fail to indicate how the child's hands might be cleaned. Braggadocchio's fate is much more easily dispatched, without recourse to the usual hermeneutical enterprise debated between Guyon and his guide; neither figure is even present in canto 3. In his letter to Ralegh, the expert poet had offered to take his readers through the bureaucratic maze of his poem,[14] but here we are deposited at a site of easy access and require no official help, since Braggadocchio poses no real threat to chivalry, to virtue, or to meaning. His aspirations are ridiculed by Trompart, Belphoebe, Brigadore, and the poet, and it is because he is excluded so strenuously from the allegorical world that Braggadocchio seems more of a mistake than a digression.

Spenser's reluctance to mystify Braggadocchio's personal failure is unusual when he fashions legends about it nearly everywhere else in the poem.[15] Still, this episode's importance in Book II might be construed more fully as part of a narrative in which Spenser has enfolded the story of Arthur's failed initiation and complicated the meaning of knightly victory, switching a contest with Maleger in canto 11, more appropriately geared for Guyon, with the rescue of Verdant in canto 12, better suited to Arthur. Included with such veiled failures and shuffled victories, the problematic destruction of Acrasia's Bower is just one of a series of events in Book II, which also assumes a place in a carefully withheld legend of courage (none of the other knights, with the exception of Braggadocchio and Arthur, really aims to rise in rank).[16] But if this unwritten legend still supplies knightly failure with a location, in Braggadocchio's case it is given a name.

Braggadocchio's significance is not only to designate knightly failure, however, for the utterly delimited representation of his character reveals a great deal about the prince's own obscure development. Both Arthur and Braggadocchio are deprived of allegorical footing in the poem since their presence interrupts rather than advances it. More crucially, like Braggadocchio's unsuitable postures, Arthur's unconscious or secret experiences and sensations prove obstacles to any official sanction of his destiny.[17] Both figures are cut off from a public realm which might recognize or restore value to a knightly quest, or at least read that quest allegorically. As a result of this deprivation, both characters threaten to transform courtly aspirations into narrowly personal aims.

THE PRINCE'S TWO BODIES

If Arthur, as Mueller notes, seems separated from the rest of Spenser's knights, his deprivation is graphically represented in Braggadocchio who, besides lacking manners, is called a "Peasant" (st. 43.1) and likened to a eunuch ("kestrell kind," st. 4.4). The poet even refers to his "bastard armes" (st. 42.6). Provided with all of Guyon's tools for symbolizing himself, but ignorant as to how to wield them, Braggadocchio in his self-representation ends up being incoherent. While it still might be going too far to call him an idiot, Lionel Trilling reminds us that *idiot* was used simply to denote a private person, that is, someone not holding an official position or disconnected from the affairs of state.[18] Rather than simply parodying Arthur's quest, it appears that Braggadocchio's limitations more deeply parallel Arthur's own limitations. Lawrence Stone devises the term "bogus genealogy" to describe the fictional lineages designed by the new gentry in an effort to clothe their "social nakedness" (p. 16),[19], and we might easily view Braggadocchio as similarly naked. Yet, as critics like Josephine Waters Bennett point out, the Arthur of *The Faerie Queene* is not really recognizable as the legendary King Arthur (p. 62);[20] actually, he is left only with the "clothes" Stone might have us see: his insignia, sword, and shield. In addition, Arthur frequently must explain his actions to the knights he rescues, reminding them of the chivalric ideals which have become obscured, for them, by the face of Gloriana (see, for instance, 8 st. 56).[21]

Similarly, many of Arthur's private experiences are often viewed as eluding any convention of narration. His dream of the faery queen makes use of a personal lexicon of feelings and wishes, whereas the chronicles take no account whatsoever of those subjective ambitions. This discrepancy is noted by Prays-Desire when she encounters Arthur at Alma's Castle and asks him:

> How is it, that this word in me ye blame,
> And in your selfe do not the same aduise?
> Him ill beseemes, anothers fault to name,
> That may vnwares be blotted with the same.
> (9 st.38.1–4)

As Prays-Desire indicates, Arthur is "not himself" because he is unable to recognize himself in others or see how others see him. Substituting for this form of public recognition, in canto 10 the chronicles register Arthur's private dilemma in print, opening it thereby to everyone while simultaneously shutting him out. The chronicles make his dream a matter of political import, and they install a rhetoric of publicity in place of Arthur's incoherent sensations. Once again, the consequence is that Arthur is unable to identify with the disembodied public subject parallel to himself: whether in the guise of the faery queen's promise in Book I or represented in *Briton moniments* as a dynastic avatar.[22] Over and over again, Arthur comes to us as an inimitably dispossessed hero: without a love, without a clue, and without a knightly agenda.

Arthur's privacy does not facilitate introspection, since his secret destiny is both revealed and withdrawn from him as he sleeps. But Braggadocchio cannot even imagine himself in solitude. While Braggadocchio's desire to publicize himself does not therefore involve doing or being anything different from what he already is, his elemental wish for 15 minutes (or cantos) of fame assumes too much about publicity in construing it merely as a form of acceptance or reification. In its earliest sense, that definition probably held true, since "publicity," like "public," comes from the Latin stem *pubes*—puberty or pubescence—and thus basically referred to an unorganized group of adult men, or the male population at large: conceivably all potential knights of Gloriana, except for Braggadocchio.[23] With this early definition in mind, we might also perceive the interruption of Arthur's lovemaking in his dream as a call to duty, even an admonition, which restores him to the group of knights. But later, Prays-Desire's comments reflect a "public opinion" critical of his overweening ambition, as if to suggest that it is an obstacle to his search for the faery queen. Like Braggadocchio, Arthur appears divided by these encounters and he learns almost nothing from them.[24]

Was it possible, however, for the sixteenth-century body to truly enjoy privacy? Four hundred years ago, the body served as document, a storehouse, and a thoroughfare. It stood or slept or swung from the gallows as a singularly ordered instrument supplying the locus for all other likeness, containing similitudes to plants, the heavens, and animals: all resemblances had to pass through this body, described by Foucault as "saturated with analogy" (p. 22).[25] In *The Faerie Queene*, however, Spenser's multiplication of likeness is part of an almost systematic disavowal of the body and materiality in the poem. From the start we see that Braggadocchio is trapped by his vulgar body, a creature of weight (a "base burden" st. 46.9) and tired, graceless form (he "crauld," stands "stoutly"; when he meets Belphoebe "his lofty crest / Did fiercely shake, and rowze, as comming late from rest" [st. 35.6–9]). Likewise, Arthur's body is often paralyzed, spied on while asleep, or teased and subjected to discipline; and while his readers learn to be gentlemen or noble persons through the "vertuous and gentle discipline" offered by his model, their progress implies a simultaneous perception of the uselessness and excrescence of Arthur's material body. His own sensations become increasingly problematic, making it impossible for him to determine whether he's dreamed of the faery queen or not. The result of this process is that in his isolation—even from himself—Arthur becomes a dead metaphor inhabiting and guiding *The Faerie Queene*.[26]

It seems that his ghostly, unmarked body resembles the empty forms of many other characters in the poem, however; Amoret, locked in the heart of Busirane's castle, appears as empty as its horrifying center; Alma is the superfluous hostess of a self-regulating machine; Arthegall becomes an incapacitated image of Britomart when he is imprisoned and forced to wear women's clothing. The debate over Guyon's "slombred corse" in canto 8, when the paynim brothers attempt to steal his chivalric equipment, is the clearest example of a suspect and disciplined "public" body, at once exposed and lifeless. Spenser's pedagogy is now punitive, almost too anxious to establish the equivocal nature of human bodies and the space they occupy.[27] In such an arena, the knights' efforts to steal Guyon's armor and the palmer's attempt to repel them alternately resemble a dry philosophical inquiry and cruel anatomy experiment, sidestepping empiricism to finger bodies and their extent. Their discussion raises such questions as: Is Guyon dead? Is he still responsible for the crimes the paynim knights allege, or does his "bad death" satisfy their "greedy hunger" (st. 15.3–4)? Just when does Guyon's guilt or honor cease to exist? Unsuccessful at first, the palmer seeks to resuscitate chivalric ideals by detaching them from Guyon's mortal body, but Pyrochles claims these too have died, proof of which lies in the "outcast carkasse" itself searched as evidence: "Loe where he now inglorious doth lye, / To proue he liued ill, that did thus foully dye. . . . Palmer thou doest dote, / Ne canst of prowesse, ne of knighthood deeme, / Saue as thou seest or hearst" (st. 12.8–9; st. 14.1–3). When Arthur eventually arrives to join their debate, he assumes Guyon's defense and becomes his "dayes-man" (st. 28.2) by ignoring these issues, taking up the sleeping knight's weapons coveted by the two brothers in order to defeat them.

But Arthur's heroic and eager identification with Guyon also highlights the prince's own repeated failures to coincide with his public image. This gap is duplicated in canto 9 by Alma's Castle, an image of the body and wholeness, verging on disunity and collapse, which "growes a Monster, and incontinent / Doth loose his dignitie and natiue grace" (9 st. 1.7–8). Upon arriving at Alma's, Arthur and Guyon are jointly locked out of the castle. In a sense, Guyon has been repeatedly denied access in Book II and only discovers his body in the

141

palmer's rebuke at Acrasia's Bower. But Arthur never learns to recognize his body; as we witness in Prays-Desire's comments, his other selves merely chastise him. That private experience is at odds with public knowledge is nowhere more clearly written than in their conversation; in other places in *The Faerie Queene*, privacy is just written out of the poem so as to prevent embarrassment, and Scudamour and Amoret are allowed to move underground when Britomart and Arthegall go public.[28] Typically, Spenser's other strategy is to ritualize privacy, as in the *Epithalamion*, where his format prevents lovers from being alone with each other, and together, like Arthur and Prays-desire, feeling mutually embarrassed.[29]

BUREAUCRACIES OF IDENTITY

Whether underground, asleep, or in private, when removed from official locales like the court, the pronouncements of public knowledge—which deem the apparently obvious or certify the clearly evident—are more difficult to retrieve and decipher. Outside of court, for instance, Belphoebe and Braggadocchio easily mistake each other's identity and intentions, so that Braggadocchio's admiration is now defined by presumption, while Belphoebe's beauty can in no way be construed as an erotic signal. Their uncomfortable encounter is replicated in Arthur's interrupted dream, where his unconscious wish is awkwardly substituted by harder physical evidence, the dream-vision of lovemaking replaced by the pressed grass beside him. Like Braggadocchio's voyeuristic pleasures, Arthur's privacy reiterates his deprivation. By reimagining the courtly realm, moreover, their two private experiences also offer proof against its existence, so that Gloriana's court increasingly appears as the most secret and hidden place of all. In contrast, the other knights' quests have already been validated at the beginning of the poem, as the events of the projected Book XII would describe the poem's origins. At that final stage, furthermore, their historical knowledge of struggle would be, as Frank Whigham might suggest, pushed aside—like the hard-to-read imprint left alongside Arthur's warring, sleeping form—by agreements founded on public knowledge of hierarchy and status. As the examples of Braggadocchio and Arthur make clear, though, such public knowledge can in itself be a final goal and not a source. Their shared dilemma indicates a revised conception of the social order Berger describes,[30] one more indicative of a bureaucratic order produced by documentation, certification, and publication, which typically envisions the "court" as not the first but the last place of appeals.

For most of the sixteenth century, the court had not only provided publicity but legislated all forms of it, articulating rules about courtship and flattery and issuing sumptuary codes which dictated how many courses one might serve at a banquet or whether one was entitled to wear silks or furs—codes to which Arthur seems immune but which Braggadocchio flaunts.[31] These regulations create opportunities within a public sphere unlike those provided by courtly masquerade or theatrical spectacle, in which actors might only borrow the clothes of the personages they were portraying; sumptuary regulations were designed to broadcast rank, not disguise it, and unlike rules for courtship and flattery, they authorized personal difference, not equality. Although the earliest sumptuary laws were enacted by Parliament in Chaucer's time during the reign of Edward III, most codes were established, elaborated, and abolished within the 118 years of Tudor reign.[32] Before they were all overturned by James I, their specifications had grown increasingly complex, so that Tudor citizens found themselves operating through more and more official procedures in order to announce private objectives (one can only speculate that wearing cat fur was faddish for this reason). In contrast to other courtly strategies, the sumptuary system required the participation of the entire kingdom because individuals were rewarded for reporting each other's infractions: these exclusionary practices enfranchised everyone, and they were representative and revelatory of each.

In his study of sumptuary codes Wilfrid Hooper suggests this shared responsibility and access, reporting that "when a lawyer, after being summoned before the privy council to answer for another offense presented himself with 'a guilt rapier, extreame greate ruffes & lyke unseemlie apparell,'" he was not only fined but nearly thrown out of his profession (p. 445).[33] What is signified by this case is not the unqualified authority of the royal center but its fragmentation, since the notion that a specifically public forum supplied the most efficient way to read evidence about personal identity was something upon which the lawyer and his courtly accusers agreed. We might speak of a Renaissance self-"clothing," when what is subjectively modeled is a model. As John Mowitt explains:

fashion is understood to exemplify the historical development wherein society has so splintered that history itself can no longer embrace the efforts to narrativise experience. Splintering is not used pejoratively here. Instead, . . . it reflects the multiple articulation of the social whose very theorisation can be counted among the various social responses to the withering away of the historical dimension of experience.[34]

The innovations of fashion introduced by sumptuary codes coincide with the transition occurring in the seventeenth century when Foucault claims the body ceases to be a locus for analogy, its similarity impaired, its resemblances disappeared. The development of a public body which knows itself through sumptuary codes at once disguises and highlights the collapse of the analogical body. Sumptuary codes describe how people are not what they imagine themselves to be. They replace the function of the court to indicate roles and confer identity and provide a site where order, hierarchy, even chaos are made visible and intelligible in Elizabeth's body.

This new form of publicity shapes many incidents in *The Faerie Queene*, where through six different versions of knightly discourse and behavior, courtly rhetoric is given a chance to review itself. Replacing a prior and evanescent discourse of gossip, designed primarily to "prolong or multiply [the] single point of view of the queen," the elaborations and revisions of a public discourse, clarified by the frequent alterations of sumptuary codes, designate a revised ethic for which "being seen and being heard by others derive their significance from the fact that everybody sees and hears from a different position."[35] Allegory breaks down under such a bureaucracy, as meaning merely explodes rather than accumulates in the confrontation of the twin Florimells. While nearly all the other characters finally agree about the false Florimell, that she herself needs the presence of the real Florimell to assert who she really is, demonstrates how she is now provided with physical, not moral, evidence in order to vanish into thin air. It is the false Florimell, not "public opinion," who is ultimately discovered to be "evanescent."[36] She is false because she is superficial, but she was also never material to begin with, just as the real Florimell is genuine because she has a body that is more recalcitrant, not Platonic.

If Braggadocchio is not permitted an allegorical figuration, Arthur's body, like that of the false Florimell, is shadowy and debilitated, completely at odds with his allegorical status in the poem. For this reason, when Arthur reads the chronicle of British kings, Spenser's poem, once conduct book, is now transformed into a work of fiction—something to help Arthur merely pass the time in Alma's Castle. Its official status has been altered because Arthur is unable to "actualize" or verify faery land; indeed, his own empirical data explicitly refute it. Presented with the fragments of his biography, Arthur deconstructs the epic of *The Faerie Queene* by reading it, and the chronicles are abruptly ended by his presence (st. 68.2), not completed by it. In fact, he calls himself a "foster childe" of the history Spenser records (10 st. 69.5), personifying the opposite of what Wolfgang Iser terms the "implied reader" or typical member of a reading public, those members of Spenser's audience who might formulate ideas about moral behavior or human conduct from a disembodied ideal (8 st. 2).[37]

CONCLUSION

Through the parallels offered by Arthur's and Braggadocchio's portraits, a new form of publicity is articulated in *The Faerie Queene*. Spenser had reasoned in his letter to Ralegh that public opinion might rally around the figure of Arthur as the subject of least "envy or suspition," as object of common knowledge who does not embody knowledge; but, like Braggadocchio, Arthur is a point of consensus rather than an allegorical source of information who possesses none. Yet, although he is repeatedly "disseuered" in the poem, Arthur never was a single entity in Spenser's original conception. His letter to Ralegh details two figures who do not coincide: one, a subject, "most fitte for the excellency of his person," and another, a text "[b]eing made famous by many mens former workes":

> first Homere, who in the Persons of Agamemnon and Vlysses hath ensampled a good gouernour and a vertuous man, the one in his Ilias, the other in his Odysseis; then Virgil, whose like intention was to doe in the person of Aeneas; after him Ariosto comprised them both in his Orlando; and lately Tasso disseuered them againe, and formed both parts in two persons[.]

145

In the same way that Montrose describes Elizabeth's royal body, Arthur's body is a "cultural corpus," a site for public pressures and discourses, who is mediated and constituted by the same language he inaugurates (pp. 324–25).

Still, Arthur seems less a collection of texts than a collision between them, his strengths most clearly demonstrated in his final battle with Maleger and his men when he wages a war against a bloodless specter with a team of ghosts. In the hollowed, doubled, shadowed, and bewildered figure of Arthur is represented the breakdown of a public realm operating by allegorical codes and their replacement by wider sites of evaluation, which do not provide information but confirmation, which enforce identity by evacuating subjectivity, and which are grounded not on virtue but on public knowledge. Promoting a uniformity of perception, this public is not taught how to act, but what its members have in common.[38] In fact, the public who would criticize Braggadocchio for lacking virtue, or coherence, is also comprised of those people "who have ceased [by identifying themselves as members of a public] to be individuals" (Warner, p. 379). But already, the self-unity inherent in individuals is rendered archaic in the poem: all the other knights are more like each other than themselves—a situation which Archimago as impresario repeatedly, gleefully exploits. And Elizabeth, as aging queen, is more like the Gloriana or Belphoebe she impersonates than like herself, whoever she might be.

NOTES

1. A version of this essay was first presented at the special session on "Spenser at Kalamazoo" at the Twenty-Seventh International Congress on Medieval Studies, Western Michigan University, May 1992. I am especially grateful to Professor Rob Stillman and Professor Jon Quitslund as well as to Ross Zucker for their comments on the essay and advice for its improvement.

2. Their "homosocial" relation, here mediated by the iconic Belphoebe, resembles the triangular relations described by Eve Kosofsky Sedgwick in *Epistemology of the Closet* (Berkeley: Univ. of California Press, 1990), p. 15, and *Between Men: English Literature and Male Homosocial Desire* (New York: Columbia Univ. Press, 1985). Since Belphoebe is the only figure of the three for whom the court is accessible, her privacy is an imposition upon Braggadocchio's and Trompart's.

3. All citations are to the Variorum edition of *The Works of Edmund Spenser. The Faerie Queene, Book II*, ed. Edwin Greenlaw et al. (Baltimore: Johns Hopkins Univ. Press, 1933).

4. See Harry Berger's discussion of this "conspicuous irrelevance" in *The Allegorical Temper: Vision and Reality in Book II of Spenser's Faerie Queene* (New Haven: Yale Univ. Press, 1957), pp. 133–49. That Spenser's description of Belphoebe—which employs the language of the Petrarchan lover—might also be a way simultaneously to neutralize or dismember her awesome body is suggested by Louis Montrose in "The Elizabethan Subject and the Spenserian Text" in *Literary Theory/Renaissance Texts*, ed. Patricia Parker and David Quint (Baltimore: Johns Hopkins Univ. Press, 1986). See pp. 324–28.

5. *The Analogy of the Faerie Queene* (Princeton: Princeton Univ. Press, 1976).

6. Elizabeth J. Bellamy, "Reading Desire Backwards: Belatedness and Spenser's Arthur," *South Atlantic Quarterly* 88:4 (Fall 1989), 801.

7. Michael Warner, "The Mass Public and the Mass Subject" in *Habermas and the Public Sphere*, ed. Craig Calhoun (Cambridge: MIT Press, 1992), p. 379.

8. Jürgen Habermas, *The Structural Transformation of the Public Sphere: An Inquiry into a Category of Bourgeois Society*, trans. Thomas Berger with the assistance of Frederick Lawrence (Cambridge: MIT Press, 1989), pp. 32–33, 34.

9. The opposition between "official" and popular culture, nowhere more clear than during the carnival which inverts them, is treated by Michael D. Bristol, "The Social Function of Festivity" in *Carnival and Theater: Plebian Culture and the Structure of Authority in Renaissance England* (New York: Methuen, 1985), pp. 26–39.

10. *Renaissance Self-Fashioning from More to Shakespeare* (Chicago: Univ. of Chicago Press, 1980).

11. Roy Strong, *Art and Power: Renaissance Festivals 1450–1650* (Woodbridge, Suffolk: Boydell Press, 1984), pp. 3–4.

12. See Roy Strong, *The Cult of Elizabeth: Elizabethan Portraiture and Pageantry* (Berkeley: Univ. of California Press, 1977).

13. "'Infinite Desire': Spenser's Arthur and the Representation of Courtly Ambition," *English Literary History* 58 (1991), 747–771.

14. See Frank Whigham's discussion of courtly "bureaucratic" aid in *Ambition and Privilege: The Social Tropes of Elizabethan Courtesy Theory* (Berkeley: Univ. of California Press, 1984), pp. 30–31.

15. I borrow the phrase from Whigham, whose account explores how tropes of courtesy "mystify the various levels of personal failure" (p. 21).

16. See Hannah Arendt's discussion of the marginalization of courage in early-modern conceptions of virtue in *The Human Condition* (Chicago: Univ. of Chicago Press, 1958).

17. Bellamy comments that "[u]nlike Britomart and Arthegall, Arthur is the only dynastic avatar in *The Faerie Queene* who is given no prophetic validation of his imperial destiny" (p. 794).

18. *Sincerity and Authenticity* (Cambridge: Harvard Univ. Press, 1972).

19. *The Crisis of the Aristocracy 1558–1641*, abr. ed. (London: Oxford Univ. Press, 1977). See also Laurence Stone, "Social Mobility in England, 1500–1700" *Past and Present,* 33, pp. 16–55.

20. *The Evolution of The Faerie Queene* (Chicago: Univ. of Chicago Press, 1942).

21. In taking account of such discrepancies, my reading of Arthur's problematic positioning differs therefore from investigations which assume the entire project of *The Faerie Queene* to be a critique of chivalry. Mueller, for instance, reads Arthur's characterization as itself part of a much larger programme: "the figure of Arthur functions to isolate and problematize the whole notion of an overarching Platonic significance. . . . Arthur's actions emblematize a virtually constitutive pattern of questing and failure" (p. 749).

22. For a discussion of the body of the "public subject," see Warner, "The Mass Public and the Mass Subject," p. 381.

23. Habermas considers the earliest definitions of the "public" in *The Structural Transformation of the Public Sphere*.

24. In contrast to Arthur, Britomart, as William Oram states, "may not meet herself as Redcrosse does when he meets Sans Joy or Despair, but she exists in a world peopled largely by fragmentary personalities, clarified and simplified versions of the drives present in herself and the other major characters of the poem" (p. 38). "Elizabethan Fact and Spenserian Fiction." *Spenser Studies,* 4 (1983), 33–47.

25. Michel Foucault, *The Order of Things: An Archaeology of the Human Sciences* (New York: Vintage Books, 1973). See chapter 2, "The Prose of the World."

26. The excrescence of the seventeenth-century body, which had, a century earlier, been the locus for analogy and similarity, is described by Francis Barker in *The Tremulous Private Body: Essays on Subjection* (New York: Methuen, 1984), pp. 21–23.

27. The twinned meanings of discipline as pedagogy and punishment were explored in Andrew Murphy's response to M. Lindsay Kaplan's paper "Spenser's Slander of Lord Grey," presented at the Twenty-Sixth International Congress on Medieval Studies. Western Michigan University, May 1991.

28. Donald Cheney refers to this movement underground in "Spenser's Fortieth Birthday and Related Fictions," *Spenser Studies,* 4 (1983),3–31. See also Elizabeth Mazzola, "Marrying Medusa: Spenser's *Epithalamion* and Renaissance Reconstructions of Female Privacy," *Genre,* 25 (Spring 1992), 193–210.

29. Christopher Ricks, in *Keats and Embarrassment* , (New York: Oxford Univ. Press, 1984) explains how love protects two people from that particular state, so that they are enough at ease to even do something as private and hidden as sleep together (p. 13).

30. Perhaps for this reason Berger (*The Allegorical Temper*) curiously dismisses the Braggadocchio episode in exploring its "conspicuous irrelevance." He finally concludes: "As in any comic form, the characters [of Braggadocchio

and Trompart] are basically inadequate to upset or even to cope with the order in which they exist; to this extent, the order is secure" (p. 143).

31. Whigham (*Ambition and Privilege*) claims the development of sumptuary laws indicates a transition during which "national centers began to grasp to themselves the determination and licensing of actions of all sorts, [so that] the conceptual screens of bureaucracy fell between ordinary people and the practices of their everyday lives" (p. 30). I would see the elaboration of these laws as registering an arena for a new form of mutuality, the kind Habermas claims takes shape two centuries later.

32. Frances Elizabeth Baldwin, *Sumptuary Legislation and Personal Regulation in England* (Baltimore: Johns Hopkins Univ. Press, 1926), pp. 9–12.

33. "Tudor Sumptuary Laws," *English Historical Review*, 30 (July 1915), 433–49.

34. "The Coming of the Text: The Text of Publicity," *History of European Ideas,* 11 (1989), 574–75.

35. Arendt explores revisions of official discourse in *The Human Condition*, p. 57.

Rumor is another way such "splintering" can be described. Richard Abrams suggests that rumor was "the *lingua franca* of a troubled England in the last years of Henry's reign": "To discuss Rumor's parodic status as royal householder usurping Henry is thus to explore a crisis in the kingmaking process whereby the country normally epitomizes its group personality in a single representative, a human synecdoche" (pp. 467–68). But Abrams too easily associates the fragmentation of rumor with decline in royal power: "[A]t Shrewsbury, Henry's device of multiplying the royal image in the counterfeits who reduce his personal risk in battle bankrupts the majesty of the institution of kingship itself, setting the stage for Rumor's corporate personification in which many are represented yet none elevated, none vouchsafed by reflection a glimpse of his own potential divinity." See "Rumor's Reign in 2 *Henry IV*: The Scope of a Personification," *English Literary Renaissance*, 15 (Autumn 1986), 467–95. If the negative aspect of fragmentation is depicted in *The Faerie Queene* by the blatant beast, there is a positive side as well, exemplified by Spenser's Arthur, the model on whom all of the other virtues are based.

36. This particular episode of "evacuated" subjectivity collapsing around a single identity counters Whigham's description of "evacuated authority" in courtly society, where subjectivity is generally already hollow. First describing the predicament of Thomas More, who judged himself against his idea of himself, "in many more ordinary cases," Whigham claims, "the typical courtier's dominant Other will be the embodiment of a nonexistent 'public opinion,' readable in the mirroring responses of witnesses but dangerously evanescent" (*Ambition and Privilege*, p. 39).

37. Iser is clear to situate the change historically: "While other literary forms induced the reader to contemplate the exemplariness [he] embodied, the novel confronted him with problems arising from his own surroundings, at the same time holding out various potential solutions which the reader himself had, at least partially, to formulate" (p. xi). *The Implied Reader: Patterns of*

Communication in Prose Fiction from Bunyan to Beckett (Baltimore: Johns Hopkins Univ. Press, 1987.

    38. See John Barrell, *The Political Theory of Painting from Reynolds to Hazlitt: The Body of the Public* (New Haven: Yale Univ. Press, 1986), p. 63.

6 ARTHURIAN ILLUMINATIONS IN MIDDLE DUTCH MANUSCRIPTS

Martine Meuwese

This article aims to discuss all Arthurian illustrations in Middle Dutch manuscripts, which may seem more ambitious than it actually is. There are only four manuscripts containing such illustrations, only two of which are real Arthurian romances, and together they contain no more than seven Arthurian illuminations.[1]

The best-known Middle Dutch Arthurian illustration is probably the full-page opening miniature of the *Roman van Walewein* (Leiden, UB, Letk. 195, f. 120v) (fig. 6.1).[2] This original Middle Dutch romance was started around the middle of the thirteenth century by Penninc, and subsequently completed by Pieter Vostaert. The Leiden manuscript is the only complete manuscript that has survived. At the end of the manuscript, the copyist gives 1350 as the year in which he completed his work.[3]

The full-page miniature shows how Walewein (Gawain) pursues the flying chessboard on horseback. This chess set has flown into Arthur's castle through a window after the king and his knights have finished their meal. The knights are too surprised and too frightened to approach it, and when no one shows any intention of starting a game of chess, the set flies off again by the same route it had taken when it came in. Gawain goes off in pursuit of the set on his faithful horse, Gringolet. Kay calls after him that it would have been better if he had tied a cord to the chessboard, for then it could not have escaped him. The chess set keeps flying in front of Gawain for some time until it reaches a mountain and disappears into a crevice. Gawain will also enter the mountain, after which the hole will close again, and he will have to fight a number of dragons. Many other adventures follow, which will eventually lead to Gawain's return to King Arthur with the chessboard.

The miniature depicts the moment when Gawain arrives at the mountain, which here has flowers growing on it. His left hand seems to point to the face of the mountain. At the same time the illustration covers the whole of the romance, which, after all, centers on the quest for the chessboard. Gawain's arms, "argent, a lion's head gules," is depicted seven times on his armor. These arms are unusual for Gawain, who normally bears "argent, a canton gules."[4] Yvain, the knight who in Chrétien de Troyes's romance of the same name is accompanied by a lion he has befriended, usually bears a lion.[5] Lancelot bears a somewhat comparable lion's head in a *Lancelot en prose* manuscript at Oxford (Bodleian Library, Rawlinson Q B 6, f. 47v). In the depiction of the scene of the perilous bed from Chrétien's *Perceval* on the ivory caskets made in Paris at the beginning of the fourteenth century, Gawain is represented with a lion's paw on his shield, although this is not a heraldic blazon but a real paw which has been cut off.[6] The lion in Gawain's arms in the *Roman van Walewein* might be particular to the Low Countries. The romance itself associates Gawain with a lion at one point, and in another original Arthurian romance, *Walewein ende Keye*, Gawain is said to bear 'a lion gules.'[7]

The chess set is described as very expensive with an ivory board inlaid with precious stones; it has a silver rim and red gold legs. The chess pieces, moreover, are said to be more valuable than all of Arthur's kingdom. All this splendor, however, does not show in the miniature; the chess pieces are not even depicted. The flying chessboard seems to be unique to the *Roman van Walewein*. Magic chess sets are found in other Arthurian romances; however, these do not fly but are capable of playing a game of chess against a human opponent by themselves, which is not the case in *Walewein*.[8] On the left side of an illustration from the *Lancelot en prose* in the Pierpont Morgan Library at New York (MS 805–06, f. 253v), for instance, Lancelot is seen playing against a magic chessboard which moves the pieces by itself. He wins the game and thereby becomes the owner of the board, which he sends to Guinevere in the middle of the picture. On the right of the picture, she is shown playing a game, which she, however, will lose.[9]

The flying chessboard has received much attention since J. Janssens recently observed that the board has only seven horizontal rows instead of eight and suggested that this might be because the miniaturist was experimenting with the use of perspective.[10] In my view, however, this would simply seem to be an error on the part of the artist. The illumination does not seem to suggest that any attempt at the use of perspective was made; moreover, the use of perspective does not make a row of squares disappear. What is conclusive, however, is the fact that the miniaturist obviously did not quite manage to fit in the last row, as there is quite a large space left at the bottom of the board, which is filled by many lines.[11] In the miniature from the Pierpont Morgan Library mentioned above, the number of rows on the chessboard differs in successive scenes, and a marginal decoration from a *Roman d'Alexandre* from the Bodleian Library at Oxford (Bodley 264, f. 92v, 1338–44) clearly shows a correct preliminary drawing, from which the miniaturist deviated when he made the illustration. This seems to suggest that such "incorrect" chessboards are of frequent occurrence and that the illuminator's primary aim was not to depict a chessboard realistically but rather to suggest one.

The miniature depicting Gawain and the flying chessboard was inserted on a single leaf of parchment, which has led many scholars to suppose that the illustration was cut from the copyist's exemplar and then inserted in the present manuscript. The illustration has been said to have originated in the Northern Netherlands, but since this claim was made because the miniature could not be placed stylistically, and since very little is known about illumination in the Northern Netherlands, nothing would seem to have been proved yet.[12] In fact, it is doubtful whether the miniature predates the manuscript, which, as has been said before, is dated 1350. It was quite common to insert single leaves with full-page miniatures which had been produced separately, and the details of Gawain's armor in particular would seem to suggest that the miniature was made around 1350.[13] The ailettes he is wearing are found especially in the period up to 1350, but the loose-fitting sleeves and the hauberk which is pointed at the lower edge were introduced precisely around that date. Similarly, the fact that the surcoat is cut short at the front but long at the back points to a short-lived fashion current in the Low Countries in the middle of the fourteenth century. Examples of this type of armor are found in depictions of knights on tombstones, which are usually dated, and on a stained-glass window from the middle of the fourteenth century.[14] It therefore seems logical to assume that the miniature was intended for the present manuscript from the beginning.

Full-page miniatures are scarce in the French secular book illumination, and certainly in French Arthurian romances. The format of the *Walewein* miniature was therefore probably not inspired by the French Arthurian romance tradition.[15] Above the miniature, in the top left-hand corner of the page, traces of a short written line are visible, which has been quite thoroughly erased. This line may have contained more information about the illustration, for instance instructions for the miniaturist, but, unfortunately, the text is now illegible.

Like the *Walewein* manuscript, the other illuminated Arthurian romance, the *Ferguut* (Leiden, UB, Letk. 191), is at Leiden. Folio 1r of this manuscript contains a historiated initial (fig. 6.2). The *Ferguut* was written around the middle of the thirteenth century and is an adaptation of the Old French *Fergus*. The Leiden manuscript is dated at around 1350 and is said to have originated in the Southern Netherlands on the basis of linguistic evidence.[16] This means that the *Walewein* miniature and the historiated initial from the *Ferguut* may have been made at around the same time.

The severely damaged initial at the beginning of the text is the only illumination in the *Ferguut* manuscript. It depicts a knight standing upright carrying a sword and a shield. This knight can be interpreted in two ways: he could either be the patron of the manuscript, or he could represent Ferguut, the protagonist of the romance. The *Lancelot en prose* from the Pierpont Morgan Library contains somewhat comparable initials in the text which represent the characters in the romance.[17] This seems to make it likely that the knight should be interpreted as the protagonist, also because the text usually refers to Ferguut as "the knight with the white shield." The little bits of color that are still visible on the shield contain traces of silver, and white and silver (argent) are the same color in heraldry. Yet it is remarkable that in iconography the Arthurian knights who carry white shields according to a text are also shown carrying white shields in the accompanying illuminations, and never silver shields, to my knowledge.[18] It is, of course, possible to assume that the illuminator of the *Ferguut* initial was not familiar with this tradition. It is not at all certain, however, that the initial originally depicted a plain silver shield. Traces of a sketch for a blazon representing an animal-like figure seem to be detectable on the severely damaged part of the shield. This raises the question whether the damage done to the initial, which mainly affected the shield, was caused on purpose, for example, to remove the arms of a former owner which were no longer wanted. Thus both interpretations of the knight's identity are still possible.[19]

The two illustrations discussed so far are the only illuminations found in Middle Dutch Arthurian romances. In order to account for this lack of illuminated texts, it has been argued that the patrons of Middle Dutch Arthurian romances belonged to the lesser nobility and did not have the means to pay for expensive illuminations. Another reason that has been put forward is the absence of a real tradition of illumination in the Low Countries.[20]

Although the above discussion may seem to suggest otherwise, there are some sumptuously illustrated Middle Dutch texts, but these usually are not romances but works of a more encyclopedic nature. A good example in the context of Arthurian illumination is the *Spiegel Historiael* (Mirror of History) written by Jacob van Maerlant around 1285 for Floris V, the Count of Holland. Only one illuminated copy of this text has survived (The Hague, KB, KA XX), containing many fine miniatures, often three columns wide. This manuscript was probably made in Ghent at the beginning of the fourteenth century.[21] The *Spiegel Historiael* is an adaptation of the *Speculum Historiale* by Vincent of Beauvais, but since this author pays very little attention to the events surrounding King Arthur, Maerlant used Geoffrey of Monmouth's *Historia Regum Brittanniae* to expand the account of King Arthur's reign. In two famous passages from his description of this period, Maerlant criticizes the fact that French romances describe Arthurian knights who are not found in Latin chronicles and who, therefore, in his view, never existed, as opposed to Gawain, Mordred and Kay, present in the Latin tradition.

Maerlant's account of the *History of King Arthur* is illustrated with four miniatures. The first miniature on f. 153v depicts festivities at Arthur's court (fig. 6.3). Maerlant's text says that Arthur marries Guinevere, and it then suddenly moves on to a detailed description of festivities. This leads the reader to think that these festivities were held on the occasion of the wedding. However, Maerlant's source, Geoffrey of Monmouth, describes them as taking place on the occasion of Arthur's coronation, which Maerlant does not mention here at all.[22] On the left-hand side of the miniature the tables are being laid for the banquet, and a large procession of nobles, returning from the mass, is approaching from the right.[23] The composition of the procession of nobles in particular links up very closely with Maerlant's text. Arthur is preceded by four kings with gold swords and is followed by a group of musicians, including a man with an organ and a fiddler, who, in turn, are followed by the queen and her ladies. It does not seem impossible to assume that the illuminator also thought he was dealing with a wedding feast. There are some details that seem to suggest this. First of all, both Arthur and Guinevere bear Arthur's arms, "three crowns gules," on their golden garments. Thus, the queen is shown to adopt her husband's arms through marriage. An illustration depicting the wedding of Arthur and Guinevere in a *Lancelot en prose* manuscript from Paris (BN, fr. 95, f. 273r) also shows the two of them dressed in golden garments, while Guinevere's ermine cloak is held open in a similar fashion by those around her. In the margin an organ player is depicted. The illustration depicting a wedding in the manuscript of *Artus le Restoré* at Paris includes a fiddler (BN, fr. 761, f. 141v). A miniature depicting the mass wedding in the *Atre Périlleux* from Paris (BN, fr. 1433, f. 60r) shows a procession of brides and grooms accompanied by an organ player and a fiddler, in which the women walk with their hands crossed, just like Guinevere in the Maerlant manuscript.[24]

During the festivities, Roman envoys arrive to demand taxes from Arthur, and Arthur decides to have Gawain and some other knights report his refusal to Lucius, the commander-in-chief of the Roman army. On the right-hand side of the illustration on f. 154r (fig. 6.4), Lucius is depicted sitting in his tent and next to him stands a Roman soldier who, according to the text, has insulted Arthur's envoys by saying that the Britons may be loudmouths but are in fact extremely cowardly. Gawain is furious and kills him with a thrust of his sword, at the same time mounting his horse to get away. Arthur's knights withdraw, which does not prevent them from attacking the Romans who pursue them, as can be seen on the left side of the miniature. This episode also occurs in the Vulgate *Merlin*, and it is depicted in a manuscript of this text in London (BL, Add. 10292, f. 206r). Here, however, the Roman soldier is not stabbed to death but decapitated, which is consistent with the account in both Geoffrey's text and in *Merlin*.[25] Maerlant, however, says that Gawain thrusts his sword through the soldier's body. This detail shows that the miniaturist also based this miniature on Maerlant's text. In the London *Merlin*, the subsequent battle with the Romans is depicted on f. 206v, but this illustration is not specific enough to be compared with the Maerlant miniature depicting this scene.

After this, Arthur's entire army is shown to enter into battle with Lucius on f. 154v (fig. 6.5). In this battle, according to the text, Gawain manages to kill Lucius and to throw the banner bearing the

Roman eagle into the sand. The miniature clearly shows the banner lying on the ground. Gawain is seen thrusting his sword into a king's heart. On the basis of Maerlant's text, one may expect this to be Lucius, but this king bears the wrong arms. Geoffrey does not say who kills the commander-in-chief, but the Vulgate *Merlin* mentioned above does say that Gawain kills his Roman opponent. Could this French text have influenced Maerlant's work, in spite of Maerlant's clear dislike of anything French?[26]

In all the miniatures depicting King Arthur he bears "or, three crowns gules." The three crowns are the shield charges usually attributed to Arthur, and they presumably symbolize Arthur's reign over his three realms, but the colors are normally the other way around: "gules, three crowns or."[27] In any case, Maerlant's text will not have provided the illuminator with information about these arms. Maerlant only says that Arthur's shield bears the Virgin Mary, which is consistent with the description given by Geoffrey. Therefore, it would be more logical to expect Mary to be depicted on Arthur's shield, as she is in the well-known illustration from the *Langloft Chronicles* in London (BL, Royal 20 A II, f. 4r). However, it was also suggested that Mary was depicted on the inside of Arthur's shield, which means that this does not say anything about Arthur's actual coat of arms.[28] In any case, the miniaturist cannot have derived the crowns he depicts from Maerlant's text. His most likely sources of inspiration were the tradition of the Nine Worthies and illuminated Arthurian romances.

The miniatures in the manuscript show Gawain bearing his usual arms: "argent, a canton gules." Maerlant's text does not describe these arms either, but they fit exactly into the tradition of the French prose romances.[29] It therefore seems reasonable to assume that the illuminator derived the knowledge of heraldry he used in making these miniatures from some such source.

After the victory of Arthur's army over the Romans, a number of miniatures follow in which Arthur does not feature. He is seen once more on f. 163v (fig. 6.6). In the meantime he has been waging war against his nephew Mordred for over thirty years.[30] We have now arrived at the final battle at Salisbury, in which both of them will be killed. In the miniature Arthur cleaves his opponent, who at the same time wounds him. This seems to depict the fight between Arthur and Mordred as it is described in the *Mort Artu*, in which each deals the other the fatal blow. Maerlant's text, just like Geoffrey's, only says that they are killed, but does not specify how or by whom. This seems to suggest that here, too, the illuminator made use of sources other than the text, or otherwise he must have known the story well enough to have added this detail himself. The miniature shows a dead knight bearing Gawain's arms lying on the ground, whereas according to Maerlant's text Gawain has been dead; and also in the *Mort Artu* he also died before this battle takes place.

On the right-hand side of the miniature, Arthur, lying on a bed on a cart, is taken from the battlefield, accompanied by the knights who have survived the battle. Here the miniature clearly deviates from the usual iconography of the scene. According to the literary tradition, only two of the knights who fought on Arthur's side survive the battle, whereas the miniature suggests a crowd of people. The explanation for this may well be in Maerlant's text, which only says that many of Arthur's knights die, but not how many of them survive. Here the illuminator again may have based himself on the text. It is remarkable that Arthur is taken away in a cart, which is not a very elevated last image to be presented of this great king.[31] Indeed, one of the most striking images in Arthurian iconography is the cart in which Lancelot has to ride if he is ever to find the queen, who has been abducted from the court. This cart is compared to that in which criminals are taken to the site of their execution, and consequently Lancelot is jeered at during the ride as if he were a criminal, and in an illumination in the *Lancelot en prose* at Amsterdam (BPH 1, vol. III, f. 31v) he is even pelted with stones. Yet it is doubtful whether the image of Arthur in the cart should be interpreted in such a negative way. The illuminator may merely have adapted an illustration depicting Lancelot in the cart, just like the illuminator of the Amsterdam *Lancelot* (BPH 1, vol. III, f. 50r) used a similar composition to depict Gawain, who, according to the text, is transported on a litter. Arthur's eyes are closed, which probably indicates that he is dead. However, this would be inconsistent with Maerlant's text, which says that Arthur "is taken to an island to recover."[32]

As far as I know, the last illustration to be discussed here has not received any scholarly attention so far. It depicts the tryst beneath the tree scene from the story of Tristan and Isolde in the Leiden manuscript of *Der Minnen Loep* by Dirc Potter (Leiden, UB, Letk. 205, f. 155v). This work, which was written at the beginning of the fifteenth century, discusses many kinds of love and lovers, and the episode of the orchard scene from the story of Tristan and Isolde is included in the section on "good love." In it Potter relates how "the king"—he does not mention the name Marc anywhere—is sitting in the lime tree under which Tristan and Isolde are reposing. Isolde sees the reflection of the king's head in the well and cleverly draws Tristan's attention to this by pointing to the fishes in the water. Now that Tristan has seen the head, the two go on to talk only of their loyalty to their lord and of his virtues, to which Tristan adds that he wishes the king were with them. The moral of this brief episode is that woman's cunning is permitted to preserve a woman's honor. This is rather a free interpretation of the episode.[33] The reference to the fishes and Tristan's wish that the king were there are particularly remarkable. Both are found on banderoles in French in the hands of several figures in the trysting scene as depicted on the oak comb from Bamberg, dating from the first half of the fifteenth century.[34]

Isolde's reference to the fish is also included in the trysting scene depicted on one of the leather slippers that were found during recent excavations of wells.[35] The slipper, found at Mechelen, which dates from the first half of the fifteenth century, has a Middle Dutch inscription around the edges saying "TRIESTRAM SIEDI NIET DAT VISELKIIN" (Tristan, don't you see the little fish). This remarkable reference to the fish is not only found on the comb from Bamberg and the leather slipper but also in a mural at St. Floret in Issoire, which dates from around 1350.[36] It would be interesting to know whether these references to the fish go back to a literary source—but if so, what text could this be—or whether the different artists concerned used the same motif independently. Potter is the only literary source known so far to mention the fishes, and it is possible that he did not make up this element in the story himself. He may have taken it from an iconographical source, comparable to the Bamberg comb, which would be a remarkable instance of art influencing literature instead of the other way around.[37]

The Leiden manuscript containing Potter's story and the miniature illustrating it (fig. 6.7) dates from 1486. The book is written on paper and the illustration is a pen drawing colored with water colors. The illustration is remarkable for a late fifteenth-century manuscript. The whole figure of the king is seen in the tree under which Isolde, wearing a crown, and Tristan are sitting on a garden seat (Isolde on the left and Tristan on the right). In between the two there is the well. Although usually only the head of the king can be seen in the tree, his being depicted in full is not unique to this illustration.[38] What is more remarkable is the fact that he bears a kind of yellow halo and that his left hand seems to be pointing to something. In the water his reflection can be seen in a simplified form, drawn as if seen from the side: three balls to the left indicate the crown; next to it there is a small round face; and to the far right we see the upper part of his body. Although it has been interpreted differently so far, the Tristan slipper found at Mechelen also shows the reflection of the king's head in the well: the head is drawn in profile and as if seen from the side, his crown to the right and his nose in the middle, facing upwards. Here Tristan and Isolde are shown playing chess, a motif which was probably taken from the iconography of the garden of love.[39]

The only other example of this scene from the Low Countries known to me besides the slippers is a sculpture on a stone console made at the end of the fourteenth century, which originally formed part of the Bruges town hall.[40] Both on the Mechelen slipper and in this sculpture it is Isolde who points at the surface of the water. This makes it even more remarkable that in the illustration accompanying Potter's text, which has a woman's cunning for its subject, it is Tristan who points to the well. Thus there does not seem to be a very close relationship between the text and the illustration here, although the illustration fits rather well into the iconographical tradition of the trysting scene. The subject was especially popular in the visual arts. However, only a few manuscript illuminations depicting this scene are known, and this miniature is a valuable addition.

Further on in the manuscript, on f. 190v, a variation on this motif seems to have been depicted in an illustration depicting the garden of love. A man playing a lute and a woman playing a harp are on a seat in the garden, and in between them there is again a well. This well does not show the reflection of a head, but it has a gargoyle in the shape of a man's head, made of stone, from which the water runs into the basin through a tube in its mouth.

The Arthurian illustrations in Middle Dutch texts may be few in number, but the subjects they depict and the ways in which they are executed are very diverse. They often visualize specific elements in the text. In addition, they make use of the iconographical and heraldic traditions, which shows that those traditions have not passed the Low

Countries by as completely as might be inferred from the scarcity of these illustrations in Middle Dutch manuscripts.

NOTES

1. I would like to thank Alison Stones, who gave me the opportunity to use some illustrations from her collection to compare with the Dutch material, and Bart Besamusca, for his valuable comments on an earlier version of this article. This translation was made by Frank van Meurs and Inge van Eijk.

2. This illustration is on the cover of *Arturus Rex*, I (Leuven: Leuven Univ. Press, 1987), for instance.

3. Ff. 1–119 contain the *Roman van Heinric en Margriete van Limborch*, and ff. 120–82 contain the *Roman van Walewein*. The date can be found on f. 182r. For a description of the manuscript and further references, see *Arturus Rex*, I, no. 5. 3. 1.

4. These arms are frequently found in miniatures from the *Lancelot en Prose*, to which I will return in greater detail later. *Sir Gawain and the Green Knight* is an exception; here Gawain's arms are "gules, a pentangle or." See *Sir Gawain and the Green Knight*, ed. J.A. Burrow (Harmondsworth: Penguin, 1972), ll. 619–620.

5. See, for example, the miniature from Chrétien's *Yvain* in Paris, BN, fr. 1433, f. 67v, which is reproduced in R.S. and L.H. Loomis, *Arthurian Legends in Medieval Art* (New York: MLA, 1938), fig. 260, for instance. For Yvain's arms, see G.J. Brault, *Early Blazon. Heraldic Terminology in the Twelfth and Thirteenth Centuries with Special Reference to Arthurian Literature* (Oxford: Clarendon Press, 1972), pp. 48–50.

6. In this episode, Gawain is attacked by a lion, and succeeds in cutting off its head and its paws, which it had thrust into his shield. For this passage, see Chrétien de Troyes, *Le Roman de Perceval ou le Conte du Graal*, ed. K. Busby (Tübingen: Niemeyer, 1993), ll. 7849–7870. For the ivory caskets, see Loomis, *Arthurian Legends in Medieval Art*, pp. 71–72, figs. 136–137.

7. See J. Janssens, "Schaken met de geest . . . Enkele bedenkingen rond de Walewein-miniatuur (hs. Leiden, U.B., Letk. 195, f. 120v)," *Ingenti Spiritu. Hulde-album opgedragen aan Prof. Dr. W.P.F. de Geest ter gelegenheid van zijn zestigste verjaardag* (Brussel: [UFSAL], 1989), pp. 117–118. Gawain bears "argent, a lion sable" in the Mons *Perceval* (Mons, BU, 331/206, p. 103), which was produced in Flanders, possibly Tournai, c. 1275. He bears "azure, a lion or" and "gules, a lion or" in the *Atre Périlleux* (Paris, B.N., fr. 1433, f. Av, f. Br, f. 55r), which was produced in Northeastern France in the first quarter of the fourteenth century. See *Les Manuscrits de Chrétien de Troyes*, ed. K. Busby, T. Nixon, A. Stones, L. Walters (Amsterdam: Rodopi, 1993), esp. Vol. 2, pp. 54, 73, 272, 285 and figs. 201, 304, 305, 307.

8. See W. Haug, "Der Artusritter gegen das magische Schachbrett oder das Spiel bei dem man immer verliert," *Strukturen als Schlüssel zur Welt. Kleine Schriften zur Erzählliteratur des Mittelalters* (Tübingen: Niemeyer, 1989), pp. 672–86.

9. See *Illustrations from One Hundred Manuscripts in the Library of Henry Yates Thompson* (London: Chiswick Press, 1916), p. 19, pl. xliv.

10. See Janssens, "Schaken met de geest . . . ," pp. 110–30, esp. pp. 118–25.

11. This is also pointed out by K. van Dalen-Oskam, following D. Weverink in 1981, in "Een schaakprobleem: de Walewein-miniatuur," *Madoc*, 1, 3 (1987), 24–26. Janssens also mentions this suggestion, but is more in favour of the perspective theory.

12. See G.J. Hoogewerff, *De Noord-Nederlandsche Schilderkunst*, I (The Hague: Martinus Nijhoff, 1936), pp. 74–77. He dates the illustration at around 1340, without putting forward any arguments.

13. G.I. Lieftinck, "De herkomst van het Walewein-handschrift," *Bulletin van den Nederlandschen Oudheidkundigen Bond*, 5e serie, jaargang 1 (1947), 12–18, already pointed out that the insertion of single leaves was a very common practice, and that it is not surprising, therefore, that the parchment of the miniature differs from that of the rest of the manuscript, since the miniature was made by someone other than the copyist. He thought that the reasons for locating the miniature in the Northern Netherlands were not very convincing. Lieftinck's article seems to be somewhat forgotten in the discussion about the *Walewein*. Separate full-page miniatures were often inserted in psalters, but they are also found in Middle Dutch literary works; see, for instance, Groningen, UB, 405, f. 163r from 1339, a miniature at the beginning of the *Wrake van Jerusalem* by Jacob van Maerlant; and Leiden, UB, BPL 14A from c.1360, which represents St. Christopher and a patron at the beginning of Jacob van Maerlant's *Der Naturen Bloeme*.

14. The ailettes with the knight's blazon on them were worn from 1270 to 1350. See H.M. Zijlstra-Zweens, *Of His Array Telle I No Lenger Tale. Aspects of Costume, Arms and Armour in Western Europe 1200–1400* (Amsterdam: Rodopi, 1988), p. 93, fig. 22, 23; and E. van Caster, R. op de Beeck, *De grafkunst in Belgisch Limburg. Vloerzerken en -platen met persoonsvoorstellingen (13e tot 17e eeuw)* (Assen: Van Gorcum, 1981), p. 108. For the armor with loose-fitting sleeves, the surcoat which is cut short at the front and the hauberk which is pointed at the lower edge, compare the grave of Egidius van Hamal from 1354 in the St. Stevenskerk at 's Herenelderen in Zijlstra-Zweens, p. 91, and Van Caster, op de Beeck pp. 74–77. Another tomb depicting a knight wearing a surcoat which is cut short at the front is the grave of Guillaume de Chastelier (d. 1352) at Moulbaix (van Caster, op de Beeck, p. 76). See also a stained-glass window from c. 1350 (Brussels, Koninklijke musea voor kunst en geschiedenis) which might represent William the Rich, count of Namur.

15. In general, an influence from the French tradition on book illumination in the Low Countries is clearly demonstrable, but, as far as format is concerned, there is no such influence here. For the scarcity of full-page miniatures in French secular book illumination, see M.A. Stones, "Secular Manuscript Illumination in France," *Medieval Manuscripts and Textual*

Criticism, ed. C. Kleinhenz (Chapel Hill: North Carolina Studies in the Romance Languages and Literatures, 1976), p. 92–93.

16. See W. Kuiper, *Die riddere metten witten scilde* (Amsterdam: Schiphouwer en Brinkman, 1989). This manuscript contains the following six texts: *Ferguut* (f.1–32), *Floris ende Blancefloer*, *Der Hystorien Bloeme*, *Esopet*, *Die Bediedenisse van der Missen in Dietsche*, *De Dietsche Doctrinael*. See *Ferguut and Galiene. A Facsimile of the Only Extant Middle Dutch Manuscript, Univ. Library Leiden, Letterkunde 191*, with an Introduction by M.J.M. de Haan (Leiden: New Rhine Publ., 1974), p. 7.

17. An initial in New York, Pierpont Morgan Library, 805–06, f. 49v depicts a similar knight, who in this case represents Lancelot.

18. For some examples of plain white shields in Arthurian miniatures, see Amsterdam, BPH 1, vol. III, f. 50r; Bonn, UB, S 526, f. 113r; New York, Pierpont Morgan Library 805–06, f. 39r, f. 239r, f. 241r. For the miniatures from the Pierpont Library, see *Illustrations from One Hundred Manuscripts*. . . .

19. Kuiper, *Die riddere metten witten scilde*, p. 17, assumes that the color of the shield was originally plain silver and that this has partly worn off. He thinks the knight is Ferguut. De Haan, *Ferguut and Galiene* . . . , p. 7, is of the opinion that the shield once bore the arms of an owner of the manuscript, and that these were, therefore, removed on purpose at a later stage.

20. It will first have to be determined how many Arthurian romances in French were illuminated in Flanders or for Flemings. The sumptuously illuminated *Lancelot* manuscript New Haven, Yale Univ. Library 229 may have been made for William of Dendermonde, son of the Flemish count Guy of Dampierre at the end of the thirteenth century. Robert de Béthune also owned a *Lancelot*, according to his inventory. See Stones, "Secular Manuscript Illumination, . . ." pp. 85–87. It would not be surprising if illuminated French Arthurian romances did indeed circulate in these parts. Consequently, the tradition need not have been so unfamiliar that it could not be adapted or adopted for Middle Dutch Arthurian romances. The lack of illuminated manuscripts may, therefore, be more to do with the fact that the patrons belonged to the lesser nobility.

21. I am preparing a dissertation in which this manuscript, its date, and the place where it was produced will be discussed in great detail. The only edition of the *Spiegel Historiael* is based on this manuscript. See M. de Vries, E. Verwijs, *Jacob van Maerlant's Spiegel Historiael, met de fragmenten der later toegevoegde gedeelten bewerkt door Philip Utenbroeke en Lodewijc van Velthem* (Leiden: von Hellwald, 1861–1873; rpt. Utrecht: HES, 1982).

22. For the coronation festivities in Geoffrey of Monmouth, see Book IX.12–15 of *The Historia Regum Brittannie of Geoffrey of Monmouth. Bern, Burgerbibliothek Ms. 568*, ed. N. Wright (Cambridge: Brewer, 1985), pp. 109–12.

23. In the space behind the table which is in between the two servants, traces can be seen of a preliminary drawing which has not been executed. Possibly, small pillars or a throne were supposed to be painted here. Festive

banquets are a popular theme in Arthurian illustrations. A well-known example is the banquet in London, BL, Royal 14 E III, f. 89r; reproduced in R.S. and L.H. Loomis, *Arthurian Legends in Medieval Art*, fig. 242, for instance.

24. The wedding miniatures from Paris, BN, fr. 95 and fr. 761 are reproduced in Th. Briant, *Le testament de Merlin* (Nantes: Bellanger, 1975), figs. 58, 49. The wedding from fr. 1433 can be found in Loomis, *Arthurian Legends in Medieval Art*, fig. 259, for instance.

25. Geoffrey relates this episode in Book X.4. See *The Historia* . . . , p. 119. For this passage in the *Merlin*, see H.O. Sommer, *The Vulgate Version of the Arthurian Romances. II. Lestoire de Merlin* (Washington: Carnegie Institution, 1908), pp. 432–433. I would like to thank Ludo Jongen for drawing my attention to this miniature.

26. Vincentius does not say that Lucius is killed by Gawain either. In "L'Episode de la guerre contre les Romains dans la *Mort Artu* néerlandaise," *Mélanges de Langue et de Littérature du Moyen Age et de la Renaissance offerts à Jean Frappier*, I (Geneva: Droz, 1970), pp. 337–49, W.P. Gerritsen suggests that a possible explanation for Maerlant's addition might be that he wanted to supplement the account in his source without contradicting it, and that he was partial to Gawain. Yet it is remarkable that the *Merlin* says that Gawain kills his Roman opponent. Could this text, or Maerlant's knowledge of it, have played a part in Maerlant's addition, in spite of his dislike of French romances, possibly without his being conscious of this influence?

27. I know of only one other example where these arms are also used for Arthur: Paris, BN, fr. 749. See Brault, *Early Blazon*, p. 44.

28. This miniature is reproduced in Loomis, *Arthurian Legends in Medieval Art*, fig. 386, for instance. For the depiction of Mary on the inside of Arthur's shield, see K.H. Göller, "Die Wappen König Arthurs in der HS. Lansdowne 882," *Anglia*, 79 (1961), 256.

29. For Gawain's arms, see M. Pastoureau, "Etude d'héraldique arthurienne: les armoiries de Gauvain," *Archivum Heraldicum*, 97 (1984), 2–10; and Brault, *Early Blazon*, pp. 40–43.

30. For this extremely long war, see Gerritsen, "L'Episode de la guerre contre les Romains . . . ," p. 346.

31. See M.A. Stones, "Aspects of Arthur's Death in Medieval Illumination," *The Passing of Arthur. New Essays in Arthurian Tradition*, ed. C. Baswell and W. Sharpe (New York and London: Garland, 1988), pp. 52–101. On p. 66, Stones makes the following comment on this miniature: "the Hague image is a particularly interesting instance because of its unusual emphasis on the ignominy of Arthur's death, showing his wounded body taken away in a cart after the battle."

32. It is not unusual for texts to describe the dead as being transported in carts. In Arthurian illuminations, however, the depiction of a knight in a cart seems to be exclusively restricted to the *charrette* episode. Maerlant's text does not mention this cart, so the use of an iconographical source depicting the scene of the *charrette* seems likely. A depiction of Lancelot in the cart which is closely related iconographically to Arthur in the cart is the *charrette* on f. 296r in

Bonn, UB, S 526. Here the usual dwarf on the horse has been replaced by a knight in a coat of mail, just as in the Hague manuscript. This miniature can be found in L. Olschki, *Die romanischen Literaturen des Mittelalters* (Potsdam: Akademische Verlagsgesellschaft Athenaion, 1928), fig. 64.

33. See *Der Minnen Loep door Dirc Potter*, I, ed. P. Leendertz (Leiden: Mortier, 1845), pp. 256–57. Here the king is sitting in the lime tree by himself. Eilhart also mentions a lime tree. Both in Béroul and in the *Folie d'Oxford* the tree is a pine tree, and in Gottfried von Strassburg it is an olive tree. Potter, however, does not follow Eilhart in every respect, for then the dwarf should also be up in the tree. It is not unusual for Potter to change the stories he tells. See A.M.J. van Buuren, "Een middeleeuwse Ovidius," *Literatuur*, 1 (1984), pp. 149–55.

34. See D. Fouquet, "Die Baumgartenszene der Tristan in der mittelalterlichen Kunst und Literatur," *Zeitschrift für Deutsche Philologie*, 92 (1973),360–70; H. Frühmorgen-Voss, "Tristan und Isolde in mittelalterlichen Bildzeugnissen," *Deutsche Viertel- Jahrsschrift für Literaturwissenschaft und Geistesgeschichte*, 47 (1973), 645–63.

35. See H. Sarfatij, "Tristan op vrijersvoeten? Een bijzonder versieringsmotief op laat-middeleeuws schoeisel uit de Lage Landen," *Ad Fontes. Opstellen aangeboden aan Prof. Dr. C. van de Kieft* (Amsterdam: Verloren, 1984), pp. 371–400. In this article, Sarfatij discusses five slippers with decorations depicting the tryst beneath the tree.

36. See Loomis, *Arthurian Legends in Medieval Art*, figs. 96–98. See also M. Curschmann, "Images of Tristan," *Gottfried von Strassburg and the Medieval Tristan Legend. Papers from an Anglo-North American Symposium*, ed. A. Stevens and R. Wisbey (Cambridge: Brewer, 1990), pp. 1–17. The murals at St. Floret are based on Rusticiano da Pisa's *Meliadus*, but the trysting scene does not occur in this text at all.

37. Winkelman thinks that Potter may have based himself on an iconographical source. See J.H. Winkelman, "Tristan en Isolde in de minnetuin. Over een versieringsmotief op laatmiddeleeuws schoeisel," *Amsterdamer Beiträge zur älteren Germanistik*, 24 (1986), 163–88.

38. King Marc is depicted in full in the tree on a North German piece of embroidery dating from the first half of the fifteenth century, which is now kept at Danzig. For a picture of this embroidery, see Frühmorgen-Voss, "Tristan und Isolde in mittelalterlichen Bildzeugnissen," fig. 8. The king is also depicted in full on the Wienhausen III tapestry; see Loomis, *Arthurian Legends in Medieval Art*, fig. 79. Thus the miniature in *Der Minnen Loep* bears some resemblance to the German tradition (see also note 33). However, Marc can also be seen in full in a miniature in London, BL Add. 11619 f. 8r. For this miniature, see T. Hunt, "The Tristan Illustrations in MS London BL Add. 11619," *Rewards and Punishments in the Arthurian Romances and Lyric Poetry of Medieval France. Essays presented to Kenneth Varty on the Occasion of his Sixtieth Birthday*, ed. P.V. Davies, A.J. Kennedy (Cambridge: Brewer, 1987), pp. 45–60. The god of love, too, is often depicted in full in a tree under which two lovers are reposing. He also wears a crown, and throws arrows at the lovers. This motif is often

found on ivory mirror cases as well as in miniatures in manuscripts of the *Roman de la Rose*. See, for instance, E. König, *Die Liebe im Zeichen der Rose* (Stuttgart-Zurich: Belser, 1992), p. 54. For the motif of the man in a tree in a parable, see J.W. Einhorn, "Das Einhorn als Sinnzeichen des Todes: Die Parabel vom Mann im Abgrund," *Frühmittelalterliche Studien. Jahrbuch des Instituts für Frühmittelalterforschung der Universität Münster*, 6 (1972), 381–417.

39. See Winkelman, "Tristan en Isolde in de minnetuin."

40. See *Arturus Rex*, I, no. 2.2.5, fig. 3.

Fig. 6.1. Gawain pursues the flying chessboard. Penninc-Vostaert,
Roman van Walewein. Leiden, UB, Letk. 191, f. 1r.
Reproduced by permission.

Fig. 6.2. Initial with a knight. *Ferguut*. Leiden, UB, Letk. 191, f. 1r.
Reproduced by permission.

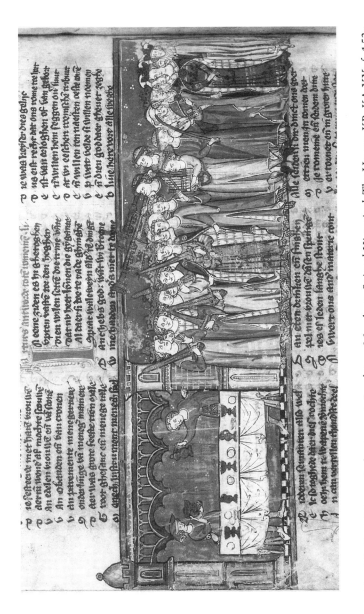

Fig. 6.3. Festivities at Arthur's court. Jacob van Maerlant, *Spiegel Historiael*. The Hague, KB, KA XX, f. 153v. Reproduced by permission.

Fig. 6.4. Gawain kills a Roman soldier. Jacob van Maerlant, *Spiegel Historiael*. The Hague, KB, KA XX, 154r. Reproduced by permission.

Fig. 6.5. Arthur's army in battle with the Romans. Jacob van Maerlant, *Spiegel Historiael*. The Hague, KB, KA XX, f. 154v. Reproduced by permission.

Fig. 6.6. Arthur's death. Jacob van Maerlant, *Spiegel Historiael*. KB, KA XX, f. 163v. Reproduced by permission.

Fig. 6.7. The tryst beneath the tree. Dirc Potter,
Der Minnen Loep. Leiden, UB, Letk. 205, f. 155v.
Reproduced by permission.

THE DISCOURSE OF THE FIGURAL NARRATIVE IN THE ILLUMINATED MANUSCRIPTS OF *TRISTAN* (c. 1250–1475)

Jacqueline Thibault Schaefer

In a fair number of the surviving medieval Tristan manuscripts, the verbal text is accompanied by images which may range in number from a single one to a full cycle. Yet, there exists no comprehensive study of this pictorial component of the reception of the myth.[1] The pages which follow represent a first attempt at an analytical survey of that corpus. While our investigation does not claim to be exhaustive, it encompasses most of the illuminated Tristan versions from the first extant manuscripts of the thirteenth century up to the incunabula of the fifteenth century, when the advent of the printing press inflected the popular story and its iconography.

FIELD OF INVESTIGATION

The iconographical body we have examined groups two verbal traditions, one in verse, the other in prose, of the same mythic narrative. But since neither the unique manuscript extant of Beroul's poem nor the Thomas fragments carry miniatures, the illuminations accompanying the verse version are to be found only in the German texts.[2] Three illluminated manuscripts contain Gottfried von Strassburg's unfinished poem with Ulrich von Türheim's Continuation: Munich, Bayerische Staatsbibliothek, Cgm. 51 (mid-thirteenth century),[3] Cologne, Stadt Historisches Archiv W* 88 (1323),[4] and Brussels, Bibliothèque Royale ms. 14697 (c. 1435). In the latter case, the fragment known as *Tristan als Mönch* is inserted between Gottfried's and Ulrich's texts.[5] There subsists but one manuscript with images of Eilhart von Oberge's *Tristrant* (Heidelberg, UB, Pal. germ. 346) a copy made c. 1460 of a manuscript dated 1403 according to the inscription on Tristan and Isolde's grave in the last miniature.[6]

Much more numerous are the illuminated manuscripts of the prose version, of French, Italian, English and Flemish provenance.[7] We have examined ourselves the following complete texts: Paris, BN, fr. 758 (thirteenth century); Malibu, Getty Museum, Ludwig XV 5 (c. 1320–1340);[8] Paris, BN, fr. 100–101 (c. 1400); BN, fr. 335–336 (1400); BN, fr. 97 (fifteenth century); BN, fr. 99 (1463); BN, fr. 103 (fifteenth century); Chantilly, Musée Condé 645–646–647 (fifteenth century). We relied on the thorough descriptions available for four other complete manuscripts: Vienna, Österreichische National-bibliothek (ÖNB) 2542 (c. 1300, except ff. 500–550v dating from the third quarter of the fifteenth century) illustrated with 4 large miniatures and 197 historiated initials;[9] Vienna ÖNB 2537 (before 1416) counting 144 miniatures;[10] Vienna, ÖNB 2539–2540 (second and third quarter of the fifteenth century) totaling 190 colored pen drawings.[11] We have also examined first hand a number of illustrated incomplete manuscripts: Paris, BN, fr. 750 (1278), BN, fr. 759, BN, fr. 772, BN, fr. 776, BN, n. a. fr. 6579 (all of French provenance, thirteenth century) and BN, fr. 1463, BN, fr. 12599 (also thirteenth century, but of Italian provenance); for the fourteenth century, Paris, BN, fr. 334, BN, fr. 349 with planned but unexecuted miniatures, and London, British Library, Add., 5474 (all three of French provenance), also Paris, BN, fr. 755, BN, fr. 760, London, BL, Harley 4389 (all three from Italian workshops), and London, BL, Royal 20 D. ii (in a Flemish hand); finally, for the fifteenth century, Paris, BN, fr. 102, BN, n. a. fr. 6639, Chantilly, Musée Condé 648 (all three of French provenance), and London, BL, Add. 23929 (of Italian execution).

APPROACH AND METHOD

The 38 manuscripts examined constitute a large iconographical corpus, which brings together *Tristan* versions produced over several centuries within the medieval period, and written in different languages or genres, while illustrating the same basic narrative. Our approach to this corpus differs from that of the art historian or the philologist; rather, we wish to consider it as would a mythologist with a particular interest in one aspect of the phenomenology of myth, namely, the modalities of its transtextuality. Under this light, the iconography of a given myth at any point of its reception appears as one of the transtextual virtualities of that myth. So, the purpose of the present analysis is to determine how the images narrate the myth in the illuminated manuscripts of the medieval *roman de Tristan,* that is to say at a specific moment in the evolution of a particular iconographic genre in which text and image share the diegesis.[12]

In order to arrive at a synthesis based on a broad spectrum of specific examples, the investigation had to be at once meticulous and extensive. For the 29 manuscripts whose iconography had not yet been analyzed, we wrote, from direct observation, a description of each miniature accompanied by its rubric, an endeavor conducted over a number of years. A methodological process was devised to manage the large number of images repertoried. Manuscript by manuscript (along with codicological data, provenance, date, place of conservation, number of folios, number and type of images, specific version), each illustration was entered in an episodic matrix which divided the narrative into 19 main sequences.[13] Such a system allows for both a vertical, diachronic reading of the figural narrative of each manuscript, and a horizontal, thematic reading, tracing the visualization of particular mythemes throughout the corpus under examination.[14]

FORMS OF REPRESENTATION

Among the three methods of rendering literary contents through illustration in rolls and codices, the closest to the text is, according to Kurt Weitzmann,[15] the cyclic representation, which first appeared in the Hellenistic period. It is the method prevailing in the manuscripts under study, but within this category one may distinguish different types according to the place of the images in relation to the layout of the page.

Miniatures may be detached from the script in varying degrees. In Munich, BSB, Cgm. 51, the figural narrative appears on both sides of separate folios, inserted singly (with one exception)[16] and bound. The images show from two to six scenes on the same page and visualize the story in units usually, but not always contained within the two sides of each folio.[17] The interpretation of the scenes is guided by inscriptions placed either in the image on streamer-shaped balloons, or in between the image frames; they identify the figures,[18] or comment on the situation, not without humor and sometimes in Latin.[19] Since the comprehension of the miniatures depends to some degree on the reader's ability to decipher the accompanying inscriptions, the illustrative program cannot be meant to provide an easy access to the story substituting for the verbal text. But, these conflated scenes strewn over the manuscript may be intended as sporadic recapitulations, as synchronic pauses in the diachronicity of the verbal narrative, or as reference marks which, taken together, also provide a quick reviewing of Gottfried's and his continuator's lengthy poem. In frontispieces,[20] prefatory miniatures occur either singly (Paris, BN, fr. 103, 355, n. a. fr. 6579; Vienna, ÖNB 2539; London, BL, Add. 23929), or in various combinations of compartments which count from the most common four (Paris, BN, fr. 99, 100, 101, 334; Vienna, ÖNB 2537, 2542) to as many as nine (Paris, BN, fr. 102). First-page illustrations occupy a privileged space which is put to use in essentially two different manners. Some contribute not to the understanding of the narrative but to the modalities of its reception. The auctorial miniature conforms to the pictorial modulus of *translatio studii* by representing the author seated, absorbed in the task of writing, copying, or dictating, that is to say of producing the text.[21] Sometimes, combined with the author-image, a dedicatory miniature (Paris, BN, fr. 355; Vienna, ÖNB 2539), by showing the presentation of the book to a crowned figure, fictitious or not, addresses the destination of the work to its intended public. The other illustrative approach to the frontispiece privileges the contents of the book. It may concentrate on Tristan's pre-history (Chantilly, Musée Condé 648; Vienna, ÖNB 2542; Paris, BN, fr. 334), or combine it with the extra-diegetic auctorial illumination described above (Paris, BN, fr. 97, 100, 102; Vienna, ÖNB 2537). Less often, it illustrates exclusively the hero's story, which it may develop in four miniatures (Paris, BN, fr. 99, 101) or summarize in one composition as the well-known single illustration of ms. Paris, BN 103.[22] To exemplify the complexity of interaction between verbal and figural narratives in the prefatory image, let us pause on a lesser known codex, Malibu, Getty, Ludwig XV 5. It opens on an hexapartite illumination reading from left to right and down, as a verbal text, thus flowing into the red rubric underlining it (fig. 7.1). The three scenes on the upper register concern the story of Tristan's ancestors, succinctly evoked in the first sentence of the rubric: "Ci commence li Roumans du bon chevalier Tristan fils du bon Roy Melyadus de Leonois et de Sadoch." The lower register is devoted to Tristan, as the four other sentences of the rubric. First, the hero's liberating engagement against the Morholt: "Et comment Tristan tua le Morholt dYrlande qui estoit .i. des bons chevaliers dou monde quant il vint querre le treu du seruage que li Roys Mars de Cornoaillle li deuoit chascun an." [23] In accordance with the implicit intent rather than the formulation of the verbal text, the image focuses on the moment when Tristan, his lance lowered, unsaddles his adversary. The rubric then turns to the tragedy: "Et comment li roys mars enuoya querre Yseult la blonde en Irlande pour avoir la reine. Et comment Tristans but en la nef le buurage amoureux pour le quel il ne se pout puis partir de lamour Yseult." Here again, the miniature sets before our eyes the pivotal scene: on the boat at sea, in Brangien's presence, Iseut proleptically crowned and Tristan in full armor extend their arms towards each other; but, even scrutiny under the magnifying glass fails to reveal the presence of the love potion mentioned in the rubric. [24] The selection process in the last sequence is less obvious. The rubric reads: "Et comment le Roy Marc li lanca par une fenestre .i. dart enuenime dont il morut et de pluseurs auentures quil fist par sa cheuallerie." However, the image, instead of representing the assassination or the death of the hero, harks back to Marc's visit at Arthur's court where— but neither the rubric nor the image makes this explicit—the treacherous king swears on the Bible not to make further attempts on his nephew's life.[25] In all evidence, the artist preferred to extrapolate, and, through an analepsis in relation to the diachronics of the rubric, he grounded on Marc's mendacious duplicity the cowardly murder foretold in the rubric. One notices also that the repeated mention of Marc in the rubric and the choice of images bring to the fore Tristan's victimization. This prefatory illumination and the pre-text of its rubric taken together constitute in fact a complex proleptic and exegetic metatext.

In some of the Tristan manuscripts of Italian provenance one encounters a type of illumination at once separated from the verbal narrative and integrated with it. Here, the miniatures appear on both the recto and verso sides of each folio, most often at the bottom, but not exclusively.[26] They occupy the entire width of the written text and resemble frescoes, sometimes simple or even crude (Paris, BN, fr. 760, 1463; London, BL, Harley 4389),[27] sometimes spectacularly rich and refined (Paris, BN, fr. 755). Generally, when there are no rubrics, the onlooker is guided by inscriptions giving the names of characters and places, in full or in abbreviated form (Paris, BN, fr. 760), but rubrics and inscriptions may appear together in the same manuscript (Paris, BN, fr. 1463). The illustration of a single episode may extend over several folios, such as the triple sequence of Tristan's fight with

Morholt (London, BL, Harley 4389, ff. 17, 18, 18v) or the five scenes of Tristan's encounter with Lancelot at the "Perron Merlin" (Paris, BN, fr. 1463. ff. 17, 17v, 18, 18v, 19). Characteristic of these manuscripts are architectural structures which, roughly sketched and touched with color in the earlier codices or lavishly executed in the later ones, soar up in the margins of the page. High campaniles with delicate bells (over the lovers' monumental grave in Paris BN, fr. 760, f. 126; fig. 7.2) or tall towers sometimes peopled with onlookers (witnessing the plight of the knight with the harp in Paris, BN, fr. 755, f. 15; fig. 7.3), they frame the text, even crowd it at times, as if the illustration took precedence over the words in the composition of the page, and the verbal narrative was added as a gloss to the images.

The relation of the written to the pictorial element is reversed in those manuscripts in which the figural narrative is framed in historiated initials. Fully integrated in the visual disposition of the verbal narrative, this type of illustration may be monoscenic, in which case the illustrator selects one scene as the most representative of an episode and the difference with miniatures in the column becomes a matter of size (Vienna, ÖNB 2542, Paris, BN, fr. 776 and fr. 334, all three with grotesques; London, BL, Add. 23929, Royal 20. D ii). Pluriscenic historiated initials—for instance, in Paris, BN, fr. 750 (1278)—deconstruct the episode, sometimes on two registers, as Iseut's attempt at suicide (f. 123v), more often on three registers, and in four scenes (f. 300, Tristan's arrival at Morgain's castle), five scenes (f. 304v, the tournament at Roche Dure), even six scenes (f. 173v, Tristan's madness). One is reminded of the compartmented arrangements of Munich, Cgm. 51 of the same period.

Yet another type of miniature spans the columns of the verbal narrative. It may be placed above a small decorated initial or stand on its own. In such a disposition, an interesting single scene framed within the column width serves to visualize the episode of the "perron Merlin" on f. 107v of Paris, BN, fr. 12599, an Italian manuscript from the North-East (fig. 7.4); the moment chosen is not the fierce battle which opposed Tristan and Lancelot, who had not recognised each other, but its conclusion. Beneath the fountain flowing near the "perron," the two heroes in full armor, leaning on swords whose points rest against the ground, sit at peace side by side, clearly engrossed in a lively chat. It seems the illuminator wanted to show two sides of the same scene, for the knights have their backs to the stone, which is seen from another angle in the upper compartment. Often, the time sequence of an episode is expressed over several miniatures, but temporal as well as spatial relations may also be compressed into a single image. One finds an interesting exemple of this figural narrative technique on f. 37 of Getty, Ludwig XV 5 (fig. 7.5). The rubric preceding lists five segments of the episode concerning the attempt made by Tristan's stepmother on the hero's life: "Comment la royne de Loonois appareilla le venin pour enprisonner [*sic*] Tristan et comment son petit fils en morut par une damoiselle qui li en donna a boire Et comment la royne fu iugiee a mort et Tristan len delivra." The miniature shows, reading from right to left, the dismayed crowned murderess with the head of her dead child resting limply on her lap, then the executioner—with his back and leg protruding on the other side of the frame—laying hold of the queen, who stands facing a brightly burning stake, while Tristan in chain-mail reaches from behind her to lay a protective left hand on her shoulder. Not only did the artist reduce further the already condensed narrative of the rubric, but in choosing these two particular moments he managed to render the contrast not expressed in the rubric between the queen's unforgivable crime, both intentional and accidental, and the hero's exemplary forgiveness, in short the real meaning of the episode. On f. 107 of the same manuscript (fig. 7.6), both the despatching and the reception of a letter are shown in a single illustration which is also to be read in the opposite direction from the verbal text. Here again, the absence of separators between the two segments contributes to the impression of continuity, further reinforced by the movement of the sender's arms outstretched towards the direction in which the message was sent. The joy caused by the message at the receiving end is expressed with uplifted arms, even before the contents have been read, so it seems, since the messenger delivering it on bended knee still holds it unopened in her hand.

Finally, one should cite the case, unique in our corpus, of Brussels, BR 14697. Colored drawings illustrating single scenes fill the page facing the text, at the beginning of the sections signaled by numbers and rubrics in red (figs. 7.10 and 7.13).

Rubrication does not appear on all manuscripts. When it does, it may announce or underline the images. Far from merely providing instructions to illuminators as it has sometimes been suggested, rubrics may, as we have already seen in the first-page illustration of Getty,

Ludwig XV 5, share in a complex interrelation between the verbal text and the images. The latter, however, do not necessarily depend on the mediation of rubrics and often contradict them flagrantly.[28]

DIEGETIC CONTENTS AND FUNCTIONS OF THE FIGURAL NARRATIVE

In attempting to define the discourse of the figural narrative in the illustrated manuscripts of Tristan, one must consider not just *what* the images tell of the story, but *how* they tell it. Discourse, when relating to narrative, does not mean simply expressing something, but, in the Genetian acceptance of the term,[29] it implies the presence of an enunciative system. In an illustrated narrative, two enunciative systems are at work simultaneously, one carried by the flow of the script, the other by the iconographic program. In this particular form of art, the text is the result of the combined effect of these two systems of different substance. In other words, the fruitful reading of an illuminated manuscript entails a double decoding process which will reveal the various types of intratextual relations between words and images.

Of the illuminated manuscripts we have examined, some contain a large number of repeated formula-images. It seems to be particularly the case with the most voluminous manuscripts of the prose romance, such as the monumental three volumes of Chantilly, Musée Condé 645–646–647. Throughout 900 or so folios, bloody battles rage against a background of motley tents; individual encounters of mounted assailants are relentlessly pursued on foot; tournaments unfold their colorful pageants of matching shields and caparisons, extravagant crests, and streaming pennons, under the blank gaze of courtiers and royal couples. In manuscripts designed for less pugnacious patrons, stereotyped dynamic hunting parties and static banquets account for the more peaceful side of life: under a tree or two, stags run away from horsemen blowing their horns, excited dogs are on the scent, squires follow, masters of the hunt lead; or, facing the onlooker, commensals sit in hierarchic order on one side of long boards resting on trestles, covered with a cloth and laid with the same display of trenchers, knives, and drinking vessels, fish and fowl rest on platters set at precarious angles, while more is preferred on bended knee by dwarfish attendants, and canines share in the scraps of the feast. Italian illuminators who, as we have seen, need to cover the bottom part of each folio, often resort to such scenes which lend themselves to elongation, as do "cortèges," processions of knights escorting ladies and their retinues from castle to castle through forests emblematized by a single tree whose representational credibility is duly guaranteed by the inscription "sylva." The abundance of these formulistic images may be explained by a variety of factors: the magnitude of the illuminators' task in some instances, in others perhaps the necessity to comply with formal constraints or the dictates of a patron, or the prevalent taste of the time. Be it as it may, such scenes are not negligible. They supply a visual context for the verbal narrative. They set the general mood, as a stage backdrop does for drama.

Then, there are the situational images one encounters from manuscript to manuscript: one could cite, among others, the carrying or delivering of messages, abductions, and visits. They too correspond most of the time to set patterns. For instance, the visitor and the host repeatedly appear seated, engaged in a conversation made improbable by their positions facing full front the reader. Yet, upon close examination, such images reveal small but noteworthy variations. These may concern the rapport of the interlocutors: when Gaheriet visits Iseut to bring her news of Tristan, a scene frequently illustrated in the prose versions, she may extend her hand to him in a regal gesture while he looks up on bended knee (Vienna, ÖNB 2537, f. 204), or she may welcome him as an equal by sharing her seat, bench or edge of the bed, with him (Vienna, ÖNB 2539, f. 216v; Paris, BN, fr. 102, f. 223v, BN, fr. 335, f. 317v), or even eagerly meet him at the door (Malibu, Getty, Ludwig XV 5, f. 306v).

Formulaic and situational images are based, as most illumination of profane literature, on moduli which can be traced to the well-honed iconographic tools of sacred literature. But one must not be too hasty in underestimating the paratextual function of these images with respect to the verbal narrative. Accessory signs[30] are still signs.

This becomes all the more evident in the case of the wedding scene. It is characterized by a formal paradigm: on either side of an officiating cleric or his equivalent, the future spouses stare at each other, flanked by their respective bevies of witnesses. There are several such wedding scenes in the Tristan manuscripts. In their compositional structure, they seem repetitive, but careful study of the "gestuelle" uncovers subtle yet pregnant nuances of meaning. Happy brides, Blanchefleur (Munich, BSB, Cgm 51, f. 11, lower register; fig. 7.7) or Iseut Blanches Mains (Vienna, ÖNB 2537, f. 71; Paris, BN, 102, fol.

73v; Chantilly, Musée Condé 645, f. 125) signify their acceptance by holding their arms crossed in front of them. By contrast, Iseut's reluctance to becoming Mark's wife is expressed in the same ms. Chantilly, Musée Condé 645, on f. 99v, by her uncrossed arms, contrasting with Marc's, while Tristan's hand, slipped from behind under her left arm, signals his own consent and encouragement (fig. 7.8).[31] It is through the dialectics of these nuances that the modulus acquires specific pertinency to the verbal narrative it illustrates.

This type of illustration plays on the principle of sameness with a difference. By bringing to bear on a given situation a wide and varied background of referential accumulation, such miniatures fulfill an explanatory, sometimes even an exegetic function. They constitute a commentary on the verbal narrative with which they entertain a relation of metatextuality. One would also classify in this category other situational images also based on moduli but which have become Tristanian images by adaptation: for example, in the verse version, Tristan's combat with the "serpent," patterned after Saint George's fight with the dragon (particularly Heidelberg, UB, Pal. germ. 346, f. 32v, and Munich, BSB, Cgm. 51, f. 67), or the lovers' tryst observed by the king hidden in the tree, a configuration reminiscent of Adam and Eve and the serpent (Munich, BSB, Cgm. 51, f. 76 lower register, and Heidelberg, UB, Pal. germ. 346, f. 66); in prose and verse versions, Tristan in the bath exposed to the wrath of Morholt's womenfolk, partially modeled on baptism scenes (for instance, Vienna, ÖNB 2539, f. 34v, and Munich, BSB, Cgm. 51, f. 67v, lower register), or Iseut and Tristan's voyage to Cornwall and the sharing of the love potion, all the more similar to the stereotype of navigation images as the cup is sometimes shown (Cologne, Stadt Historisches Archiv W* 88, f. 142; Paris, BN, fr. 103, f. 1; Vienna, ÖNB 2537, f. 50v with even two cups),[32] sometimes not (Malibu, Getty, Ludwig XV 5, f. 1; Paris, BN, fr. 100, f. 71 in spite of the rubric "coment ilz beurent le boire amoureux"; Heidelberg, UB, Pal. germ. 346, f. 49v, shows the result, i.e. the love-sick heroes in bed in separate chambers with Gorvenal and Brangien lamenting in the middle).

Whether the figural narrative illustrating the Tristan manuscripts entertains with the verbal narrative it accompanies a relation of para- or metatextuality, it also fulfills a mnemonic function. While the practice of using pictures as aids to memory[33] may be observed in other types of enlumined manuscripts, it must have proved particularly useful with stories, unraveling themselves at considerable length, such as that of Tristan. Here also, images serve as links in the recollective chain. Punctuating the narrative, they recall milestones in the action. This is achieved in essentially two ways. Either images cue single actions by visualizing them in a sequence of snapshots,[34] each corresponding to an isolated moment, or they cue entire episodes by synopsizing the action in a synthetic composition. The ocular recapitulative technique is most readily evident in multiscenic historiated initials, or multi-scenic arrangements in general, but it is not limited to them, as we have seen. The same process is at work in synthetic yet mono-scenic images, whether different moments of the episode are shown simultaneously and parallelly like the alternate "mansions" of the medieval stage (the "knight with the harp," fig. 7.3), or whether the illuminator conflated different spatio-temporal instances (the attempt on Tristan's life by his stepmother, fig. 7.5, and Iseut's letter to Guenievre, fig. 7.6).

TRISTANIAN ICONEMES

What has been said above concerning the types and the functions of the images encountered in the *Tristan* manuscripts, is not limited to the latter but would hold true of similar secular texts, for instance of other illustrated romances, as far as the present stage of research seems to indicate. The question then arises whether, if images followed recognizable models and migrated from codex to codex, there could be any specific Tristanian images at all. According to Kurt Weitzmann, "a medieval artist invents only when he has to do so."[35] One might wonder whether there were instances in which the illuminator of a Tristan text had to invent, at least partially, perhaps even completely. Four cases come to mind which we shall briefly investigate. They are common to both verse and prose versions, albeit with variations.

Tristan's madness, whether feigned or real, appears to be frequently, and at times lavishly, illustrated in both versions. It evolved, as we have shown elsewhere,[36] from an image inspired by sacred iconography, the "insipiens" of Psalm 52, and developed into mini-cycles of miniatures playing on the theme of the topsy-turvy world of mental imbalance. The topic obviously inspired illuminators, who often used the simultaneous presence of a court fool, Daguenet, to juxtapose different kinds of folly and blur the distinction between them. Thus the artist of Paris, BN, fr. 102, f. 161v (fig. 7.9) invented for Tristan gone mad a garment at once close to a fool's costume and to the clothing of the shepherds. Amidst their flock, the latter sit observing the maniac's wild dance measured by the swing of his club, at whose end the replica of his own face seems to stare at him. Later in that manuscript (f. 162v), Daguenet similarly clad, but for the addition of stripes, brandishes a similar club while executing in front of Marc the very same dance. Two of the illuminated verse versions containing the episode add to the images of "folatrerie," the lovers' reunion and the discovery of the stratagem (Munich, BSB, Cgm. 51, f. 101v lower register and f. 104 upper register; Heidelberg, UB, Pal. germ. 346, f. 164v) essentially adapted from standard bed scenes.

When Iseut, for fear that Brangien may betray her, orders two men to kill the maid, the verbal narrative dwells at length on the "clean shift" Brangien lent the queen on her wedding night, an allusion to the necessary substitution in Marc's nuptial bed. In the manuscripts we have examined, there is no image to render this metaphor, central as it is to the articulation of the entire episode. Instead, most of the time, the illuminators represent a form of arrest scene (Heidelberg, UB, Pal. germ. 346, f. 55). Even, against the logic of the story since Iseut's plot is at first unknown to the victim, we find in Brussels, BR 14697 (f. 336v; fig. 7.10) an image conflating the moment of Iseut's order and its execution. The queen's unquestionable authority is expressed by the disproportionate height of her figure, Brangien's submissiveness by her crossed hands, and the mixed feelings of the fellow on her left by the conflicting positions of his hands—one arresting, the other comforting. Often, in the prose versions, the miniatures illustrate the plight of the poor girl, left bound, sometimes by the hair, up, or around a tree (Paris, BN, fr. 102, f. 60v; Malibu, Getty, Ludwig XV 5. f. 86v). Occasionally, by showing the henchmen hastening away from Brangien tied to the tree, the image focuses on the executioners' change of mind and its consequence, thus combining cause and effect (Vienna, ÖNB 2539, f. 552; Paris, BN, n. a. fr. 6579, f. 118v). As for the resolution of Brangien's predicament, rather than emphasizing the reconciliation of the two women as in the verbal narrative (we have found so far only one such image, in Heidelberg, UB, Pal. germ. 346, f. 57v), there is a marked preference in the prose versions for adapting a "knight rescues damsel in distress" scene, with Palamedes "armé de toutes armes" coming upon a most elegant Brangien and freeing her from her tree (Chantilly, Musée Condé 648, f. 56; fig. 7.11).

The episode of the lovers' life in the forest afforded a chance to illustrate a love idyll in a natural setting, free from the constraints of society. It is interesting to note that an effort is made in this direction in manuscripts of both prose and verse versions, namely Paris, BN, fr. 97, f. 62a, (fig. 7.12) and Brussels, BR 14697, f. 441, (fig. 7.13), as well as Heidelberg, UB, Pal. germ. 346, f. 85, even though the latter two are poems by different authors. In spite of the rubric of the Brussels ms. which states that the pair lived in a waste land, "in der wüste,"and suffered such deprivation that they grew thinner, "und grossen mangel litten umb ir lip narunge," the artist did not show any of this. As with the other two manuscripts, the emphasis is on the couple and its ostensible irrelevance to the surroundings. Iseut's crowned and groomed hair, Tristan's pink and green feather head-dress, the lovers' fine clothing contrast with the stylised vegetation which seems to cradle their intimacy. Unconventionality is also the mark of the illumination of Paris, BN, fr. 97: again in the fine array which signals the incongruity of their presence, Tristan and Iseut emerge out of an elementary dwelling surmounted with a chimney, "lostel de la saige damoiselle en la forest de cornouaille," nestled among dense trees. They are both holding a long, narrow object pointed downward, which defies identification, even when magnified, unless it were a sword. The illustration of Munich, BSB, Cgm. 51, f. 90, second register (Loomis and Loomis, fig. 365), points to another unusual situation. Under some nondescript shelter, separated by a significantly huge sword, the lovers sleep, head to foot, directly on the ground. A scene all the more striking as, elsewhere in the same manuscript, the illuminators show the adulterous couple embracing on regal couches. True, in the episode of Tristan's jump into Iseut's bed (f. 76v, lower register, left), and when the false fool rejoins the queen (f. 101v, lower register), the scenes take place inside the castle, but the inclusion of that piece of furniture is not easily justified when the meeting of the lovers takes place in the garden (90v, upper register).

In both versions, the visual narrative of the lovers' end unfolds in two stages: Iseut joining Tristan in death and the lovers' monument. Essentially these are images meant to convey the overt manifestation and the public recognition of the couple's irrepressible fate. While in the poems, Iseut is shown grieving by Tristan's bier just before life leaves her in turn (Munich, BSB, Cgm. 51, f. 107v, middle register; Heidelberg, UB, Pal germ. 346, f. 173), the illuminators of the prose manuscripts choose the actual moment of their common death. According to the prose version, in front of Marc and the court assembled, Tristan dying takes Iseut into his arms as we see in Chantilly, Musée Condé 647, f. 262 (fig. 7.15), "lors estreint la royne contre son pis de tant de force comme il avoit si quil le fist le cuer partir et il meismes morut en tel point si que bras abras et bouche a bouche morurent les ii amants et demourerent en telle maniere embraciez tant que ceulx de layens endoient qui seult en pamoison." [37] A damaged but fascinating image in Paris, BN, fr. 1463, f. 102v (fig. 7.14) shows Iseut's torso bent over Tristan's chest, their arms on each other's shoulder, and their heads resting cheek to cheek on the pillow. [38] The expression "bouche à bouche" is clearly represented in the corresponding miniature of another Paris manuscript, BN, fr. 99 (f. 760b). The image must have been considered highly representative of the Tristan story, for we find it in a fragment of a *Lancelot* (Paris, BN, fr. 112, f.145b), accompanied by a rubric which sums up the entire episode: "Coment messire tristan et la royne yseult morurent bras a bras dont le roy marc fit grant dueil." It is precisely this tragic scene which the artist of Paris, BN, fr. 97 illustrates: the pair is lying on the bed, side by side, rigidly, their arms locked, while the bearded king looks on, his hands raised in amazement (f. 543; 7–16). Sometimes, this phase of the episode is synopsized in one mourning image of the lovers' bier returning to Cornwall on a ship (Paris, BN, fr. 103, first page miniature; Munich, BSB Cgm. 51, f. 107v, upper register) or a wake scene, as in Vienna, ÖNB 2542, f. 489v. Variations also occur in the representation of the lovers' tomb, but essentially the same illustrative principle is applied: the point is to iconize the lovers' exemplarity through their "ymages," as in Italian manuscripts, Paris, BN, fr. 760, f. 126 (fig. 7.2), and BN, fr. 1463, f. 104, [39] or to signify their eternal reunion in afterlife through the symbol of the entwined trees growing out of their separate graves (Cologne Stadt Historisches Archiv W* 88, f. 263), or out of their common tomb (Munich, BSB Cgm. 51, f. 107v, lower register; Heidelberg, UB, Pal germ. 346, f. 174.)

Obviously, the illuminators did not always choose the same segment of the episode, in the four cases we have examined. Yet, the frequency of occurrence of these sets of images and their relative specificity to the Tristan manuscripts warrant their being considered as key articulations in the ocular enunciative system, visual narremes, that is to say, iconemes. It is interesting to note that they differ from the contemporaneous figurations which decorated a variety of luxurious artifacts, psalters, combs, caskets, and others, and were recognized as unmistakenly Tristanian without the support of a verbal narrative. Of course, the primary function of the latter was not to tell a story, although they contributed a great deal to its dissemination.

At the conclusion of so brief a survey of an extensive corpus, is it possible to discern a Tristanian figural discourse? We have encountered a number of interchangeable images which constitute the visual backdrop of medieval romance, others which had been adapted and appropriated by our texts, and yet others apparently specific to them. Far from being naive, these images appeal to a complex system of signs, a semiotic code difficult for us to decode which are not meant to be mimetic. The visual discourse progresses according to its own dynamics. In the illuminated manuscripts of *Tristan,* the heroes' saga is told through a relatively constant figural chain, in other words through a particular paradigmatic figural discourse which will definitely mark the ocularisation of the myth, and hence its reception.

NOTES

1. For the most recent general bibliography on medieval manuscript illumination, see Jonathan J.G. Alexander, *Medieval Illuminators and Their Methods of Work* (New Haven and London: Yale Univ. Press, 1992). However, to Alexander's recapitulative list should be added two important titles: Maurits Smeyers, *La Miniature* (Brepols: Turnhout, 1974), and Jean Wirth, *L'Image médiévale, Naissance et développements* (VIe-XVe siècle) (Paris: Méridiens Klincksieck, 1989); also the seminal contributions of François Garnier, *Langage de l'image, Vol. I. Signification et symbolique, Vol. II. Grammaire des gestes* (Paris: Le Léopard d'Or, 1982–1989), and *Thesaurus iconographique, système descriptif des représentations* (Paris: Le Léopard d'Or, 1984).

2. The first attempt at an overview of the illustrated German *Tristan* manuscripts is to be found in Doris Fouquet, *Wort und Bild in der mittelalterlichen Tristantradition, Der älteste Tristanteppich von Kloster Wienhausen und die textile Tristanüberlieferung des Mittelalters* (Berlin: Schmidt, 1971), pp. 16–21.

3. The illuminations of Munich, Bayerische Staatsbibliothek, Cgm. 51 (mid-thirteenth century), are painted on both sides of 15 sheets inserted at intervals in the text: a total of 118 scenes, arranged on 3 registers on each page and according to 11 different schemas. See the excellent description and analysis accompanying the facsimile edition: Paul Gichtel, "Die Bilder der Münchener Tristan-Handschrift (Cod. germ. 51)," *Gottfried von Strassburg "Tristan und Isolde" mit der Fortsetzung Ulrich von Türheim, Faksimile Ausgabe des Cod. 51 der Bayerischen Staatsbibliothek München, Faksimile und Textband,* ed. Paul Gichtel and Ulrich Montag (Stuttgart: Müller und Schindler,

1979), pp. 391–457. For a study of ff. 46, 46v, 67, 67v, of the same manuscript, see Michael Curschmann, "Images of Tristan," in *Gottfried von Strassburg and the Medieval Tristan Legend*, ed. Adrian Stevens and Roy Wisbey (Cambridge: Brewer, 1990), pp. 1–17. Images of this manuscript have been often reproduced, for instance in Roger Sherman Loomis and Laura Hibbard Loomis, *Arthurian Legends in Medieval Art* (New York: MLA, 1938; rpt. New York: Kraus, 1975), figs. 359–366.

4. The nine colored drawings of Cologne, Stadt Historisches Archiv W* 88 (1323), are placed in the columns of the text and are underscored with a rubric. Seven appear in Gottfried's text, two in Ulrich's Continuation. In "Mittelhochdeutsche weltliche Literatur und ihre Illustration, Ein Beitrag zur Überlieferungsgeschichte, mit 13 Abbildungen," *Deutsche Vierteljahrsschrift für Literaturwissenschaft und Geitesgeschichte*, 43 (1969), 23–75, Hella Frühmorgen-Voss published three miniatures (f. 44, Tristan plays the harp for Marc, f. 142, Tristan and Isolde share the love potion, f. 164, Tristan takes Isolde from Gandin (and not the reverse as Frühmorgen-Voss. writes)—and a fourth (f. 263, the lovers' tombs with the mingling trees) in *Text und Illustration im Mittelalter. Aufsätze zu den Wechselbeziehungen zwischen Literatur und bildender Kunst*, ed. Norbert H. Ott (Munich: Beck, 1975), pp. 119–39.

5. Besides a large initial, the 91 illuminations of Brussels, Bibliothèque Royale, 14697 (c. 1435) are full-page, colored pen drawings, executed in the workshop of Dieboldt Lauber at Hagenau in Alsace. There are 79 images for Gottfried's text (ff. 10–510v), 10 images for *Tristan als Mönch* (ff. 511–584), and 2 for Ulrich von Türheim's Continuation (ff. 584–end); the latter does not include the "madness" episode and is incomplete at the end. For a succinct identification of each miniature, useful but not always reliable, see Camille Gaspar and Frédéric Lyna, *Les Principaux manuscrits à peinture de la Bibliothèque Royale de Belgique II* (Paris: Société française de reproduction des manuscrits à peinture, 1937–1945), pp. 89–95. One finds interesting remarks on the history of the Brussels manuscript in Karl Marold, *Gottfried von Strassburg: Tristan* (Berlin: De Gruyter, 1969), pp. XLVII–XLVIII.

6. For a detailed description of the 91 colored pen drawings, see "Verzeichnis den Bildhalten, cod. pal. germ. 346," in Doris Fouquet, *Die Illustration der Heidelberger Tristanhandschrift Pal. germ. 346 und des ersten Tristandruckes von 1484* (Cologne: Assessorarbeit am Bibl. Lehrinstitut, 1970), pp. I–XIII. Eleven miniatures were published in black and white in Danielle Buschinger and Wolfgang Spiewok, *Eilhart von Oberge, Tristrant und Isalde, hochdeutsche Übersetzung* (Goppingen: Kummerle, 1986), namely f. 17, the fight with Morholt; f. 21v, Tristrant is put to sea; f. 32v, the fight with the dragon; f. 49v, Tristrant and Isalde love-sick; f. 54v, double wedding night scene; f. 64, Marke discovers the lovers; f. 73v, Tristrant jumping from his bed to Isalde's; f. 85, the lovers' hut in the forest; f. 95, Tristrant's fight with Delekors; f. 164v, Tristrant the fool discovered in Isalde's bedroom; f. 174, the lovers' common grave with the two trees. Two other miniatures were published:

f. 118, Dynas playing chess with Isolde and Marke, by Loomis and Loomis (1938, fig. 376), and f. 66, the tryst under the tree, by Frühmorgen-Voss.

7. One finds a precious list of the prose Tristan manuscripts in Brian Woledge, *Bibliographie des romans et nouvelles en prose française antérieurs à 1500* (Geneva: Droz, 1975), pp. 122–25, and *Supplément*, pp. 99–104; however, there is no specific indication which manuscripts contain miniatures.

8. Malibu, Getty Museum, ms. Ludwig XV 5 and its miniatures are described in Anton von Euw and Joachim M. Plotzek, *Die Handschriften der Sammlung Ludwig, Band 4* (Cologne, 1985), pp. 207–21, Abb. 117–142.

9. For Vienna, ÖNB 2542, see H.J. Hermann, *Die westeuropäischen Handschriften und Inkunabeln der Gotik und Renaissance, 2. Englische und französische Handschriften des 14. Jahrhunderts (Beschreibendes Verzeichnis der illuminierten Handschriften in Österreich, Neue Folge 7, 2),* (Leipzig: Hiersemann, 1936), pp. 1–17, with eight reproductions in Tafel I-III; also Otto Pächt and Dagmar Thoss, *Französische Schule I, (Die illuminierten Handschriften und Inkunabeln der Österreichischen Nationalbibliothek I, 1 = Österreichische Akademie der Wissenschaften, Philos.-hist. Klasse, Denkschriften 118)* (Vienna: Österreichische Akademie der Wissenschaften, 1974), pp. 20–21. Further images are reproduced in the edition directed by Philippe Ménard, *Le Roman de Tristan en prose,* I–VII (Geneva: Droz, 1987–).

10. See for Vienna, ÖNB 2537, H.J. Hermann, *Die westeuropäischen Handschriften und Inkunabeln der Gotik und Renaissance, 3. Französische und Iberische Handschriften des ersten Hälfte des 15. Jahrhunderts (Beschreibendes Verzeichnis der illuminierten Handschriften in Österreich, Neue Folge 7, 3),* (Leipzig: Hiersemann, 1938), pp. 44–64, with 19 reproductions in Tafel XIII–XVI; also Otto Pächt, *Französische Gotik und Renaissance in Meisterwerken der Buchmalerei, Ausstellung der Handschriften- und Inkunabeln der Österreichischen Nationalbibliothek* (Graz: Akademische Druck- und Verlaganstalt, 1978), pp. 103–105, with one reproduction not in Hermann (1938), f. 474v, the death of Tristan. Some 60 miniatures of ÖNB 2537 are beautifully reproduced in color in *Tristan et Iseut, commenté par Michel Cazenave et Edmond Pognon, adaptation en français moderne de Pierre Dalle Nogare* (Paris: Lebaud, 1991). Unfortunately, the comments accompanying each miniature cannot always be trusted.

11. Otto Pächt and Dagmar Thoss described ÖNB 2539-2540 in *Französische Schule I, (Die illuminierten Handschriften und Inkunabeln der Österreichischen Nationalbibliothek I, 1 = Österreichische Akademie der Wissenschaften, Philos.-hist. Klasse, Denkschriften 118)* (Vienna: Österreichische Akademie der Wissenschaften, 1974), pp. 13–20, with 13 reproductions in Tafelband, Abb. 1–13.

12. Tristanian images appearing in heterodiegetic context evoke other problems, and must be analyzed within a double tradition, that of the host text and their own, whether these images appear singly or as a cycle. The series inserted in London, BL, Add. 11619 was studied by Tony Hunt, see "The Tristan Illustrations in ms. London BL Add. 1119," in *Rewards and Punishments in the Arthurian Romances and Lyric Poetry of Medieval France:*

Essays Presented to Kenneth Varty on the Occasion of his Sixtieth Birthday, ed. Peter V. Davies and Angus J. Kennedy (Cambridge: Brewer, 1987), pp. 45–60. We are only beginning to collect single insertions of Tristanian iconography, such as the tryst under the tree in the Leiden UB, Letk. 205, f. 155v, of Potter's *Der Minnen Loep,* presented by Martine Meuwese in this volume.

13. For a structural approach to the Tristan myth and its semantic components, see our articles: "Tristan," in *Dictionnaire des mythes littéraires* (Paris: Editions du Rocher, 1988), pp. 1306–19, esp. p. 1337; "The French Modern Remaniements of *Tristan,*" in *Arturus Rex II,* ed. W. Van Hoecke, G. Tournoy, W. Verbeke (Leuven: Leuven Univ. Press, 1991), pp. 462–78, esp. 470–71; "Mythocriticism, Computer-based Mythanalysis and the Case of Tristan," in *Littérature comparée/Littérature générale,* ed. Paul Chavy et György Vajda (Bern: Lang, 1992), pp. 135–43, esp. p. 138.

14. Needless to add, only computers allow for easy manipulation of such a bulk of material.

15. Kurt Weitzmann, *Illustrations in Roll and Codex, A Study of the Origin and Method of Text Illustration* (Princeton: Princeton Univ. Press, [1947] rev. ed. 1970), pp. 17–18.

16. Ff. 10, 10v, and 11, 11v, Gichtel (1979), p. 397.

17. The last image of f. 76v concerns an episode continued in f. 82 (Tristan's wound opening and bleeding in Isolde's bed); so with f. 82v into f. 86 (Tristan and the giant Urgan); f. 104v into f. 107 (Kaerdin and Cassie).

18. At times erroneously, for example on f. 45v, the physician attending Tristan is labeled as "Ysolt."

19. On f. 15 and f. 67v, the same quote from Virgil, "omnia vincit amor sed nos cedamus amori,"glosses two very different scenes, respectively, Blanchefleur's burial and Iseut's ineffectual attempt to kill Tristan in his bath.

20. On this particular type of illustration, see Elizabeth Salter and Derek Pearsall, "Pictorial Illustration of Late Medieval Poetic Texts: The Role of the Frontispiece or Prefatory Picture," in *Medieval Iconogaphy and Narrative, A Symposium* (Odense: Odense Univ. Press, 1980), pp. 100–23.

21. A number of these cases have been analyzed by Emmanuèle Baumgartner, "La «première page» dans les manuscrits du «Tristan en prose»," in *La Présentation du livre, Littérales 2, Cahiers du Département de Français,* Paris X Nanterre (1987), pp. 51–63. One should note, however, that the description and the reproduction of the miniature ascribed in this article to Chantilly, Musée Condé 648 (pp. 57–58, and Planche 1) belong in point of fact to ms. 645 (anc. 315) of the same collection.

22. Loomis and Loomis (1938, fig. 304.)

23. Von Euw failed to perceive the link between image and rubric, judging by his description: "Tristan besiegt einen Ritter im Schwertkampf zu Pferde," op. cit., p. 207.

24. It seems von Euw thought he could see it: "Tristan begleidet Isolde auf der Fahrt übers Meer nach Cornwall, auf der sie ihm den Liebenstrank reicht," ibid.

25. Von Euw's description merely signals: "Begegnung zweier Küniger mit Gefolge." It is interesting to note that the actual episode of the oath, starting on f. 370, is preceded by a rubric and a pertinent miniature different from that of the first page illustration (see von Euw, p. 216).

26. For instance, the miniatures of London, BL, Harley 4389 are placed at the top or the bottom of the page, and in the middle as well.

27. For a study of BL, Harley 4389 and BN, fr. 1463, see Bernhard Degenhart and A. Schmidt, "Frühe angiovinische Buchkunst in Neapel. Die Illustrierung französischer Unterhaltungsprosa in neapolitanischen Scriptorien zwischen 1290 und 1320," in *Festschrift Wolfgang Braunfels*, ed. Fol. Piel and J. Traeger (Tübingen: 1977), pp. 71–92; 89, n. 8. For another *Tristan* manuscript illuminated in comparable style, Venice, Biblioteca Marciana, fr. Z. XXIII (234) dated 1280–1290, see Francesca D'Arcais, "Les illustrations des manuscrits français des Gonzague à la Bibliothèque de Saint Marc," in *Essor et fortune de la chanson de geste, Actes du IXe congrès international de la Société Rencesvals* (Modena: Mucchi, 1984), pp. 585–616, esp. pp. 586–87.

28. Rubrics deserve a study of their own.

29. The concepts and terms used in our approach to narratology, verbal or visual, are borrowed from three works of Gérard Genette, "Discours du récit, essai de méthode," in *Figures III* (Paris: Seuil, 1972), pp. 65–273; *Palimpsestes, La littérature au second degré* (Paris: Seuil, 1982); *Nouveau discours du récit* (Paris: Seuil, 1983). For the equivalent terminology in English, see Gerald Prince, *A Dictionary of Narratology* (Lincoln: Univ. of Nebraska Press, 1987).

30. The function assigned by Genette to illustrations is that of paratexts, defined as "signes accessoires" (*Palimpsestes*, p. 9), even though he concedes that this is one of the privileged areas of the "pragmatic dimension of the work, that is of its action on the reader" and that the study of this field of relations is yet to come.

31. See François Garnier's models (1982) for the three types of gestures, pp. 185–87, 175, 178–79, and 190, 193, respectively.

32. The cup also appears, with the addition of the chess game, in a *Lancelot* manuscript, Paris, BN, fr. 112, f. 239 (reproduced in Loomis and Loomis, fig. 298.)

33. On the "visual gate" to memory, see particularly the chapter entitled "Memory and the Book," in Mary J. Carruthers, *The Book of Memory, A Study of Memory in Medieval Culture* (Cambridge: Cambridge Univ. Press, 1990), pp. 221–57; also Sylvia Huot, "Visualization and Memory: The Illustration of Troubadour Lyric in a Thirteenth-Century Manuscript," *GESTA*, 31/1 (1992), 3–14.

34. Our translation of the expression "une séquence d'instantanés," used by Mireille Mentré in "Remarques sur l'iconographie des romans arthuriens à propos de quelques exemples," *Cahiers de civilisation médiévale*, XXIX (1986), pp. 231–42.

35. Weitzmann (1970), p. 19.

36. Angelika Gross and Jacqueline T. Schaefer, "Tristan, Robert le Diable und die Ikonographie des Insipiens: der Hund als neues Motiv in einem alten Kontext, I. Die Narrheit im religiösen Kontext, II. La folie dans le contexte profane," in *Schelme und Narren in den Literaturen des Mittelalters,* ed. Danielle Buschinger and Wolfgang Spiewok (Greifswald: Reineke, 1994), pp. 55–7.

37. The passage is quoted from Paris, BN, 101, f. 386b, which has no corresponding image.

38. The forms are more easily made out if one turns the image sideways.

39. See also the reproduction of Venice, Bibliotheca Marciana, fr. XXIII, f. 62, in D'Arcais, op. cit. p. 601.

Fig. 7.1. First page miniature. *Le Roman du bon Chevalier Tristan, fils au bon roy Meliadus de Leonois*. Malibu, Getty, Ludwig XV 5, f. 1. Reproduced by permission.

Fig. 7.2. Tristan and Iseut's tomb with effigies. *Le roman en prose de Tristan.* Paris, BN, fr. 760, f. 126. Reproduced by permission.

Fig. 7.3. Episode of the knight with the harp at King Arthur's court. *Le roman en prose de Tristan.* Paris, BN, fr. 755, f. 15. © cliché Bibliothèque Nationale de France, Paris. Reproduced by permission.

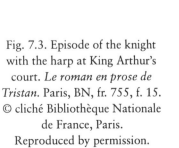

Fig. 7.4. Tristan and Lancelot at the "Perron Merlin." *Le roman en prose de Tristan.* Paris, BN, fr. 12599, f. 107v. © cliché Bibliothèque Nationale de France, Paris. Reproduced by permission.

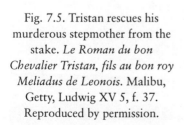

Fig. 7.5. Tristan rescues his murderous stepmother from the stake. *Le Roman du bon Chevalier Tristan, fils au bon roy Meliadus de Leonois.* Malibu, Getty, Ludwig XV 5, f. 37. Reproduced by permission.

Fig. 7.6. Dispatching and arrival of a letter from Iseut to Guenievre. *Le Roman du bon Chevalier Tristan, fils au bon roy Meliadus de Leonois.* Malibu, Getty, Ludwig XV 5, f. 107. Reproduced by permission.

Fig. 7.7. The wedding of Rivalen and Blancheflor. Gottfried von Strassburg's *Tristan.* Munich, BSB, Cgm. 51, f. 11, third register. Reproduced by permission.

Fig. 7.8. The wedding of Marc and Iseut. *Le roman en prose de Tristan*. Chantilly, Musée Condé 645 (anc. 315), f. 99v. Reproduced by permission.

Fig. 7.9. Tristan mad, among the shepherds. *Le roman en prose de Tristan*. Paris, BN, fr. 102, f. 161v. © cliché Bibliothèque Nationale de France, Paris. Reproduced by permission.

Fig. 7.10. Iseut's attempt on Brangien's life. Gottfried von Strassburg's *Tristan*. Brussels, BR 14697, f. 336v. Reproduced by permission.

Fig. 7.11. Iseut's attempt on Brangien's life. *Le roman en prose de Tristan.* Chantilly, Musée Condé 648 (anc. 404), f. 56. Reproduced by permission.

Fig. 7.12. The lovers' exile in the forest. *Le roman en prose de Tristan.* Paris, BN, fr. 97, f. 62. © cliché Bibliothèque Nationale de France, Paris. Reproduced by permission.

Fig. 7.13. The lovers' exile in the forest. Gottfried von Strassburg's *Tristan.* Brussels, BR 14697, f. 441. Reproduced by permission.

Fig. 7.14. The lovers' death.
Le roman en prose de Tristan.
Chantilly, Musée Condé 647
(anc. 317), f. 262.
Reproduced by permission.

Fig. 7.15. The lovers' death.
Le roman en prose de Tristan.
Paris, BN, fr. 1463, f. 102v.
© cliché Bibliothèque
Nationale de France, Paris.
Reproduced by permission.

Fig. 7.16. The lovers on their deathbed. *Le roman en prose de Tristan.*
Paris, BN, fr. 97, f. 543. © cliché Bibliothèque Nationale de France, Paris.
Reproduced by permission.

8 THE ILLUSTRATIONS OF BN, FR. 95 AND YALE 229

PROLEGOMENA TO A COMPARATIVE ANALYSIS

Alison Stones

The Yale manuscript, containing *Agravain, Queste* and *Mort Artu,*[1] is among the least known of the densely illustrated copies of the five-part prose *Lancelot* (also known as the *Lancelot–Graal* or Vulgate Cycle) that enjoyed a huge wave of popularity in northern France and surrounding territories from the 1220s to the end of the fifteenth century.[2] Roger Sherman Loomis included only a brief mention of the Yale manuscript in the great book *Arthurian Legends in Medieval Art* by himself and Laura Hibbard Loomis;[3] and in the literary essays he edited, he referred only, and indirectly, to one of its miniatures.[4] The miniature concerned (fig. 8.8) is one of the most intriguing in the entire picture cycle of 166 illustrations because of its unique depiction—or more properly its non-depiction—of the Holy Grail, but Loomis left it without comment, a situation I propose to rectify below.[5] One reason why the Yale manuscript has received relatively little attention is that for many years it remained inaccessible among the *Nachlass* of the great English bibliophile Sir Thomas Phillipps, in whose collection it was MS 130.[6] While Lilian Randall was the first scholar to devote serious attention to it in her seminal study of Gothic marginalia in 1966,[7] it was only with the publication of Barbara Shailor's catalogue of Beinecke Library manuscripts in 1984 that a full description of the manuscript and a list of its narrative illustrations has become available.[8] Better published, in some ways, is its sister manuscript, Paris, BN, fr. 95, which contains two of the other branches of the *Lancelot–Graal: Estoire and Merlin.* Not only did the Paris volume figure quite extensively in the Loomis's *Arthurian Legends,*[9] but it had also been treated from the stylistic point of view in Georg von Vitzthum's magisterial 1907 study of northern French illuminated manuscripts in the thirteenth and early fourteenth centuries;[10] and it was in Jean Porcher's 1955 exhibition of French Gothic manuscripts held at the Bibliothèque Nationale, as well as appearing in most of the popular books on Arthurian art.[11] Even so, there is still no list in print of its 163 illustrations.[12] The rest of the *Lancelot* proper, up to the beginning of *Agravain*, is now missing.[13]

The two books are so closely similar in dimensions, ruling patterns, number of columns and lines, script, pen-flourishing, champie initials, in the several formats selected for their illustration and in its style (figs. 8.1, 8.2, 8.8, 8.15, 8.16, 8.23, 8.24, 8.26–29, 8.31)[14] that, since Loomis first assumed the two volumes were made as parts of the same set, the idea has met with little challenge.[15] Two factors may cast shadows of doubt on the question, though neither is conclusive evidence against the notion, and should be offered as possible qualifiers rather than as disclaimers. One is the presence in BN, fr. 95 of two non-Arthurian texts, the *Sept Sages* and the *Pénitence Adam*. Non-Arthurian texts in the same volume as one or more branches of the Vulgate Cycle are rare, but they do occur,[16] and there are also some instances in the manuscript tradition of Chrétien de Troyes where other textual material was included, from the beginning, in the same volume as a text by Chrétien, so the arrangement in BN, fr. 95 is not without parallel.[17] However, it is worth noting that *Sept Sages* begins a new folio at the beginning of a fresh quire (f. 355) and that the previous quire was expanded to 10 instead of the usual 8 folios in order to include the end of the *Suite Vulgate* as though that were the end of the volume; so the parts could also have been made separately, by the same team, for another purpose—possibly "on spec," and brought together later. Numerous scenarios are possible. The patron could always have decided to buy a ready copy of the *Sept Sages* and the *Pénitence Adam* as well as his commissioned *Estoire* and *Merlin* while waiting for the team to produce the rest of the prose *Lancelot*. Perhaps he did not live to see the latter completed, and it was acquired by someone else.

Whether because of the patron's death, or for some other reason, BN, fr. 95 and Yale 229 seem not to have shared quite the same history. BN, fr. 95 was in the library of Filippo Maria Visconti, Duke of Milan, by 1407,[18] while the whereabouts of Yale 229 at this date is unknown. Iconographic links suggest, however, that Yale 229 or a close copy was also in Italy in the fifteenth century, providing a channel of iconographic influence on *Queste* and *Mort Artu* cycles in

Italy. Indeed, Delisle pointed to several items of Arthurian content among the books in the 1459 inventory of the Sforza, later Dukes of Milan, which might in general terms fit Yale 229 (though he did not mention any possible candidates for the references),[19] and Delcorno Branca has pointed to similar references in the 1470 inventory of the Sforza.[20] And there is no evidence in Yale 229 to suggest that it came to France in 1499 or 1500 when BN, fr. 95, together with other manuscripts of the Sforza library in Pavia was seized by Louis XII and brought to Paris.[21] Whatever the original circumstances of their production, and whatever the ways in which their subsequent peregrinations may have differed, Yale 229 and BN, fr. 95 are so obviously close that it is clearly useful to consider them together.

The painting in both volumes is qualitatively highly distinctive, engaging, and entertaining. As Jean Porcher, writing in 1955 about BN, fr. 95, put it, "L'abondance et la richesse de l'illustration, la sûreté du dessin, son élégance, la vivacité des coloris et aussi l'excellent état de conservation font de ce manuscrit l'un des monuments les plus importants de la peinture du Nord de la France dans la seconde moitié du XIIIe siècle."[22] These volumes offer such a quantity, a variety, and a quality of illustration that they hold a special place among manuscripts of the Vulgate Cycle (or *Lancelot–Graal*) tradition and in French vernacular illustration in general. Between them, they contain a very large corpus of illustration—more pictures, for the *Mort Artu,* than any other extant copy, as I have shown elsewhere; and for the other branches they are among the most densely illustrated copies; in some respects their iconography follows received Arthurian tradition, or borrows from biblical or other religious subject-matter; yet in many instances what is selected and depicted in these volumes is new and original.[23]

Two illustrators were responsible, I believe, one of whom can be identified as working personally on at least one other book and giving rise to a stylistic phase that encompasses another dozen or more manuscripts; and the other, whose personal style is rather harder to define individually, and difficult to interpret chonologically, nonetheless adds another important dimension to the stylistic pool to which these books belong. The stylistic relations between the work of these painters and other products they or related painters made, coupled with some hints contained in the heraldic shields in the manuscripts, allow an attribution of date and place to be advanced, along with suggestions about who the patron may have been. What I propose to do here is to explore these dimensions of inquiry in order to determine, as far as possible, what the cultural context of these books was.[24]

TYPES AND LEVELS OF ILLUSTRATION

I begin with a simple analysis of how the illustrations are presented in the volumes, in terms of decorative format and density of distribution, both of which offer unusual and distinctive features that set them apart from the rest of French vernacular illumination, whether of Arthurian texts or other material. Like all copies of the prose *Lancelot,* these are large and heavy volumes in which the primacy of the written text is paramount, even on openings containing illustration. In these volumes, the images make a striking impact, partly because of their artistic qualities, vibrant colors and attractive design of the pictures, as Porcher noted; and also because most of them are accompanied by a border running all or part of the way down the text column and ending at top or bottom, or both, with curvilinear terminations of leaves and gold balls, usually supporting or ending in human figures, animals, birds, or hybrids, some of which complement the main narrative, others of which offer a visual inversion of it, and still others seem to be of uncertain significance, as I show below. Most French vernacular illuminated manuscripts reserve this kind of treatment for opening pages only.

Much of the narrative illustrations take the rare form of rectangular miniatures about 12 lines high, placed in one text column and subdivided into two registers (figs. 8.1, 8.2, 8.10, 8.24), a format derived from a type common in the full-page miniatures of the small devotional books like psalters and books of hours (and occasionally the larger picture-bibles). But full-page miniatures are rare in French vernacular manuscripts,[25] unlike the German vernacular tradition, which offers numerous examples of epic and romance texts, and even of poetry, with full-page pictures.[26] Although BN, fr. 95 and Yale 229 lack full-page miniatures as such, and despite their compression of the picture space into a single column, the use of subdivided miniatures allows a sense of continuous narrative in which a sequel to the event depicted in the top compartment can be included below, or the top subject can lead up to the one beneath it. Curiously, hardly any other French vernacular illustration is presented in this format.[27] It was repeated (with some variations) only in one other surviving Vulgate Cycle manuscript, Geneva, Bodmer 147 (ex-Philipps 1046).[28]

Sometimes in BN, fr. 95 and Yale 229 the miniatures lack subdivisions and a single scene is depicted (fig. 8.15); at other times, a smaller format is preferred, five or six lines high and less than a full text column wide (figs. 8.8, 8.26, 8.27), often with the top right corner cut out so that the first initial of the accompanying text can be included in the picture space rather than occupy its own space beneath the miniature, as is the rule with the full-column miniatures.[29] Sometimes historiated initials, occasionally large (fig. 8.29), more usually small (fig. 8.28), replace the smaller miniatures, most notably on the opening page of BN, fr. 95 (fig. 8.16).[30] To some extent, then, the illustration is parcelled out within a hierarchy of decoration in which some scenes can be more extensively treated because of the bigger space allotted. This variation of decorative format is also relatively unusual and contributes a subtle dimension to the question of how each particular picture and its subject might be interpreted.

THE CHOICE AND PLACING OF THE PICTURES

To a considerable degree, the selection of episodes to be depicted and the precise position of each picture in the text in BN, fr. 95 and Yale 229 were governed by considerations of tradition: these manuscripts were made, as I shall show below, in the last decades of the thirteenth century, by which time several recensions of a pictorial tradition had already been elaborated for Vulgate Cycle manuscripts. I outline a few general points in order to situate the two volumes within the broader illustrative tradition to which they belong and on which in part they depend; this background will also help to define the ways in which the pictures in these books depart from received models and make original contributions to the illustrative tradition.

The chronological evolution of *Lancelot–Graal* picture-cycles is a matter whose development is not just one that moves in a sequential pattern from simple to complex. I have shown elsewhere that the patterns of the *Queste* and the *Mort Artu* illustration as a whole do show that the earliest surviving manuscripts were sparsely illustrated, that a fairly full cycle of pictures had emerged by c. 1250 in BN, fr. 339 and Brussels, BR 9627–28, followed by a more extensive picture-cycle, incorporating the earlier cycle and expanding upon it, by 1274 in BN, fr. 342; and that the placement of the pictures in that manuscript is adopted and enlarged upon to a significant degree in several of the later manuscripts, including BN, fr. 95 and Yale 229.[31] But copies with short picture cycles—or with still fewer illustrations—continued to be produced from the thirteenth into the fifteenth centuries. Furthermore, the patterns of evolution followed by the other branches are not the same as for the *Queste* and the *Mort Artu*. In the case of the *Estoire,* for instance, the earliest surviving copy is already quite fully illustrated in the 1220s; and comparative work still needs to be done on the *Merlin* and the *Lancelot* proper.[32]

At what stage or stages in the emergence of the picture-cycle the decisions about placement and content were taken, and by whom, is something that is not yet entirely clear. What can be said about the picture cycles of the *Lancelot–Graal* tradition is that there is a close link between the positioning of large decorative initials—large pen-flourished initials or champies in gold on pink and blue grounds—in the text in the earlier unillustrated or sparsely manuscripts and the locations of pictures in illustrated ones. The distribution pattern of miniatures within the body of the text is often irregular, so that, at times, the pictures cluster together, and at other times there are many pages of text with no illustration at all; and, at the same time, manuscripts which share certain clusters of illustrations may diverge from each other in their inclusion or omission of others, and in their treatment of the same subject. But full comparative charts still have to be made before final conclusions can be drawn.

The decisions about whether the picture-cycle of the model would be followed, abandoned, reduced, or expanded in any one particular copy were obviously made at the planning stage, before or during the copying of the text, since the scribe had to leave spaces for them. In the case of BN, fr. 95 and Yale 229, the decision about the size of each space had to be made at the same time—depending on whether a full-column miniature, a half-column miniature, or a smaller initial, was to be inserted by the painters in the space left for it.[33] Whether these decisions were made by the scribe himself, one of the illuminators, or a third individual, is unclear as far as these volumes are concerned. There are no notes, assembly marks, or other indications of how the process worked, nor, unusually, do the manuscripts include rubrics, which in other cases offer clues about how the picture-cycle was put together and how individual scenes were interpreted.[34]

In BN, fr. 95 and Yale 229, large miniatures tend to emphasize particularly important and especially memorable episodes in the text— or at least, episodes which someone in the planning stage of the volume considered important—while less significant ones were relegated to an image in a smaller format. As I have shown elsewhere,[35] Lancelot's discovery that he had made love with King Pelles' daughter, not with Guinevere, is shown in Yale 229, f.50, in a small historiated initial. I think the choice of this very small pictorial format attests to a desire to minimize the love-making incident itself and to stress Lancelot's remorse; it is part of the deliberate exclusion of all scenes of overt love-making that characterizes Yale 229's *Agravain* sequence. Possibly such subject-matter, considerably more prominently illustrated in other copies, was considered unsuitable for, or unwanted by, the book's patron.[36] And the numerous tedious battles and single combat scenes depicted with boring repetition towards the end of the *Mort Artu* also occupy small miniatures or historiated initials;[37] but there are also some very important scenes that share the small format, so that the relation between size and significance is a complex one. I consider some examples below.

LANCELOT FINDING THE HEAD OF HIS ANCESTOR

Often, a full-column miniature is accompanied in the opposite column by a smaller miniature or a historiated initial, so that decoration is concentrated on one page and a subsidiary episode can be related visually to the main picture. In one instance, the only one, there are two double-register miniatures on one page, and marginalia as well (fig. 8.1). The focus of the this painted double-page opening is the head episode, a crucial step in Lancelot's process of self-recognition, where Lancelot retrieves a head from a fountain of boiling water and re-unites it with a body in a tomb guarded by lions, a motif which draws as well upon ancient mythology;[38] the head turns out to belong to King Lancelot, father of King Ban and Lancelot's grandfather and namesake.[39] The choice of double miniatures on facing pages gives this episode more visual prominence than any other in the two surviving volumes. Its treatment here is also much more elaborate than in any other instance in the illustrative tradition, so far as I know. To someone—patron? planner? painter?—this was the high-point of the entire narrative, but this view was apparently not shared by other patrons or manuscript makers before or after.

On f. 110v (fig. 8.1) in Yale 229, the left-hand miniature presents, like a visual foil, subsidiary events that lead up to the main sequence. At the top Lionel, now cured of an illness, thanks to hearing news of Lancelot, bids farewell to the monks of the abbey and rides off; below, having dismounted, he is embraced by the other knights (shown in civilian clothes) at the Tertre.[40]

An ape seated on a chair in the bottom margin, wearing an academic hat and robe, holding a urine-flask, and examining the beak of a stork, plays off visually on Lionel's illness; a hare sits on the left border, turning its back on the activities behind it, but possibly alluding to the lasciviousness of the marginal scene on the facing page, where a towering woman puts a crown of flowers on the head of a kneeling lover. The crown in the marginal scene goes on the lover's head; the major scene above also has to do with a head, but in quite a different context. In the top border, a head is also involved: a man caught in the jaw of a dragon terminal wounds it in the head with his sword, a visual allusion to the killing of the lions by Lancelot. The hooded male terminal in the top centre plays on the hermit, also shown in the second major scene, and who there is bare-headed, with his hood over his shoulders—another play on heads and head-gear.

The two scenes in the second major miniature focus on Lancelot, who figures only indirectly, as the reason for Lionel's cure, in the opposite miniature. At the top, Lancelot (housing, surcoat, and shield white) meets a dwarf[41] who warns him of the dangers that await in the Perilous Forest; Lancelot, having dismounted and put on his red helm, fights two lions who guard the blue marble tomb, whose lid is splatted with drops of blood; below, Lancelot (having taken off his helm) lifts the head out of the basin of the fountain of boiling water, shows it to the hermit who stands in the doorway of his hermitage and points to the tomb, shown a second time; then Lancelot lifts the lid of the tomb to reveal the headless shrouded body inside.[42] In this short version of the text, Lancelot spontaneously recognizes the head and headless body as those of his ancestor; the letter relating the identity of head and body, featured in the long version of the story, is also omitted in the picture.

The identification is confirmed by the hermit and the body and head buried before the altar where King Lancelot's wife's remains had been interred; but none of that is depicted in the miniature. Even so, the Yale manuscript's treatment of this episode is considerably more detailed than the treatment of the same episode in Add. 10293, the most densely illustrated of the *Agravain* manuscripts: on f. 334v in Add. there are three scenes, the first showing Lancelot (not Lionel) greeted by knights; the second shows Lancelot, riding and meeting the dwarf; the third shows him defeating the two lions at the bleeding tomb by the fountain with the head; the sequel occurs on f. 335v and shows Lancelot talking to the hermit, but includes no head. So in Add., the major event—Lancelot removing the head from the boiling water— is not shown at all. In fact, this complex episode is scarcely illustrated at all in the rest of the iconographical tradition.[43]

The Magic Carole

Indicative of the great complexities in the iconographic relationships among these illustrative cycles is the varying treatment of the Magic Carole, also shown as part of a double-register large miniature in Yale 229, f. 66v (fig. 8.2). At the top, Lancelot has joined five dancing ladies;[44] below, an episode from the story of the origins of the Magic Carole, which directly follows in the text, is shown. Before Lancelot breaks the spell by sitting on the throne and being crowned with his father's crown, the text explains how the dance came into being: a magic spell was cast on the dancers by a clerk so that he might obtain the favours of a beautiful king's daughter, who sat in the middle of the dance on a throne. Here, the clerk and the beautiful damsel play chess together on the Magic Chessboard, which they do until death;[45] the breaking of the spell is not shown. This time the point of the marginalia is not quite as evident as before; while a pair of embracing male and female heads on dragon terminals in the left border refer to the love of the clerk for the beautiful damsel, the hooded man leaning on a stick with a basket containing two baby apes on his back is more problematical; a ready explanation does not come to mind.

This is a subject which, unlike the finding of the head, is rather popular in other *Agravain* manuscripts. What is interesting is that there is considerable variation in which bit of this story is depicted. No other copies exactly match what is shown in Yale 229.[46] The dance, where it is illustrated again, is shown as a circular affair: in London, BL, Roy. 20. D. iv, f. 237v (c. 1310–20) (fig. 8.3) and Paris, BN, fr. 122, f. 137v (1344) (fig. 8.4),[47] and the participants include men as well as women. These examples each treat the scene as a long miniature over two columns and include supporting scenes. In The Royal manuscript, the breaking of the spell is shown in part: Lancelot, still wearing his closed helm, is assisted by two ladies as he sits on the throne. Marginalia of a young man terminal shooting an arrow at a dragon may anticipate Lancelot's defeating the powers of evil by breaking the spell, and the musician playing pipe and tabor sets a horse to dance like the dancers in the main miniature (for whom no music plays); a shaggy-dog creature butts its head against a post, of unclear significance, possibly the frustration of the powers of evil at being defeated?

In BN, fr. 122 (fig. 8.4), what is shown to the right of the dance itself is a group of men receiving Lancelot; in the upper left corner is a curious detail showing a damsel seated on the ground in a forest, and a stag placing its front leg in her lap. This section of the miniature is separated from the rest of the dance by a stream that runs from the bottom left corner all the way round the top of the miniature. It is not clear from the textual context just what this is. Of course a stag—but white, not brown, as here—does figure in the story of the *Agravain*, but not at this point, [48] and accompanied by lions, not in association with a lady. Might the pair be a misquoted Virgin and unicorn from the illustrated Bestiary tradition?[49] If this interpretation is correct, it would parallel the Pelican in her Piety which Boort sees in the *Queste*, and which is very occasionally illustrated;[50] I know of two examples, in BN, fr. 342, f. 112, and in the manuscript made in Southern France in 1319, on f. 53 (fig. 8.5). Most eccentric of all in BN, fr. 122 is the treatment of the throne and the crown—placed at the top of an enormous column as tall as the figures and surrounded by lavish acanthus motifs. The crown is placed on top of a leaf finial that rises between two architectural pinnacles at the back of the cushion placed on the seat of the throne. Again, I see no textual justification for this odd arrangement which seems curiously to evoke the foliage motif used to support the manger of the Christ Child in English Psalters of the late thirteenth century. [51]

The breaking of the spell, without the dance, is what was chosen in Add. 10293, f. 301 (fig. 8.6) and Rylands, f. 46v (fig. 8.7). Both elaborate on this episode to include one of the ladies placing the crown on Lancelot's head (although in Add., he still wears his mail coif); in Rylands, two other ladies watch.[52] Particularly noticeable is the falling idol, naked in Rylands, through described as "fait en samblance de roi," and robed and crowned, as he should be, in Add.[53] Both topoi derive from biblical imagery: motifs both of a naked idol and of a falling king are commonly depicted in the bibles of the third quarter of the thirteenth century made in Paris, Artois and Flanders, in the context of the illustration to IV Kings (II Chronicles), where King Ochozias (Ahaziah) falls to his death. [54]

In BN, fr. 333, f. 51v, Lancelot dances in the Magic Carole with three ladies, and is shown again in the same miniature, enthroned, being crowned by two ladies; he sees the idol, shown as the head of a king, suspended in mid-air.

In M 806, f. 253v, three sequential episodes about the chessboard are depicted, and the dance is omitted: not the clerk and the beautiful lady playing chess, as in Yale 229, but Lancelot, watched by the ladies he has freed from the Magic Carole, winning the game, and with it the board itself; a messenger delivers the chessboard to Queen Guinevere, who sits enthroned beside King Arthur, watched by a group of male and female courtiers who stand behind them; the queen, watched by her courtiers, plays and is defeated by the magic chessboard.

The Holy Grail in the Queste del saint Graal

One might expect in a textual cycle in which appearances of the Holy Grail are so frequent and, particularly in *Estoire* and *Queste,* so central in importance, that illustrated copies would visually emphasize the Grail as well. In fact, the opposite is the case: as in the illustrative tradition of the *Perceval* of Chrétien de Troyes and its Continuations,[55] there is considerable reluctance to represent the Grail as such in the *Estoire* and the *Queste.* Nevertheless, the examples in BN, fr. 95 and Yale 229 are particularly interesting cases and allow me to turn to the fascinating image that Loomis first reproduced from the liturgy of the Grail in the *Queste* (fig. 8.8).

Several things are extraordinary about this image. The first is that it is there at all: for only five manuscripts in the entire tradition of *Queste* illustration include an image showing the enactment of the Grail liturgy that occurs towards the end of the story: the other three are the Southern French copy made in Avignon in 1319, mentioned above for its Pelican in her Piety, Florence, Laur. Ash. 121(48) (fig. 8.9); Ars. 3482, made in Paris at about the same date; the well-known copy from Tournai, Arsenal 5218, written, illuminated, and bound by Pierart dou Thielt in 1351; and last is the *Tavola Ritonda,* not strictly speaking a *Queste* manuscript, but an Italian version based in part on the *Queste,* Florence, BN, Pal. lat. 556 (figs. 8.11, 8.12). Most manuscripts omit an illustration altogether, so that the climactic Grail liturgy is left to the imagination to picture—a deliberate ploy that was also used in the illustration of Chrétien.[56]

Even in Yale 229, the Grail liturgy is discreetly shown in the format of a small, half-column miniature, a striking contrast to the two-part miniature that precedes it, showing the death of King Mordrain and Galaad bidding farewell to Lancelot (fig. 8.10). In the depiction of the Grail liturgy (fig. 8.8), five men grouped on the left of a long draped table watch a mitred figure, supported by three angels, two of whom hold lighted candles, the group flanked by two floriated crosses, giving the host to a kneeling male figure, Galaad, who kneels at the short end of the table; in the middle of the table sits a shrine-like house-shaped gold container on a six-footed stand, decorated with arcading and finials, behind which a bleeding lance stands vertical. Outside the miniature, two angels holding incense boats swing thuribles from the top border and from the terminal below into the picture-space. A hybrid creature wearing a Jew's hat stands on the bottom border, possibly a topsy-turvy allusion to Josephe's Jewish ancestry.

There are some problems with the iconographical interpretation presented in the miniature, as the mitred figure shown in the image must be Josephe, son of Joseph of Arimathea, who in the text is the celebrant at the beginning of the Grail liturgy; whereas, according to the text, the person who distributes the communion is Christ Himself.

> Lors fist Josephes semblant que il entrast ou sacrement de la messe. Et quant il i ot demore un poi, si prist dedenz le saint Vessel une oublee qui ert fete en semblance de pain. Et au lever que il fist descendi de vers le ciel une figure en semblance d'enfant, et avoit le viaire auisi rouge et ausi embras come feu; et se feri ou pain, si que cil qui ou pales estoient virent apertement que li pains avoit forme d'ome charnel. Et qant Josephes l'ot grant piece tenu, si le remist ou saint Vessel.[57]

Josephe then invites the knights to sit at the table, promising them "haute viande" from their Saviour. Josephe then disappears, and Christ emerges from the Grail and Himself adminsters the sacrament to the knights, "Lors regardent li compaignon et voient issir del saint

Vessel un home ausi come tout nu, et avoit les mains saignanz et les piez et le cors . . . lors prist il meismes le saint Vessel. . . ."[58] This is what should be shown in Yale 229, but the bishop figure can only be Josephe, and the artist (or planner) has misinterpreted the text.

Ash. 121 (48) treats the episode as two sequential single-column miniatures, the first showing Josephe raising his hands in prayer as he celebrates mass at an altar with a chalice-shaped vessel on it; on the left, behind Josephe, stand angels with two candles behind them; one of the angels holds the lance, resting its foot on the floor. On the other side of the altar kneel three knights. In the second miniature (fig. 8.9), Christ, holding a large chalice-like vessel, administers the host to the three kneeling knights, Galaad, Perceval and Boort (wearing hooded robes). A long table is shown behind them draped with a patterned cloth.[59]

In Ars. 3482 (f. 538v), Galaad, alone, receives the sacrament from Josephe, robed as bishop; but the miniature accompanies the account of Galaad's death, just before which he receives the sacrament from Josephe; other manuscripts where this is illustrated tend to focus on Galaad's death before the Grail which I discuss below.[60]

Pierart dou Thielt's version in Ars. 5218, made in 1351, is different again.[61] Placed earlier in the text, at the spot where the Yale manuscript has the death of King Mordrain, it focusses on the Grail procession and the transubstantiation.[62] The central pivot of the miniature is the figure of Christ in the vessel, which floats in mid-air, between the two kneeling, candle-bearing angels, in front of the horizontal bleeding lance; both lance and chalice stand out against the white cloth on the table, behind which are grouped the eleven knights. Josephe sits, holding his crozier, on a throne at the left short end of the table, and the space on the right of the composition is occupied by two standing angels, one of whom carries an object draped with a red cloth, while the other holds a lance. The composition is ingeniously arranged so that the narrative climax, the transubstantiation, is enclosed within the rest of the pictorial depiction of the procession, as though the preceding action were taking place around it, ". . . et ot l'uis de la chambre ouvrir . . . et en voient issir les anges qui Josephes avoient aporté; dont li dui portoient deus cierges, et li tierz une touaille de vermeil samit, et li quarz une lance tote droite sus le saint Vessel, si que li sans qui contreval la hanste couloit chaoit dedenz. Et si tost come il ont ce fet, Josephes se leva et trest un pot la lance en sus dou saint Vessel et le covri de la toaille."

Pierart dou Thielt has apparently re-arranged the items carried by the angels so that the Grail is covered by the "touaille de vermeil samit" carried by one of the angels on the right, while the lance is borne separately by the other, and does not drip into the vessel. In the central depiction of the Grail with the figure of Christ inside it, the lance is again placed so that the Grail does not receive the dripping blood—its horizontal position perhaps governed by the desire to make it stand out against the long horizontal white of the table-cloth and the floating effect (not in the text) may at the same time underline its supernatural quality.

The only other manuscript to devote comparable attention to the illustration of the Grail liturgy of the *Queste del saint Graal* is in the Florence copy of the closely related Italian compilation, the *Tavola Ritonda,* Florence, BN, Pal. lat. 556 (figs. 8.11, 8.12).[63] Produced in 1446 by two craftsmen from Cremona, the scribe or editor (or both) Zuliano di Anzoli[64] and, in all likelihood, the artist Bonifacio Bembo,[65] the manuscript contains no fewer than 9 tinted drawings depicting the various stages in the enactment of the liturgy. Not only is this concentration of images unprecedented in the illustrative Arthurian tradition, but, as Breillat has noted, more prominence is given in the manuscript itself to this section of the text than to any other.[66]

The Grail liturgy begins on the lower half of f. 147v with the appearance of Josephe, in bishop's robes, holding a crozier and supported by three angels, before the knights; they sit elegantly robed and some wearing fashionable hats, their arms crossed over their chests, at the far side and the near end of a draped table placed diagonally in the right half of a room whose walls are patterned with large cinqfoil flowers. The Grail procession enters on f. 148 (upper miniature), passing alongside Josephe: the first angel carries two candles, the second a cloth with a band of decoration and a fringe at the end; the third holds the lance, held at an angle over the angel's shoulder, so that its tip is poised directly above the Holy Grail, which the fourth angel raises high in veiled hands in order to catch in it the blood of the lance, ". . . quatro angieli l'uno como doi dopieri acesi in mano l'altero como una toalia vermelia, lo terzo como una lanza tuta sanguanenta, que continuo la ponta di la lanza gotava sangue senpre; lo quarto portava uno vasello . . ."[67] The Grail is extraordinary in shape: like a huge round ceramic pot with a heavy torus moulding at the rim and base, each decorated with a band of small circles; the rounded body of the vessel is patterned with a ring of cinqfoil flowers, matching in shape and size the ones on the walls of the room! The lower miniature on the same page shows the angels kneeling beside and behind Josephe, two of them now holding the candles, while the Grail rests on the table with the lance standing vertical inside it "e miseno la lanza intello vasello";[68] the knights watch the moment of transubstantiation as Josephe holds up high the small blessing figure of Christ (fig. 8.11).

Then Josephe, having replaced the transubstantiated bread in the vessel (in which the lance still stands), bends over to give Galaad the Kiss of Peace (f. 148v, top), which Galaad should then transmit to the other knights; the four angels stand behind Josephe, two holding candles, the other two holding their arms crossed over their chests like the knights. As in the *Queste,* Josephe then disappears (not represented in the illustration), and Christ appears, and administers the sacrament to the knights. Here (f. 148v, bottom, fig. 8.12) Christ, lifesize, revealing the wounds of the Passion, "uno homo nudo chi avea sue mane e piedi ello costato tuto perforato et insanguinato,"[69] actually stands on the table next to the Grail (no lance in the Grail this time), and blesses the knights. After that (f. 149) Christ leans over, his hand on the rim of the vessel, about to lift it up for Galaad to drink from it; Galaad bends over the vessel, still with crossed arms, "Alora vene lo vasello e portolo a Galasso e fecilo gustare et a Princivallo et a Borzo et apresso tuti li altri chevalieri."[70] Then (f. 149, bottom) Christ flies up towards the window (shown here for the first time). Outside, Lancelot, not permitted to witness the events, sits on the ground by the door, the head of his horse peering at him round the corner of the building.

The scene shifts altogether to the outside of the Grail palace on f. 149v as Lancelot, still seated on the ground facing the closed door, looks up at Christ, now transformed into a sitting stag, who has emerged from the window above the door and is borne away on a cushion by three angels. The castle's exterior walls are patterned on the ground storey with a diaper pattern of quatrefoils alternating with the same cinqfoil flowers as on the inside; four decorated Gothic double-lancet windows with pierced spandrels are set back behind an arcaded string course and the upper storey is capped by forked crenelation. And Lancelot's horse still peers round the corner, as in the next scene

(f. 150) where Lancelot sees the four angels carry away the two candles and the lance, still dripping blood into the Grail which is borne by the last angel who is still emerging through the window above the door of the castle.

Although Josephe consecrates the bread in the *Tavola Ritonda,* the substance that is meted out to the knights not flesh, as in the *Queste,*[71] but blood. As Breillat pointed out, much more attention is given to blood as an underlying motif throughout the *Tavola Ritonda*. Not only does the description of the Grail liturgy make clear that the blood of the lance actually falls into the vessel, as is also shown in the illustrations, but the Christ is the Christ of the Passion, revealing his wounds in both text and picture much more explicitly than in *Queste.*[72] In the final appearance of the Grail in the *Tavola Ritonda* (f. 151), the nails of the Passion and the Crown of Thorns are also included; they all accompany the dead body of Perceval's sister on the boat (bottom), and are transferred by the knights to the altar in the Grail chapel, before which Perceval's sister is buried (top) and where Galaad, having ruled as king for a year, will also be buried (not illustrated).[73] And, as in *Queste,* Perceval's sister died from donating her blood, with which a maiden with leprosy was cured. But in the *Tavola Ritonda* version of this episode, the leper is cured by drinking the blood, not by having it splattered on her breast as in *Queste,* discussed below. [74]

Several visual parallels for these final scenes in the Pal. lat. *Tavola Ritonda* can be found in *Queste* manuscripts, though not the Yale copy. The most striking later version of the knights in the Grail chapel is the splendid illustration commissioned by Jacques d'Armagnac in BN, fr. 112, f. 179v,[75] where the three knights kneel before a spectacular jewelled polygonal ciborium-like Grail with a knot in the centre of the stem and surmounted by a polygonal turret with a jewelled cross on top. As Galaad dies before the Grail (f. 181v), supported by Perceval and Boort, the vessel has become a round ciborium on a splayed stem, with scalloped motifs on bowl and cover, and beading on the rim of the foot, the base of the lid, and the top of the lid below a finial of four balls supporting another ball on top of which is a cross. As described in the text,[76] a hand appears and miraculously carries off the Grail and the lance.

Ash. 121 (48) has a simpler version: Galaad, crowned, lies beside the altar on which is the chalice-like Grail from which the lance projects vertically. The miniature is badly rubbed, like many in this manuscript, and one cannot be sure whether Galaad has a halo or whether his head rests on a cushion.

This southern French manuscript is the one that, iconographically, comes closest to the Pal. lat. *Tavola Ritonda* in terms of the number of miniatures included at the end of *Queste*, which serve to emphasize visually the importance of the Grail; and the Grail is always shown as a chalice, whose shape evokes the element of blood. This is also one of the rare manuscripts that illustrates the transfusion through which the blood of Perceval's sister is donated to the dying leper. This subject is not illustrated in Yale 229; curiously, the only parallel is in the Bonn manuscript.[77] The Avignon version shows the surgeon making the incision as Perceval's sister holds the bowl to catch the blood, watched by three standing figures; the leper (her face rubbed out—because it was disfigured?) lies on a patterned bed in front of the scene. In the Bonn manuscript's version the tourniquet, wound, blood, and supporting staff stand out, as does the application of the blood to the breast of the leper.

Relics of the Holy Blood were allegedly preserved in Northern Italy since at least the ninth century. Joanna Woods-Marsden has argued that the particular interest of the Gonzaga of Mantua in the cult of the Holy Blood at Mantua, one of the earliest documented in Western Europe,[78] was a governing factor in their choice of an Arthurian subject about Boort, the only one of the Grail heroes to produce any progeny, for the painting of the Camera by Pisanello. Because of the presence of the relic of the Holy Blood in Mantua, the Gonzaga considered themselves guardians of the relic, even as present-day Grail kings and successors of Boort.[79] The Pal. lat. *Tavola Ritonda*, illustrated by Bembo, has been attributed to the same artistic current as the Camera paintings, and Benedetti has identified an earlier *Queste* manuscript of Italian manufacture, Udine B. Arcivescovile 177, in the Gonzaga inventory of 1407.[80]

Although Yale 229 has no known medieval provenance, apart from what can be deduced stylistically and from the heraldry in its decoration,[81] Delcorno-Branca has suggested the possibility that it or another copy from the same workshop might well have also been in the Visconti-Sforza library and could have been available to Bembo during one of his visits to Milan to work for the dukes of Milan.[82] What Bembo saw would be likely to have been a copy whose illustrations emphasized the Grail; so Yale 229 itself would be a likely candidate. Other cases show that books made by the same team of scribes, decorators, and artists do not always transmit the same picture cycle, nor do they necessarily treat the same subject in the same way; so other possible copies made by the same team as Yale 229 and now lost, would not necessarily have given the same pictorial emphasis on the Grail liturgy.[83]

I argue below that BN, fr. 95/Yale 229 were most likely made in the region of the diocese of Thérouanne. Boulogne-sur-Mer, in the diocese of Thérouanne, and Bruges, in the neighboring diocese of Tournai,[84] also boasted Holy Blood relics; and Ars. 5218 was made in Tournai. The Bruges relic was allegedly acquired by Thierry of Alsace from the Patriarch of Jerusalem in 1148, in appreciation of his valour in the Second Crusade, and housed in a crystal cylinder with late thirteenth-century metal terminations;[85] the Boulogne relic is a piece of cloth supposedly donated to his native Boulogne-sur-Mer by Godefroi de Bouillon in 1101 and now preserved under rock crystal in the splendid translucent enamel disk made to house it in the last decade of the thirteenth century, its workmanship attributed to the Parisian goldsmith Guillaume Julien, and its patron Philippe le Bel, king of France. It is housed today at the church of St-François-de-Sales in Boulogne-sur-Mer.[86] At about the same time BN, fr. 95 and Yale 229 were made.

Of course, an interest in the Holy Blood need not necessarily result in the production of illustrated *Queste del saint Graal* or *Estoire* manuscripts: England also boasted a flourishing cult of the Holy Blood in the thirteenth century, sponsored by eminent royal and noble figures, which seems to have had a certain impact on Last Judgement iconography;[87] yet there is no comparable surviving tradition of illustrated *Queste* or *Estoire* manuscripts with extensive liturgical cycles to match what northern France, Flanders, Avignon, and Italy were producing.[88] Even in France, it is not until the fifteenth century that the cult of the Holy Blood is fully developed pictorially, as in the remarkable devotional image of the wound of Christ in a chalice, with accompanying explanatory caption, in fifteenth-century Books of Hours like Carpentras, Bibliothèque Inguimbertine 59 (fig. 8.13). The inscription reads, "C'est la mesure de la playe du coste nostre seigneur laquelle fut aportee par deux anges de Constantinoble au noble empereur Charlemanie dedans une chasse d'or afin que nulz enemis ne peussent nuyre en bataille." [these are the measurements of the wound in the side of Our Lord, which was brought by two angels from Constantinope to the noble emperor Charlemagne in a shrine of gold so that no enemies could do it harm in battle]. [89]

This wound-filled chalice is a spectacular counterpart to the images of the Miraculous Bleeding Host that occupy a singular place in certain fifteenth-century books of hours from Burgundy (fig. 8.14).[90] In the *Queste*, the Grail cult is essentially based on the bread of the Eucharist rather than on the wine-blood. In the *Estoire* the elements are both present, though the emphasis on transubstantiation again, as in *Queste*, gives greater weight to the bread than to the wine.[91] It is in the illustration of the *Estoire* liturgy, again celebrated by Josephe, that occur the only other parallels for the extraordinary Grail liturgy in the Yale manuscript's *Queste*. The mass is preceded by Josephe's coronation by Christ and followed by lengthy explanation of the significance of the vessels and vestments used, presented like a kind of catechism.

THE GRAIL LITURGY IN *Estoire*

In Rennes 255, made in Parisian royal circles c. 1220, none of this is illustrated, and it can again be claimed, as with the liturgy in the *Queste*, that the representation of the *Estoire*'s liturgy is not intrinsic to the illustrative tradition.[92] In Rennes 255, the Grail, described in the text as an "escuelle," is shown only once: as it it borne away to Norgales by Joseph of Arimathea, Josephe his son and their company much later in the story (fig. 8.17).

Only four manuscripts, so far as I know, illustrate the Grail liturgy in *Estoire* at the place in the text where it occurs, all showing slightly different episodes.[93] In BN, fr. 95 (fig. 8.15), the focus is the mass celebrated by Josephe. What is shown is a conventional representation, at the moment of the elevation of the host, with Josephe bareheaded and his followers kneeling on the ground behind. But for the inclusion of the populace, the representation is of a type common in liturgical illumination for the beginning of the canon of the mass in missals.[94] Josephe elevates a eucharistic wafer: there is no sign of the "cors autre tel comme d'un enfant" that Josephe finds in his hands, and that Christ orders him to tear apart.[95] But the host in this miniature is not blank: it is inscribed with the letters IHS of the Name of Jesus, so there is a cryptographic reference, if not a literal one, to the transubstantiation. On the altar is the partly veiled Grail, shown as a eucharistic chalice. This is all rather tame compared with some of the more exotic earlier examples of the Christ in the host, such as the one in the miracles of St. Edward the Confessor as recorded in *La estoire de seint Aedward le rei* in Cambridge, UL Ee.3.59, p. 37.[96] Somewhat comparable is the right-hand part of the opening miniature of the *Estoire* in Yale 227, written by Jehan Deloles in 1357,[97] where Josephe, robed as bishop and bareheaded, stands with outstretched hands celebrating mass at an altar on which are a draped chalice and a large eucharistic host with a cross between dot motifs inscribed on it. Three knights kneel on the left. These two miniatures, in BN, fr. 95 and Yale 227, are striking and, as far as *Estoire* illustration is concerned, relatively rare reflections of standard liturgical iconography. Another instance of borrowing an image from a liturgical context in BN, fr. 95 is its opening illustration that depicts a *Gnadenstuhl* Trinity surrounded by angels in a historiated initial 'C' (fig. 8.16). The illustration of Psalm 109, "Dixit Dominus" [The Lord said unto my Lord] provides many examples by the late thirteenth century,[98] as also do books of hours.[99]

The most extensive treatment of Josephe's liturgy in the *Estoire* occurs in the Amsterdam and Royal copies, made by the same craftsmen c. 1315.[100] Both have two scenes of Josephe's liturgy; but their third product, Add. 10292, omits illustrations of the liturgy altogether. The first image in Amsterdam, f. 18 (fig. 8.18) shows Josephe in the ark, robed as a bishop, urging his father Joseph not to touch him.[101] The text describes what Joseph sees as he looks past his son into the ark, whereas we view the whole scene from a different perspective that includes the entire building in which the ark is placed, framed by a rounded cusped arch (possibly evoking the dome of the Holy Sepulchre?) at the crossing of a church-like structure, beneath an elaborate tower with a rose window, flying buttresses, and an exterior passage at the level of the upper windows. Interesting here is the placement of the ark in the centre of the composition, not at the east end of the church where the high altar would be if one could see it; but that part of the building as viewed from the outside, while the transept end has been peeled away to show us the scene which Joseph would also see from his position beneath the cusped arch and pointed gable in the nave, whose north wall has again been removed to reveal him and the angel holding the silver ewer. Two more angels kneel to the left of the ark, one holding an incense-boat and swinging a thurible. What Joseph sees as he looks into the ark is a small altar covered with a white cloth and a red cloth of "samit" (the red altar-cloth is omitted in the miniature); on the altar are three bleeding nails and the top of a bleeding lance (the head and part of the shaft), a silver chalice-like vessel on a stem with a lid, mostly covered by a cloth painted red in the miniature but white in the text, and partially veiled from our sight (especially in a black and white photograph) but revealed to Joseph; and the silver "escuelle" that Joseph himself had brought, into which Josephe, a little before this in the text, had seen drip the blood of Christ on the cross. This bowl-shaped vessel must be the Grail.

Joseph does not see the crucified Christ, so no representation is shown here; but there is no attempt to include the hands holding candles and a cross,[102] which Joseph does see—though a cross is shown on top of the arch above the altar, and others are on the triangular gable above Joseph and on the roof at the east end of the church; further angels with rich draperies round their necks and more vessels are also omitted in the miniature. The Royal 14. E. iii version (f. 15v) is similar but much simpler in treatment, omitting the elaborate architectural setting, reducing the censing angels to two busts in the top corners, and eliminating the lance and nails; but it does include a red cross held by a hand above the altar; the hands holding candles are omitted. One of the other pictorial versions of Josephe's liturgy, BN, fr. 113, f. 18v, does include the hands holding cross and candle, shown emerging from the reredos behind the altar, on which rest a round ciborium-like vessel (the Grail), a paten, the three nails and the tip of the lance. Josephe, wearing civilian clothes and bare-headed, kneels, alone, before the altar; back in the doorway behind him stand four wingless angels, one of whom holds a situla and aspergillum, another a processional cross. Here the emphasis is very different from the treatment in the Amsterdam manuscript's scene, where sacred objects, as in the text, are presented from the point of view of Joseph rather than Josephe, who even turns his back on them in the image; and the psychological interaction between the two men is a significant part in the miniature that is especially underlined in the rubric. Clearly added after the miniature, as its letters avoid the pinnacles of the church structure which project into its space, the rubric says "Chi canta iosephus messe et mist son pere hors du tabernacle." [Here Josephe sang mass and put his father out of the tabernacle].[103] In BN, fr. 113, both picture and rubric focus on Josephe contemplating the Grail, "C[i] iosephez estoit devant le saint Graal a genoulx." [Here Josephe knelt before the Grail.].[104]

The second miniature in Amsterdam, on f. 21 (fig. 8.19), shows Christ and Josephe administering the sacrament, shown as a eucharistic host, to the kneeling assembly. The rubric says "Chi acummenie dieus et iosephus le sieucle" [Here God and Josephe give communion to the world].[105] Christ, framed by the open transept of a church, has a crossed halo and is robed as a priest, as described in the text,[106] and even tonsured (not in the text); Josephe, also robed as a priest, still wears his mitre. They each hold a shallow bowl painted in silver (or tin), like the one on the altar in the previous miniature; two angels are also included, one holding another shallow bowl which is his incense boat; in the other hand he swings a thurible, while the second angel, in a stooping pose on the left next to Christ, uses both hands to support a huge silver (tin?) chalice-like object. This angel, wearing an orange robe, is the one described in the text as "cil qui porta la sainte escuelle fu tous daarains" [the one who carried the holy bowl was all of brass].[107] Clearly there is some confusion about the shape of the Grail which, this time, is shown as a chalice not as a bowl. The Royal 14. E. iii version is simpler and shows the altar which has a gold chalice and wafers on the altarcloth; Christ holds a gold bowl-shaped vessel and blesses a kneeling man, probably Joseph, while Josephe, robed as bishop, administers the host to the rest of the assembly.

What is shown in the Le Mans manuscript (fig. 8.20) is a slightly earlier episode in this sequence where Josephe, at Christ's invitation, enters the ark and sees Christ Himself surrounded by five angels (only four shown in the image).[108] The text says the angels hold a blood-red cross; three bleeding nails, a lance with a bleeding tip, a bloody cloth, and a bleeding scourge, and describes the objects as "les armes par qui li iugieres del monde uenqui la mort" [the arms with which the judge of the world conquered death].[109] Here the cross, nails and lance only are shown. Even so, both text and picture represent an extremely early version of the "arma Christi" which only in the early fourteenth century come into prominence as devotional images;[110] this manuscript was probably made c. 1285,[111] yet in this text passage the Instruments of the Passion, explicitly referred to as "arms" are expanded beyond the usual limited selection of cross, lance and nails which are otherwise the only ones that play a prominent rôle in the *Estoire* and the *Queste*;

and a man on horseback holding a white shield and raising his sword against a snail provide a play on the notion of "arms."[112] Christ and the angels are described as flame-red in the text, and, like the brass angel in Amsterdam's version, they are all painted orange-red in the Le Mans manuscript and so Josephe and the draped white altar with veiled chalice/Grail before which he stands contrast sharply with the heavenly figures. Christ blesses Josephe who is robed as a bishop, justifying the explanation of the scene that is given in the accompanying caption: "C'est ci si come nostre sires ordena yosephe a ueske" [Here this is how Our Lord ordained Josephe as bishop]; the ordination indeed follows. [113]

It is the Amsterdam manuscript's first image (fig. 8.18) that comes closest to what is shown in the Yale liturgy in the *Queste* (fig. 8.8), and the comparison emphasizes all the more the peculiar treatment of the Grail in the Yale version. On the table rests a large shrine-like object, behind which the bleeding lance is poised. It is hard to believe this is meant to be the Grail itself: it is more likely to be a container for the Grail, and here it functions effectively to preserve the mystery of the Grail itself—most commonly done by not depicting it at all, or by partially concealing it beneath a draped veil—and shield the sacred vessel from the viewer's gaze. But for the absence of figured decoration, the house-shaped object looks very much like a miniature version of the body-sized shrines that were popular in the thirteenth century as receptacles for the relics of saints, such as the shrine of St. Taurin at Evreux made between 1240 and 1255 and that of St. Romain, Rouen, of about the same date;[114] a new shrine was made c. 1250 for the relics of saint Omer, housed at the collegiate church in St-Omer, not far from Thérouanne and in its diocese,[115] and there were many more in the region, of which the most spectacular was that of St. Gertrude of Nivelles (dioc. Liège), commissioned in 1272 from Colart de Douai, Jaquemon de Nivelles and Jakemez d'Anchin, and sadly decimated in the bombing of Nivelles 1940.[116] Certainly this solution to the problem of how to display the Grail, or rather to conceal it while revealing its potency, is quite ingenious; it is surprising that others did not copy it.

Another, related set of associations is just coming into prominence at this time: the use of a miniature architectural structure as a device to enhance, draw attention to, and protect, a cult statue, particularly of the Virgin Mary. Looking rather like a miniature decorated sentry-box with wrap-around doors, such objects must once have been extremely prevalent on thirteenth-century altars, on a large scale as well as small.[117] Most interesting for our present purpose is the adaptation of the statue-tabernacle as a miniature shrine for the reservation of the eucharist, whose special devotion, already mentioned above in relation to the question of transubstantiation, was further developed in the course of the thirteenth century, with the founding of a feast in the diocese of Liège in 1246, the authorization of the feast of Corpus Christi by papal bull in 1264, which had become a universal feast by 1317, date of the publication of the new collection of canon law, largely drawn up under Clement V (d. 1314).[118]

It is in the tabernacle for the reservation of the eucharist, of course, that the spiritual associations of the Yale Grail-shrine find their closest analogy, although the shape is closer to that of a reliquary shrine, a phenomenon that Andrieu has also noted in relation to the emergence of the monstrance, the earliest example of which is the one made for the abbey of Herkenrode in 1286.[119] Braun lists no examples of tabernacles or monstrances of the right date in sculpture or metalwork, though the St-Omer monstrance from Clairmarais is an interesting early example of a vessel on a stem through which the eucharistic element was presumably intended to be (just) visible.[120] More interesting examples for our purpose are to be found in painting, including manuscripts very close in style to BN, fr. 95/Yale 229: the hours of Thérouanne (after 1297) in Baltimore, Walters 90, f. 148v (fig. 8.21) has a tabernacle containing a host in a chalice, held by St. James the Great (identified by the two cockle-shells on either side of him in the background);[121] or, closer still in style, the closed tabernacle held by an unidentified saint in Marseille 111, who points to it as he preaches to a seated crowd, watched by the dove of the Holy Spirit emerging from a cloud as if to protect the tabernacle and the saint from the evil gaze of the hybrid terminal head directly above it (fig. 8.22).

In fact, this tabernacle motif also occurs in another context in Yale 229, on f. 248 (fig. 8.23). It is held up high above his head by a marginal figure who stands on one foot on the top left corner of a small miniature. Sacramental associations are conveyed by the words of the adjacent text which are Calogrenant's dying prayer addressed to Christ, before Lionel kills him; the miniature shows the following episode, where fire from heaven comes between Lionel and Boort, who fight without recognizing each other, and prevents them from killing each other. The tabernacle, as in Marseille 111, remains closed, its contents screened from public view much like the shrine which conceals the Grail (fig. 8.8). Both the Grail-shrine and the tabernacle are further interesting cases of a formal motif invented for one context being used in another, thereby endowing the new context with additional transferred meaning derived from the original context.

The pictorial evidence suggests that the painter of the Yale manuscript (the Grail liturgies and this marginal tabernacle are all the work of the chief artist) was quite deliberate in his choice of container for the Grail in the *Queste*: the puzzle of it is that he seems to have been so much less inventive in his *Estoire* version of the Grail liturgy. Was it that, after a career spent primarily on illustrating devotional books, he was at first not very adventurous in his iconography in BN, fr. 95, then, by the time he reached the end of Yale 229, his ideas had developed in more interesting directions?

STYLISTIC CONSIDERATIONS

Two painters participated in the execution of both volumes. The Master Painter did most of the illustration in both (figs. 8.8, 8.10, 8.15, 8.16, 8.23, 8.26), but was assisted in both by a second artist (figs. 8.1, 8.2, 8.24, 8.27, 8.28, 8.29) whose work occurs sporadically in BN, fr. 95 and more frequently in Yale 229. Of the 163 illustrations in BN, fr. 95, 35 are by the inferior assistant, all except one (f. 343v) of which are small miniatures or historiated initials; all of them occur in quires in which the major painter also participated, and in two cases (ff. 309 and 350), both painters worked on the same folio. In Yale 229 the major painter did the illumination in 22 out of 46 quires, collaborating only in quires 22, 24, and possibly 40 and 41, and only once on the same folio as the assistant (f. 325, where the assistant—or possibly another assistant—did the borders); the assistant was responsible for at least 77 of the 166 illustrations (in 3 cases it is difficult to decide which painter was responsible, on ff. 169, 174v, 175)—just under half of the total number, and certainly a much higher proportion than in BN, fr. 95, suggesting that his participation had increased in proportion to the development of his skill, and/or of his responsibilities in the atelier. His rôle has also increased in importance in Yale 229 as in that manuscript he did major miniatures as well as minor ones, assuming that it was executed after BN, fr. 95 and represents a development in the career of the assistant, at a point when the major painter was occupied with other commissions.

The format of the illustrations is comparable in both volumes and in the work of both painters, suggesting that the major master planned all of the layout. The inner backgrounds are usually of gold, generally plain in BN, fr. 95 (except on f. 1, fig. 8.16) and patterned in Yale 229, suggesting a slightly later date for the latter; both manuscripts also have some miniatures and initials with plain coloured backgrounds in deep blue or dusty pink. Historiated initials are set against backgrounds of pink and blue diaper (figs. 8.16, 8.29) or occasionally of plain blue or pink. Bars of initials and occasionally of miniatures are filled with geometrical motifs in pink, blue and white, or a plain blue or pink with white and red pen-flourished decoration; a few of the borders of the miniatures in both volumes are in gold with foliage motifs outlined in black (fig. 8.29); but most of the miniatures are framed by a thin band of gold, a significant hall-mark of the unusual arrangement adopted for most of the miniatures in both volumes. The rest of the palette includes orange-red, maroon, grey-green, deep blue, grey and white, with gold prominently used alongside colors.

What distinguishes the work of the two painters one from the other is above all their treatment of human figures, especially heads, hair and faces, where the main artist's figures have more symmetrically curling hair, the faces of the assistant tend to be somewhat more sallow; but there would seem to be some variation in the work of both painters, so that one sometimes wonders whether yet more painters were involved; similar differences are evident when the work of the two major artists are compared in other products. The main painter's drapery modelling is more sophisticated; he uses different kinds of realistic foliage motifs, and prefers certain other characteristic motifs like knotted fabric covers on thrones (figs. 8.16), fringed cloths on altars (fig. 8.15), tombs with a shallow arch beneath (fig. 8.26). The two painters differ in their treatment of details of arms and armour: main painter likes helmets which are gently conical on the front face with rectangular sights (fig. 8.23); those of the second painter have sights that end in a trefoil (figs. 8.1, 8.27); the major painter likes rolled-up saddle blankets attached to saddles (fig. 8.10, 8.23). The assistant has a few mannerisms in his treatment of architecture, notably his treatment of arches (as in doorway openings) in profile (fig. 8.24), and of round towers with polygonal roofs (figs. 8.1, 8.2, 8.24).

The major work by the principal artist, as has long been recognized, is the Franciscan psalter, Paris, BN lat. 1076.[123] Its illumination consists entirely of historiated initials with patterned gold backgrounds and borders with copious leaf motifs and marginalia; its flourished line-endings and pen-flourished borders include motifs like those in BN, fr. 95 and Yale 229. The smaller format of the psalter may account for the increase in foliage and pen-flourished decoration, but these are features which seem to be a stylistic development and might suggest that the book represents the next commission executed by the major BN, fr. 95/Yale 229 painter, undertaken perhaps at the point at which work was also beginning on Yale 229. This additional commission would explain why so much work in Yale 229, as opposed to BN, fr. 95, was done by the assistant.

Closely related, as Porcher observed, is the Hours of Thérouanne, Marseille, BM 111 (figs. 8.22, 8.25, 8.32),[124] whose use provides the closest approximation to a fixed locus of production for itself, BN, lat. 1076, BN, fr. 95/Yale 229. Similar to BN, lat. 1076 in its reliance on historiated initials and border illustration, it shares many motifs with the main illustration of BN lat. 1076 and BN, fr. 95/Yale 229 while standing slightly apart, I believe, in its treatment of faces and hair; perhaps it represents a later phase of development of the major painter's work or the work of a close collaborator (cf. figs. 8.22, 8.23, 8.25, 8.26). However, it also has the same distinctive pen-flourishing (cf. figs. 8.31, 8.32).

While the use of Marseille 111 suggests the (rather broad) geographical area of the diocese of the (now destroyed) suffragan of the arch-diocese of Reims, Thérouanne, as the region where that book was made to be used—and possibly, therefore, where other stylistically related books might also have originated or found their way to the homes of patrons living in the region—neither book contains firm evidence about its date. The only hint is that the feast of St. Louis (25 August), canonized in 1297, is absent in the calendar of BN lat 1076 and St. Louis is not invoked in the litany of either book, by contrast with Walters 90, a later book of hours of St-Omer (dioc. Thérouanne) whose illumination can be seen as a later outgrowth of the style of the main painter, where the saint is commemorated (discussed above in the context of the tabernacle, fig. 8.21). [125]

The additional activities of the assistant painter are most clearly represented by the puzzling psalter in Brussels attributed, on the basis of the shields in the borders, to the patronage of Gui de Dampierre, count of Flanders (1280–1305), BR 10607 (Van den Gheyn 592) (fig. 8.30). [126] Immediately striking is a combination of motifs that recall the style of BN, fr. 95/Yale 229 hand 2: similar framing devices (gold with black leaf patterns, cf. figs. 8.29, 8.30); similar folded acanthus motifs and cusped borders with gold balls, and similar faces and hair, particularly of curly-haired men shown in profile (cf. figs. 8.24 border, 8.30).

Both painters of BN, fr. 95 and Yale 229 collaborated again on a manuscript that Kerstin Carlvant has connected with BN, fr. 95: Bruges, Grote Seminaar 45/144, where the opening historiated initial is possibly by the major painter and the figures in the borders by the second artist of BN, fr. 95/Yale 229 (fig. 8.33). [127]

Here I wish only to draw attention to a stylistic sub-group, to which I can now make an addition, that broadens slightly our picture of the geographical range of places where patrons of these painters lived. In 1970 I drew attention to the Florence French literary miscellany, Laur. Ash. 125, that is closely related to BN, fr. 95/Yale 229 in many stylistic ways, yet also contains work by other painters who did not participate in the *Lancelot*. The hands that painted its Brunetto Latini and one of those who did the *Turpin* are both very close to BN, fr. 95 and Yale 229 (figs. 8.34, 8.35) with similar figures, faces, chain mail; the patterns in the backgrounds—geometrical for the Brunetto Latini part (fig. 8.34), flowers in scroll-work for the Turpin (fig. 8.35) suggest a closer link with Yale 229 than with BN, fr. 95, while both have gold frames with black patterns, of a type that occurs from time to time in both BN, fr. 95 and Yale 229 (figs. 8.29, 8.36). The third hand in the Florence manuscript stands somewhat apart from the rest and finds its closest parallel in the Paris *Guillaume de Tyr*, BN, fr. 2754 (figs. 8.37, 8.38). This hand I suggest was also responsible for a tiny book of hours with a calendar that probably indicates Arras use before 1297 in the Museum in Lille, SA 367 (figs. 8.39, 8.40). This book of hours has an exceptional series of full-page miniatures that include substantial Old Testament illustration (fig. 8.40) as well as historiated initials and marginalia (fig. 8.39). The distinctive use of roundels on the corners of these miniatures is a formal link with the third hand in the Florence miscellany; and the distinctive sallow faces are another hall-mark of this sub-group.[128]

THE PATRON: GUILLAUME DE TERMONDE?

BN, fr. 95 and Yale 229 can be shown with reasonable certainty to have been produced somewhere in the diocese of Thérouanne in the last decade or so of the thirteenth century for a patron whose wealth is attested to by the enormous size of the volumes, the quantity of illustration and the very substantial amount of gold used on the backgrounds of the miniatures, their frames and borders. Such an undertaking would almost certainly have been made on commission. It is unfortunate that neither volume contains the name of the patron, a situation all too common in the thirteenth century. Most books of this period were rebound in later centuries and provided with new flyleaves, which no doubt explains the general absence of ownership marks contemporary with the books: BN, fr. 95 was rebound in the eighteenth century and bears the arms of Louis XV; Yale 229 was also rebound in the eighteenth century. The only hints of possible early ownership are the heraldic shields that occur sporadically in the margins of both books, coupled with what surviving inventories tell us about the kinds of patrons who owned copies of the prose Lancelot in this period. Again, none of them is specific enough for the identification of either of these manuscripts.

With great enthusiasm I many years ago suggested that the arms of the marginal knight on f. 187 in Yale 229, on the opening folio of *Queste: or a lion sable, a bend gules*, were those of a cadet of the house of Flanders, Guillaume de Termonde (c. 1248–1312), second son of Guy de Dampierre, count of Flanders (1280–1305),[129] who might possibly have been the owner.[130] The horse's housing is *or a lion sable*, with a *bend gules* just visible in good light on front and hindquarters; the knight, who has dismounted and kneels before a lady, is wearing a surcoat *or*, and an ailette that is rubbed but just might have borne a *lion sable*. If this is a portrait of the patron, it is a very discreet one, and it might equally be that these arms are there for another purpose. Much of the ecclesiastical diocese of Thérouanne is politically in the county of Flanders, and so the presence of the arms of Flanders, and of members of the family and associates of the counts, might be included for purposes of flattery rather than as indications of specific ownership. In general, the shields of knights in the miniatures are differently treated that those in the margins: they are coloured and patterned, particularly burrely, checky or lozengy in a lighter shade of the main tincture of the shield within a bordure of the main colour or a bordure engrailed; and they often ignore basic rules of true heraldry by using colour on colour. Frequently the colors of shields in the miniatures bear no relation to those of housings or surcoats, nor do knights consistently bear the same arms or wear the same colors.[131] The prime function of that heraldry would seem to be to enhance the general colouristic effect of the miniatures.

It is in the borders that some of the shields—but not all—seem to correspond to what is found in contemporary rolls of arms. The arms of Flanders appear several times in both volumes,[132] and one marginal shield, in addition to the horse's housing referred to above, may be that of Guillaume de Termonde, though the ground is plain parchment not gold.[133] The others are much more difficult to identify in terms of their owners on the one hand and their purpose on the other. Shailor, using identifications given in Gaspar and Lyna for the shields in the so-called psalter of Guy de Dampierre, BR 10607,[134] listed five more in Yale 229 : *or a cross sable* (ff. 1, 126, given as Gruythuse of Bruges); *or a lion gules* (f. 100v, Bergen); *or a cross gules* (f. 100v, Mortaigne); *argent a lion gules* (f. 100v, Court ?); *argent a lion sable* (f. 347, Northwyck, Bouchorst, Crechy or Fiennes).[135]

Unfortunately a glance at the contemporary sources produces other results: selecting from Jéquier's tables only those armorials that are closest to BN, fr. 95 and Yale 229 in period and region, the Wijnberghen, Chifflet Prinet and Ost de Flandre rolls,[136] one arrives at the following: *or a cross sable*: WN 546 Renier de Creüe, peer of the bishop of Verdun (1278–1289) and WN 1254 Geltholf (without further identification); *or a lion gules*: CP 71 le châtelain de Bergues and WN 32 Anseau de Garlande, seigneur de Tournon (1269–1274); *or a cross gules* : WN 566 Jean de Velaines (Bar, 1270), WN 657 Bergheim, WN 1136 Val d'Isère (Savoie), WN 1195 Crainhem; *argent a lion gules* : OF 168 le sire de Wallincourt; *argent a lion sable*: OF 156 Foucant M[. . .]gny (source defective) and WN 1160 le sire de Franchelein. None of these additional shields occur in the margins of BN, fr. 95; and four shields found in the margins of the latter do not occur in Yale 229: *or 3 chevrons sable* (ff. 149v, 238v): WN 131 Guy III de Levis, maréchal d'Albigeois and WN 563 Renaut le sauvage (possibly of Louvigny); *or 3 besants sable* (f. 199v): not in WN CP or OF; *or a saltire sable* (f. 199v): not in WN, CP or OF; *sable a lion or* (f. 78): OF 17 le conte de Hainaut and WN Bardoyn de Milly (Milly en Gâtinais) and WN 1170 le duc de Brabant. This selection does not appear to add up to any coherent pattern. The Count of Hainaut and the Duke of Brabant ruled territories immediately ajoining Flanders; the Châtelain of Bergues held a châtellenie of Flanders located northeast of Saint-Omer, in the diocese of Thérouanne; but why the others are there, always assuming the identifications are the intended ones, is not self-evident. What these findings show above all is that, unfortunately, identification of ownership on the basis of this kind of heraldry is at best precarious; at the same time, it is also clear that recognizable arms of other possible patrons among the rulers of neighbouring regions to the west and south, such as a member of the royal house of France or of the countess of Artois or the count of Ponthieu, are entirely absent.

The inventories that survive from the late thirteenth and early fourteenth centuries do not include that of Guillaume de Termonde, so an independent corroboration of whether or not he owned Vulgate Cycle manuscripts is not possible. Nor does the inventory made at the death of his father Gui de Dampierre, Count of Flanders and Marquis de Namur, in 1305 include a Vulgate Cycle manuscript among the books listed. [137] I have found just a few references to prose *Lancelot* volumes which do give a certain picture of what kinds of people had them in their possession around 1300. Jean d'Avesnes, count of Hainaut, oldest son of Guy de Dampierre's mother Marguerite, countess of Flanders, and her first husband Bouchard d'Avesnes, had a "grand roumans a rouges couvertures ki parolle de Nasciien de Mellin et de Lancelot dou Lach," which is listed among the 18 books in the inventory of possessions made at his death in 1304. [138] This sounds like a single volume containing the *Estoire*, the *Merlin* and part or all of the *Lancelot* proper; the only single-volume survivor with these contents made before 1304 is Rennes 255 (c. 1220), probably made in Paris, which contains no indications of early ownership. [139] It is of course possible that a volume like this, which would have been very large, might have been subsequently broken up into two; but there is not enough information for it or them to be identified. [140] Robert de Béthune, older brother of Guillaume de Termonde and count of Flanders 1305–1322, had a "livre de Merlin," listed among 15 books in the inventory of his possessions at Courtrai at his death.[141] A "Lancelot du Lac" is included in the list of 10 "roumans qui sont monseignieur" copied onto the last folio of a manuscript containing the *Chevalier au Cygne* and *Antioche,* Paris, BN, fr. 12569; there are no hints as to who "monseigneur" might have been, but he was clearly a person whose social class allowed him to have his book-list drawn up by a member of his household, a clerk, chaplain, or secretary.[142] Curiously, the other great bibliophile of the right period whose library is known, Mahaut, countess of Artois (1302–1329), does not appear to have had a Vulgate Cycle manuscript in her otherwise excellently stocked library, furnished by booksellers in Arras and in Paris, and unusually well documented.[143]

The last third of the thirteenth century is a period in which there begins to be evidence that the ownership of fine—presumably illuminated—books was no longer the exclusive province of the nobility. Wills of townspeople of Douai in 1272, 1274, 1287 and 1320 indicate that both men and women were in a position to bequeath books to their relations, though not one Vulgate Cycle manuscript is mentioned.[144] Tournai wills of 1294, 1297, 1303, 1311, 1316, 1319, 1324, 1325, also include mention of books, mostly devotional items like psalters and hours, but in one case, among the seven "roumans" bequeathed by Jean Cole to his son Jehan, is included a copy of the *Merlin.*[145]

We shall probably never know what the full histories of BN, fr. 95 and Yale 229 really were—whether they were made for the same or different people, for Guillaume de Termonde, his children, or another member of the family of the counts of Flanders, or for someone else altogether. But the two surviving volumes and their illustrations will continue to fascinate, and I hope their rich illustration will soon become much better known.

ACKNOWLEDGMENTS

Photographs are acknowledged as follows: Figs. 8.1, 8.2, 8.8, 8.10, 8.23, 8.24, 8.26–8.29, 8.31, photos Alison Stones, reproduced by permission of the Trustees of the Beinecke Library, Yale University; figs. 8.3, 8.6 reproduced by permission of the Trustees of the British Library; figs. 8.4, 8.15, 8.16, 8.37, 8.38 reproduced by permission of the Bibliothèque Nationale, Paris; figs. 8.5, 8.9, 8.34, 8.36, photos Alison Stones, reproduced by permission of the Biblioteca Laurentiana,

Florence; fig. 8.7 reproduced by permission of the John Rylands University Library, Manchester; figs. 8.11, 8.12 reproduced by permission of the Biblioteca Nazionale, Florence; figs. 8.13, 8.14, 8.20 reproduced by permission of the Institut de Recherche et d'Histoire des Textes; fig. 8.17, photo Alison Stones, reproduced by permission of the Bibliothèque Municipale, Rennes; figs. 8.18, 8.19, photos Alison Stones, reproduced by permission of the Biblioteca Philosophica Hermetica, Amsterdam; fig. 8.21 reproduced by permission of the Walters Art Gallery, Baltimore; figs. 8.22, 8.25, 8.32, photos Alison Stones, reproduced by permission of the Bibliothèque Municipale, Marseille; fig. 8.30 reproduced by permission of the Bibliothèque Royale, Brussels; fig. 8.33, photo Alison Stones, reproduced by permission of the Grootseminarie, Bruges; fig. 8.39, 8.40 photos Alison Stones, reproduced by permission of the Musée de Lille.

ABBREVIATIONS

Ars.	Bibliothèque de l'Arsenal
Ash.	Ashburnham
BI	Bibliothèque Inguimbertine
BM	Bibliothèque Municipale
BN	Bibliothèque Nationale, Biblioteca Nazionale
BPH	Biblioteca Philosophica Hermetica
BR	Bibliothèque Royale
f.	folio
Fr., fr.	French, français
GS	Grootseminarie
Laur.	Laurenziana
MM	Médiathèque Municipale
Ryl.	Rylands
UB	Universitätsbibliothek
UL	University Library
Walters	Walters Art Gallery
Yale	New Haven, Yale University, Beinecke Library

NOTES

1. New Haven, Yale University, Beinecke Library, MS 229 (*Agravain, Queste, Mort Artu*); see particularly Barbara A. Shailor, *Catalogue of Medieval and Renaissance Manuscripts in the Beinecke Rare Book and Manuscript Library, Yale University*, 2 vols. (Binghamton: SUNY, 1984, 1987), I, no. 229, with references to previous literature. I first studied it in the context of my

Ph.D. dissertation, "The Illustrations of the French prose Lancelot," 1250–1320 (Univ. of London, 1970–71), pp. 20, 41, 62, 77, 81, 109, 164–5, 169–73, 175–76, 180, 185, 204, 230–31, 238, 312–21, 323, 326–37, 340–58, 33, 370–82, 430–39, 441–42, 448, and have mentioned it a few times since, in "Secular Manuscript Illumination in France," in *Medieval Manuscripts and Textual Criticism*, ed. C. Kleinhenz (University of North Carolina, Chapel Hill, Dept., of Romance Languages, Symposia, 4) (Chapel Hill, 1977), pp. 83–102, esp. p. 87, and "Some Aspects of Arthur's Death in Medieval Art," in *The Passing of Arthur: New Essays in Arthurian Tradition*, ed. Christopher Baswell and William Sharpe (New York: Garland, 1988), pp. 52–101. The opportunity to study the manuscript very much more closely came during my tenure of the H. P. Kraus Visiting Fellowship at the Beinecke Rare Book and Manuscript Library in 1992. I extend my warm thanks to Mrs H. P. Kraus and to Dr. Ralph Franklin and Dr. Robert Babcock and their colleagues and staff at the Beinecke Library, and to Drs. Pamela Blum, Walter Cahn, William Clark, Mary Dean and Barbara Shailor for their kindness during my stay. Research for the documentary component was furnished by a summer research grant from the Faculty of Arts and Sciences of the University of Pittsburgh to whom my thanks are also due. Parts of this paper were delivered at the Oxford Seminar in the History of the Book conference in 1988, the Lancelot–Graal conference in Austin, Texas, in 1992, and as a keynote address at the XVIIth International Arthurian Congress held in Bonn in 1993. Special thanks to Martine Meuwese for helpful comment and criticism of various iconographic problems.

2. Some 180 manuscripts of all or parts of the five-part cycle (*Estoire, Merlin, Lancelot proper, Queste* and *Mort Artu*) are listed (under the heading *Lancelot*) by Brian Woledge in his indispensable *Bibliographie des romans et nouvelles en prose française* (Geneva: Droz, 1954), *Supplément* (Geneva: Droz, 1975). No mention is made of illustrations, and indeed not all of them are illustrated. More detailed descriptions of the manuscripts are given in Alexandre Micha, "Les manuscrits du *Lancelot* en prose," *Romania*, 81 (1960), 145–87; *Romania*, 84 (1963), 28–60 and 478–99; "La tradition manuscrite du *Lancelot* en prose," *Romania*, 85 (1964), 293–318 and 478–517, and in the the text editions and studies by Micha and others. The only edition of all five branches, based on London, BL, Add. 10292–4, with variants from certain other manuscripts, is H. O. Sommer, *The Vulgate Version of Arthurian Romances*, 7 vols. (Washington, D.C.: Carnegie Institution, 1909–1913, rpt. New York, 1979). For the text of *Estoire*, see Sommer, I. For discussion, see F. Bogdanow, "The Relationship of the Portuguese *Josep Abarimatia* to the extant French mss. of the *Estoire del saint Graal*," ZRP, 7 (1960), 343–75, ead., *The Romance of the Grail: A Study of the Structure and Genesis of a Thirteenth-Century Romance* (Manchester: Manchester Univ. Press and New York: Barnes and Noble, 1960) and Alison Stones, "The Earliest Illustrated prose Lancelot Manuscript?" *Reading Medieval Studies*, 3 (1977), 3–44. A complete list of *Estoire* manuscripts is given by Jean-Paul Ponceau, *Étude de la tradition manuscrite de l'Estoire del saint Graal, roman du XIIIe siècle*, Thèse du Doctorat de Troisième Cycle, Université de Paris-IV-Sorbonne, 1986; and for a

discussion of the iconography, see Martine Meuwese, *L'Estoire del saint Graal*. *Een studie over de relatie tussen miniaturen en tekst in het eerste deel van de Vulgaatcyclus uit de Biblioteca Philosophica Hermetica te Amsterdam*, 2 vols., M.A. Diss, Rijksuniversiteit Leiden, 1990. For the text of *Merlin* see Sommer, and A. Micha, *Merlin, roman du XIIIe siècle* (Geneva: Droz, 1979), where BN, fr. 95 is MS 'D'; for *Lancelot*, see Sommer; A. Micha, *Lancelot : roman en prose du 13e siècle*, 9 vols. (Geneva: Droz, 1978–83); and for the non-cyclical version, see Elspeth Kennedy, *Lancelot do Lac : the Non-cyclic Old French Prose Romance*, 2 vols. (Oxford: Clarendon Press/New York: Oxford University Press, 1980); for *Queste* see A. Pauphilet, *La Queste del saint Graal* (Paris: Champion, 1965); for *Mort Artu* see J. Frappier, *La Mort le Roi Artu* (Geneva: Droz and Paris: Minard, 1964). For my lists of thirteenth-century copies, which revise the dates proposed by these scholars, see "The Earliest," 42–44. Other key studies are C.E. Pickford, *L'Évolution du roman arthurien en prose vers la fin du moyen âge d'après le manuscrit 112 du fonds français de la Bibliothèque Nationale* (Paris: Nizet, 1960), and Susan A. Blackman, *The Manuscripts and Patronage of Jacques d'Armagnac*, Diss. University of Pittsburgh, 1993, and in this volume.

3. Roger Sherman Loomis and Laura Hibbard Loomis, *Arthurian Legends in Medieval Art* (New York: MLA, 1938), pp. 95–97, no illustrations.

4. Roger Sherman Loomis, ed., *Arthurian Literature in the Middle Ages, A Collaborative History* (Oxford: Clarendon, 1959/1974), pl. B, facing p. 302.

5. Michael Camille, *Image on the Edge: the Margins of Medieval Art* (London: Reaktion and Cambridge: Harvard Univ. Press, 1992), pp. 107–08, concerned about the expansion of the action into the border through the marginal position of the censing angels, also passed over the treatment of the Grail in silence (while confusing the celebrating Josephe, first Christian bishop, with his father, Joseph (no 'e') of Arimathea).

6. Sotheby's 1.vii. 46, lot 66, 2 plates.

7. Lilian M. C. Randall, *Images in the Margins of Gothic Manuscripts* (Berkeley/Los Angeles: Univ. of California Press, 1966), figs. 4–6, 41, 87, 97, 157, 172, 178, 183, 195, 236, 245, 299, 303, 334, 414, 457, 487, 499, 542, 561, 583, 706, 709. Randall also mentioned it in two important articles, "A Medieval Slander," *Art Bulletin*, 42 (1960), 25–40 at p. 27, and "The Snail in Gothic Marginal Warfare," *Speculum*, 37 (1962), 358–57 at 359.

8. Full citation in note 1. Yale 229 had also received a brief notice in the *Yale University Gazette* (1955), 110, with one reproduction, and had been mentioned by Woledge, *Bibliographie*, p. 72. Shailor's list of subjects omitted the small historiated initial on f. 143 (at Sommer V: p. 271.34 and Micha V: 187) which shows a knight (surcoat and housing white) and a damsel with a veiled head riding up to a castle where a man stands in the doorway and greets them. The depiction of the woman is an error as no damsel is mentioned in the text at this point, whereas Bohort and Gavain are; the man could be either the valet who directs them to the house of a rich bourgeois or the rich bourgeois himself. Other minor errors in Shailor's identifications are as follows: f. 15v Gaheriet unhorses Guinas himself, not one of his knights; f. 25 Lionel (not

Lucan) addresses the King; the Queen with Lionel (not Elysabel); the Queen in a swoon (not asleep); f. 43 this scene should depict Lancelot and the knight of the tent in bed together, but the second figure in the image is an error as it is clearly female and wears a hair-net; f. 110v Lionel (not Lancelot) takes his leave and Lionel (not Lancelot) greets the prisoners; f. 132v either Hector and Lionel or Galehodin and one of his men recognize Mordret among the wounded knights; f. 164v King Brangoire (not Carados) and his division; f. 167 Bohort and Hector with Claudin's (not Claudius') horse; f. 175 Mellic del Terte is not named in this version of the text; f. 183v botttom part: Perceval, Lancelot and their host at a banquet (not Helaine as the third figure is clearly male); f. 187 the damsel sent by King Pelles (not Pelles himself) arrives at Camelot; the damsel (not Pelles) departs with Lancelot; f. 199 the table is laden not empty; f. 29v Josephe, not Christ, is shown giving the sacrament to Galaad; f. 356 text is Sommer p. 373: 24; f. 357v text is Sommer p. 376: 24.

    9. *Arthurian Legends,* pp. 95–97, 114, pl. 224–36.

    10. Georg von Vitzthum, *Die Pariser Miniaturmalerei von der Zeit des heiligen Ludwig bis zu Philipp von Valois und ihr Verhältnis zur Malerei in Nordwesteuropa* (Leipzig: Quelle und Meyer, 1907), p. 143.

    11. *Manuscrits à peintures du XIIIᵉ au XVIᵉ siècle,* ed. Jean Porcher (Paris: Bibliothèque Nationale, 1955), no. 57, pl. X (f. 273). See also Woledge, *Bibliographie,* p. 7, Micha, *Manuscrits du Merlin,* MS 'D'; Randall, figs. 72, 246, 305, 367, 368, 403, 44, 447, 459, 460, 556, 557, 582, 631, 636, 671, 708. Stones, *The Illustrations,* pp. 20, 30–31, 41, 51–53, 62, 78 n.92, 81–82, 85–86, 103, 116, 165, 167–78, 180, 182–83, 204, 208, 209–210, 221 n.3, 212, 217, 230–31, 237–38, 261, 165, 272, 427, 429–30, 438–39, 448.

    12. A full study of both surviving components is in preparation.

    13. Woledge, *Bibliographie,* p. 72, lists several composite sets of volumes, and other now separated manuscripts can be rejoined as sets, such as the one comprising Manchester, The John Rylands University Library fr. 1, Oxford, Bodleian Library, Douce 215, and Amsterdam, Biblioteca Philosophica Hermetica MS 1. The Amsterdam part was formerly in the possession of H. P. Kraus, and published in *Cimelia. A Catalogue of Important Illuminated and Textual Manuscripts Published in Commemoration of the Sale of the Ludwig Collection. Catalogue 165* (New York: Kraus, 1983), no. 3, pp. 12–15 and, earlier, in his *Catalogue 159* (New York: Kraus), no. 31, and, before that in the Phillipps Collection as MS 1045/7 (one volume; for this problematic number see my "Another Short Note on Rylands fr. 1," in: *Romanesque and Gothic, Essays for George Zarnecki,* ed. Neil Stratford (Woodbridge: Boydell and Brewer, 1987), pp. 185–94, esp. p. 186, n. 7), and MS 3630 (two volumes). As has long been recognized, the same production team of scribes, decorators and illuminators also made London, BL, Add. 10292–4 (c. 1315) and Royal 14.E.iii. Further examples of multiple copies made by other craftsmen, in roughly chronological order, are discussed in Stones, *The Illustrations*: Paris, BN, fr. 748 *Joseph, Merlin*) and 754 (*Lancelot* proper and *Merlin* resumé); Le Mans 354 (*Estoire*), BN, fr. 770 (*Estoire, Merlin*), and Oxford, Bodleian Library, Digby 223 (*Lancelot, Queste, Mort Artu*) cf. also BN, fr. 342

(*Agravain, Queste, Mort Artu*), written in 1274; Bonn UB 526, written in 1286, and Paris, BN, fr. 110 (both complete in one volume), cf. also London, BL, Add. 5474 (fragment of *Lancelot* in a *Tristan*); BN, fr. 19162 and 24394 (both *Estoire* and *Merlin*); BN, fr. 344 (complete in one volume) and ex-Phillipps 1047 (*Estoire, Merlin,* present whereabouts unknown); St. Petersburg, Saltykov-Shchedrin State Public Library, Fr.F.v.XV, 5 (*Estoire* with fragments of *Josephe*) and Oxford, Bodleian Library, Rawl Q. b. 6 (*Agravain, Queste, Mort Artu*); BN, fr. 105 and 9123 (both *Estoire* and *Merlin),* cf. also Ars. 3481; BN, fr. 117–20 (complete) and Ars. 3479–80 (complete); BN, fr. 113–6 (complete) and BN, fr. 112 (special version), see Pickford and Blackman; Brussels, BR 9246 (*Estoire,* special adaptation) and Paris, BN, fr. 91 (*Merlin,* adapted by Guillaume La Pierre), see Avril in François Avril and Nicole Reynaud, *Les Manuscrits à peintures en France, 1440–1520,* exh. cat. (Paris: Bibliothèque Nationale and Flammarion, 1993), no. 83. In all cases, it can be demonstrated that copies of the prose *Lancelot* are merely one component of the output of the craftsmen, who also made all kinds of other illuminated books, devotional and often liturgical as well as secular in type.

14. Summary information: BN, fr. 95: iii + 394 + iii, 470 × 330 mm, written space 319 × 223; text written by one hand in a formal Gothic textura, 2 columns, 40 lines, capitals touched in red on f. 1 and sporadically thereafter. Yale 229: i (paper) + 33 + i (paper) 475 × 343, written space 325 × 220; text written by one hand in a formal Gothic textura, 2 columns, 39–40 lines. Both volumes: single vertical rulings at left and right of columns, double horizontals at top, middle, and botton of written space, across margins; centre space ruled across. Pen-flourished borders in red and blue with 'J' motifs and spiral terminals with windmill tendrils and flower and leaf motifs, by one hand in BN, fr. 95 and by several hands, perhaps as many as six, or of six different types, in Yale 229. Both volumes have champie initials in gold against a partly maroon and blue ground, with predominantly cinqfoil flower motifs, folded acanthus and scroll-work in red and white. Less commonly fleur-de-lis, sycamore-leaf motifs, the occasional dragon, stork, bird, eagle and human head appear.

15. *Arthurian Legends,* p. 95; Randall, *Images in the Margins,* p. 38; Stones, "Secular Manuscript Illumination," 91.

16. There is no check-list. Woledge, *Bibliographie,* gives no indication of the presence of additional texts; the following list is based on my notes. Berkeley, UCB, 106 (ex Phillipps 3643) includes a *Vie des pères,* Gautier de Coincy's *Vie de Théophile* and other religious poems before its *Estoire, Merlin* and *Suite Vulgate;* Berkeley UCB, 107 (ex Phillipps 1279), has a calendar of indeterminate use, probably not intrinsic to the manuscript, before its *Lancelot* proper; Paris, BN, fr. 12581 includes Brunetto Latini's *Trésor* together with the *Lancelot* proper; Geneva, Bodmer 147 (ex-Phillipps 1046) includes in its *Estoire* and *Merlin* numerous biblical interpolations, the *Histoire de Troie* and *Sermons* of Maurice de Sully, followed by the *Queste* and the *Mort Artu,* see Françoise Vielliard, *Manuscrits français du Moyen Age* (Cologny-Genève: Fondation Martin Bodmer, 1975), pp. 46–60; Paris, BN, fr. 770 also includes *Prise de Jerusalem;* the *Queste* manuscript made by Pierart dou Thielt in 1351,

Paris, Ars. 5218, also contains chronicles, see Lori Walters in this volume. For literary compendia that group texts by Chrétien de Troyes with other works, see Les Manuscrits de Chrétien de Troyes, eds. Keith Busby, Terry Nixon, Alison Stones, Lori Walters (Amsterdam: Rodopi, 1993), Appendix I, pp. 249–62: Bern, Burgerbibliothek 354 includes the Sept Sages, see ibid., p. 260, and Paris, BN, fr. 1450 includes the verse version by Herbert entitled Dolopathos (ibid., p. 255).

17. I have not come across another copy of Pénitence Adam in the context either of Chrétien or of the prose Lancelot.

18. See Elisabeth Pellegrin, La Bibliothèque des Visconti et des Sforza (Paris: CNRS, 1955), p. 117; it was also in the 1426 inventory as item A 198, "De sanguine graduale in galico," identified by A. Thomas, "Les manuscrits français et provençaux des Ducs de Milan au Château de Pavie," Romania, 40 (1911), 571–609 and 41 (1912), 614–15, at p. 577, cited by Pellegrin, ibid.

19. Léopold Delisle, Le Cabinet des manuscrits de la Bibliothèque impériale, 4 vols. (Paris: Imprimerie Nationale, 1868–1881), I, pp. 135–36.

20. See "Arthur's Death," 71. A thorough investigation was made by Daniela Delcorno Branca in "Tradizione italiana dei testi arturiani. Note sul 'Lancelot'," in Medioevo Romanzo 17 (1992), 215–50. Delcorno Branca lists (p. 245) several entries in the Visconti-Sforza inventories whose titles could correspond to a volume with the same contents as Yale 229: B 817–820, B 823–824; and she also cites A.G. Cavagna, "'Il libro desquadernato: la carta rosechata dai rati'. Due nuovi inventari della libreria Visconteo-Sforzesca," Bollettino della società pavese di storia patria, 89, n.s. 41 (1989), 27–97: I, 670, 672, 673, 675, 681–683, 686, 692; but the descriptions are not precise enough to prove the case. For further discussion of the iconography of the Grail liturgy of Queste in relation to the Tavola Ritonda, see below.

21. BN, fr. 95 bears the notation, added at the end of the text, on f. 394v, "De Pavye au roy Loys XII" (Delisle, 126).

22. Porcher (1955), cat. no. 57, p. 32.

23. There are no published comparative figures from which to calculate exactly how many more pictures the BN, fr. 95/Yale 229 volumes have than other copies. For a complete assessment of this question, variant long and short text versions and lacunae would have to be fully taken into account, along with complete tallies for every single manuscript and every branch, a task that remains to be completed. My comparisons therefore represent a sample rather than an exhaustive list, but the figures given below will give some idea of the relative density of pictures across the pictorial cycles. The numbers are more or less accurate but I count composite miniatures as one; and errors of elementary arithmetic are all too easy to make. I omit the sparsely illustrated manuscripts. For the Estoire there are 41 illustrations in BN, fr. 95 and BN, fr. 9123; 63 in Add. 10292 and Roy. 14. E. iii, 50 in BN, fr. 105, 44 in Bonn 526, 39 in BN, fr. 344, 33 in BN, fr. 749, 31 in Rennes 255, 28 in Yale 227, 27 in Amsterdam BPH 1, 26 in BN, fr. 19126 and Tours 951, 25 in BN fr. 12582, 23 in BN, fr. 24394, 17 in Le Mans 354, 8 in BN, fr. 770 and BN, fr. 110; for the Merlin and the Suite Vulgate, 120 in BN, fr. 95 and Bonn 526, 143 in Yale 227, 127 in

BN, fr. 9123, 117 in BN, fr. 770, 94 in BN, fr. 749, BN, fr. 344, Ars. 3482, 76 in BN, fr. 105, 62 in Add. 38117, about 60, counting gaps, in Tours 951, 57 in BN, fr. 19162, 48 in BN, fr. 24394, 19 in Add. 10292, 16 in BN, fr. 110; *Agravain* (not always distinguished in the literature from the rest of the *Lancelot* proper and difficult to assess on its own without more work) 78 in Yale 229, 188 in Add. 10293, 49 in BN, fr. 119–120, 47 in Rylands/Douce and BN, fr. 115, 45 in BN, fr. 122, 38 in Bonn 526, 37 in BN, fr. 1422, 36 in BN, fr. 333, 35 in BN, fr. 12573, 26 in Rawl. Q. b. 6, 22 in M 806 (counting historiated initials and miniatures each as one), 8 in BN, fr. 110; these patterns are especially interesting as in Micha, "MSS du *Lancelot,*" Add. is classified as belonging to the short version of the text, yet it has more illustrations than any other copy including long version manuscripts. For the *Queste* there are 38 illustrations in Yale 229, 45 in BN, fr. 342, 33 in BN, fr. 112, 31 in Roy. 14. E. iii, 29 in BN, fr. 116, 24 in Add. 10294, 21 in BN, fr. 111, 18 in Bonn 526, 17 in BR 9627–8, 16 in Rylands/Douce 215 (incomplete) and Ars. 3482, 15 in BN, fr. 339, 344, 1423–4, 12573, 14 in BN, fr. 120, 13 in Rawl. Q. b. 6, 7 in BN, fr. 110; for the *Mort Artu* there are 49 illustrations in Yale 229, 47 in Add. 10294, 33 in BN, fr. 342, 31 in BN, fr. 112, 28 in BN, fr. 12573 and BN, fr. 111, 25 in BN, fr. 116, 23 in Bonn 526, 22 in BR 9268, Roy. 14. E. iii, BN, fr. 1424, Rylands/Douce 215 (incomplete), 16 in BN, fr. 339, 4 in BN, fr. 110.

24. My methodology is old-fashioned and could be described as "positivistic," in that it relies on first-hand observation of a large corpus of illustration of the same texts, and of others that contain illumination in a similar style; but I prefer the term "empirical" which implies a neutral outcome, in that patterns will not always be clear, nor links direct, nor developments sequential. The comparative material drawn upon here has been assembled over many years, with the help of the holdings of the major research collections; for some outlines and examples of my comparative approach that encompasses iconography as well as style, see "Notes on Three Illuminated *Alexander* Manuscripts," in *Alexander and the Medieval Epic, Essays in Honour of David J. A. Ross,* ed. Peter Noble, Lucie Polak and Claire Isoz (Millwood, N.Y., London and Nendeln: Kraus, 1982), pp. 193–241; "Arthur's Death," 54–56, discussion of diachronic and synchronic approaches; "The Illustrated Chrétien Manuscripts and Their Artistic Context," in *Les Manuscrits de Chrétien de Troyes,* pp. 227–322, esp. pp. 227–31, and "Illustrating Lancelot and Guinevere" (forthcoming). See also n. 35.

25. The best-known exception is the *Roman de la Poire,* where the full-page sequence of famous lovers is mostly depicted in double-register geometrical frames; and the rest of the illumination includes single-register full-page miniatures and historiated initials, see C. Marchello-Nizia, *Thibaut, Le Roman de la Poire* (Paris: SATF, 1984); recent articles are Véronique Guilhaume, "Le manuscrit illustré du *Roman de la Poire,* XIIIe siècle," *Histoire de l'Art* 23 (1993), 3–14; and Hans-Erich Keller, "La structure du Roman de la Poire," in *Conjunctures: Medieval Studies in Honor of Douglas Kelly,* ed. Keith Busby and Norris J. Lacy (Amsterdam: Rodopi, 1994), pp. 205–17, where a date of soon after 1259 is proposed for the composition of the main body of the

text (based on the apprearance of Guy de la Roche, Duke of Athens, at the court of St. Louis, to request the king to arbitrate in his dispute with Guillaume de Villehardouin, prince of the Morea, following Guy's defeat), and a date of c. 1270–1280 for the prologue in BN, fr. 2186 and the production of that manuscript and its illustrations ("quand la vie parisienne sous saint Louis, tellement vantée par l'auteur de l'original [voir les vv. 1327–85], appartenait déjà 'au bon vieux temps.'"). For my most recent list of other vernacular texts with full-page miniatures, see "The Illustrated Chrétien Manuscripts," p. 258, n. 124, and for full-page opening miniatures, see p. 263, n. 152 and Lori Walters, "The Use of Multi-Compartment Opening Miniatures in the Illustrated Manuscripts of Chrétien de Troyes," ibid., pp. 331–50.

26. Berlin, Staatsbibliothek, MS germ. fol. 282, f. 11v, Heinrich von Veldecke, *Eneide. Die Bilder der Berliner Handschrift*, ed. Albert Boeckler (Leipzig: Harrassowitz, 1939). Rudolf von Ems, *Wilhelm von Orlens*, c.1270/75 from Strassburg, Munich, Bayerische Staatsbibliothek Cgm 63, f. 38v, reproduced in colour in *Codex Manesse, Katalog zur Ausstellung*, ed. Elmar Mittler and Wilfried Werner et al. (Heidelberg: Braus, 1988), no. H 18, pp. 300 and 612–13; *Parzival, Titurel, Tagelieder: Cgm 19 der Bayerischen Staatsbibliothek München*, ed. G. Augst et al. (Stuttgart: Müller and Schindler, 1970); *Gottfried von Strassburg, "Tristan und Isolde" mit der Fortsetzung Ulrichs von Türheim. Facsimile-Ausgabe des Cgm 51 der Bayerischen Staatsbibliothek München*, ed. Ulrich Montag and Paul Gichtel, 2 vols. (Stuttgart: Müller and Schindler, 1979. For the *Carmina Burana*, Munich, Bayerische Staatsbibliothek Clm 4660 and 4660a (4660, f. 72v); see the facsimile ed. B. Bischoff, 2 vols. (Munich: Prestel, 1967); for the *Weingartner Liederhandschrift, Stuttgart, Württembergischer Landesbibliothek HB XIII 1*, facsimile ed. Ottfried Ehrismann et al., 2 vols. (Stuttgart: Müller and Schindler, 1969) and the *Manessische Liederhandschrift, Heidelberg, Univ. Bibl. Cod. Pal. Germ. 848*, facsimile ed. W. Koschorrek and W. Werner (Frankfurt: Insel, 1975–9, Kassel, 1981); Rudolf von Ems, *Weltchronik, Der Stricker, Karl der Grosse, HS 302 der Kantonsbibliothek (Vadiana) St. Gallen*, facsimile ed. H. Herkommer and E. J. Beer (Luzern: Faksimile-Verlag, 1982).

27. The closest approximation to this double-miniature effect in other vernacular books would be the long miniature spread out horizontally across two or three columns, which also allows more than one scene to be included. This is a format in fairly common use in other Vulgate Cycle manuscripts, such as BN, fr. 342, written in 1274, as well as several later copies, like Oxford, Bodleian Library, Ashburnham 828 (c. 1300), whose treatment of single-column illustrations and of borders is otherwise very close to BN, fr. 95/Yale 229; London, BL Roy. 20.D. iv (c. 1310), Paris, BN, fr. 122 (1344), Paris, Ars. 5218 (1351), all copied, like BN, fr. 95/Yale 229, in two columns; and New York, M 805–6 (c. 1315), copied in three columns. Other three-column Vulgate Cycle manuscripts, BN, fr. 105, Paris, Ars. 3482, BN, fr. 333 (second quarter of the fourteenth century) have miniatures across two columns except on the opening page which includes a miniature across all three columns; but there are also three-column manuscripts which have only single-column, single-register

miniatures, such as BN, fr. 110 and Bonn 526, Add. 10292–4 and Rylands/Douce/Amsterdam. And the long horizontal miniature format is not restricted to Vulgate Cycle manuscripts.

28. Reproductions of two-register miniatures in "Arthur's Death," fig. 4. 9, and Sotheby's 1.vii. 46, lot 8, pl. XIII; for a half-column miniature (without cut-out corner), ibid. pl. XIV. See also Vielliard, cited in note 16.

29. For comparisons, see part of Paris, BN, fr. 12576, ff. 201v, 208v, 218, 219, 225, 230v, 238v, the first four of which are the last of the eleven illustrations to Gerbert de Montreuil's Continuation of *Perceval*, and the other three, followed by a historiated initial and a larger miniature "hors texte" are the five illustrations to Manessier's Continuation of *Perceval* (*Les Manuscrits de Chrétien*, II, figs. 121–127); this format is also found in the *Roman de Jules César*, Rouen BM 1050 (U.12), see Stones, ibid., I, p. 239, fig. 23, where this formal link with Yale 229, fig. 24, is made.

30. I have shown elsewhere that it is common (though not universal) in French vernacular illustration for the opening illustration to be of a different format than the rest: so books whose illustration is mostly historiated initials will generally have a miniature at the beginning, while books with mostly miniatures will have either a historiated initial, or a composite miniature; see "Secular Manuscript Illumination," p. 93.

31. See Stones, *The Illustrations*, ch. 10, and "Arthur's Death."

32. See Stones, "The Earliest."

33. We do not know what the direct model was. Nothing with an identical set of illustrations survives. Micha, *Merlin*, p. 78, gave BN, fr. 95 the siglum 'D' and classified it with his beta version, consisting of 12 manuscripts of the 'grand cycle' or *Lancelot–Graal* (p. 145), and subgroup x1 (p. 174). In his articles on the *Lancelot* propre, he classified it with BN, fr. 112, 123, 12573 and more distantly with Rawl. Q. b. 6 and BN, fr. 12580 (p. 344), an oscillating group; for Sommer V, Micha groups it with BN, fr. 122, 123, 12573 (p. 231). Pauphilet (p. v) did not assign it a siglum; nor did Frappier (p. xxii).

34. For discussions of this question see Alison Stones, "Indications écrites et modèles picturaux, guides aux peintres de manuscrits enluminés aux environs de 1300," *Artistes artisans et production artistique* (Colloque international 1– mai 1983), ed. X. Barral I Altet, 3 vols. (Paris: Picard, 1988–90), III, pp. 322–49 and the contributions by P. Stirnemann and J. J. G. Alexander in the same volume, and, in relation to the Bonn manuscript, see "Illustrating Lancelot and Guinevere" (forthcoming); see also L. Sandler, "Notes for the Illuminator: The Case of the *Omne Bonum*," *Art Bulletin*, 71 (1989), pp. 551–64. Jonathan Alexander has included some examples from the Rylands fr.1 group in his *Medieval Illuminators and Their Methods of Work* (New Haven-London: Yale Univ. Press, 1992). In relation to the quire structure of each volume, the distribution of the various pictorial formats or types of illustration would appear to be somewhat haphazard. In BN, fr. 95 there are between two and seven illustrations per quire (except in the *Sept Sages* and *Pénitence Adam* texts, which have only one illustration each); small format miniatures and initials are more common in the *Merlin* and the *Suite Vulgate*

than in the *Estoire* where all the illustrations except one (f. 49v) are large miniatures; but there is always at least one large miniature in each quire. In Yale 229, the distribution patterns differ in that there are two quires (8, 10) with a single large miniature, and one quire (45) with 9 miniatures; several quires (3, 6, 19, 31) have only small historiated initials.

35. "Images of Temptation, Seduction and Discovery in the prose *Lancelot*: A Preliminary Note," *Wiener Jahrbuch für Kunstgeschichte*, 46–47 (1993–1994), 725–35, at 733 and fig. 15.

36. Perhaps Guillaume de Termonde, as suggested in my "Secular Manuscript Illumination," p. 87. He would have long reached adulthood by the time the book was made; possibly he might have had it made for one of his children. See also below.

37. See "Arthur's Death," fig. 4. 8.

38. On the head-motif in Celtic tradition, see Anne Ross, *Pagan Celtic Britain, Studies in Iconography and Tradition* (London: Routledge and Kegan Paul/New York: Columbia Univ. Press, 1967), ch. 2, pp. 61–126; Miranda J. Green, *Dictionary of Celtic Myth and Legend* (London: Thames and Hudson, 1992), under "head"; and the motif is of course also significant in Christian hagiography, in relation to the martyrdom of St. John the Baptist and the numerous other cephalophores. I thank Ruth Mellinkoff for stimulating discussion of heads and head-hunting, and for references.

39. Micha V, pp. 116–18.

40. Micha V, p. 116.

41. No colour is specified for the dwarf's horse in this version of the text; the picture shows it painted pink; cf. Micha, V, p. 117, where the horse is black.

42. Micha V, pp. 117–18.

43. It is omitted in BN, fr. 342, Bonn 526 and BN, fr. 110, M 806, and Jacques d'Armagnac's books, BN, fr. 118–120, 112, 113–116; in BN, fr. 123, f. 140, Lancelot arrives at a tomb guarded by two lions (F. Avril and P. Stirnemann, *Manuscrits enluminés d'origine insulaire, VII-XXe siècles* [Paris: Bibliothèque nationale, 1987], no. 152); in BN, fr. 12573, f. 107v, Lancelot fights two lions by a building, with no sign of the head; similar treatment in Oxford, Bodleian Library, Rawl. Q. b. 6, f. 290b; BN, fr. 122, f. 169, Lancelot fights two lions, head episode omitted; in BN, fr. 333, f. 866v, Lancelot fights two lions and opens the tomb, but the head episode is omitted. BN, fr. 111, f. 204 has two miniatures and includes the head episode: it is so far the closest to Yale 229. But this examination is not complete, and checking for textual variants and omissions is needed.

44. Micha, IV, p. 286.

45. Micha, IV, p. 292.

46. BN, fr. 110, f. 358v, comes closest by showing Lancelot dancing with three ladies.

47. The circular formation may be in part due to stylistic developments after 1300 and a greater interest in rendering space that is not a feature of Yale

229. For BN, fr. 115, f. 476, see Micha, IV, plate facing p. 232; the episode is not in BN, fr. 112 or BN, fr. 119, nor BN, fr. 342.

48. Micha V, pp. 133, 204. The latter episode is commonly illustrated, cf. Yale 229, f. 126; Oxford, Bodleian Library, Rawl. Q. b. 6, f. 274v; Rylands f. 90; cf. also *Estoire*, Roy. 14. E. iii, f. 78, and no doubt many more.

49. Very common thoughout the tradition and on its own, see T.H. White, *The Book of Beasts* (London: Cape, 1954), p. 20.

50. Pauphilet, p. 168; White, p. 132.

51. Such as the psalter Blackburn Public Library, Hart Collection, MS 091.21001, f. 1, reproduced in an analogous context in Michael Camille, *The Gothic Idol* (Cambridge: Cambridge Univ. Press, 1989), fig. 107; see also Nigel J. Morgan, *Early Gothic Manuscripts, II, 1250–1285* (London: Miller, 1988), no. 160. But the cushion, crown and finials do not fit. Could they echo a motif such as the mosaic thrones with books of Ravenna mosaics and Carolingian bibles, or a tabernacle drawn from Old Testament iconography such as the examples in Helen Rosenau, *Vision of the Temple. The Image of the Temple of Jerusalem in Judaism and Christianity* (London, 1979) ?

52. Also of note is the heraldry: in Add., Lancelot's ailettes are orange with white saltires, a motif used by the same painter in the so-called Psalter-Hours of Margaret of Beaujeu, New York, M 754 and London, BL Add. 36684 (facsimile of the Morgan Library part, ed. Madame Th. Belin, *Les Heures de Marguerite de Beaujeu* [Paris: Belin, 1925]; in Ryl, they are *arg* (white) *a lion gu*. Although these books are closely related stylistically, this image, as most of Add. 10293, is illustrated by a painter who does not reappear in Ryl./Oxford/Amsterdam or Royal 14. E. iii; see Stones, *The Illustrations*, ch. 6.

53. Micha, IV, p. 28.

54. For the bibles, see Ellen J. Beer, "Liller Bibelcodices, Tournai und die Scriptorien der Stadt Arras," *Aachener Kunstblätter*, 43 (1972), 191–226, where the falling of King Ochozias appears in Paris, BN lat. 16719–22, Basel Öffentliche Kunstsammlung U. IX. 3, Lille, BM 835–838 (1–4), written in 1264, the Marquette Bible, now Getty Ludwig I, 8, Arras BM 1 (3), Cambrai, MM 345–346. Beer's chart wrongly includes Brussels, BR II 2523, but there the fall is not shown: Ochozias is in bed beside an idol on a column and his death is foretold by Elijah and another figure, a variant that also occurs in New York Public Library 4 (not on Beer's chart). To Beer's list can be added further manuscripts from the Tournai-Cambrai region in the same period, where Ochozias's fall is shown: Manchester, Rylands 16 and London, BL, Yates Thompson 22. For a general discussion of the motif, see Camille, *The Gothic Idol*. The motif was very popular in *Lancelot* iconography: the idol is also clothed in BN, fr. 123, f. 108v (Avril and Stirnemann, no. 152); in Oxford, Bodleian Library, Rawl. Q. b. 6, f. 255: Lancelot, crowned by a lady, watched by others, and the idol (naked) falling, a mirror-image version of Rylands; BN, fr. 12573, f. 665 shows Lancelot crowned by a lady and a naked idol falling from a tower; Bonn 526 , f. 373b shows a simpler version of the spell-breaking, focussing on the crowning of Lancelot only.

55. See Emmanuèle Baumgartner, "Les scènes du Graal et leur illustration dans les manuscrits du *Conte du Graal* et des Continuations," in *Les Manuscrits de Chrétien de Troyes*, I, pp. 489–503.

56. The fifteenth-century copies other than those of Jacques d'Armagnac still need checking. Space precludes full illustration of the comparative material on the Grail: I give a more detailed analysis in a separate article, forthcoming.

57. Pauphilet, p. 269.

58. ibid., p. 270.

59. See P. Breillat, "La *Quête du Saint-Graal* en Italie," *Mélanges d'archéologie et d'histoire de l'École française de Rome*, 54 (1937), 262–300, esp. 296–300, and Lori Walters in this volume. I thank Lori Walters for sharing her views on this manuscript. My own view is more sceptical; I think the wording of the colophon, which Breillat cites only in part, precludes the book being actually made for Pope John XXII (Jacques Duèze); it was merely made during his pontificate, "[F]actum anno domini millesimo trecentesimo decimo nono secunda die mensis augusti pontificatus domini domini [sic] Iohannis pape xxii. anno tercio. in Civitate Avinonense." The arms of the shield placed between foliage do indeed appear to be his, but not originally so, in my view. I think the gold in particular shows signs of being an overpainting. For the arms, see D. L. Galbreath, *A Treatise on Ecclesiastical Heraldry*, I, *Papal Heraldry* (Cambridge: Heffer, 1930), p. 77, documented from the carving on the outer wall of his and his nephew Cardinal Jean de Via's chapel in the cathedral of Avignon (fig. 133); but the tinctures on this shield are not the same as those quoted by Galbreath, from Dom Bruno Malvesin's 1702 study of the Charterhouse of Cahors, founded by John XXII, in *Revue de l'art chrétien* (1908), p. 258: *Quarterly, first and fourth, silver a lion azure in an orle of roundels gules, second and third, gules two bars silver*; Malvesin is also quoted in Breillat, p. 297, n. 4, with a note of the tinctures found here, which are the same for the first and fourth quarters, but *or two bars gu* for the second and third. I noted in June 1995 that the shield on the chapel wall now reads *or* not *argent* in the first and fourth quarters. For the spectacular tomb of Pope John XXII in the chapel, see Julian Gardner, *The Tomb and the Tiara: Curial Tomb Sculpture in Rome and Avignon* (Oxford: Oxford Univ. Press, 1992), pp. 138–41; no mention of heraldry. And papal records do not prove the manuscript was in John XXII's library (Breillat, 296–97; F. Ehrle, *Historia bibliothecae romanorum pontificum*, Rome: Vatican, 1890, pp. 579–80). But there is no denying that the iconography is extraordinarily interesting and it is tempting indeed to see a link between this book, the North, and Italy, and between the papal interests and the liturgical elements so poignantly underlined by the illustrations in this copy, and those that surface again both textually and visually in the *Tavola Ritonda*.

60. Pauphilet, p. 278. Alternatively, the miracle of the carrying of the Grail table by a cripple is illustrated, at p. 273, as in Roy. 14. E. iii, Rylands, Add. 10294, BN, fr. 112, f. 181 (but not in Jacques d'Armagnac's other manuscripts, BN, fr. 116 and 120). Ars. 3482 has this scene as well, on f. 537, as does Ash. 121 (48), on f. 88v, and, in addition, another scene of Christ

administering communion to the three knights from a chalice-like Grail (f. 89) and the crowning of Galaad (f. 89v).

61. For the artistic context see François Avril in *Fastes du Gothique, le siècle de Charles V,* exhibition catalogue (Paris: Musées de France, 1981), no. 301, pp. 348–49.

62. See Stones, "Secular and Liturgical," p. 103, noting that transubstantiation is already a "given" concept by then, see Norman P. Tanner, S. J., *Decrees of the Ecumenical Councils,* 2 vols. (London: Sheed and Ward and Washington, D.C. : Georgetown Univ. Press, 1990), I, pp. 227–303.

63. E. G. Gardner, *The Arthurian Legend in Italian Literature* (New York: Dent-Dutton, 1930; rpt. New York: Octagon, 1971), p. 153, reproductions facing pp. 2, 112, 122, 174, 180, 190, 208, 28, 272, 286; Loomis, "Arthurian Legends," p. 121, figs. 335–39; *Mostra dei codici romanzi delle Bibliotheche fiorentine* (Florence: Sansoni, 1957), pp. 119–20. For the text, see *La Tavola Ritonda o L'Istoria di Tristano, Testo di lingua,* ed. Filippo-Luigi Polidori, I, *Testo* (Bologna: Romagnoli, 1864); Daniela Branca, *I Romanzi italiani di Tristano e la "Tavola Rotonda"* (Florence: Olschki, 1968), esp. 204–207; see also Christopher Kleinhenz, "Tristan in Italy. The Death and Rebirth of a Legend," *Studies in Medieval Culture,* 5 (1975), 145–58; M. J. Heijkant, *La tradizione de "Tristan" in prosa in Italia e proposte di studio sul "Tristano Riccardiano"* (Nijmegen: Sneldruck Enschede, 1989).

64. His name and the date are in the colophon; he is known as a Cremonan from his *Filocolo,* see D. De Robertis, "Centesimo dei manoscritti delle Rime di Dante," *Studi Danteschi,* 38 (191), 27, cited by Daniela Delcorno Branca, "Tradizione italiana dei testi arturiani: Note sul 'Lancelot'," *Medioevo romanzo,* 17 (1992), 215–50, at 243, n. 78.

65. For the attribution to Bembo, see Niccolò Rasmo, "Il Codice palatino 556 e le sue illustrazioni," *Rivista d'arte,* ser. 2–11 (1939), 245–81; Mario Salmi, "Nota su Bonifacio Bembo," *Commentari,* 4 (1953), 7–15; G. Mulazzani, *I tarocchi viscontei e Bonifacio Bembo: il mazzo di Yale* (Milan: Bocca, 1981); Joanna Woods-Marsden, *The Gonzaga of Mantua and Pisanello's Arthurian Frescoes* (Princeton: Princeton Univ. Press, 1988), pp. 28, 184, n. 81; see also L. Stephani, "Per una storia della miniatura italiana da Giovanni de' Grassi alla scuola cremonese della IIa metà del Quattrocento: appunti bibliografici," *La miniatura italiana tra Gotico e Rinascimento* (Atti del II Congressi di Storia della Miniatura Italiana, Cortona 24–26 settembre 1982), ed. Emanuela Sesti, 2 vols. (Florence: Olschki, 1985), II, pp. 823–81, esp. p. 859. A useful summary of the problems is Daniela Delcorno Branca, "Rassegna sulla letteratura arturiana in Italia (1985–1992)," *Lettere italiane* (1992), 465–97. I thank Daniela Delcorno Branca, Marie-José Heijkant, Christopher Kleinhenz, and Joanna Woods-Marsden for their generous assistance.

66. P. Breillat, "Le manuscrit Florence Palatin 556 et la liturgie du Graal," *Mélanges d'archéologie et d'histoire de l'École française de Rome,* 55 (1938), 342–73. Other aspects of the iconography are equally unusual, see Stones, "Arthur's Death," p. 71.

67. Reading the manuscript; cf. Polidori, p. 473.

68. Not quite as in ibid.

69. Polidori, p. 474, with spelling variants.

70. Cf. ibid.

71. "... la piece en semblance de pain ..." Pauphilet, p. 270.

72. Cf. Pauphilet, p. 270 "un hom ausi come tout nu, et avoit les mains saignanz et les piez et le cors"; no mention of the wounds as such.

73. Polidori, pp. 475–76.

74. Pauphilet, p. 240–41; Polidori, p. 472, "E la dama del castello, bevendo quello sangue si fue tantosto guarita."

75. Not in Jacques d'Armagnac's other manuscripts, BN, fr. 116 and BN, fr. 120. Also in BN, fr. 342, f. 145v.

76. Pauphilet, p. 279.

77. For connections with medical illustration of this subject, see my "Indications écrites," pp. 322–3, figs. 1–3.

78. Discovered in 804 in a vessel contained in a chest of leather inscribed *Jesu Christi Sanguis,* noted in *Annales Regni Francorum* ed. G. H. Pertz and F. Kurze (MGH SS, Hannover 1895), p. 119, also mentioned in J. Sumption, *Pilgrimage, an Image of Medieval Relgion* (London: Faber, 1975), pp. 46–48; subsequently lost, but another relic was discovered in 1048, see X. Barbier de Montault, *Oeuvres complètes* (Paris, 1889–1902), vii, pp. 524–37, cited in M. E. Roberts, "The Relics of the Holy Blood and the Iconography of the Thirteenth-Century North Transept Portal of Westminster Abbey," *England in the Thirteenth Century* (Proceedings of the 1984 Harlaxton Symposium) ed. W. M. Ormrod (Grantham: University of Evansville, 1985), pp. 129–42. The relic was allegedly brought to Mantua in the first place by Longinus, the soldier who pierced the side of Christ at the Crucifixion and who, according to apochryphal sources, regained his sight, cured by the Holy Blood from the wound of Christ. The relic was preserved in the church of S. Andrea, Mantua. Pope Sixtus IV granted indulgences in three briefs of 1475 to Lodovico Gonzaga and Barbara of Brandenburg and their descendants, see Woods-Marsden, pp. 54, 63–64, 212, n. 126, citing I. Donesmondi, *Dell'istoria ecclesiastica di Mantova* (Mantua, 1612), pp. 4–12 (which was not available to me); R. J. Peebles, *The Legend of Longinus, Its Ecclesiastical Tradition in English Literature and Its Connection with the Grail* (Baltimore: Furst, 1911); H. Horster, "Mantuae sanguis preciosus," *Wallraf-Richartz Jahrbuch* 25 (1963), 162–71, see also Konrad Burdach, *Der Gral* (Stuttgart: Kohlhammer, 1938, rpt. Darmstadt: Wessentliche Buchgesellschaft, 1974) pp. 93–129, 151–180, 209–449. Venice also possessed a relic, housed at San Marco: see *Le Trésor de Saint-Marc de Venise* (Paris: Grand Palais, 1984), cat. no. 128, pp. 116–18; Marie-Madeleine Gauthier, *Les routes de la foi* (Fribourg: Office du Livre, 1983), no. 65, pp. 116–117, before 1283. For Holy Blood relics in France, see below.

79. What is shown is the victory of Boort over King Brangoire in a tournament, followed by his deception, thanks to a potion, by the king's

daughter, which resulted in the conception of Helain le Blanc, future emperor of Constantinople, see Woods-Marsden, *The Gonzaga.*

80. R. Benedetti, "'Qua fa' un santo e un cavaliere...'. Aspetti codicologici e note per il miniatore," *La grant Queste del Saint Graal. Versione inedita del XIII secolo del ms. Udine, Biblioteca Arcivescovile 177* (Tricesimo: Vattori, 1990), pp. 32–47, cited by Delcorno-Branca, "Sette anni," 470.

81. See below.

82. Delcorno Branca, pp. 244–45, citing Stefani, "Per una storia," pp. 853–64, for Bembo's activities for the Visconti-Sforza. See also above for the possibility that Yale 229 was in the Sforza library by 1470.

83. A glance at the numbers I give in note 23 shows, for instance, that the picture-cycles in Add. 10292–4, Royal 14. E. iii, and Ryland/Oxford/Amsterdam, produced by the same team, are not identical; similarly Bonn 526 and BN, fr. 110; and BN, fr. 112 and BN, fr. 113–116 (although the textual versions are different); and the treatment of the same subject may also differ, as in the case of the carole illustrated above, and that of the *Estoire* liturgy discussed below.

84. The most reliable maps are the ones in E. Moreau, *Histoire de l'Église en Belgique*, 5 vols. (Brussels: Édition universelle, 1945–52); see also L. H. Cottineau, *Répertoire topo-bibliographique des abbayes et prieurés*, 2 vols., (Mâcon: Protat, 1939); *Supplément* ed. G. Poras (Mâcon: Protat, 1970).

85. J. Toussaert, *Le sentiment religieux en Flandre à la fin du Moyen Age* (Paris, 1963), pp. 259–67.

86. Marie-Madeleine Gauthier, *Les émaux du moyen âge occidental* (Fribourg: Office du Livre, 1972), no. 158; *Trésors des Églises de France*, ed. J. Taralon (Paris: Hachette, 1966), no. 42, pl. 111. The reliquary was a gift from Philippe le Bel to Notre-Dame de Boulogne in commemoration of the marriage in 1308 of his daughter Isabelle to Edward II of England. See also the extremely useful and well-illustrated survey by Vloberg (M. Vloberg, *L'Eucharistie dans l'art*, 2 vols., Grenoble and Paris: Arthaud, 1946), with reference (p. 149) to Mgr. Malou, *Du culte du Saint Sang de Jésus Crist et de la Relique de ce Sang qui est conservé à Bruges* (Bruges, 1851, rpt. 1927), which was not available to me. Vloberg, pp. 149–51, also discusses the Fécamp relic of the Holy Blood, allegedly hidden, in a vial, in a hollow fig tree by Isaac, nephew of Nicodemus and carried by water to Fécamp (Fici Campus).

87. See the useful survey with copious references in Roberts, "The Relics of the Holy Blood" (where the impact of the relics on Last Judgement iconography seems rather overplayed). The focus is the relic of the Holy Blood acquired by Henry III in 1247, and its influence on the sculpture of the central portal of the north transept of Westminster Abbey, reflected in the south porch at Lincoln Cathedral in the way in which the Christ of the Last Judgement draws special attention to the wound in his side. For the procession on St. Edward's Day, related by Matthew Paris and accompanied by a drawing in Cambridge, Corpus Christi College, MS 16, f. 215, see Suzanne Lewis, *The Art of Matthew Paris in the Chronica Majora* (Berkeley and Los Angeles: Univ. of California Press, 1987), pp. 408, 414, 432, 456, pl. X. Edmund, Earl of

Cornwall purchased a relic from the Countess of Flanders in 1266, of which he gave part to Ashridge priory and half to Hayles Abbey, see St. Clair Baddeley, "The Holy Blood of Hayles," *Transactions of the Bristol and Gloucestershire Archaeological Society*, 22 (1900), 276–84. For further discussions of the wound, see Vladimir Gurewich, "Observations on the Iconography of the Wound in Christ's Side, with Special Reference to Its Position," *Journal of the Warburg and Courtauld Institutes*, 20 (1957), 358–62; id., "Rubens and the Wound in Christ's Side, a Postscript," ibid., 26 (1963), 358; A. A. Barb," The Wound in Christ's Side," ibid., 34 (1971), 320–21; and, with an emphasis on manuscripts of c. 1400, Nigel Morgan, "Longinus and the Wounded Heart," *Wiener Jahrbuch für Kunstgeschichte* 46–47 (1993–94), pp. 507–18. Another example of the Measure of the Wound illustration, this time with the three nails, is in the Playfair Hours, on which see the facsimile by Rowan Watson, *The Playfair Hours, a late Fifteenth-Century Illuminated Manuscript from Rouen* (London, V & A ms. L 475-1918), London: Victoria and Albert Museum, 1984, p. 118, pl. XXVII (f. 169v). Watson cites further references on the subject: John Harthan, *Books of Hours*, New York, 1977, p. 170, and W.P. Simpson, "On the Measure of the Wound in the Side of the Redeemer," in *Journal of the British Archaeological Association*, 30 (1874), 357–74.

88. See my summary in "Arthurian Art Since Loomis," pp. 27–30.

89. I came across this extraordinary image while browsing through the slides at the Institut de Recherche et d'Histoire des Textes, Section iconographique, Orléans. My thanks to Odile Lépinay for her kind reception there. Of course the wound is represented much earlier, in images of the Instruments of the Passion, beginning c. 1320, see R. Berliner, "Arma Christi," *Münchner Jahrbuch der bildenden Kunst*, 3e ser. 6 (1955), 35–152; R. Suckale, "Arma Christi. Überlegungen zur Zeichenhaftigkeit mittelalterlicher Andachtsbilder," *Städeljahrbuch*, n.s. (1977), 177–208; and my summary in Wace, *La Vie de sainte Marguerite* (Tübingen; Niemeyer, 1990), pp. 195–96. See also Morgan, "Longinus," and, for lances true and false, Stephen Runciman, "The Holy Lance found at Antioch," *Analecta Bollandiana* 68 (1950), 197–209.

90. Useful discussion in Lilian M. C. Randall, assisted by C. Clarkson and J. Krochalis, *Medieval and Renaissance Manuscripts in the Walters Art Gallery* (London and Baltimore: Johns Hopkins Univ. Press and the Walters Art Gallery, 1992), II, France, 1420–1540, ii, under cat. no. 180, W. 291, to which a miniature of the Miraculous Bleeding Host was added after 1505. The Host, which allegedly bled when a Jew attempted to desecrate it, was presented to Philip the Bold of Burgundy in 1433 by Pope Eugene IV in gratitude for the duke's support of the pope at the Council of Basel, and displayed in a special monstrance. Six representations are listed by Randall. Another passed through Sotheby's on 22.vi.93 as lot 61, and the Sotheby catalogue refers to an eighth example, Johns Hopkins University, Evergreen House, ms. 10; I reproduce the image from Beaune 60, f. 26v. See also Vloberg, II, pp. 187–224, and Rubin, cited in n. 98 below.

91. Sommer, I, p. 40.

92. For a complete list of subjects, see "The Earliest ?" 37–41.

93. A few more include a simplified version as part of a multi-compartment opening miniature: Geneva, Bodmer 147; Yale 227 (1357), see below. A full study is needed.

94. Victor Leroquais, *Les sacramentaires et les missels manuscrits des bibliothèques publiques de France,* 2 vols. (Paris: Protat, 1924). At the time of the composition of the text of the *Estoire* at least as early as c. 1220 (because of the likely date of Rennes 255 made at about that time), the elevation was a relatively recent phenomenon, decreed at the synod of Paris between 1205 and 1208, and surrounded by considerable debate about the precise moment of transubstantiation in relation to the two elements of the eucharist. See V. L. Kennedy, "The Moment of Consecration and the Elevation of the Host," *Mediaeval Studies* 6 (1944), 121–50, esp. pp. 146–47. See also E. Dumoutet, *Le désir de voir l'hostie et les origines de la dévotion du Saint-Sacrement* (Paris, 1926), noting also the critical analysis of Dumoutet in André Wilmart, *Auteurs spirituels et textes dévots du Moyen Age latin* (Solesmes: Bloud and Gay, rpt. Paris: Études augustiniennes, 1971), p. 371, n. 2; and Michele Maccarone "Innocenzo III teologo dell'Eucharistia," in *Studi su Innocenzo II* (Studi e documenti di storia ecclesiastica 17) (Padua, 1972), pp. 341–431, and Peter Browe, S.J. *Die Verehrung der Eucharistie im Mittelalter* (Munich, 1933, rpt. Sinzig, 1990), esp. pp. 70–88. Further studies that were not available to me are E. Dumoutet, *Corpus Domini, Aux sources de la piété eucharistique médiévale* (Paris, 1942); H. Thurston, "L'Eucharistie et la saint Graal," in *Revue du clergé de France,* 56 (1908); P. Browe, *Die eucharistische Wunder des Mittelalters* (Breslau, 1938).

95. Sommer, I, p. 40.

96. See Vloberg and Miri Rubin, *Corpus Christi: The Eucharist in Late Medieval Culture* (Cambridge: Cambridge Univ. Press, 1991), pp. 118–42, noting that the presence of the Christ figure in the chalice in Ars. 5218 needs no exclamation mark (p. 13) as it depends directly on the text, see above; and that liturgical illustrations of the priest elevating a child (p. 138) also depend directly on the word "anima" that follows the opening words "ad te levavi": the priest's own "anima," shown as a child, iconography also common in death scenes for the representation of the soul as distinct from the body (cf. the death of King Mordret, discussed above). And surely the Cistercian elements in the interpretation have been overplayed in the literature.

97. Colophon on f. 31,"Cis livres fu par escript l'an mil.ccc.lvii. le premier samedi de guillet et le fist Jean Deloles escriven nes de hainnaut (de haumaut ?) pries pour lui et ce que vous endires puissiez."

98. The Gnadenstuhl, or "Throne of Mercy" type shows God the Father holding the crucified Christ with the dove of the Holy Spirit between. Günter Haseloff, *Die Psalterillustration im 13. Jahrhundert* (Kiel: n.d.[1938]); Victor Leroquais, *Les psautiers manuscrits des bibliothèques publiques de France,* 3 vols. (Paris: Protat, 1940–41); missing in the psalter BN, lat. 1076, closely related to BN, fr. 95 and Yale 229 and discussed below.

99. Victor Leroquais, *Les livres d'heures manuscrits de la Bibliothèque nationale*, 3 vols. (Paris: Protat, 1927). See also the hours of Saint-Vaast, Arras, Lille, Musée, S. A. 367, discussed below; but not in Marseille 111, also discussed below. I know of only one other example of the Trinity in an opening *Estoire* illustration: BN, fr. 749, f. 1, where the Trinity as two Persons and a dove are part of a three-part image in which the other two scenes have to do with the hermit and Joseph, as is more usual in *Estoire* opening scenes; and BN, fr. 748 has Christ enthroned, holding and orb, and blessing, as the lower part of its opening historiated initial "B," in which the upper part has three indeterminate male figures. Might they be a three-person Trinity? The initial is badly rubbed and its subject not clear. This is however an important example because it must date very early in the iconographical tradition: its text is written above the top line of ruling; see Neil Ker, "From 'above top line' to 'below top line,' a change in scribal practice," *Celtica*, 5 (1960), 13–16. No reflection of this subject in Rennes 255, however, where Christ hands a book to the author, one of the standard subjects for the opening of the *Estoire*, of which the angel handing the scroll in Yale 227 is a common variant. I reserve a full study of the *Estoire* for another occasion.

100. The date carved on the tomb in Add. 10292, f. 65 (Sommer, I, frontispiece) made by the same craftsmen, and an approximate date for all three copies, Add. 10292–4, Royal 14. E. iii and Rylands/Oxford/Amsterdam.

101. Sommer, I, p. 33–34. Royal 14. E. iii, f. 15v has a space for a rubric that was never added.

102. p. 34.

103. As on most pages in this manuscript and the others made by the same team, notes for the rubricator, in a compressed cursive hand, and a second set of notes, for the illuminator, in a larger, less compressed script, are found in the bottom margin beneath the picture; see my "Indications écrites," figs. 19–20, and Alexander, *Medieval Illuminators*, pp. 112–15.

104. No image of the liturgy is in BN, fr. 112 or BN, fr. 117–120, Jacques d'Armagnac's other Vulgate Cycle manuscripts.

105. Traces of erasure beneath the word "siecule" which possibly explains what looks like a "t" instead of an "l". An unfilled space for a rubric again in Royal 14. E. iii, f. 17v.

106. Sommer, I, p. 34.

107. p. 41.

108. Sommer, I, p. 32; complete edition based on this manuscript is E. Hucher, *Le Saint Graal*, 3 vols. (Le Mans: Monnoyer, 1877–78).

109. Sommer, I, p. 32.

110. For "arma Christi," see note 89 above.

111. For discussion of Le Mans 354 in relation to BN, fr. 342 of 1274 and BN, fr. 770, see Stones, *The Illustrations*, ch. 3 and ead., "Illustrated Chrétien," pp. 237–38, for the signature of the same scribe, Walterus de Kayo, and the date of 1282 in an *Image du Monde*, Paris, BN, fr. 14962. BN, fr. 770 and BN, fr. 342 are treated in the very incomplete study by Andreas Brähm, "Ein Buchmalereiatelier in Arras um 1274," *Wallraf-Richartz Jahrbuch*, 54

(1993), 77–104, which omits Le Mans 354 and numerous other books I have identified as part of this stylistic group; and the attribution to Arras is certainly open to challenge.

112. For other examples of this motif, see Randall, "The Snail."

113. Sommer, I, pp. 35–37.

114. *Trésors des églises*, nos. 217 and 210 respectively.

115. A study by Rosemary Argent is forthcoming.

116. Documents include the contract for the work, which names the craftsmen and gives the beginning date: Brussels, Archives générales du Royaume, AE no. 1417, f. 493, edited by A. Mottard, "La châsse de sainte Gertrude de Nivelles," *Annales Nivelles* 20 (1949), 33–476; R. Hanon de Louvet, "L'inspection des ossements de sainte Gertrude eut-elle lieu en 1292 ou 1293 ?" *Annales Nivelles*, 17 (1946), 249; C. Donnay-Rocmans, *Gazette des Beaux-Arts* (1961), 185–202; summary in Bernard Wuillaume, *La châsse gothique de Sainte Gertrude de Nivelles (Rif tout dju* [sic], numéro spécial, no. 348), Nivelles, 1992. There is considerable debate on how long the work took; the translation of the relics seems to have occurred only in 1298. On view in its fragmentary state during the 1970s, the shrine was restored at the Institut royal de la Patrimoine artistique in Brussels, where excellent photographs made before the destruction are available; a modern copy is on view in the abbey church. The restored shrine was exhibited at Cologne and Paris in 1995–1996, see *Schatz aus den Trümmern: Der Silberschrein von Nivelles und die europäische Hochgotik* (catalogue) ed. H. Westermann-Angerhausen (Cologne: Schnütgen Museum, 1995). I thank Robert Didier for helpful discussion of the shrine and for the privilege of seeing the fragments in course of restoration.

117. Few large-scale examples survive; the frame in which is now set a crucifix at Hedalen, Norway, is one mid-thirteenth-century example, whose Virgin and Child statue is in the museum in Oslo; see Martin Blindheim, *Main Trends of East-Norwegian Wooden Figure Sculpture in the Second Half of the Thirteenth Century* (Oslo, Dybwad, 1952), p. 46, for the crucifix; photo of the entire inside at the Ikonografiske registrant for Norge, Oslo Museum, showing the double arched niches that once held sculptures (now empty except for later painting of fruit and flowers) in three registers on double hinged panels on either side. See also Mikjel Sørlie, *Hedalskyrkja i Valdres* (Sjøvik: Mariendals Offsettrykkeri, 1984), pp. 11, 12, 18. The painted panel of St. Peter also at the Museum, Oslo, but done under English influence, or possibly of English manufacture, of the 1240s, is allegedly the outside of a side panel from another such large-scale wooden shrine (*Age of Chivalry*, ed. Jonathan Alexander and Paul Binski [London: Royal Academy and Weidenfeld and Nicolson, 1988], no. 311, with bibliography, and reference to another such tabernacle at Fröskog, Sweden). I thank Erla Bergendahl-Hohler and Christopher Hohler for their kindness in Norway and for stimulating discussion of these shrines. For the small-scale shrines, in ivory or metal, see O. von Falke, "Ein frühgotischer Marienaltar aus Tournai," *Amtliche Berichte aus den Königlichen Kunstsammlungen*, 39 (1917–18), 158–67; S. L. Faison, Jr. "A Gothic Reliquary in the Metropolitan Museum of Art, New York City," *Revue belge*

d'archéologie et d'Histoire de l'art, 66 (1936), 133–35; Virginia Wylie, "A Copper-Gilt Shrine in the Museo Sacro of the Vatican Library," Art Bulletin, 27 (1960), 195–204. For a comparable example in metalwork see M.-M. Gauthier "Du tabernacle au retable: une innovation limousine vers 1230," Revue de l'art 40–41 (1978), 23–42.

118. See Vloberg and Rubin; for the impact of the new feast on iconography, in particular the representation of Christ as priest, see F. Avril, "Une curieuse illustration de la Fête-Dieu: l'iconographie du Christ prêtre élevant l'hostie et sa diffusion," in Rituel. Mélanges offers à Pierre-Marie Gy, o. p., ed. Paul de Clerck et Éric Palazzo (Paris: Cerf, 1990), pp. 39–54; fig. 1 shows a Parisian manuscript illustration of a Corpus Christi procession in which the host is displayed in a monstrance, dated c. 1340–50 by Avril who notes (p. 41) that the subject first emerges at about this date. Joseph Braun, Das christliche Altargerät in seinem Sein und in seiner Entwicklung (Munich: Hueber, 1932), p. 355, notes a considerable lapse of time between the institution of the feast and the widespread use of the monstrance.

119. See M. Andrieu, "Aux origines du culte du Saint-Sacrement. Reliquaires et monstrances eucharistiques," Analecta Bollandiana, 68 (1950), 379–418. An inscription claims it was made at the abbey of Herkenrode in 1286 by prioress Heilewigis (p. 403, citing "l'ostensoir de l'abbaye de Herkenrode" in Le Beffoi, arts, héraldique, archéologie, 3 [Bruges, 1866–1870], pp. 347–48, which was not available to me). It is now at the church of Saint-Quentin in Hasselt, Belgium.

120. Gauthier, Les routes de la foi, no. 66, in the treasury of the church of Notre-Dame, St-Omer (Pas-de-Calais); see also Trésors des églises de l'arrondissement de Saint-Omer (Saint-Omer: Musée Sandelin, 1992), no. 3, pp. 42–45, where it is identified as a pyx, a type of vessel that is not normally perforated.

121. I thank Martine Meuwese for suggesting this example.

122. This outline is derived in part from Stones, The Illustrations, ch. 4. There, building on Vitzthum's 1907 and Porcher's 1951 and 1955 juxtapositions, I related BN, fr. 95/Yale 229 to BN lat. 1076 (Franciscan psalter, calendar without St. Louis), Marseille 111 (hours of Thérouanne, no calendar), adding Florence, Laur. Ash. 125 (literary miscellany in French), BN, fr. 2754 (Guillaume de Tyr, Histoire de la guerre sainte, linked with BN, fr. 95 by Porcher [1955], no. 57), three copies of Brunetto Latini's Trésor: BN, fr. 567 (Vitzthum, p. 142, linked with BR 11040), Leningrad, Fr. F. v. III, 4, BL, Yates Thompson 19; BN, Smith-Lesouëf 20 (psalter, calendar without St. Louis, Porcher [1951], no. 72), three copies of the Roman d'Alexandre in French prose: BR 11040 (Vitzthum, p. 141, linked with BN, fr. 567), Berlin, Kupf. 78.C.1, BL, Harley 4979; two more volumes of the Vulgate Cycle: BN, fr. 749 (Estoire, Merlin), Oxford, Bodleian Library, Ash. 828 (Lancelot proper); two copies of Vincent of Beauvais' Speculum historiale: Boulogne-sur-Mer 130 and 131 (the latter copied in 1297, also in Porcher [1951] as nos. 66 and 67); the psalter at S. Marienstern, Oct. 3, and the psalter-hours Baltimore W 90 (calendar including St. Louis, so after 1297). I treated sub-components of this

group separately in two articles, "Alexander," cit. n. 24, to which another *Alexander* manuscript in a private collection should now be added, and in "Prolegomena to a Corpus of Illustrated Vincent of Beauvais Manuscripts," in *Vincent de Beauvais: Intentions et réceptions d'une oeuvre encyclopédique au Moyen Age* (Actes du XIVe Colloque de l'Institut d'études médiévales, organisé conjointement par l'Atlelier Vincent de Beauvais (A. R. Te. M., Université de Nancy II) et l'Institut d'études médiévales (Université de Montréal), 27–30 avril 1988), ed. Monique Paulmier-Foucart, Serge Lusignan and Alain Nadeau (Saint-Laurent: Bellarmin and Paris: Vrin, 1990), pp. 302–344. Here I add several further manuscripts to the broad group and modify the stylistic subdivisions somewhat, particularly in relation to the stylistic origins and the rôle of the psalter of Guy de Dampierre, Brussels, BR 10607, in the group, to which important contributions have been made by Kerstin Carlvant, see note 126 below.

123. Haseloff, p. 48, Tab. 9, pl. 12–13, where its closest stylistically relevant associate is Arras, Grand Séminaire 47, on loan to the Bibliothèque Municipale, Arras (similar decorative format and many identical marginalia, but differences in figure style), Leroquais, *Psautiers,* II, p. 63; *L'Art du Moyen Age en Artois* (exh. cat.) ed. Jean Porcher (Arras, 1951), no. 53; Porcher (1955), no. 81. Porcher did not actually make the connection in the Paris catalogue, though he included both books.

124. Connected with BN, lat. 1076 by Leroquais, *Psautiers,* II, pp. 63–66; Porcher (1951), no. 74; made, according to Porcher (1955), no. 81, for a lady particularly devoted to St. Francis. See also J. Billioud, "Très anciennes heures de Thérouanne," *Trésors des Bibliothèques de France,* 5 (1935), 165–85, pl. LX-LXIV.

125. I can see no justification for supposing BN, fr. 95 to have been made in Amiens, as several scholars have suggested, see Loomis, *Arthurian Legends,* p. 97; Eleanor S. Greenhill, "A Fourteenth-century Workshop of Manuscript Illuminators and Its Localization," *Zeitschrift für Kunstgeschichte,* 40 (1977), 1–19, at p. 1; Karen Gould, *The Psalter and Hours of Yolande of Soissons* (Cambridge: Mass., 1978), p. 56; Vitzthum and Porcher did not say Amiens, as reported by Rolf Hasler, "Die Miniaturen des Breviculums," in *Raimundus Lullus-Thomas le Myésier, Electorium parvum seu Breviculum, HS St. Peter perg. 92 der Badischen Landesbibliothek Karlsruhe* (Wiesbaden: Reichert, 1988), pp. 33–59 at p. 47, n. 99. Vitzthum rightly (p. 143) derived the style of BN, fr. 95 from the *Liber Floridus,* BN, lat. 8865, presumably a product of St-Omer (dioc. Thérouanne) made after the death of Blanche of Castille in 1250 and before that of St. Louis in 1270 as the former is an original entry and the latter an addition (p. 114); Vitzthum did not put BN, fr. 95 in Maastricht, as Gould, p. 56, and Greenhill, p. 1 report); and Porcher grouped BN, fr. 95 much more generally under the broad heading "Artois, Picardie" in his 1955 catalogue. The style has also been discussed by Patrick de Winter, who invents the term "style Graal" for much of vernacular illustration in northern France, including these volumes and many others. I disagree with his breakdown of stylistic groups and I also find the term "style Graal" misleading

in that Arthurian, and vernacular texts in general, invariably consititute only a part of the output of artists who, in every case, can be shown to have worked on devotional and liturgical books as well. See Patrick M. de Winter, *La Bibliothèque de Philippe le Hardi, duc de Bourgogne (1364–1404), étude sur les manuscrits à peintures d'une collection princière à l'époque du style gothique international* (Paris: CNRS, 1985).

126. L. Destrée, "Le psautier de Gui de Dampierre," *Messager des sciences historiques de Belgique,* 64 (1890), 377–90 and 65 (1891), 81–88, 129–32; Vitzthum, p. 138, grouped it with Brussels, BR 11220–21 (2320); Camille Gaspar and Frédéric Lyna, *Les principaux manuscrits à peintures de la Bibliothèque royale de Belgique,* 2 vols. (Paris: Bulletin de la Société française pour la reproduction de manuscrits à peintures, 1937), I, no. 95, pp. 219–28, dated it between 1280 and 1297 because of the absence of the arms of Margaret, countess of Flanders, d. 1280, and because Jean de Dampierre adopted a *bend gu* in 1297, not shown on his shield in the manuscript, and also because the canonization of St. Louis in 1297 is not commemorated in the calendar; these dates have been challenged by L. Stijns, "Het Psalter von Gwijde van Dampierre," *De Vlaamse Gids* (1953), 85–94, on the grounds that the shields shown in the borders include that of Jean de Namur on f. 8v (b. 1266) and that of Baudouin (d. 1275) on f. 7v, to give a date of between 1266 and 1275. This is what has been accepted by all subsequent writers such as L. M. Delaissé in *Miniatures médiévales* (Geneva: Deux-Mondes, 1959), no. 9, p. 50, who dates it c. 1270; Kerstin Carlvant, *Thirteenth-Century Illumination in Bruges and Ghent* (Ph.D. diss., Columbia Univ., 1978), p. 7; and de Winter, p. 72; and I myself thought that c. 1275 is a fairly reasonable date for the book: "Arthur's Death," p. 85, n. 51. But an examination of the manuscript with Pierre Cockshaw in 1990 convinced me that the present state of the shields is such, because of overpainting, that they cannot be the basis for a dating argument. In view of this, Stijns's arguments, and equally those of Gaspar and Lyna, rest on thin ground; c. 1275–1285 could well be the best compromise position, and would have the advantage that it would allow a link between BR 10607 and the books associated with BN, fr. 412 and BN, fr. 15106, both dated 1285.

127. Carlvant, pp. 68, 73, and *De Vlaamse Kunst Op Perkament,* ed. W. LeLoup, Bruges: Gruuthusemuseum, 1981, no. 80. Other additions to the group are mentioned on p. 68: a psalter published in H. P. Kraus, *Catalogue 77,* no. 88, which Carlvant compares to Bruges, Stadtbibl. 373, a canon law book written in 1283 in Bruges; Berkeley UCB 28, a psalter-hours; and a manuscript in Aschaffenburg, reproduced in J. Merkel, *Die Miniaturen und Manuscripte der Königlich Bayerischen Hofbibliothek in Aschaffenburg* (Aschaffenburg, 1883), pl. X, to which should now be added Josef Hofmann and Hans Thurn, *Die Handschriften der Hofbibliothek Aschaffenburg* (Aschaffenburg, 1978), MS 5, pp. 12–16. Several further psalters have passed through sale rooms: Drouot, 17. vi. 60, lot 2; Danon 21. iii.73, lot 13; Sotheby's 4. vi. 74, lot 2916; Drouot, 1980; Sotheby's 7. xii. 82, lot 44; Sotheby's 7. xii. 92, lot 50. London, BL, Add. 24681, 29407; Paris, BN, lat.

1394, BN, n.a.lat. 406 (before 1297); BN, n. a. fr. 6245; Oporto 623, should be added in one way or another; I reserve them and a few others for more detailed treatment elsewhere.

128. A psalter with a calendar adapted for the use of the Chartreuse of Val-Ste-Aldegonde near Saint-Omer, would appear to be another member of this group; it passed through Sotheby's on 7.xi.82 as lot 44.

129. On Guy de Dampierre's children, see T. Luykx, "Rond het eerste huwelijk en de daaruit gesproten kinderen van Gwijde van Dampierre," in *Oudheidkundige Kring van het Land van Dendermonde, Gedenkschriften*, 3 s., II (Dendermonde: van Lantschoot-van Criekinge, 1946), pp.161–79, and id., *Het grafelijk geslacht Dampierre en zijn strijd tegen Filips de Schone* (Leuven, n.d.). Luykx notes that Guillaume was given the lands and title of Crèvecoeur upon his marriage in 1286 to Alix, daughter of Raoul de Clermont, seigneur de Nesle and connétable de France, also a book collector, see below (Raoul's second wife was Isabelle, daughter of Jean d'Avesnes, count of Hainaut, and Philippine de Luxembourg). If BN, fr. 95 and Yale 229 were made for Guillaume de Termonde in the 1290s as I think was most likely the case on stylistic grounds, it is curious that the arms of Alix de Clermont-Nesle do not also appear in the book; possibly this adds weight to the idea that he might have commissioned it for his children. That would also help to explain the de-emphasis on amorous encounters in the illustrations, discussed above.

130. "Secular Manuscript Illumination," 87. Guillaume is a more attractive candidate for this book than his brother Jean de Namur, who may also have borne the arms of Flanders *a bend gu.* Guillaume is also known for a literary commission, of *La noble chevalerie de Judas Machabé et de ses nobles frères*, extant in one copy, BN, fr. 15104, ed. J. R. Smeets, *La noble chevalerie de Judas Macabé et de ses nobles frères* (Assen: van Gorcum, 1965); and another book in which his shield and that of his wife, Alix de Clermont-Nesle, appear is the Tournai Cathedral psalter Scaldis H 12/2, on which see L. Fourez, "Le psautier de Louis le Hutin," in *Revue belge d'archéologie et d'histoire de l'art*, 15 (1945), 101–15 and Stones, *The Illustrations*, pp. 483–4. The identification of Guillaume's arms is based on WN 1235, ed. Paul Adam-Even and Léon Jéquier, "Un armorial français du XIIIᵉ siècle, L'armorial Wijnbergen," *Archives héraldiques suisses* 65 (1951), 49–62, 101–110; 66 (1952), 28–68, 103–111; 68 (1954), 55–80. But see also WN 1236 and the discussion of Jean de Namur's arms in my "Stylistic Associations: Evolution and Collaboration: Charting the Bule Painter's Career," *The Journal of the J. Paul Getty Museum* 23, 1995, pp. 11–29 at p. 25. The starting-point for heraldic invesigations is now Léon Jéquier, "Tables héraldiques de dix-neuf armoriaux du Moyen Age," in *Cahiers d'héraldique*, 1 (Paris: CNRS, nd), XXXVI-XLII, 1–147. The arms *or a lion sa a bend gu* surface again on the dead knight in the added section in the Bute Psalter, now J. Paul Getty Museum 46 (92.MK.92), but this miniature must date in the early fourteenth century and is more likely to show a member of the house of Juliers (Jülich) than a member of the house of Flanders, see Stones, "Stylistic Associations," p. 25.

131. For more on early Arthurian heraldry see my "Les débuts de l'héraldique dans les romans arthuriens," presented at the Colloque "Les Armoriaux" in Paris in 1994 and forthcoming.

132. BN, fr. 95: ff. 78, 249v, 268v (the latter with a cream-colored ground rather than gold); Yale 229: ff. 23v, 66 (on a cream-colored ground), 100v, 126, 260v (? on a plain parchment ground).

133. Yale 229, f. 260v.

134. For references and caveats, see note 126.

135. This one I think has been overpainted. The shield noted by Shailor on f. 15v as *or a bend cottised gules* I read as brown *a bend cottised* maroon; and it occurs in the miniature as the shield of Guinas, defeated by Gaheriet, and unlikely therefore to be intended as historical.

136. For Wijnberghen (WN) see note 131; Chifflet Prinet (CP): M. Prinet, "Armorial de France composé à la fin du XIIIe siècle ou au commencement du XIVᵉ siècle," *Le Moyen Age* (1920), 3–49; Ost de Flandre (OF): Paul Adam-Even, "Rôle d'armes de l'ost de Flandre (Juin 1297)," *Archives héraldiques suisses*, 73 (1959), 2–7. The other important rolls listed in Jéquier are less pertinent in date and provenance.

137. I thank Robert-Henri Bautier and Janine Sornay for helpful discussion of the sources. Much of what follows is based on my early analysis in "The Illustrations," ch. 1, supplemented by first-hand examination of the documents in Ghent, Mons and Lille. For the sources, see particularly Chrétien Dehaisnes, *Documents et extraits divers concernant l'histoire de l'art dans la Flandre, l'Artois et le Hainaut avant le XVᵉ siècle,* 2 vols. (Lille: Danel, 1886), I, pp. 170: Rijksarchief, Ghent, inv. Gaillard 746; it includes, in addition to "i espectacle pour lire bordé de laiton," a chess book, a Chronicles of Flanders, a *Vie des pères,* a book of Saints Peter and Paul and Simon Magus, and a *Miracles of Our Lady.* Other references to the making of books for Guy de Dampierre are the payment in 1270 "a maistre Gilon de Bruges, pour un missel et un troper acate xxii l x s" (Dehaisnes, p. 63, RA Ghent, inv. Gaillard 3); the reference to a payment in the period 1270–1275 to "Bauduin, l'enlumineur pour r...ans 12 lb; paie 6 lb. par le frere P(ieron)" cited in J. Buntinx, *Het memoriaal van Jehan Makiel, klerk en ontvanger van Gwijde van Dampierre* (Brussels: Commission royale d'histoire, 1944), p. 101 (RA Ghent, Raad van Vlanderen no. 8731, among the earliest known documents on paper [p. xi]); and the payment "Pour aler a Male pour 1 escrivent, ke me dame de Namur avoit mandé a Lille pour son breviaire escrire 3 s. " on 25 May, 1273 (Buntinx, p. 143; Dehaisnes, p. 66, with the variant reading "par" for "pour"). Lists of the surviving accounts of Guy de Dampierre, his successor Robert de Béthune (1305–1322) and their wives and children, mostly in the Archives de l'État in Ghent, are given in R.-H. Bautier and J. Sornay, with F. Muret, *Les sources de l'histoire économique et sociale du Moyen Age, II, Les États de la maison de Bourgogne, I, Archives des principautés territoriales, 2. Les principautés du Nord* (Paris: CNRS, 1984), pp. 58–64. My examination of the documents revealed that several of those listed were destroyed in the Second World War: notably inv. Gaillard 31, 32, 40, 42, 45, 46, 55, 59. The sources that survive

include several payments for parchment and for writing, noting, and binding liturgical books for the chapel c. 1276–1279 according to Dehaisnes, or 1299 according to Bautier et al. (inv. Gaillard 24, 27, 29, cited in part by Dehaisnes, pp. 70–72); chapel books comprising a missel, a breviary in two parts, a gradual, a troper, are listed in inv. Saint-Genois 1056; and among the possessions of Mlle de Brabant towards the end of the thirteenth century listed in inv. Wyffels 281 are a breviary, a psalter, a book of hours, a diurnal and an epistolary; no mention of romances. This reference to a psalter is the only mention of anything that might correspond to the so-called psalter of Guy de Dampierre, BR 10607; but see note 126 for the problems of the book's heraldry.

138. Dehaisnes, p. 156 (Mons, Archives de l'État, Cartulaire de la Trésorerie des Comtes de Hainaut, cart. 19, f. 117v-122, ed. in part by M. Devillers, "Extrait d'un Cartulaire de la Trésorerie des Comtes de Hainaut (fol. 117v)," in *Bulletin de la Commission royale d'histoire de Belgique*, 3e sér., XII [1871], 447–57.)

139. See "The Earliest."

140. Similarly imprecise are the references in the general evaluation of the romances in the possession of Philippine de Luxembourg, countess of Hainaut, at her death in 1311, to the value of ii cxxv lb; they had been purchased by her deceased husband Jean d'Avesnes. The same document has another general entry "Pour XIX pieches de rommans" (no specified value) (Dehaisnes, p. 195, AE Mons, Trés. cart. 19, ff. 172–176; general outline of the contents of the document in Bautier et al., pp. 530–31, 563).

141. Dehaisnes, pp. 238–48, Lille, Archives départementales du Nord, Fonds de la Chambre des comptes B 278 (no. 5475), general description in M. Bruchet, *Inventaire sommaire Série B* (Chambre des Comptes de Lille) (Lille: 1931).

142. Stones, *The Illustrations*, p. 127. The list appears to be otherwise unpublished. I deciphered it (with difficulty) as "premierement sergant (?) et puis maregnos (?) et puis ii..de..trosses (?) et puis Anseiz de Cartagie et puis Auberi le Bourgainginon et puis Lanselot du Lac et puis le Lehoiranc (Loherain?) Guerrier et puis les x commandeman de la foi et puis le Chevalier qui ala an anfer et puis Partenopre de Blois." The manuscript dates around the middle to third quarter of the thirteenth century, and the list would seem to have been added by another hand in the late thirteenth or early fourteenth century.

143. Dehaisnes, p. 235 and Jules-Marie Richard, *Une petite-nièce de saint Louis, Mahaut, comtesse d'Artois et de Bourgogne* (Paris: Champion, 1887), pp. 99–106. The libraries of other prominent book-collectors like Margaret, queen of Jerusalem and Sicily and countess of Tonnerre, Robert de Nesle, connétable de France and father-in-law of Guillaume de Termonde, and Godefroi, seigneur de Naste and Oosterzeele, seem also not to have owned copies of the prose *Lancelot* (Dehaisnes, pp. 135–49, 166, 319–20).

144. For Gérard Mulet, documents of 1272 and 1287, see Dehaisnes, p. 65; for Marguerite Baudaine, wills of 1274 and 1320 which include a "rouman," p. 67.

145. I have referred to it in "Another Short Note," p. 191, citing A. de la Grange, "Choix de testaments tournaisiens antérieurs au XVIe siècle," in *Annales de la Société historique de Tournai* 2 (1897), 1–365, at pp. 35, 36, 37–38, 39, 41, 43, 45, 47, 48. I found among the documents at the RA, Ghent, a reference in inv. Gaillard 24, dated 10.iii-28.ix, 1279, to a payment by Madame de Namur (Isabelle de Luxembourg, second wife of Guy de Dampierre) to a lady named Cole: "Adont a dame Cole sour son livre preste x s." This offers an interesting insight into the circulation of books. The payment does not indicate where Dame Cole lived, but Tournai is in the county of Flanders, so one is tempted to assume the lady was related to Jean Cole and that the book borrowed by the countess of Flanders might therefore have been one of his romances.

a lesauer. Beaus amis. va si ma
pareille vn cheual. Sire dist il q̃ feries
vous de cheual. ia faues voz q̃ la voie
du tertre est si anuerse quil na el mon
de cheual qui monter ypuist. Et q̃nt
voz venistes au pie du tertre vous lais
sastes vo cheual ou voz le trouerois sa
chies de voir. or te comant dont a dieu
fait lanc. Lors sen part lanc. delaueus
t auale le tertre. t vait tant quil vint
a larbre ou il auoit laisse son cheual
si le trouue t li oste le frein t la sele t
le laisse vn petit paistre t puis li remist
la sele t le frein t remonte sus. si sa che
mine vers la forest perilleuse. Si lais
se ore li contes aparler de lui t retorne
aparler des compaignons q̃ sont ou ti
tre deuec.

Or dist li contes que q̃nt li com
paignon furent au matin leue.
t il ne trouerent lanc. si enfu
rent mout corrouce. Ches q̃nt il vire
q̃ autrement ne por estre. Si deman
derent gens du pais dluee entour si
sont atorner la voie du tertre q̃ on
ipuet bien aler a pie t a cheual. Et
q̃nt honel qui en labere guoit mala
des oi ceste nouele q̃ li tertres estoit co

nus si estu mout lies. t dist q̃ ore
ne seent nul maladie quil ait eue. Si
se vest au mieux quil pot t saparella
t sen ala tout droit au tertre la ou il
troua tous ses compaignons de la que
ste. Et q̃nt il le virent. si li furent mb
grnt iote. mais il ne trona mie lancl.
Si en fu mour corrouces t tout li com
paignon. Si demanda ou il estoit ales.
t il li rendient teux noueles com il en
sauoient. Et q̃nt il vit quil ni perdroit
plus si sen conforta au plus bel quil
pot t dist a ses compaignons quil ne
sesmaraissent mie de lui. car il na gra
de se diex plaist en lui ou il viegne. car
nus ne li puet fosfaire darmes sil nest
soupris par traison. Ensi sen reconfor
terent li compaignon t demeurent laiens
en tel maniere. t dient quil larendront
tant quil reuendra. Si laisse ore li con
tes aparler daus tous t retorne a lanc.

Or dist li contes que q̃nt lanc.
fu entres en la forest perilleuse
t il eut tant cheuauchie q̃ la
nus fu passee t li solaus leues. Si en
contra vn nain qui cheuauchoit vn pale
froi sile salue. t li nains li demande
ou il vait. Et lanc. li dist quil vait q̃

Fig. 8.1. Yale 229, f. 110v.
Reproduced by permission.

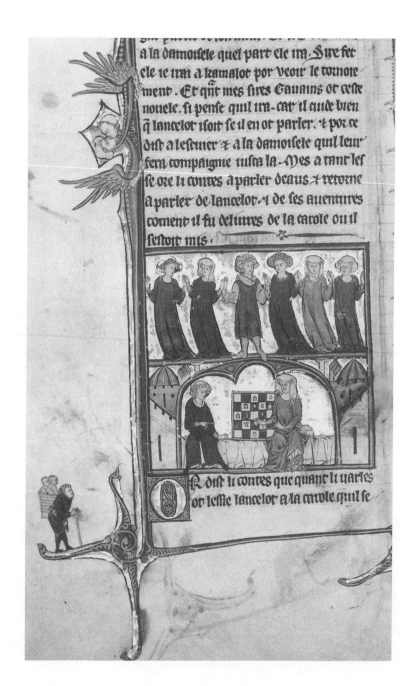

a la damoisele quel part ele ira. Sire fet
ele ie irai a kamalot por veoir le tornoie
ment. Et qūt mes sires Gauains ot ceste
nouele. si pense quil ira. car il auide bien
q̄ lancelot isoit se il en ot parler. ⁊ por ce
dist a lescuier ⁊ a la damoisele quil leur
fera compaignie iusta la. Mes a tant les
se ore li contes a parler deaus ⁊ retorne
a parler de lancelot. ⁊ de ses auentures
coment il fu deliures de la carole ou il
sestoit mis.

O R dist li contes que quant li uarles
ot lessie lancelot a la carole qiul se

Fig. 8.2. Yale 229, f. 66v.
Reproduced by permission.

Fig. 8.3. London, BL, Roy. 20. D. iv, f. 237v.
Reproduced by permission.

Fig. 8.4. Paris, BN, fr. 122, f. 137v.
Reproduced by permission.

Top. Fig. 8.5. Florence, Laur. Ash. 121 (48), f. 53.

Center. Fig. 8.6. London, BL, Add. 10293, f. 301.

Bottom. Fig. 8.7. Manchester, Ryl. Fr. 1, f. 69.

Reproduced by permission.

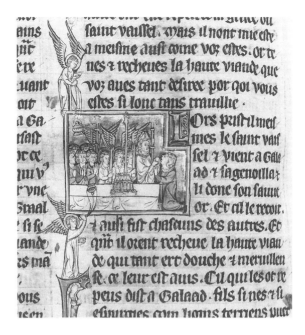

Fig. 8.8. Yale 229, f. 269v.
Reproduced by permission.

Fig. 8.9. Florence, Laur. Ash. 121 (58), f. 86v.
Reproduced by permission.

Fig. 8.10. Yale 229, f. 267v.
Reproduced by permission.

Fig. 8.11. Florence, BN, Pal. lat. 556, f. 148.
Reproduced by permission.

Fig. 8.12. Florence, BN, Pal. lat. 556, f. 148v.
Reproduced by permission.

Fig. 8.13. Carpentras,
BI 59, f. 84.
Reproduced by permission.

Fig. 8.14. Beaune,
BM 60, f. 26v.
Reproduced by permission.

Top. Fig. 8.15. Paris, BN, fr. 95, f. 18.

Bottom left. Fig. 8.16. Paris, BN, fr. 95, f. 1.

Bottom right. Fig. 8.17. Rennes, BM 255, f. 76v.

Reproduced by permission.

le. ẽuais chelui dott la mains estoit ne
vit il mie. Chu   canta tosephuse mes
se. t mist son   pere hore du tã
bernade

Fig. 8.18. Amsterdam, BPH 1, f. 18.
Reproduced by permission.

Car qui usera mon cors t buuera mon lãc.

Fig. 8.19. Amsterdam, BPH 1, f. 21.
Reproduced by permission.

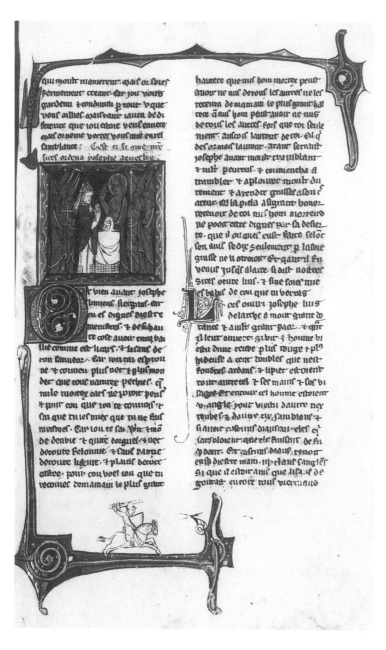

Fig. 8.20. Le Mans, MM Louis Aragon 334, f. 30.
Reproduced by permission.

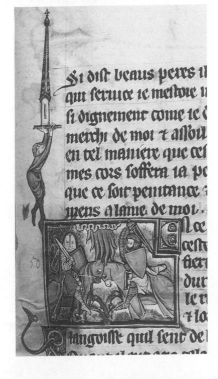

Top.
Fig. 8.21. Baltimore, Walters,
W 90, f. 151.

Center.
Fig. 8.22. Marseille, BM,
111, f. 61v.

Bottom right.
Fig. 8.23. Yale 229, f. 248.

Reproduced by permission.

mout lies qͤt il oi ceſte nouele.
Mais a tant laiſſe oie li contes a
parler du meſſage ⁊ ſen retorne au
roi artus ⁊ a ſa compaigne.

Or dist li contes que qͤt li
Rois artus et ſis en tor la
cite de Gaunes entor·ij·
vois. ſi come li contes nos a ferme
vraiement. Si ſe reconut mout treſ
bien que ou ſiege nauroit il ia niu
le honor en toute ſa vie. car cil de
dens ſe defendoient ſi tres bien·⁊

eſgardes que nos enp
ques. car ie vos di bie
nos wortons aſſes pl
que gaaignier a ce qͤ
terres ⁊ entre lor am
aus vone chie a mou
Et ſi ſachies tout vn
nues Gau·fait donq
car ſe il nos haiſſent
noʒ haons aus·nos
le tout perou a ce qͤ
de mout gͤt pooir ⁊
⁊ de mout gͤt chie·
ques que nos ferons
ſur fait mes ſires G
ſeillerai a mot meſm
en ſauru a reſpondr
demain.

Celui ior fu
penſis de gͤ
ne ſoloit ⁊ a
uant. Et qͤt il or t
pela vn de ſes valles
ten va mout toſt la

Fig. 8.24. Yale 229, f. 333.
Reproduced by permission.

Fig. 8.25. Marseille, BM 111, f. 139.
Reproduced by permission.

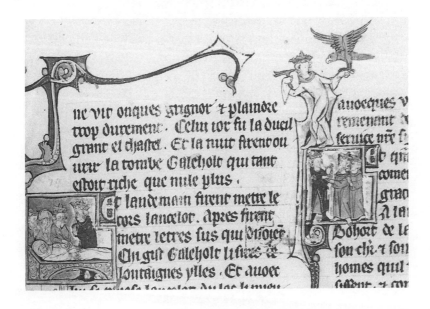

Fig. 8.26. Yale 229, f. 363.
Reproduced by permission.

enuoies · iiij · batailles
aes
t qut li rois
qui deuan
les uit ven
mes · ore
batailles
en sele · Et illi dient qui
a lassembler veissies lan
abatre si durement que
est conuers · Mais qut l
quil furent si hastinemet
uerent tel ciriie que mill

Fig. 8.27. Yale 229, f. 164.
Reproduced by permission.

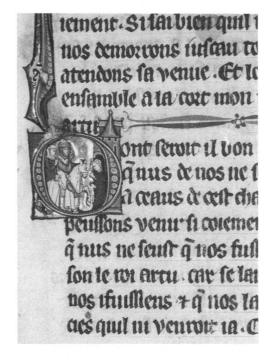

ternent · Si sai bien quil i
nos demorrons tusctau to
atendons sa venue · Et le
ensamble a la cort mon
Artu
ont seroit il bon
q nus de nos ne s
i ceaus d cest che
peussons uenir si coiemet
q nus ne seust q nos fus
son le roi Artu · car se lai
nos isuissiens + q nos la
aes quil ni uenroit ia · C

Fig. 8.28. Yale 229, f. 123.
Reproduced by permission.

Fig. 8.29. Yale 229, f. 14.
Reproduced by permission.

Fig. 8.30. Brussels,
BR 10607, f. 7v.
Reproduced by permission.

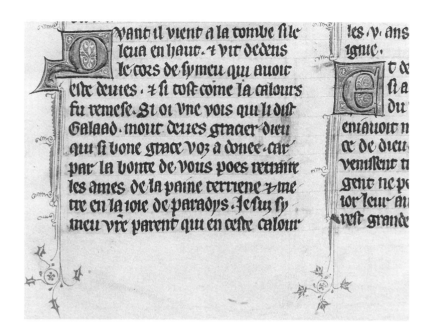

Fig. 8.31. Yale 229, f. 268.
Reproduced by permission.

Fig. 8.32. Marseille, BM 111, f. 19v.
Reproduced by permission.

Fig. 8.33. Bruges, GS 45/144, f. 2.
Reproduced by permission.

Fig. 8.34. Florence,
Laur. Ash. 125, f. 1.
Reproduced by permission.

Fig. 8.35. Florence,
Laur. Ash. 125, f. 16 (31).
Reproduced by permission.

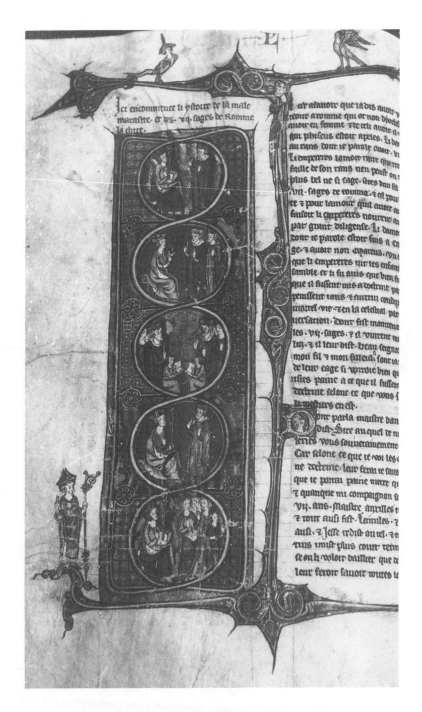

Ict encoumence li ystoire te la male
marastre. er les. vij. sages te Romme
la cite.

est asavoir que la dis avoir v
tour a romme qui or non dyoclc
avoir eu femme ree teu avoie c
qui phiseus estoit apxcis. la de
au rans dont te parole avoir. vi
Le emperetes lamoir tant que tre
saule te son rans tien peust on
plus bel ne si sage. Ares dan su
vij. sages te romma. a est pou
te z pour lamour quil avoir a
sanoit li empereirs nourru ar
par grant diligense. Li damo
tout te parole estour suis a ca
ge. z avoir non chartus. ont
que li empereirs vir les enfan
sanble er li su avis que bien su
que il sussent mis a tochine z
preussent tans z autru condy
morrel vie zen la celestal par
uerrarion. dont sist mamena
les. vij. sages. z il vinreur m
luj. z il leur dist. treau seigne
mou sil z mon suleul. sont ra
te leur eage si uproie bien qu
usties paine a ce que il sussen
tochrine selone te que vous s
le mestiers en est.

dont parla maistre van
dit. Sire au quel de n
leries vous souveraineme
Car selone ce que te voi les c
ne tochrine. leur seroit te sano
que te porrai paine mitre qu
z quanque mi compaignon s
vij. ans. maistre anrilles v
z tout aussi sist. Lemiles. z
aussi. z Jesse rodist au tel. zn
ruis imist plus cour retin
se on li volott bailler que a
leur seroir savoir routes te

Fig. 8.36. Florence, Laur. Ash. 125, f. 136v (155v).
Reproduced by permission.

Fig. 8.37. Paris, BN, fr. 2754, f. 1.
Reproduced by permission.

Fig. 8.38. Paris, BN, fr. 2754, f. 21v.
Reproduced by permission.

Fig. 8.39. Lille, Musée SA 367 (folios unnumbered).
Reproduced by permission.

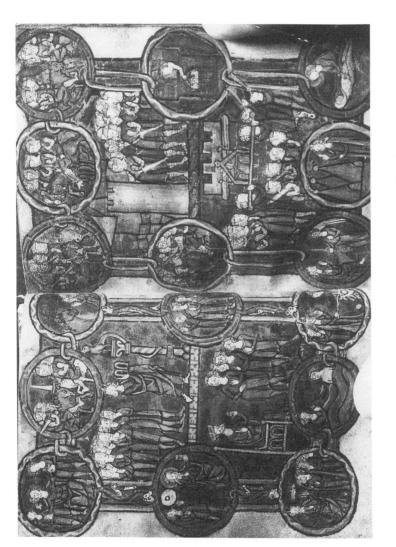

Fig. 8.40. Lille. Musée SA 367 (folios unnumbered). Reproduced by permission.

9 DISCURSIVE ILLUSTRATIONS IN THREE TRISTAN MANUSCRIPTS

Stephanie Cain Van D'Elden

The story of Tristan and Isolde was one of the most popular in the Middle Ages. Resonances of it appear in other narratives, in poetry, and especially in art.[1] In this essay I will examine three manuscripts (now located in Munich and Cologne) with illustrations of the verse *Tristan*, that is, versions of the story in the tradition of Eilhart von Oberge (between 1170–1190), Thomas d'Angleterre (around 1175), Béroul (between 1176 and 1202), Gottfried von Strassburg (about 1210), and his continuators Ulrich von Türheim (1235) and Heinrich von Freiberg (1290) as well as Brother Robert's Norse saga (1226) and the English verse *Sir Tristrem* (late thirteenth century).

On the surface these manuscripts look dissimilar; they present the story of Tristan and Isolde in quite distinct formats, possibly for different reasons. In each case, however, the illustrations promote discourse with the viewer, and in some cases this discourse is not the same as that provided in the written text. Series of illustrations such as these provide the artist with an opportunity to engage in discourse with his viewer(s), to present his own version of the basic story or a different version, or to put an explicit slant on the story for moral or didactic or even entertainment purposes.

The Munich *Tristan* manuscript, Bayerische Staatsbibliothek Cgm. 51, contains the *Tristan* of Gottfried von Strassburg from around 1210 and the continuation composed by Ulrich von Türheim about 1235. The manuscript may have been copied in Strassburg between 1230 and 1240 under the auspices of Meister Hesse, a notary,[2] the illustrations conceived at a later date. In her dissertation Julia Walworth questions both the customary dating and the origin of the manuscript and its illustrations. Though her evidence tends to be negative without specific alternatives, she suggests that we might look towards the eastern Upper Rhine (Swabia and the Bodensee) and southern Bavaria rather than Strassburg, while maintaining a general dating of the 1240s to 1250s.[3] Of the 109 extant folios of the Munich manuscript, 15 are full page illustrations. The dimensions of the folios are approximately 23.5 × 16 cm. There are two to six scenes per page arranged in two to three horizontal registers[4] for a total of 84 to 118 scenes (depending upon how one counts them, since it is difficult to distinguish scene boundaries). Unlike most illuminated manuscripts, the illustrations are quite far removed from the corresponding text. Only in three instances is the picture leaf approximately in the middle of the text it covers. It appears that the scribe and illuminator were not working in close collaboration. In fact, the illuminators could have been using an entirely different text (*Vorlage*) or, perhaps, relying on their memory of an oral retelling of the story.[5] Between ff. 71 and 72, at least eight leaves (one quire) are missing with lines 11599–13574[6]; these leaves probably included one leaf of illustrations, including the important love potion scene. And between text ff. 100 and 102 lines 461–2584[7] (i.e., more than half of Ulrich's continuation) are missing; f. 101r shows illustrations for which there is no text. Since illustrations pertaining to parts of the text are missing, it may be assumed that they were lost at a very early state.

The illustrations were rendered in a delicate pen and wash technique with vividly colored backgrounds and designed with space for inscriptions. Art historians, such as Paul Gichtel and Bettina Falkenberg,[8] for example, deplore the lack of talent displayed by the artists after the first three folios.[9] The inscriptions are in several different hands, none of which are those of the scribes of the text. There is annotation in the form of names, animals, or subjects or four lines in rhyme pairs in German or in Latin. The text of the annotations does not match Gottfried, Ulrich, or the earlier Eilhart von Oberge. Nor does there seem to be a connection between the illuminators and the writer of the inscriptions.

The importance of the church and the court are emphasized throughout the cycle. For example, Tristan does not receive his sword from King Mark as in Gottfried's lengthy description, but rather from a priest, indicating the prominence of the church (f. 30r, lower register; fig. 9.1). Jörg Hucklenbroich describes the cycle of Tristan receiving his sword from a priest, then Tristan about to mount his horse (a scene that would make more sense at the conclusion of the sequence), and finally Tristan receiving his shield from Mark as cinematographically united. The progression of the series of 45° turns by Tristan emphasizes to the viewer the continuity of action.[10] Mark is frequently portrayed in his role as judge sitting with crossed legs on his throne. During the ordeal episode (f. 82r; fig. 9.2), for example, Mark sits on his throne consulting his ecclesiastical advisors (middle register). In the next scene (bottom register) Isolde seems to be agreeing to the trial. After being rescued by Tristan disguised as a pilgrim (f. 82v; fig. 9.3), she is shown swearing the oath facing Mark, his right hand in a speaking gesture with his outstretched index finger raised; her right hand is in the form of an oath gesture stretched upward; behind Mark stands the bishop with a book in his hand. In the next scene Isolde stands in front of the bishop, he with his arms stretched out before him, she with two fingers stretched out in an oath; the glowing iron is missing. Nevertheless, Friedrich Ranke[11] interpreted the scenes as depicting the proof that her hand was not burned by the glowing iron. (Interestingly, Gottfried does not mention the bishop's role in this episode.) More specifically, Isolde's clothing symbolizes the course of events: in the first scenes, in which we observe a contrite Isolde, she is wearing appropriately plain clothing, but in the final scene she wears a crown and a red robe as signs of her regained status.

According to Falkenberg the pictures are word illustrations[12] that reflect the abundance of details in the text. The choice of illustrations demonstrates an endeavor to comprehend not only the action of the plot but also psychological relationships between the characters. The artist's primary tools are gesture and demeanor. The first folios are divided into two registers and set the courtly atmosphere of the May festival at King Mark's court in which Riwalin and Blanchfleur fall in love.[13] Folio 7r (fig. 9.4) one of the most reproduced illustrations, features a cluster of youths in the center, several energetically gesturing and one dancing to the accompaniment of a viol player. On the left is the seated Riwalin, a falcon tied to his hand; on the right King Mark sits with his legs crossed holding a scepter in his right hand. In the lower register feasting maidens celebrate at a table on either side of a crowned woman, labeled "regina" (a later addition). No queen is mentioned in the text, and "blancheflur" is assigned to one of the maidens in the corner. Under the same billowing canopy Blanchfleur observes Riwalin for the first time (f. 7v; fig. 9.5) and hands him a note while he is participating in a tournament in the lower register. On the surface this scene is reminiscent of the miniature of Walther von Klingen in the Manesse manuscript. There is nothing in the text to indicate the gesture or objects of mourning found in this illustration. Behind Blanchefleur is a woman with her head in her left hand, holding in her right hand a veil (a symbol of widowhood) above Blanchefleur's head. Thus the first meeting of the lovers is marred by signs of death.[14] Next, in a frenzied battle Riwalin is pierced through his blue shield by an enemy spear (f. 10r; fig. 9.6). Blanchefleur hears about his presumed fatal wound from her "Meisterin" and, in the next scene, throws herself into Riwalin's arms while the "Meisterin" weeps in distress beside the two lovers. On the verso (f. 10v; fig. 9.7) Riwalin and Blanchefleur consummate their love beneath wildly moving covers. Upon the report of Duke Morgan coming into Riwalin's land, Blanchefleur faints, then discusses her plight (she is pregnant) with Riwalin, and he takes his leave from King Mark. The young couple sail to Parmenia in a crowded boat with Blanchefleur kneeling, her upraised arms around Riwalin and her eyes fixed languishingly on his (f. 11r; fig. 9.8). Hand in hand Riwalin and Blanchefluer greet Rual, who is recognizable by his steward's staff; in the lower register a tonsured priest marries them while their horses are waiting; and Blanchefleur rides sidesaddle along with Rual, labeled as "Foitenant," to Canoel for her protection. The verso (f. 11v; fig. 9.9) shows a mounted Duke Morgan delivering the fatal blow to Riwalin in a fierce battle in which both lances and swords are employed. The bottom register formally depicts the burial of Riwalin in the presence of clerics and weeping women. His body is lifted into a sarcophagus. On the top register of f. 15r (fig. 9.10) Blanchefleur, upon hearing of Riwalin's death, gives birth to Tristan and dies. Her sorrow and suffering are graphically portrayed in increasing intensity. The bottom register mirrors the top register, depicting Floraete simulating giving birth to Tristan. In the middle the burial of Blanchefleur corresponds to that of Riwalin; both burials resemble contemporary versions of the burial of Christ. The alternation of the deaths of Riwalin and Blanchefleur and the true and simulated birth of Tristan provide a visual harmony. Floraete carries Tristan to church for baptism (f. 15v; fig. 9.11). The center register is devoted to Tristan's courtly training, the intellectual pursuits symmetrically flanking the martial arts: Tristan learns to read from a huge book balanced on a three-legged stand with the words *Beatus Vir, Deus, Veni sancte Spiritus*; he throws a stone, an accomplishment not specifically mentioned by Gottfried although it is by Eilhart; he aims a spear; and he learns to play the harp. In the bottom register he is shown seated before the chessboard on the Norwegian ship. His abductors hold hawks on their wrists. One foster brother is shown just leaving the ship, another and his foster father stand on land; Curvenal, his tutor, remains on the ship. These are the first twenty-four scenes of the illustrative cycle.

While the illustrator omits many of the rich details of the written text, he elaborates on others not included in the text, such as the burial of Riwalin. According to Falkenberg, here the illustrator is complying with the expectations of the viewer.[15] In other words, the illustrator is more verbose than the poet. On many occasions the artist skillfully connects two scenes with speech bands (*Spruchbänder*) containing texts not found in Gottfried.[16] Thus the illustrations are suitable in their detail and clarity, serving as mnemonic devices for the viewer who is familiar with the text. The illustrations were drawn for the connoisseur of the written text, including of its theoretic excursions. The cycle seems therefore less an additional illustration of the romance than a replacement for those recipients who prefer the picture to the word,[17] a second discourse. In this sense it is entirely imaginable that the illustrated leaves were originally meant to stand on their own separated from the written text, not as a "illustrated book similar to comics"[18] (as Volker Schupp would have it), which would not presuppose any knowledge of the text, but rather more like a secularized Paupers' Bible.

A somewhat similar situation is involved in illustrations from a British Library manuscript. Recently, Tony Hunt has examined London, British Library, Add. 11619. The manuscript contains 277 folios, approximately 11 × 8 cm. According to Hunt it is "a monastic book designed for edification, combining religious and theological texts with didactic *exempla* such as the *Fables* of Aesop or the *Disciplina clericalis* of Petrus Alfonsi."[19] Hunt suggests that the manuscript must have been created at the beginning of the 14th century.[20] Folios 6r–9v consist of eight illustrations pertaining to the Tristan story, of varying quality and unaccompanied by a written text. The illustrations are located between two quires and are bound together as separate single leaves, though numbers 1–6 are sewn together. It appears that at least one leaf (possibly two) has been cut out after f. 9. Furthermore, at least one leaf was cut out of the book after it was bound. In addition, the pictures were probably originally on much larger folios.[21] Hunt believes that they were either part of the original manuscript or inserted at a very early stage.

There are eight scenes, one per folio side, pen drawings tinted in yellow, brown, green, blue, and red. The first probably depicts Tristan at King Mark's court following his first trip to Ireland and before he sets off to woo Isolde for Mark (f. 6r; fig. 9.12). Mark, bearded and crowned, is seated with legs crossed and dressed in green with a brown cape, two counselors standing at his side. Tristan, dressed in green with a hood, is accompanied by two bare-headed followers dressed in green and brown. The scene resembles a disputation between a monk (Tristan) and a Jew (one of the counselors wearing the typical pointed "Jew's hat"), a king mediating. The second scene portrays Tristan in the bath (f. 6v; fig. 9.13), his hands in praying fashion, threatened by Isolde, dressed in red, being restrained by Brangaene, dressed in green. The notch in the blade of Tristan's sword is clearly visable. This scene is followed by Tristan on horseback thrusting his spear through the dragon's gullet (f. 7r; fig. 9.14). The next scene (f. 7v; fig. 9.15) is more problematic: Hunt identifies it as Tristan attempting to regain his lands by beheading the seated unarmed Duke Morgan. According to Gottfried, Tristan attacks Morgan while hunting in the forest. In Bedier's reconstruction, however, Tristan kills Morgan in the main hall in the midst of his court after Morgan has struck him in the face. The only color in this illustration, aside from the pale green wash of Morgan's robe, is the bright red halo of blood gushing from his head and patches of red anger on Tristan's and his companions' faces. The trysting scene (f. 8r; fig. 9.16) shows a crowned Mark in the tree and a dwarf beneath the tree rather than a reflection in the water of both Mark and Melot. Isolde, dressed in red and blue, gestures to Tristan whose left hand is not drawn. Gottfried mentions an olive tree, Beroul a pine tree, and in this manuscript there seems to be a pear tree, colored green with ochre pears. Next follow two sketchy sea voyages (ff. 8v-9r; figs. 9.17 and 9.18). In both cases the composition is structured around a boat, two figures, with a mast forming a triangle. There is very little color except for the bright green sea in f. 9r. The final scene (f. 9v; fig. 9.19), hardly more than an uncolored sketch, possibly shows Tristan presenting Isolde to Mark after he has brought her from Ireland to be Mark's bride. The crowned, and here unbearded, Mark is seated with legs crossed in a similar position to the first scene.

Hunt was able to identify the subject matter of the folios from the two specific scenes, Tristan threatened in the bath and the trysting episode, combined with the dragon scene. We notice a certain symmetry, the first and last pictures depicting a court with a king, presumably King Mark. In between, the scenes represent the bride-winning as well as the trysting scene. This sequence is not particularly unusual; it also occurs in the Wienhausen I and II tapestries and the Erfurt tablecloth, which I have discussed in another forum.[22] The series begins and ends with Mark as king and judge (note again the crossed legs). The two specific scenes depict Tristan wooing Isolde for Mark and Tristan with Isolde deceiving Mark. The poorly executed ship scenes extend the symmetry. Ship scenes provide a visual structure in many of the Tristan cycles.

Hunt maintains that the Tristan illustrations were included in the generally didactic Add. 11619 "for their didactic value as a reminder of the negative element of the legend received as an exemplum."[23] Not surprisingly, this interpretation coincides with Hunt's concept of Thomas's *Tristan*, written in the milieu of court politics surrounding Henry II of England and his wife Eleanor of Aquitaine in the 1170s. Hunt suggests that Thomas wrote as a "response to a situation in which (1) Henry had both a mistress and a wife, (2) his wife became jealous and, further, betrayed him, and (3) the mistress died (according to legend at the hands of his wife)." Thus, according to Hunt, *fin 'amor* (*minne*, or courtly love) was as uninteresting to Thomas as it was to Eleanor. Hunt considers Thomas, the inspiration for these illustrations, "a moralist who shows all his protagonists behaving dishonourably under the influence of passion, when they are not plunged in gloom. So far as the lovers are concerned, it is not *fin 'amor* but *thanatos* which dominates this poem. It is therefore right . . . to contend that Thomas's poem is a pessimistic account of the vicissitudes of purely human love in the perspective of traditional Christian morality. . . ."[24]

Douglas Kelly, on the other hand, surmises that a preacher may have used the diverse exemplary material in this manuscript to help him prepare sermons. Kelly points out the circularity of Hunt's argument: "There is nothing in the illustrations that suggests any kind of reading for or against the lovers and their love (or that they even refer to Thomas's version of the legend)."[25]

It is not clear whether the illustrations were designed to be interleaved in a text (such as in Munich, BSB, Cgm. 51) or, perhaps, to stand alone. The scenes as we have them presented today in BL, Add. 11619 are not significant individually, but collectively they invoke the entire story of Tristan and Isolde, a negative exemplum based on Thomas's *Tristan*, according to Hunt's interpretation. The viewer of the illustrations or the teller of the story based on the illustrations could, of course, choose to tell it differently. I disagree with Hunt's neat explanation of a negative exemplum placed fortuitously near the beginning of a compilation of didactic works. First, the story is too sensually tantalizing to be used as such a pessimistic moral. And, secondly, the medieval audience tended to concentrate on the love story (here Tristan winning a bride for Mark) and forget the negative (such as adultery and deceit) details. And finally, even if the illustrations are based on Thomas, which is debatable, Thomas, in the spirit of Gottfried, may have wanted to portray a positive exemplum based on the virtues of faithfulness and constancy.

Thirdly, the Cologne manuscript, Stadt Historisches Archiv W 88, Perg. 8° (21 × 14.4 cm) from 1323 contains 263 pages, with Gottfried's *Tristan* and the continuation of Ulrich von Türheim. There are nine colored pen sketches drawn on a background of filigree scroll work, washed in either red or green, one column wide and ten lines high. The manuscript belonged to the treasury of Blankenheim castle in the Eifel, which was broken up and dispersed during the French Revolution. In 1815 it was acquired by Gerhard von Groote after whose death it was given over to the Cologne City Library, later the Cologne City Archive.

The illustrations begin with Tristan's birth (p. 22; fig. 9.20), Blanchfleur reclining on a bed, a female attendant handing baby Tristan to a male figure. Tristan plays a harp before King Mark (p. 47; fig. 9.21), crowned and seated, holding a scepter in his right hand. The duel between Tristan and Morolt is portrayed with the triumphant Tristan (wearing a boar on his tunic and shield) pursuing Morolt who seems to be attempting to mount his horse. Both men have swords in their hands (p. 89; fig. 9.22). Unlike the preceding illustrations that have red backgrounds, the scene showing Tristan killing the dragon (p. 112; fig. 9.23) is green with red accents such as the fire spurting out from the dragon's mouth and the tongue of his companion dog. The love potion scene (p. 142; fig. 9.24) depicts Tristan and Isolde in blue on a red background in a boat on a green sea, drinking from a huge vessel that looks as though it were modeled after the urine specimen bottles depicted so often in medieval medical manuscripts. Isolde offers the vessel to Tristan whose arm is very crudely drawn. The next illustration shows Tristan on horseback taking Isolde away from the standing Gandin who has kidnapped her (p. 164; fig. 9.25). Gandin in yellow is shown with his harp behind him. Tristan in blue and red armor has his arms around Isolde wearing a brown robe. The background is pale green. The next illustration shows an armored and visored Tristan pushing Urgan from the bridge (p. 199; fig. 9.26); both men are holding swords. A large standing Tristan is shown clubbing the false Pleherin (p. 257; fig. 9.27), who is on horseback wearing armor and a red tunic. The final illustration, again with a green background, depicts Tristan and Isolde lying in two graves with a rose bush and a grape vine growing out of their chests (p. 263; fig. 9.28). The grape vine has large green leaves, the rose bush flowers with bright red centers.

The Cologne manuscript contains approximately the same number of illustrations as the British Library manuscript. Here also, if the illustrations were isolated from the text, one would recognize them as Tristan from two specific scenes, the love potion scene and the grave scene with the grape bush and rose vine springing up from the couple's hearts. The scenes of Tristan with the dragon (which looks like a jolly winged sea monster accompanied by an equally jolly dog) and Tristan playing the harp support the identification but alone are insufficient for identification. There is a definite resemblance between the dragons in the British Library and Cologne manuscripts where Tristan, according to Gottfried's description, is shown thrusting his sword through the dragon's mouth and out his head; the Munich manuscript (f. 67r; fig. 9.29) portrays a similarly friendly dragon that sticks out its tongue to be cut off, thus specifically identifying the episode. There does not appear to be a particular political or moral motive for the choice of the scenes in the Cologne manuscript. Nor are we likely to be able to answer very satisfactorily why these particular scenes were chosen out of the many other possibilities. The generic scenes are easily recognizable by their placement within the written text. Isolated from the text, only the love potion and death scene are specific. The birth scene could be anyone's birth. And, indeed, Blanchfleur looks happy and healthy, certainly not about to expire. In comparison, in the

Munich manuscript (f. 15v; fig. 9.11) she is depicted sadly swooning. Tristan is further identified by the boar in his coat of arms in the combat scene with Morolt (p. 89; fig. 9.22), attributed to him and elaborated upon by Gottfried (see Marjodoc's dream, ll. 13,511–13,536). In the British Library manuscript, on the other hand, he is depicted wearing a green lion (the color is probably arbitrary since it is the primary color of the illustrations); the *Tristramssaga* and the Middle English poem, which were based on Thomas's version, state that Tristan bore a shield, "gules a lion rampant or,"[26] thus connecting Tristan to Henry II of England.

While the background of the Cologne illustrations, consisting of a series of circles, a sort of vine motif, is very decorative, there is at the same time definite narrative discourse. If they were isolated like the British Library illustrations, we would perhaps find an even better negative exemplum, beginning with Tristan's birth and concluding with Tristan's and Isolde's deaths. The two specific scenes, the love potion and the death scene, could be linked, the love potion leading inexorably to the death of the lovers. Certainly an exemplum! The Cologne manuscript concludes with the depiction of the two graves from which grow a rose and a grape vine, thus linking the two lovers even in death. But is this a glorious death or punishment for their sinful lives on earth? A positive or a negative exemplum? The same scene, while much drawn out, also appears in the Munich manuscript (f. 107v; fig. 9.30). Here the artist depicts the dying Tristan sending for Isolde who comes by ship; Isolde arrives at the church where she finds the already dead Tristan with Isolde Whitehands watching over him; she dies also; Mark brings the dead Tristan and Isolde by boat back to Cornwall; Tristan and Isolde are buried in a cloister, and Mark plants a rose bush and grape vine on their grave; and finally Mark builds a cloister for the two lovers, removes his crown, and enters as a monk.

To reiterate: the illustrations in the Munich manuscript do not stand next to the text they are portraying, but it is possible to follow the story based on rubrics and *Spruchbänder*; the illustrations in the British Library manuscript have no accompanying text, and only parts of the story can be established; and the miniatures in the Cologne manuscript are firmly attached to their text. Each of these illustrative cycles contains specific scenes that can be identified without relying on a written text. In addition, they all contain generic scenes only recognizable in context or, in the case of Munich, by rubrics. Because of their physical placement within the manuscript, we can say that the illustrations of the Munich manuscript and the British Library manuscript act as a second discourse between the viewer and the illustrations, based on the viewer's understanding or memory of the text. The designers conceived the illustrations as mnemonic devices for someone who knew the story very well and was prepared to retell it based on the pictures. If the Cologne illustrations were isolated from their written text, we could probably make the same assertion, for they too represent a retelling of the story independent of the written text. Since they are an integral part of the manuscript, it will be useful at another time to examine them again in conjunction with later manuscripts and incunabula, where there are many more intertextual illustrations. Nevertheless, the viewers of these three pictorial cycles could choose an interpretation based on their own understanding of the written text, their memory of a written text, or an oral retelling of the story; or they could rely on the discourse of the illustrations.

NOTES

1. Hella Frühmorgen-Voss, "Tristan und Isolde in mittelalterlichen Bildzeugnissen" and "Katalog der Tristan-Bildzeugnisse. zusammengestellt von Norbert H. Ott," in *Text und Illustration im Mittelalter: Aufsätze zu den Wechselbeziehungen zwischen Literatur und bildender Kunst* (Munich: Beck, 1975), pp. 119–39 and 140–81.

2. Friedrich Ranke, "Die Überlieferung von Gottfrieds Tristan," *ZfdA*, 55, NF 43 (1914), 157–278 and 381–438, esp. 405–17; *Tristan and Isold* (Munich: Bruckmann, 1925).

3. Julia Caroline Walworth, "The Illustrations of the Munich *Tristan* and *Willehalm von Orelns*: Bayerische Staatsbibliothek Cgm 51 and Cgm 63" (diss. Yale, 1991), pp. 270–75.

4. Walworth demonstrates how the "artists encourage the viewer to go from one scene to the next while at the same time maintaining the compositional integrity of the register and the page," pp. 10, 81–136.

5. The facsimile edition, Gottfried von Strassburg, *Tristan und Isolde. Mit der Fortsetzung Ulrichs von Türheim. Faksimile-Ausgabe des Cgm 51 der Bayerischen Staatsbibliothek München* (Stuttgart: Müller und Schindler, 1979), contains an essay by Ulrich Montag describing the contents and state of research (pp. 5–72) and an essay by Paul Gichtel describing the illustrations (pp. 73–144).

6. The line numbering is from Friedrich Ranke, Gottfried von Strassburg, *Tristan und Isold*, 14th ed. (Berlin: Weidman, 1969).

7. The line numbering is from Thomas Kerth, Ulrich von Türheim, *Tristan* (Tübingen: Niemeyer, 1979).

8. Bettina Falkenberg, *Die Bilder der Münchener Tristan-Handschrift* (Frankfurt am Main/Bern/New York: Lang, 1986).

9. Only Roger Sherman Loomis and Laura Hibbard Loomis, *Arthurian Legends in Medieval Art* (New York: MLA, 1938; rpt. New York: Kraus, 1975), p. 134, have the peculiar theory that the single artist became careless through hastiness: "The progressive coarsening of the first illustrator's style can be easily observed. He worked more and more rapidly, with increasing resort to the one- or two-figure type of scene, and in the figures themselves, increasingly careless of modeling or proportions, he continued to accent, almost to the point of caricature, the backward slant of the body, the fashionable protuberant stomach."

10. Jörg Hucklenbroich, "Einige Bemerkungen zum 'Münchener Tristan,'" in *Diversarum artium studia. Beiträge zu Kunstwissenschaft, Kunsttechnologie und ihren Randgebieten: Festschrift für Heinz Roosen-Runge zum 70. Geburtstag am 5. Oktober 1982* (Wiesbaden: Reichert, 1982), pp. 55–73; see pp. 72–73.

11. Ranke, *Tristan*, l. 1925, p. 281.

12. Falkenberg, pp. 178–79. See also Stephanie Cain Van D'Elden, "Reading Illustrations of Tristan" in *Literary Aspects of Courtly Culture*, ed. Donald Maddox and Sara Sturm-Maddox (London: Boydell and Brewer, 1994), pp. 347–55.

13. Hucklenbroich, pp. 57–58, points out the optimism of the early scenes and the absolute harmony between man and nature that is later repeated in the grotto episode.

14. Hucklenbroich, pp. 62–63.

15. Falkenberg, p. 179.

16. Falkenberg, pp. 172–77, gives a good description of how the *Spruchbänder* in the early folios neatly incorporate design and meaning.

17. Volker Schupp, "Kritische Anmerkungen zur Rezeption des deutschen Artusromans anhand von Hartmanns 'Iwein'. Theorie-Text-Bildmaterial," *Frühmittelalterliche Studien*, 9 (1975), 405–42, see p. 428: "der Zyklus . . . scheint . . . weniger zusätzliche Illustration des Romans zu sein, als dessen Ersatz für Rezipienten, die dem Bild den Vorzug vor dem Wort gaben."

18. Schupp, p. 29: "Der Bildteil des Münchener Tristan also ist, so könnte man dieses Nebenergebnis, das freilich noch abzusichern wäre, zusammenfassen, entweder das Musterbuch eines Malers bzw. die Kopie eines solchen oder ein textunabhängiges Bilderbuch, eine Art säkularisierte Armenbibel . . . ein selbständiges, Comics-ähnliches Bilderbuch . . . das seine Autarkie verloren hat."

19. Tony Hunt, "The Tristan Illustrations in MS London, BL, Add. 11619," in *Rewards and Punishments in the Arthurian Romances and Lyric Poetry of Mediaeval France. Essays Presented to Kenneth Varty on the Occasion of his Sixtieth Birthday*, ed. Peter V. Davies and Angus J. Kennedy (Cambridge: Brewer, 1987), pp. 45–60, see p. 51.

20. Hunt, "The Tristan Illustrations . . . ," p. 46.

21. Many thanks to Karen Pratt of Kings College, London, for her codicological research. She hypothesizes that there were eight illustrations per folio (i.e., four recto and four verso) and that these were cut up and inserted in BL, Add. 11619. Because of the obvious lacunae in the plot, it is difficult to determine in which direction the pictures were read, if there were four per folio side.

22. "You Can Tell It Is Tristan When . . . ," a paper delivered at the annual meeting of the Medieval Academy of America, Columbus, Ohio, 20 March 1992.

23. Hunt, "The Tristan Illustrations . . . ," p. 60.

24. Tony Hunt, "The Significance of Thomas's *Tristan*," *Reading Medieval Studies*, 7 (1981), 41–61, see p. 50.

25. Douglas Kelly, "*Fin' amor* in Thomas's *Tristan*," in *Studies in Honor of Hans-Erich Keller. Medieval French and Occitan Literature and Romance Linguistics*, ed. Rupert T. Pickens (Kalamazoo: Western Michigan Univ., 1993), pp. 167–80, esp. pp. 179–80.

26. Loomis, p. 47, figs. 43–44. See also Chertsey tiles, Elizabeth S. Eames, *Catalogue of Medieval Lead-glazed Earthenware Tiles in the Department of Medieval and Later Antiquities British Museum* (London: British Museum, 1980), 2 vols., pp. 141–71.

Fig. 9.1. Munich, BSB, Cgm. 51, f. 30r.
Reproduced by permission.

Fig. 9.2. Munich, BSB, Cgm. 51, f. 82r.
Reproduced by permission.

Fig. 9.3. Munich, BSB, Cgm. 51, f. 82v.
Reproduced by permission.

Fig. 9.4. Munich, BSB, Cgm. 51, f. 7r.
Reproduced by permission.

Fig. 9.5. Munich, BSB, Cgm. 51, f. 7v.
Reproduced by permission.

Fig. 9.6. Munich, BSB, Cgm. 51, f. 10r.
Reproduced by permission.

Fig. 9.7. Munich, BSB, Cgm. 51, f. 10v.
Reproduced by permission.

Fig. 9.8. Munich, BSB, Cgm. 51, f. 11r.
Reproduced by permission.

Fig. 9.9. Munich, BSB, Cgm. 51, f. 11v.
Reproduced by permission.

Fig. 9.10. Munich, BSB, Cgm. 51, f. 15r.
Reproduced by permission.

Fig. 9.11. Munich, BSB, Cgm. 51, f. 15v.
Reproduced by permission.

Fig. 9.12. London, BL, Add. 11619, f. 6r.
Reproduced by permission.

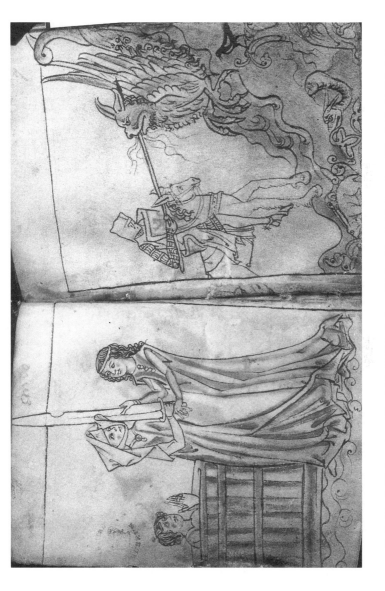

Left. Fig. 9.13. London, BL, Add. 11619, f. 6v.   *Right.* Fig. 9.14. London, BL, Add. 11619, f. 7r. Reproduced by permission.

Left. Fig. 9.15. London, BL, Add. 11619, f. 7v. *Right.* Fig. 9.16. London, BL, Add. 11619, f. 8r.
Reproduced by permission.

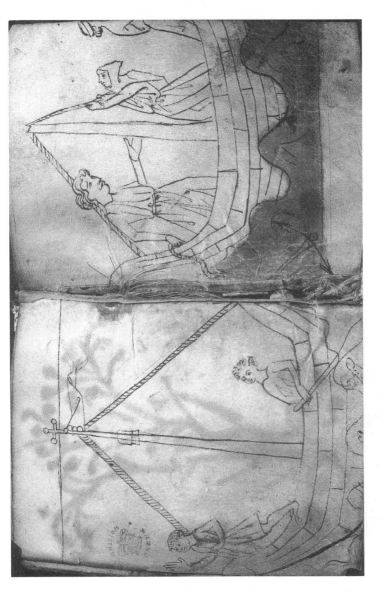

Left. Fig. 9.17. London, BL. Add. 11619, f. 8v.   *Right.* Fig. 9.18. London, BL, Add. 11619, f. 9r. Reproduced by permission.

Fig. 9.19. London, BL, Add. 11619, f. 9v.
Reproduced by permission.

Fig. 9.20. Cologne, Stadt Historisches Archiv *W 88, Perg. 8°, p. 22.
Reproduced by permission.

Fig. 9.21. Cologne, Stadt Historisches Archiv *W 88, Perg. 8°, p. 47.
Reproduced by permission.

Fig. 9.22. Cologne, Stadt Historisches Archiv *W 88, Perg. 8°, p. 89.
Reproduced by permission.

Fig. 9.23. Cologne, Stadt Historisches Archiv *W 88, Perg. 8°, p. 112.
Reproduced by permission.

Fig. 9.24. Cologne, Stadt Historisches Archiv *W 88, Perg. 8°, p. 142.
Reproduced by permission.

Fig. 9.25. Cologne, Stadt Historisches Archiv *W 88, Perg. 8°, p. 164.
Reproduced by permission.

Fig. 9.26. Cologne, Stadt Historisches Archiv *W 88, Perg. 8°, p. 199.
Reproduced by permission.

Fig. 9.27. Cologne, Stadt Historisches Archiv *W 88, Perg. 8°, p. 257.
Reproduced by permission.

Fig. 9.28. Cologne, Stadt Historisches Archiv *W 88, Perg. 8°, p. 263.
Reproduced by permission.

Fig. 9.29. Munich, BSB, Cgm. 51, f. 67r.
Reproduced by permission.

Fig. 9.30. Munich, BSB, Cmg. 51, f. 107v.
Reproduced by permission.

10 THE "ROI PESCHEOR" AND ICONOGRAPHIC IMPLICATIONS IN THE *CONTE DEL GRAAL*

Michèle Vauthier

All those who have turned their attention to the material used by Chrétien to elaborate the character of the Roi Pescheor at the Grail Castle have sought similarities in the cultural environment of the poet between details of the story and features pertaining to the world of his time. To accomplish this, they have followed diverse hermeneutic lines of inquiry.

Those such as Brown,[1] whose studies have led them to make phonetic comparisons, have been inclined to see in Nodens, the Breton king descendant of the god of the sea named Bran, also called Brion in certain later works like the Didot-*Perceval* and the Welsh bardic folktales of the Mabinogi, the prototype for this same Fisher King.

Visual comparisons have led to various conclusions. Among advocates of the Celtic theories, Jean Frappier[2] has identified the "prudhomme mehaignié" enthroned on a sick bed as an avatar of the sea gods Bran and Nuada of Welsh and Irish mythology. These gods "appear simultaneously as rich Fisher Kings and 'rois méhaigniés'"owning rich and powerful talismans of which the Grail would be the result of a romance transformation. W.A Nitze[3] establishes a relationship between the flame burning brightly in the center of the Grail Castle and that which burnt in the halls of Tara as it was recounted in the legends of Ireland. Following upon M. Coyabee and T.F. O'Rahilly, Jean Marx[4] feels tempted to see an affinity between all the "fishers" appearing in legends all over the world. In some of the Irish tales belonging to the hypothetical Ossian Cycle of Leinster for instance, the hero has to fish the Salmon of Knowledge to be endowed with prophetic vision; in one of the Iranian legends, the hero's grandfather is said to be waiting for his grandson with whom he is supposed to reign. Nitze strengthens the Celtic theory by suggesting a connection between two fires burning in the center of a fortress: one in the Castle of the Grail, the other one in the palace of Tara in the Irish legends.

A different approach is taken by Paule Le Rider,[5] who sees a relationship connecting the anglers who appear in Pope Gregory's legend recounted in the *Gesta Romanorum,* the fisher king associated with the Vandres, the Vandals, in a certain number of legends from Bourgogne, the Rhône Valley, the Parisian Basin and Gascony, and the anglers depicted in mosaic iconography. She especially singles out three special works: a miniature of the *Hortus Deliciarum*[6] showing God fishing in the Levant, the "Alton Towers" mosaic triptych enamel now in the Victoria and Albert Museum, and the stained glass of the ancient Châlons sur Marne cathedral showing the Crucifixion.[7]

Helen Adolf,[8] Urban T. Holmes, Sister Amelia Klenke[9] and Moses Gasper[10] follow the same analogical process to study the topography of places and liken the plan of the Castle of the Grail to that of Solomon's Temple in the Holy City. Following the same procedure, Martin de Ríquer[11] sees a connection between the meal offered to Perceval and the Jewish Passover liturgy.

Far from this means of study being imposed on the text, it follows from one of the methods Chrétien himself prescribes in his prologue. In fact, the essence of the introductory verses of the *Conte du Graal* is consecrated, as I have already indicated myself a number of times,[12] by comparison of an historic personage who has passed into legend (the emperor Alexander) and an actual character of the times (Philippe of Alsace), between an object that has become mythological (the Grail) and a man's inner personal adventure (the *metanoïa* of the count of Flanders), the transformation of a knight questing for human glory into a Christian knight whose heart finally becomes one with the God of Love "dwelling in God, and God in him" (l. 50)[13] to take the Johannine expression used by Chrétien (I John 3: 24, 4:16).

The poet's introductory discourse indicates the precise hermeneutic forms to be followed: metaphor in its widest sense— consisting of telling a real story (the life of Philippe of Alsace) in poetic form to create a fictional universe, a "conte" (l.63)—the "metaphora ex contrariis" in the Plotinian and Dionysian sense of the term, as it is developed by Pseudo-Dionysius.[14] This consists in suggesting the ineffable (a *metanoïa*) by defined terms, and the theological theme of the discourse which differentiates the mythical Alexander ("l'en dist" [l. 15]) from the historical character seen in the light of the revealed Word ("Alexandres . . . ne chalut / de charité ne de nul rien" [ll. 58–59]).

Strengthened by these indications, our proposal is for another possible comparison to be made between the image of the Roi Pescheor in his castle and two very similar figures, both known to Chrétien's contemporaries and the entourage of the benefactor commissioning the work: two typological representations of Christ often present in the iconography of the time and essential to Northern European chivalry from the end of the eleventh century. Those two figures are David and Solomon.

In the first place, using the same analogical, theological, and metaphorical procedures, and in the light of the sense given in the prologue, the relationship will be explored between the outline suggested by the story and that of the two images implied. Then, following the same procedure, the emphasis will be put on identifying the place and position of the person of the king in the *Conte du Graal*. Finally, an attempt will be made to appreciate the similarities and differences observed in the scene drawn in the text and the iconographical references, while investigating the underlying implications.

THE ICONOGRAPHIC PROTOTYPE OF DAVID AND SOLOMON IN THEIR CASTLE

The Roi Pescheor is immediately presented in the guise of a *prudhomme* "anchapelez" (l. 3078), "apoiez . . . desor son coute" (l. 3093), enthroned on a bed, under an immense light (ll. 3187–89) in the center of a great square hall. Apart from this, a square tower ("tor quarree" (ll. 3054–56)) dominates the scene standing above the stronghold which is defended by turrets ("tornelles" (l. 3055)).

The image of a man enthroned in royal attire in the middle of a square emplacement fortified by small turrets will remind the reader of a classical iconographic arrangement of the Romanesque period in Northern Europe. A few typical examples include f.13v. of ms. 14 of the Cîteaux Bible (in the Bibliothèque Publique of Dijon), f.138 in the Gebhart or Admont Bible (ser. nov. 2071/2 in the Österreichische Nationalbibliothek in Vienna), and f.128v of ms. 559 in the Saint-Vaast Bible (in the Bibliothèque Municipale in Arras). In the first manuscript, King David sits in his palace surrounded by battlements where foot soldiers are fighting. In the second miniature, the same King David is represented dying in the heart of his palace, where the walls make a frame for the figure. In the third, the soldiers who were on the ramparts in the first picture are at the feet of the dying king.

This depiction of a sovereign behind the walls of his fortress lying on a couch under a great lamp echoes another sovereign found in exactly the same position, similarly lying under a lamp, who was just as familiar to Chrétien's contemporaries: that is, King Solomon. When he is represented reclining on his couch under a lamp, he is placed in the center of his palace, suggested by the tower and wall which frame the scene, and accompanied by Israel's 60 warriors. For example, on f.109v of the Greek manuscript in the Bibliothèque Nationale[15] and on f. 204v of the *Hortus Deliciarum* where the gloss makes it clear that we are in the presence "de requie Solomonis."

Such visual comparisons are no more audacious than all the mythological suppositions proposed so far.

David and Solomon as Chivalric References

Furthermore, such comparisons point to the involvement of David and his son Solomon as models for the code of chivalry of the age and examples of Christian virtues. From the work of J. Flori we know the place occupied by these two kings in the liturgy of armorial rites encouraging the transference of "the mission, the rituals and the formulas which, until then, where those of the King."[16] David and Solomon are both evoked and invoked as exemplary militant defenders of the faith ("milites, defensores ecclesiæ").

Ecclesiastical writers contribute abundantly to this institutionalization of knights as a class for whom the two Old Testament kings provide the measure of perfection. So does Petrus Comestor, following Saint Jerome,[17] who finds the names of David (signifying "merciful, friendly, comely to behold") and Solomon ("pacific") congruent with Christ,[18] and for whom the edification of the temple announces that of the militant and triumphant church.[19] Similarly Honorius Augustodunensis, in his *Speculum Ecclesiæ,* considers that these "milites" form the combative arm of the church defending the royal prerogative.[20] Again John of Salisbury, in *Policraticus,* sees the "miles" primarily as a man of the church, leading the virtuous life of a knight, faithful to his duty and to God's law, a way leading to holiness.[21] Likewise Lambert d'Ardres considers the *milites* and the princes as peers; in Flanders at this time young nobles simultaneously received both an academic and a military education.

That is why, in armorial liturgy, sometimes still called "ordo ad armandum ecclesiae defensorum vel alium militem,"[22] God is asked to protect the new knight as he protected David, the valiant fighter, who fought and slew Goliath the giant whom he destroyed, and who put to flight the evil spirit troubling Saul (I Kings 16:23). He is entreated to make the new knight an instrument of his justice and his peace, as in the case of Solomon the wise "sicut Salomonem fecisti regnum obtinere pacificum." It is indeed even in the form of another David that William of Flanders is depicted on his tombstone at Saint-Omer.[23]

David and Solomon as Visual Models of Christian Virtues

The same ideal spiritual virtues of knighthood are extolled by miniaturists when they represent both kings in their palaces under a burning lamp, almost always defended by soldiers at arms.[24]

The glosses inspired by the Holy Scriptures, like those of f. 204v in the *Hortus Deliciarum* already referred to, allow an appreciation of the value of these pictorial elements which contribute to representing the King of Jerusalem and the rules governing their disposition on the page.

THE TOWER OF THE CHURCH

The tower or the castle enclosure is seen as another "turris David" as in the *Psalms,* a symbol of the church.

CHRIST, THE KING RECUMBENT

The recumbent king represents Christ, "verus Solomon." The article of furniture refers to the mental attitude of the king in this allegorical palace. When it is a couch, the image is of the king who "requiescit in lectulo, id est in ecclesia." When it is a dais, the emphasis of the miniaturist is on reigning in glory.

THE LAMP OF DIVINE LIGHT

The lamp "lucerna" at the center of the parables of the ten virgins (Matthew 25:4) *alias* the kindled light evoked in the Book of Mark (Mark 4: 21) and in Saint John's vision of the throne of God (Apocalypse 4:5) before which seven lamps of fire burn is, according to Rabanus Maurus,[25] the resplendent sign of charity and the presence of the Holy Ghost for whom the preeminent mediator is Christ.[26] "Lampadis nomine, mediator Dei et hominum homo Christus Jesus intelligitur," maintains Garnier de Saint-Victor.[27] While Herrade von Hohenburg for her part comments in these terms: "Lucerna ardens significat eternam lucem."

THE VALIANT MEN OF JERUSALEM, DEFENDERS OF THE SPIRITUAL SWORD

The soldiers are seen as a representation of the army of Jerusalem evoked in the Song of Songs (Song of Songs 3:7–8).

Rupert of Deutz reveals the symbolic intention. From the time of the Virgin Mary's birth (the cradle of Christ the Savior humility personified, veritable Solomon), he says, the soldiers of Israel are like the defenders of the sword of spirituality, the Word of God, against the sword of materialism. The "fortes" not only accept that the Word of God exists; they live it. The same is claimed by Garnier of Saint-Victor.[28] On f. 256 of the *Hortus,* the gloss, borrowed from Honorius's *Speculum Ecclesiæ,* expresses it in other terms: "Milites autem hujus civitatis sunt qui pro legibus sui imperatoris usque ad mortem certare contendunt."[29]

The whole iconographical effect which is formed by the king, his castle (or his tower, a metonymy for castle), the lamp and the soldiers, condenses into one image the work of the Word of God (the king) in his church (the castle tower), militant and secular, and the triumph of Christian virtues represented here by charity (the lamp) and strength (the soldiers).

The pictorial elements such as the tower, king, lamp, and soldiery are not always drawn or assembled exactly in the same manner from one picture to another.

In the particular drawings referred to, the tower of David appears in the upper right-hand side of the picture in the *Hortus.* It is only implied by battlements in the upper background of the Greek manuscript in the BN. It lies to the right and left of the figure in the upper section of the Admont Bible's illustration. It constitutes the complete border of the Cîteaux Bible's parchment. The king is found in the upper part of the page in the first manuscript. He occupies the complete lower section of the drawing in the second and is in the center of the page in the other two works. The lamp is only present in the first three cases. Its hanging point varies from one picture to another. The soldiers are always represented. They look after the king in both representations of Solomon. In the *Hortus,* they are static but armed from head to toe. In the Greek manuscript only those who are at the end of the lines carry a weapon, and they are all looking in different directions. In the Cîteaux Bible, the men are all armed and in full activity around David.

Thanks to the gloss or to the phylactery, these differences leave no doubt about the identity of the personage who is represented.

Associated with the king who foretells the coming of Christ, the tower typos of the ecclesia is drawn as a support in the *Hortus,* as a throne in the Cîteaux Bible and as the natural border of the page in the Admont Bible. These various ways of drawing seem to express different aspects of the same mystic reality. In the first case, "in order to reign Christ relies on His Church." In the second case, "the king, the center and the heart of the Church is Christ." In the third, "the very place of Christ is the Church."

The positioning of the *fortes* is not always the same either. Nevertheless, their attitude is such that there is no ambiguity in the fact that they represent the church, militant and vigilant for the peace of the Kingdom. They are armed and ready to march in the *Hortus.* They watch intently from the margins of the page in the BN manuscript like lookout men. They are standing at the foot of David's bed in the Saint-Vaast Bible. When they are more vindictive, as in the Cîteaux Bible, they demonstrate two theological points: David, for whom they are fighting, is the precursor of Christ; meanwhile, and because of his tumultuous disposition, it was right and proper to have left the building of the temple to his son (as it is largely developed in the spirituality of the Rhineland and expounded by Theophilus in the prologue of the third part of his treatise *De diversis artibus*).[30]

The lamp, which is the sign of God's omnipresence in the king's life, is always shown directly linked to this figure. In particular, we have to notice that although it is placed in different positions from one page to another (or even from one piece of stained glass, ivory, or enamel to another),[31] it is always placed vertically above the king's heart, according to a symbolism which is as cogent as it is simple.

In other terms, what prevails in the forms reproduced is the meaning conveyed. This value is determined by equating the Revealed Word with the image, thanks to the use of metaphor and metonymy. As they are always visual, these metaphors and metonymies rely on similarities of any origin.

With these design rules in mind, let us look at each of the details relating to the "Roi Pescheor "in the "sale . . . quarrée autant longue come lee." Here are certainly many of the elements designed to make the Grail king another David or another Solomon in Jerusalem. Under this double aspect of reproduction and transformation, the poem conveys a discourse that remains to be disclosed.

THE DWELLING-PLACE OF THE "ROI PESCHEOR"

"la sale . . . quarrée / . . . autant longue comme lee" (ll. 3083–84)

The king appears to Perceval in the middle of the great hall which is specifically described as square, "quarrée" [l. 3083]). We know through the work of Richard Krautheimer[32] that the use and interpretation of shape in the Middle Ages is quite different from that of our day. In particular, the polygon and circle are interchangeable to such a point that the former is often found as "a circle with angles." Now, in the text of Chrétien, the poet avoids all ambiguity because he states emphatically that the room is "autant longue comme lee" (l. 3084). Let us examine the underlying metaphor and its importance in the scheme of the narrative.

The Temple of Jerusalem = anima nostra

From the time of Saint John[33] (Apocalypse 21:16), this topography has been an iconographically common presentation of the messianic Jerusalem, of the temple as the abode of the blessed who will participate in the eternal glory of doomsday. It appears in all the illustrations and representations of the Patmos vision.[34] Often indeed, to underline the scriptural reference, the miniaturists take pains to draw angels who, like "surveyors," measure the side walls, as Saint John did with his golden reed (Apocalypse 11:1).

This image suggested by the letter of the text is significant in itself for Chrétien's contemporaries especially for those familiar with the monastic circles of the twelfth century. It is a visual metaphor referred to as a "factum mysticum"[35] or a "res mystica,"[36] as they are called by Hugh of Saint-Victor and Honorius Augustodunensis.

Even seen prophetically, the Temple of Jerusalem is not only a geographical place. When Christ compares himself to the temple (Matthew 26:6; Mark 14:58; John 2:19–21), the entrance represents his birth and the exit his death.[37] When he says to his disciples, "Manete in me et ego in vobis" (John 15:4), he is alluding to himself, he is asking each of his friends to live in heart, body and mind by him, with him and in him. He is addressing himself to each Christian "aeternus Rex . . . mentibus habitare dignatur" maintains Garnier of Saint-Victor.[38] For Christ and his church are one body and one person, a unique and great mystery (I Cor. 3:17). The church is the mystic body of Christ (I Ephesians 22), a fully real and spiritual body that has to be taken as a whole. So Rabanus Maurus recalls, after Origenes, that each person in his soul can build a Jerusalem, a "tabernaculum," a "templum," to fulfill Isaiah's prophecy "Surge, illuminare, Jerusalem" (Isaiah 60:1) "id est, a tenebris ignorantiae erigere, et illam pertingere claritatem, o anima . . . Juxta tropologiam, id est moralem sensum," [39] Jerusalem "ex quo perspicimus omnia intelligenda spiritualiter" [40] is "taberna-culum . . . corpus Domini, vel Ecclesia," [41] as it is tersely put by Saint Eucher. Its representation is a figure of the "mentis devotiæ," of the "mentis nostræ." [42]

Chrétien calls on all this theological background, much alive in his time, when he describes Perceval's arrival in the great hall in the Castle of the Grail. His entry into the *Roi pescheor*'s sanctuary marks a special moment when the knight discovers his soul.

The Underlying Romanesque Metaphor

Here again, it is important to recognize the underlying metaphor, familiar to all Chrétien's contemporaries who had heard it from the Crusade preachers.

According to Saint Augustine[43] and Duns Scotus Erigena,[44] who, together with Saint Bernard[45] and Hugh of Saint-Victor,[46] explain how the return of the soul to itself is a return to God, "not by change of place," this goes without saying, but "by the affection of the spirit." This return cannot be compared with any psychological introspection nor in any way with a withdrawal of the soul. It is a fundamental interior progression aimed at reintegrating the Holy City (as seen in the earlier reference to Saint Paul), which is in each Christian.[47] It is reintegration in the "tabernacle largely deployed not in the spacial world but in the world of the soul and its inner movements," according to the Abbot of Clairvaux.[48]

When Chrétien makes us penetrate, by imagery and imagination in the company of Perceval, to the center of the great square hall in the Grail Castle, he is escorting us at a very privileged moment: that of the return of a soul to itself, of the visit of self to self, by virtue of baptism, of the adopted child of God at home with God, of God as adopted father at the home of his child.

In the prologue, Chrétien announced the adventure of a soul, that of Philippe of Alsace. Everything happens as if in penetrating to the heart of this castle, this other Jerusalem, the poet was going to make us discover, in Perceval's company, the icon of this soul at a privileged moment of his development, and what follows appears as a description of it.

THE "ROI PESCHEOR": AN AVATAR OF THE PROTOTYPE OF THE KING OF JERUSALEM

It remains to understand what becomes of the king and his entourage in the transition from traditional image to that of this *Conte du Graal*. We could operate using classical rules of comparison: on the one hand, study the elements of the picture which are common to the illustrations referred to and the narration; on the other hand, look at those which are different. This cartesian scheme does not correspond, however, to what a story is, what language recognizes spontaneously in the term "thread of discourse." That is why our attention will be caught successively by the tower, the position of the man living in the castle, his head gear, the fire and its poet's comments, and the lamp, in their order of occurrence in the narrative.

The Tower

The tower is the first part of the castle seen by the knight. Chrétien states precisely that it is "quarrée" (v.3058).

At the outset, the allegorical value of this building and its shape was made clear from the glosses on the representations of the King of Jerusalem and in the paintings of Celestial Jerusalem. The prologue invites us to adopt and use this theological point of view. Consequently, it is suggested to us here that, on discovering this tower, we have come across a figure of the church of which the form is that of the city of the end of time.

Now, following the indications given by the narrator, this tower seems to be situated toward the front of the principal building, below the door.

La sale fu devant la tor . . .
Li vaslez cele part avale . . .
einsi vers la porte s'en va;
devant la porte un pont trova . . . (ll. 3056, 3058, 3065–66)

As certain scholars like Holmes[49] have noticed in relying on
what is said in the Book of Kings (III Kings 6–7), it is clear that the
tower of the real temple of Solomon is high up on the exterior portico,
which is not separated from the rest of the building as it is in
Chrétien's work. It should be noticed that the miniaturists such as
those already referred to appear themselves in this regard very
respectful of details taken from the Scriptures and apply themselves to
drawing this tower, making it an integral part of the temple.

Making the tower-*Ecclesia* of the temple-Jerusalem–*anima
nostra* unusually conspicuous, positioning it as a beacon in the
narrative and insisting upon its shape, associated with the end of time,
Chrétien jars the memory, while sharpening the reader's attention and
understanding. The structure of the temple of Jerusalem is shattered.
Allegorice and with regard to divine justice (suggested by the two
square forms), the tabernacle of the soul, the room "autant longue
comme lee," is outside the *Ecclesia,* the tower.

The Seated Prudhomme, "Enchapelés," "Apoiez desor son coute"

Everything follows, however, as if the unfolding of the tale describing
the *prudhomme* sitting down, made explicit what is implied by the
tower. Indeed, in the heart of what we have recognized as another
temple, the reader could expect to find the figures of David or
Solomon as has already been described. The illuminators made it
customary to expect a crowned king either seated, reigning in glory, in
the image of Christ as in the Cîteaux Bible, or reclining in the rest of
the just as on f. 204v of the *Hortus.*

Yet here, the king is not wearing a crown, neither is he really
seated nor really reclining. Perceval sees him "seoir . . . enchapelés" (ll.
3086–88) "apoiez desor son coute" (l. 3092). Let us examine each of
these particular features.

"ENCHAPELÉS"

A hat is the distinctive sign for men of the synagogue in medieval
iconography.[50] However, the Synagogue is not just the assembly for

unconverted Jews. It is also what the church and soul become when no longer succored by the gifts of the Holy Spirit and hope is lost during tempest and persecutions so that the *Ecclesia* becomes a sterile institution.[51]

So, consistent with this metaphor, it can be said that, when Perceval sees this avatar of the King of Jerusalem with the head covering required for the synagogue, he shares with the reader the image of a soul that no longer lives in hope and that, like the bad vine shoot, no longer gives fruit.

"APOIEZ DESOR SON COUTE"

The physical attitude of the *prudhomme* confirms the indication of the head covering. He is sitting, but "apoiez desor son coute." Slumped like this, he is not glorious, neither relaxed nor in the peace of God. Moreover, as Garnier suggests,[52] the hand held to his head is a sign of immense pain. Perceval has already witnessed this when visiting Arthur the first time at Carduel (l. 908).[53]

These two pieces of information taken together and seen from a theological point of view can appear complementary if they are considered in the scheme of the story taken in its continuity.

As Saint Paul advises, the church, the assembly of the faithful, the soul of every Christian, *mystice,* are the body of Christ of which he is the head (I Cor. 2:19, 12:27). If even one sins, "all the members suffer with him in a mutual solicitude" (I Cor. 12: 26). The reader cannot forget the misdeeds of Perceval, such as the abandoning of his mother, the stealing of the kiss and of the maiden's ring in the "tref," the morbid coveting of the silver gilt armor at Carduel, and the angry impatience shown prior to discovering the Grail Castle.

It is as a sinner that the knight arrives at the castle, the other temple of God, the heart of man. It is as a sinner that he discovers in the middle of the square hall, in the secret depths of this temple, the heart of the self.

If, as has been said, Perceval's quest tells of a soul looking into itself and rediscovering the image of his Creator "a quo factus est," there is also the perception here, through the expediency of the attire and position of the body deliberately modifying the iconographic prototype, of an ailing king, of God deformed into a synagogue, injured by human failings.

The Fire and the 400 Absentees

Chrétien completes the picture by adding a certain number of new elements to the initial forms. Let us consider but two: the "fu molt grant / de busche seche cler ardant" (ll. 3093–94) and the related commentary on the missing 400 soldiers.

THE FIRE

Following church tradition, fire is the sign of grace which enables what Rabanus Maurus calls the "terrena conscientia" and the "terrenas cogitationes"[54] of every man in search of God. It evokes, adds Suger in his commentary on the Burning Bush, those consumed with love of God,[55] and this by the power of the altar of the Cross.

THE HYPOTHETICAL 400

Everything happens then as if suddenly Chrétien came back to the image of Jerusalem with a reference to men-at-arms who could sit around the fire. He tells us: "Bien poïst l'en IIII. C. homes / asseoir environ le feu"(ll. 3095–96). In exegetical terms, it can also be said that "400 soldiers of Jerusalem could sit around the fire."

So here again, innovation is found in the text. The differences established in this way with the iconographic prototype are no more anodyne than the preceding ones. In contrast to those besides Kings David and Solomon, these men are absent and, moreover, are depicted as surrounding the fire and not the king. As has been seen, the defenders of Jerusalem represent those who not only acknowledge the Word of God but live by it.

Furthermore, Chrétien gives two more pieces of information: these hypothetical men could be as many as 400, sitting. "400" is the number of King David's soldiers (I Kings 22:2; 25:13). This is why Church tradition, with Bede the Vénérable,[56] sees in this a promise made to those who remain faithful to the cardinal virtues. It is the number which announces the militant church awoken by the teaching of the four Gospels and striving for eternal life.

SITTING

The poet adds that these 400 are able to sit around what has been recognized as a figment of the fire of divine love. This possibility is juxtaposed with a reality immediately described in the story; Perceval sits down. However, instead of sitting by the fire, he places himself next to this symbol of the synagogue and Pescheor, "lez lui asis" (l. 3119).

As Garnier remarks in his study on the language of the image of the Middle Ages, "the sitting position is reserved for God and real or allegorical personages who enjoy a hierarchical superiority and power. . . . This position is significant in itself, quite apart from the importance of the office. The fact of being seated on the same couch, at a ceremonial reception and not for the accomplishment of a material task, marks the equality of the two or the aspiration of one to accede, in recognition of his merits, to a titular position."[57]

Let us bring together the diverse elements of the metaphor drawn here in the text. The person whose soul is represented in the scene, by reason of the form of the number (400) is given the promise of becoming another David at the head of the militant church on condition his fervent heart (the fire) awakens to evangelical charity. The conditional form of the verbs and the place occupied respectively by the *prudhomme* and his visitor imply that the heart of the designated one, at this time, is still a long way from realizing this project.

The Great "Luminaire"

However, the project is not without hope because "laiens . . . luminaire / si grant . . ." (ll. 3187–88) lights up the room. As we have seen, according to the gloss, the lamp represents the divine light which alone can rescue the heart and mind from spiritual obscurity. As Garnier of Saint Victor says: "*Lucerna super caput . . . splendet, quia sacra eloquentia tenebras nostræ mentis irradiant.*"[58]

It is important to note that Chrétien places it in a particular location within the whole. It is "laiens," that is, immediately above Perceval and his host. Here the poet uses the iconographic tradition which always tends to situate the light vertically above the king of Jerusalem, exactly perpendicular to his heart and head, emphasizing divine vigilance and the close relationship that unites God with his creation. A place which, in the text, acts like a pause giving symbolic importance to the object evoked.

When Chrétien creates his fictional world of the *Roi Pescheor*'s castle, everything proceeds as if he were relying on images familiar to his contemporaries: those of the kings of Jerusalem. He retains the main themes like those of the tower, of the square room, of the king on his couch or throne, the soldiers and the lamp. These resemblances also act as reference points for the reader.

Details are modified. To do this, the procedures used are diverse. Sometimes, the author employs the effects of fracture (as when the tower is separated from the castle). Sometimes, he changes one object or a physical position represented in the original orthodoxy for another. This new one is equally familiar to the reader but unexpected in this setting (as with the head covering or the hand position of the royal *prudhomme*). Sometimes he deprives this dream world of elements present in the initial schema, while at the same time insisting on the fact they could be found there (such are the potential soldiers around the fire).

This manner of working from an iconographical prototypical base brings the storyteller's art close to that of the architect as it is described by Richard Krautheimer in his *Introduction to an Iconography of Medieval Architecture*. Although committed to a chosen model, Chrétien does not reproduce it in toto. He does not "copy" it, in the modern sense of the word.

Furthermore, he invites us to enter into the secrets of the world of Marvels where the effect of surprise is quintessential. The storyteller is preeminently an artist in this respect. He avails himself of images familiar to the entourage at the court of Flanders for whom the significance was precise and clear. The king of Jerusalem, whether David or Solomon, is more than just an historical personage. He represents Christ in his church, the grace at work in every baptized soul. Here, the same as for the presentation of the Castle of Marvels that I have studied elsewhere,[59] the poet uses "partial transpositions,"[60] all equally significant for the reader. The segmented model thus becomes much more than a reproduction. It is a new production consisting of a constellation of elements equally memorable and significant that requires intelligence to be read. It is through the mediation of an image perceived by the senses that the intellect reaches a more profound reality.

Here, through a broken and remade image of the king of Jerusalem, Chrétien, fulfilling the promise of the prologue, brings us to the discovery of Philippe of Alsace's soul at one moment of its development; this soul, (the castle's great hall) is a sinner's (a member of the synagogue wearing a typical head covering) who lives outside the benevolence and body of the church (the tower) and because of this, it is sterile (like the "roi mehaignié"). In spite of sins committed, grace (fire and light) remains alive.

This artistic *facere* implies a respect for the reality of man complete in body and soul (sensibility, memory, understanding, capacity to love . . .); it can only be recognized as such when the reader accepts this totality and collaborates in it, in the exact sense of the term. This manner of working, starting from a known Christian iconography and understood as such, in no way eliminates the other visual analogies already made with other traditions. It merely allows us to draw together a few more elaborate strands of the story.

Above all, the comparisons established here lay the stress on what could be called a "visual diachrony":

- a textual reading, linear, bound to the thread of the narrative, to that of the "conte" as Chrétien declares in the introduction,
- a vertical reading, eschatological, which adopts all the power of the visual element to describe the reality of the count of Flanders's soul, as promised in the opening words of the tale.

NOTES

1. A.C.L. Brown, *The Origin of the Grail Legend* (Cambridge: Harvard Univ. Press, 1943).

2. Jean Frappier, *Chrétien de Troyes et le mythe du Graal* (Paris: S.E.D.E.S., 1972), p. 194.

3. W.A. Nitze, "The Castle of the Grail—an Irish Analogue," in *Studies in Honor of A. Marshall Elliott,* I (Baltimore: Johns Hopkins Univ. Press, 1911).

4. Th.F. O'Rahilly, *Early Irish History and Mythology* (Dublin: Institute for Advanced Studies, 1946), pp. 318–31; M. Coyabee in *Journal of the Cama Oriental Institute,* 38 (1939); both are cited by Jean Marx, *La légende arthurienne et le Graal* (Paris: P.U.F., 1952), pp. 183–202.

5. Paule Le Rider, *Le chevalier dans le Conte du Graal* (Paris: S.E.D.E.S., 1978), pp. 77–79.

6. Herrade of Hohenbourg, *Hortus Deliciarum,* ed. under the direction of Rosalie Green, 2 vols. (London, Warburg Institute; Leiden: E.J. Brill, 1979).

7. Louis Grodecki, "A propos des vitraux de Châlons sur Marne. Deux points d'iconographie mosane," in *L'art mosan, recueil de travaux publiés par P. Francastel* (Paris: A. Colin, 1953), pp. 167–68.

8. Helen Adolf, "*Visio Pacis.*" *Holy City and Grail. An Attempt at an Inner History of the Grail Legend* (State College: Pennsylvania State Univ. Press, 1960); "Studies in Chrétien's 'Conte del Graal,'" *MLQ*, 8, (1947).

9. Urban T. Holmes, Jr. and Sister M. Amelia Klenke, *Chrétien, Troyes and the Grail* (Chapel Hill: Univ. of North Carolina Press, 1959).

10. Moses Gasper, "The Legend of the Grail," in *Studies and Texts* (1925–28), 2: 895, 898.

11. Martin de Ríquer, "Interpretacion cristiana de *Li contes del Graal,* " in *Hommage à M. Menendez Pidal*.

12. Michèle Vauthier, "Vers la figure de la 'Cité' au château du Roi Pescheor dans le Conte du Graal de Chrétoen de Troyes; étude topographique en situation," in *König Artus und der heilige Graal* (Greifswald: Reineke, 1994), pp. 269–88; "Vers une approche herméneutique possible du 'Conte del Graal' du manoir maternel à Beaurepaire: Images de l'amour falsifié," Communication at the International Congress on "Amour et Chevalerie chez Chrétien de Troyes," Troyes, 1992. To be published by the Presses Universitaires de Besançon, forthcoming.

13. All the references are to the edition of W. Roach (Geneva: Droz, 1959).

14. Pseudo-Dionysius, *Hier. Cæel.*, c. II, n. 2–3, ed. M. de Gandillac, SC, 58, 77.

15. This picture is reproduced by Gérard Cames in *Allégories et symboles dans l'Hortus Deliciarum* (Leiden: Brill, 1971), without any allusion to that of the Roi Pescheor.

16. Jean Flori, "Chevalerie et liturgie; remise des armes et vocabulaire chevaleresque dans les sources liturgiques du IXe au XIVe siècle," in *Le Moyen Age* (1978), p. 278; *L'essor de la chevalerie, XIe et XIIe siècles* (Geneva: Droz, 1986), esp. pp. 255–56, 296–97, 371–78.

17. Saint Jerome, *Liber interpretationis*, CC 72, 103; 138.

18. Petrus Comestor, *Cum audieris sonitum gradientis in cacumine pirorum*, Troyes, BM 1515, f° 51v, cited by Jean Longère, ibid., t. II, p. 89, n. 44.

19. Petrus Comestor, *Columnas duas posuit Salomon in vestibulo Templi*, Troyes, BM 1515, f. 54va., ibid., n. 48.

20. Jean Flori, *L'essor de la chevalerie*, pp. 255–56.

21. John of Salisbury, *Policraticus*, lib. II, c. 8, cited by J. Flori, p. 287, n. 96.

22. Mss. Köln 141 and Bamberg, cited by Flori, pp. 379–381.

23. Tombstone, Saint-Omer: Saint-Bertin Church, pavement mosaïcs, Hôtel Sandelin, reserves.

24. Louis Réau, *Iconographie de l'Art chrétien*, 3 vols., (Paris, 1954–1959), t. II, 1, pp. 264–65.

25. Rabanus Maurus, *Allegoriæ in Sacram Scripturam*, P.L. CXII, 981–82.

26. Ibid., 989–90.

27. Garnier of Saint-Victor, *Gregorianum* XVI, P.L. CXCIII, 457.

28. Garnier of Saint-Victor, *Gregorianum* VIII, P.L. CXCIX, 322–24: "quia videlicet verbum Dei non est mirabile solummodo scire, sed facere."

29. Honorius Augustodunensis, *Speculum Ecclesiæ*, "In consenta populi," P.L. CLXXII, 1095.

30. Theophilus, *De diversis Artibus,* ed. C.R. Dodwell (Oxford: Clarendon Press, 1986), pp. 61–64.

31. The same characteristics are found on all these artifacts. On the relationship between scarving, painting and goldsmith's trade see Louis Grodecki, *Les problèmes de l'Art Roman in Le Moyen Age retrouvé* (Paris: Flammarion, 1987), t. I.

32. Richard Krautheimer, *Introduction à une iconographie de l'architecture médiévale,* ed. Gérard Montfort, 1993, p. 16.

33. "Civitas in quadro posita, et longitudo ejus tanta est quanta et latitudo . . . aequalia sunt" (Apocalypse 21:16)

34. Mireille Mentré, *Création et Apocalypse, histoire d'un regard humain sur le divin,* (Paris: O.E.I.L., 1984), pp.138–45.

35. Hugh of Saint-Victor, *De Sacramentis,* Prologue CV, P.L. CLXXV, 185C.

36. Honorius Augustodunensis, P.L. CLXXII, 749A.

37. Stephan Langton "Ipse vos baptizabit Spiritu Sancto," Leipzig, UB 443, cited by Jean Longere *Œuvres oratoires de maîtres parisiens au XIIe siècle, étude historique et doctrinale,* (Paris: Etudes Augustiniennes, 1975), I, p.152; II, p.119, n. 8.

38. Garnier of Saint-Victor, *Gregorianum* VIII, P.L. CXCIII, 393.

39. Rabanus Maurus, *Allegoriæ in Sacram Scripturam,* P.L. CXII, 966

40. The expression comes from Gregorius Magnus, P.L. XLVIII, 487A.

41. Saint Eucher, *Liber formularum spiritalis intelligentiæ,* cap. X, P.L. L, 766.

42. Rabanus Maurus, ibid. 1064; 1062.

43. Saint Augustine, *Soliloques,* II, 19, 33 = *De Trinitate* XV, 7, 11; XV, XX, 40 = *In I. epist. Joann.* VIII, 6

44. Duns Scotus Erigena, *Periphyseon* V, 8; P.L. CXXII, 876A–B.

45. Saint Bernard, *De Cant.* XXV, XXVII

46. Hugh of Saint-Victor, *Didascalion* II,1; P.L. CLXXVI,751.

47. I have already amply exposed the meaning of the spritual "return" as it is easily understood by Chrétien's contemporaries in Michèle Vauthier "Les aventures de Gauvain dans la seconde partie du 'Conte del Graal' de Chrétien de Troyes: une apologie de la Croisade" (Göppingen: Kümmerle, 1989).

48. Saint Bernard, *De Cant.,* op. cit.

49. Holmes and Klenke, *Chrétien, Troyes and the Grail,* p.74.

50. *Hortus Deliciarum,* ed. Staub (Strasbourg, 1889), p.15, n. 3.

51. Rupert of Deutz, *De div. offic.* X, 28.

52. F. Garnier, *Le langage de l'image au Moyen Age* (Paris: Le Léopard d'Or, 1982), I, pp. 118–20, 182–184.

53. See my earlier articles, Michèle Vauthier, "Les âges d'Arthur dans le *Conte del Graal* de Chrétien de Troyes: le mirage de la vieillesse," in *Vieillesse et vieillissement au Moyen-Age* (Aix-en-Provence: CUERMA, 1987), p. 341 and "Vers la figure de la 'Cité' au château du Roi Pescheor dans le *Conte du Graal* de Chrétien de Troyes," pp. 282–83.

54. Rabanus Maurus, *Allegoriæ in Sacram Scripturam,* P.L. CXII, 966

55. E. Panofsky, *Abbot Suger, on the Abbey Church of Saint-Denis and Its Art Treasures* (Princeton: Princeton Univ. Press, 1946), p. 199.

56. The Venerable Bede, *Sam.,* CCL 119, 204, 235.

57. F. Garnier, op. cit., 113.

58. Garnier of Saint-Victor, *Gregorianum,* XII, *De lucerna,* P.L. CXCIII, 364–65.

59. Michèle Vauthier, "Le paradoxe des fenêtres colorées dans le 'Conte del Graal': une introduction possible à la lecture des couleurs chez Chrétien de Troyes," in *Les couleurs au Moyen-Age* (Aix-en-Provence: CUERMA, 1988), pp. 425–48.

60. The expression is Krautheimer's, op. cit., pp. 23–26.

11 WONDERS AND ILLUMINATIONS

PIERART DOU TIELT AND THE *QUESTE DEL SAINT GRAAL*

Lori J. Walters

Whereas mid-fourteenth-century Flemish manuscript production usually involved several workers who each carried out different tasks, Paris, Bibliothèque de l'Arsenal 5218, containing an illustrated copy of the *Queste del saint Graal* followed by vernacular church annals, offers rare and valuable evidence of a codex being transcribed, illuminated, and bound by the same person: "Chius livres fu parescrips le nuit nostre dame en mi aoust l'an mil trois cens et li. Si l'escrips pierars dou tielt. Et enlumina et loia. Explicit li queste del saint graal." (This book was brought to completion on the night of Our Lady in the middle of August 1351. Pierart dou Tielt transcribed it. And illuminated and bound it. Explicit *Li Queste* del saint Graal.) (f. 91v)[1] Although Pierart dou Tielt's signed statement seems to indicate that he took full responsibility for the production of Ars. 5218, the question of whether he designed the manuscript as well will best be discussed in detail at a later point in my study. It is possible that someone associated with the Benedictine monastery of St.-Martin de Tournai, such as its abbot, Gilles Le Muisit, commissioned the manuscript. In addition to reflecting the desires of the person who ordered its execution, Ars. 5218 expresses the conception of its planner or conceptualizer, the person who planned the execution of the manuscript book in its entirety.[2] Pierart's position as the head of a very active Tournaisian workshop[3] increases the likelihood that he was the planner of Ars. 5218.[4] This work is unusual in several respects: no evidence exists that Pierart ever copied and bound any of the many other manuscript books he illuminated, and no other bears his signature.

Recent studies have shown how cycles of illumination provide a "reading" or interpretation of the text; the present piece sets forth the hypothesis that the planner of Ars. 5218 (probably Pierart dou Tielt) "read" the *Queste* in the context of church history and in the light of topics of current ecclesiastical debate. The opposition established between spiritual and profane chivalry in the pictorial cycle and in the accompanying marginal decoration promotes reflection on such diverse questions as transubstantiation, clerical celibacy, and the beatific vision.[5] This study also considers the status of the historical annals that appear at the end of Ars. 5218. Linked to the *Queste* through material evidence and thematic concerns, these yield precious information about the ecclesiastical history of Tournai in the late Middle Ages, including the relationship between St.-Martin de Tournai and the Avignon papacy. The final section of this article explores the relationship between Pierart's production of Ars. 5218 and the documented case of the blindness and cure of St.-Martin's abbot, Gilles Le Muisit.

While adopting Stephen Greenblatt's approach of examining "the embeddedness of cultural objects in the contingencies of history" (p. 164), I will also address (somewhat paradoxically) Greenblatt's own "blind spot" concerning the significance of the illuminated manuscript.[6] A multilayered signifier created by the contextualization of works with other works, as well as with systems of rubrication and illumination, the illustrated medieval book is the product of numerous political, social, and intellectual forces. Ars. 5218 proves to be an especially pertinent example of a multivalent cultural artifact that generates what Greenblatt calls "resonance" and "wonder," terms to be explored further at the conclusion of this study.

PIERART DOU TIELT

Whereas relatively little is known about the majority of figures involved in book production, a great deal of information exists concerning Pierart dou Tielt, the extraordinary individual who was responsible for the production of Ars. 5218 as a completed manuscript book. Pierart, whose documented activity spanned the period from 1330 to 1351, was a prolific manuscript illuminator and book restorer based in Tournai, Belgium.[7] A thriving trade center and the site of a magnificent cathedral, Tournai was one of the most important cities in medieval Europe. The first traces of Pierart's activity appear around 1330 when he collaborated with the Master of the Ghent Ceremonial on the Tournai *Rose,* a manuscript of the *Roman de la Rose* that contains the most extensive recasting of the text undertaken by the Franciscan writing under the pseudonym of Gui de Mori.[8] Besides various other works[9] including another manuscript of the *Roman de la Rose* (Copenhagen, KB, Fr. LV, Gl. Kgl.S 2061),[10] parts of the *Roman d'Alexandre* (Oxford, Bodleian Library, Bodley 264), *Pamphile et Galatee* (Brussels, KB 4783), and a book of hours (Brussels, KB IV 453), Pierart illuminated the entire corpus (consisting of Latin chronicles and vernacular poetry) of Gilles Le Muisit (*Tres Tractatus,* Kortrijk, SOB, Fonds Goethals-Vercruysse 135; *Tractatus quartus,* Brussels, KB 13076–77; the *Lamentations* or *Registre,* Brussels, KB IV 119). Serving as abbot of the Benedictine monastery of St.-Martin de Tournai from 1331 to 1353,[11] Gilles was a significant figure in the political and intellectual life of Tournai.[12] Although not a monk himself,[13] Pierart was closely bound to the activities of the monastery: he revamped its twelfth-century gospel book (Washington, Library of Congress, De Ricci 127), and some time after 1349 replaced Jean de Bruelles as restorer of books in the abbey's library, which Vincent de Beauvais had judged to be excellent.[14] Although the date of Pierart's death is unknown, a testamentary bequest indicates that he was still alive in 1360.[15] By virtue of his position as the illustrator of the abbot's *oeuvres complètes* and as the abbey's restorer of books, Pierart dou Tielt evidently enjoyed a certain status in the influential mid-fourteenth-century city of Tournai.

THE PICTORIAL CYCLE OF ARS. 5218

The layout and pictorial cycle of Ars. 5218 indicate how its planner viewed the *Queste,* the fourth work in the vast *Lancelot–Graal* or *Vulgate* cycle (composed between 1215–1235 and comprising the *Estoire del Graal,* the *Estoire de Merlin,* the *Lancelot,* the *Queste,* and the *Mort Artu*). The *Queste* relates the quest of Galaad and other Arthurian knights for the Grail, the vessel in which Joseph d'Arimathie had collected the blood of the crucified Christ. The three scenes in the pictorial cycle of Ars. 5218 delineate the three distinct stages of the narrative first identified by Albert Pauphilet: departure for the quest, the testing of the knights—here centered on the figure of Galaad—and the final rewards, depicted in the Grail vision experienced by a group of Arthurian knights.[16]

The miniature and historiated initial (unfortunately partially damaged) on f. 1 (fig. 11.1) treat the beginning of the narrative. The miniature illustrates the following three scenes: on the left, the knights and ladies of the Round Table are reunited at Camelot on the Eve of Pentecost when a woman on horseback arrives at court and asks Lancelot to follow her; in the middle scene, Lancelot, the woman, and a squire ride to a convent; on the right, Lancelot, after having been presented to his son, Galaad, inside the convent and told to dub him a knight, puts on his son's spurs with the aid of Bohort. In the historiated initial, an aged "preudons," after having brought Galaad back to Arthur's court from the convent, appears following the first course of a meal to introduce Galaad as the "Chevalier Desirré" destined to accomplish the quest for celestial rather than for "terriennes choses." In the miniature on f. 10 (fig. 11.2), Galaad, in the course of his wanderings, arrives at the White Abbey. There he obtains a shield, not surprisingly a Crusader's shield, marked with a red cross that Josephé, Joseph d'Arimathie's son, had traced on its white background with his own blood. An opening in the abbey wall allows Galaad and the viewer to see the shield that hangs over the altar mentioned in the text. The final miniature in the pictorial cycle is the most important in the series. On f. 88 (fig. 11.3) several knights in company of Bishop Josephé (the first Christian bishop, brought back from the dead after over 300 years) enjoy a vision of the Grail. The picture translates visually the sense of wonder felt by the elect when confronted with heavenly mysteries.

The miniature provides a pictorial rendering of the following passages:

> Et il (Josephes) resgarde cele part et ausi font tuit li autre: et en voient issir les anges qui Josephes avoient aporté; dont li dui portoient deus cierges, et li tierz une touaille de vermeil samit, et li quarz une lance qui saignoit si durement que les goutes en chaoient contreval en une boiste qu'il tenoit en s'autre main. Et li dui mistrent les cierges sus la table et li tierz la toaille les le saint Vessel, et li quartz tint la lance tote droite sus le saint Vessel, si que li sans qui contreval la hanste couloit chaoit dedenz. Et si tost come il ont ce fet, Josephes se leva et trest un poi la lance en sus dou saint Vessel et le covri de la toaille.

> Lors fist Josephes semblant que il entrast ou sacrement de la messe. Et quant il i ot demoré un poi, si prist dedenz le saint Vessel une oublee qui ert fete en semblance de pain. Et au lever que il fist descendi de vers le ciel une figure en semblance d'enfant, et avoit le viaire ausi rouge et ausi embrasé come feu; et se feri ou pain, si que cil qui ou palés estoient virent apertement que li pains avoit forme d'ome charnel. Et quant

Josephes l'ot grant piece tenu, si le remist ou saint Vessel.
(Pauphilet, p. 269)

(When he (Josephé) looked in that direction and all the
others did also, they saw the angels come out that Josephé had
brought along. Two of them were bearing two candles, and the
third a piece of richest red silk, and the fourth a lance that was
bleeding so much that the drops fell down into a box that he
was holding in his other hand. And the two put the candles on
the table and the third put the piece of silk next to the holy
vessel, and the fourth held the lance upright over the holy
Vessel, so that the blood that flowed down the shaft fell into it.
And as soon as they had done this, Josephé got up and raised
the lance slightly above the holy vessel that he covered with the
piece of silk.

Then Josephé appeared to enter into the sacrament of the
mass. And a short way into it, he took out of the vessel a host
that looked like it was made out of bread. And when he raised
the object a figure that looked like a child and whose face was as
red and as glowing as fire came down from heaven. And it the
figure broke into the bread so that those who were in the palace
could then see that it had the form of a man in the flesh. And
after holding it up for a while, Josephé put it back into the holy
vessel.)

The picture depicts the lance and Grail at two different moments of the
procession: first, they appear on the right, held by two standing angels
(the Grail is covered with a piece of red silk), and next they are fully
displayed in the center of the illustration. Unlike the depiction in the
miniature, in the text the figure of Christ makes its appearance when
Josephé elevates the host, only to disappear after Josephé replaces the
host in the holy vessel; then Josephé gives the kiss of peace to Galaad
and the other knights and invites them to sit at the table. In the
illustration, Josephé is seated on a throne before the assembled group
observing the procession. In the passage in the text immediately
following the scene depicted on f. 88, Josephé disappears, to be
replaced by Christ himself, who distributes the sacrament.

The illustration insists on the effective presence of Christ in the
consecrated host. If the miniature on f. 88 is compared with a similar
depiction of the *Queste*'s Grail liturgy in Yale, Beinecke 229, a Flemish

manuscript produced in the 1290s (Stones's dating) containing three texts in which the *Queste* appears in its standard position in the *Lancelot–Graal* cycle between *Lancelot* and the *Mort Artu,* the emphasis given to the concept of transubstantiation in Ars. 5218 becomes even more striking.[17] In Yale 229 the kneeling Galaad receives the sacred host from Bishop Josephé's hands while an assembled group of knights and angels looks on. In contrast to this basically realistic rendering (discounting the angels) of a communion scene, the illustration on f. 88 focuses on the miracle itself; the small figure of Christ in the sacred vessel demonstrates visually that the host is without doubt the body and blood of the crucified savior.[18] In Ars. 5218 the planner may either have chosen to illustrate the *Queste* or have been commissioned by someone at the abbey to illustrate it because it represented St. Martin's thinking on transubstantiation, a view painstakingly highlighted in his depiction of the Grail liturgy.[19]

The three miniatures in the pictorial cycle trace a quest for the divine that culminates in the revelation of holy mysteries: Lancelot leaves Arthur's court to go to a convent, where he dubs his son Galaad a knight; Galaad receives Josephé's shield, which designates him as Josephé's spiritual successor; and several knights experience a vision of the Grail in Josephé's presence. The progression of the three miniatures indicates a moral and religious redefinition of the Arthurian world: Lancelot, an outstanding knight in the secular realm, is superceded in importance by his own son Galaad, a Christologic figure. References to the Arthurian world become fewer as the viewer advances through the pictorial cycle: whereas secular figures and institutions predominate over religious ones in the illustrations on the initial page of the text, the second illustration shows only an abbey. By the third miniature the transformation of the secular Arthurian court into a sacred space is complete. The table-like altar of the second miniature mediates between the secular dinner table depicted in the historiated initial on f. 1 and the table of the Grail liturgy in the final miniature. The group of 11 knights in the miniature on f. 88 recalls depictions of the Last Supper in which Judas has already departed from the scene. The viewer of the pictorial cycle moves from the mixed-gender grouping of the Arthurian court to the all-male assembly witnessing the Grail liturgy. Epitomized by the virgin knight, Galaad (who is associated with a Crusader shield in the miniature on f. 10), this final group evokes at once monastic, ecclesiastical, and militant Christian ideals.

Besides delineating an allegorical journey in search of sacred truths, the series of miniatures reveals that the planner of Ars. 5218 placed the *Queste* within the framework of church history.[20] If Galaad is a figure of Christ, he is also the spiritual successor of Josephé, the first Christian bishop. Bishops had a place in the larger church hierarchy, being connected to the papacy both historically, since the pope was originally the bishop of Rome, and in contemporary times, since the pope exercised his right to approve or veto ecclesiastical appointments in fourteenth-century Tournai (Guenée, p. 71, p. 88). By illustrating the Grail vision as witnessed by a group of worthy Arthurian knights rather than the individual visions of Perceval, Bohort, and Galaad, the planner focuses on the ecclesiastical community, be it the individual monastery or the church in general. The representation of Christ and Bishop Josephé in the last frame of the pictorial cycle reinforces the authority of the church as the representative of Christ on earth.

Unlike the majority of manuscripts featuring the *Queste*, in Ars. 5218, the work is transmitted separately from the rest of the Vulgate cycle. Nancy Freeman Regalado cites manuscript evidence indicating that the *Queste* was usually perceived as romance: "Only four [*sic*] of the forty-three extant manuscripts copy the Vulgate *Queste* independently of other sections of the *Lancelot* proper. Authors and compilers confirm their reading of the *Queste* not as a doctrinal treatise nor as a didactic work but as a secular romance...."[21] This valid observation only serves to emphasize the singularity of Ars. 5218, in which the *Queste* has been removed from its place in the *Lancelot-Graal* cycle in order to facilitate its interpretation as a work of ecclesiastical import.[22]

The iconography of Ars. 5218 supplies a "gloss" on the text similar to the commentary provided by the use of the formal procedures of *fabula* and *figura* that the *Queste* author borrowed respectively from the moral reinterpretation of pagan texts and religious exegesis. Regalado clarifies the meaning of the two terms:

> *Fabula* is that mode of suggesting or initiating thematic commentary whose content is quite unlike that of the literal narrative. *Figura* establishes analogies between juxtaposed narratives so that thematic commentary may be derived. Both *fabula* and *figura* cause an effect of textual doubling in which

second meanings oppose or extend the literal sense of the primary text. (p. 98)

Only one of a number of critics who see the *Queste* as fitting into the entire *Lancelot-Graal* cycle,[23] Regalado questions Pauphilet's hypothesis that the *Queste* author employed the Arthurian material as a fictional *fabula* in order to give a systematic exposition of Cistercian doctrine. Taking the opposing position, Fanni Bogdanow (p. 46) and others see a complete break between the ideology of the *Lancelot* and the *Queste* and that of the *Queste* and the *Mort Artu*. I am arguing that given its unusual context in Ars. 5218, the *Queste*—a work that no longer occupies its normal place in a cycle with a pronounced romance character and that has an idiosyncratic program of illuminations—promotes reflection on matters of interest to the monastery for which it was produced. In Ars. 5218, the *Queste* acquires a particular ideological content absent from most of the other manuscripts in which it appears (although we will see later that it has an analogue in Florence, Bibliotheca Medicea Laurenziana, Ashburnham 48).

How can we begin to account for the ideological reading of the *Queste*'s *fabula* in Ars. 5218? The *Queste* author drew not only on the Scriptures themselves, but also on some of the cardinal points of the moral and mystical thought of Saint Bernard as expressed in his sermons on the Song of Songs (Bogdanow, pp. 28–30). In a similar vein, Pauphilet explains how the central image of *la nef de Salomons* in the *Queste* is based on standard ecclesiological interpretations of the Song of Songs as an allegory of Christ and the church (pp. 151–54).[24] Since the library of St.-Martin functioned as a repository of Song of Songs commentary, it is not surprising that in Ars. 5218 the *Queste*, a work indebted to Songs commentary, becomes a vehicle for reflection on ecclesiastical questions. Among the 168 entries recorded in a late-twelfth-century inventory of the library[25] are found commentaries on the Songs by Origen (c. 185–254), Ambrose (c. 330–397), Jerome (347–420), Gregory the Great (540–604), the Venerable Bede (673–735), Anselm (1033–1109), and Bernard de Clairvaux (1091–1153).[26] Some of these authors interpreted the text as a commentary on the monk's relationship with the church and ecclesiastical matters, the same type of reading found in Ars. 5218. We will see how the planner of our manuscript, like Gregory the Great, the Benedictine monk who became the sixty-fourth pope (590–604), points to the ways in which the church falls short of its ideal. This study will further elucidate how another of Gregory's themes, the tension between monastic standards and temporal power, is also prominent in Ars. 5218. The ecclesiological interpretation of the *Queste* in Ars. 5218, then, would appear to be a logical outgrowth of the Song of Songs commentary genre popular at St.-Martin.[27]

TRANSUBSTANTIATION AND THE QUESTION OF CLERICAL CELIBACY

Reacting to references in the *Queste* to *Song of Songs* commentary and working within the context of a clearly established tradition of such commentary as reflected in the holdings of St.-Martin's library, the planner used the pictorial cycle of Ars. 5218 to indicate the abbey's (or the abbot's) views on current ecclesiastical questions. At the beginning of the thirteenth century, the mystery of transubstantiation, the real presence of Christ in the consecrated Eucharist, had stirred up heated controversy in the church. Although transubstantiation had been restated at the Fourth Lateran Council in 1215[28] as well as at the Second Council at Lyons in 1274, it was still being debated in Luther's time.[29]

Through his selection of scenes to be illustrated and their depiction in the pictorial cycle, the planner, adapting the theme of virginity so prominent in the *Queste*, also makes a statement about the celibacy of those who celebrate the mass.[30] The first two miniatures of Ars. 5218, which focus clearly on Galaad, imply that Lancelot is unworthy of obtaining the ultimate vision of the Grail mysteries because of his love of Guinevere. It is his virgin son who will succeed where he has failed. In addition to the interpretation that has Lancelot (ironically the adulterous hero of secular romance) engendering the exemplary hero of otherworldly chivalry, the miniature on f. 10 hints at a second level of meaning: because Galaad receives the shield displaying Josephé's blood, he becomes the spiritual son of Josephé, who in the *Queste* begins the celebration of the sacred liturgy before Christ assumes that office (Pauphilet, p. 102). It is this secondary level of meaning that provides an implicit commentary on clerics' lack of adherence to their vows of celibacy. In *The Mystic Vision in the Grail Legend and in the Divine Comedy*, Lizette Andrews Fisher argues that the emphasis on virginity in the Grail romances raises the larger question of the celibacy of those who celebrate the mass and thus participate in the mystery of transubstantiation (p. 70).[31] Although in the early church the majority of the clergy were married, attitudes toward this practice underwent a notable change in the Middle Ages.

The abolition of clerical marriage and the suppression of all sexual activity among the clergy were major aims of the eleventh-century church reform movement. The accession of the Benedictine Hildebrand to the papacy in 1073 (as Gregory VII) was followed by a decree that outlawed marriage among the clergy. One of the major changes effected by Gregory was the institution of the monastic life for the higher-ranking clergy who embraced chastity as a primary ideal. The Lateran decrees of 1123 and 1139 further reinforced the ban on clerical marriage, with the Council of 1139 imposing celibacy on the priesthood, the diaconate, and the subdiaconate by forbidding married clerics to perform the ministry of the altar.[32]

Despite the efforts of the reformers, clerical marriage was practiced throughout the Middle Ages. The attempt of the Fourth Lateran Council in 1215 to enforce clerical celibacy met with much criticism, with even high-placed clerics taking an open stand against the enforcement of the church's pronouncements. Concubinage and fornication by members of the clergy remained persistent problems throughout the fourteenth century (Barstow, p. 155).[33] Tournai was one of the cities that levied fines and other punishments for clerical incontinence in addition to those decreed by the official councils. By the end of the Middle Ages, many churchmen had concluded that the best they could do was to confine the clergy's sexual activity within reasonable limits since they were unable to eradicate it (Brundage, p. 537).

THE MARGINALIA OF ARS. 5218

The planner allies himself implicitly with the proponents of clerical celibacy through his rendering of the marginal decoration of Ars. 5218. The abundant images found on the edges of the manuscript pages evoke profane quests that reinforce the dialectic established between secular and spiritual quests in the pictorial cycle. Although the Flemish school of manuscript illumination of this period is characterized by irreverent marginalia, often with scatological and pornographic overtones, in Ars. 5218 these are employed with a specific agenda in mind: to intimate that the love quest is not as worthy as the quest for the divine and to discourage sexual activity and marriage on the part of the celebrants of the mass.

The first marginalia in the manuscript appear under the miniature on f. 1 (fig. 11.1). Positive identification of all the figures, especially the two near the bottom right-hand margin, prove difficult due to the damaged state of the marginalia. On the far left an ape lays a trap for birds. To the right of center another ape plays with a contraption (another animal trap or fishline?) while a hooded figure (a monk?) looks on. An indistinguishable figure advances toward the far right-hand margin. Two small furry animals are depicted running under these scenes. To a French-speaking public, such animals were euphemisms for the sexual organs (Camille, *Image*, p. 38). The marginal images on the first page of the text suggest a parody of a courtly hunt.

The well-preserved marginalia on f. 10 (fig. 11.2) offer a surer basis for interpretation. Located below the miniature showing Galaad's arrival at the White Abbey, a naked woman, mounted on a goat and carrying a distaff and spindle, charges another naked woman holding similar objects and mounted on a ram[34] to the musical accompaniment provided by apes, symbols of impure sexuality.[35] The distaff and spindle brandished by the women in place of the conventional jousting equipment employed by knights convey the theme of the world upside down; the naked women engaging in jousts present another image of lewdness.[36] Rams were considered lascivious and hermaphrodite in the Middle Ages.[37] These marginal images of parodic chivalric quests and licentiousness work in tandem with the historiated letter showing male and female faces on f. 10 to reinforce the opposition made at this point in the text between the sacred quest of Galaad and the profane quests of Lancelot, tainted by his adulterous love for Guinevere, and Gauvain, characterized by his inordinate love of women in general.

The technique of the juxtaposition of profane and sacred quests is continued in the next example from f. 20 (fig. 11.4).[38] The very ancient image of mermaids as seductresses is displayed in the top margin: on the left one plays a stringed instrument; on the right another mermaid combs her hair while contemplating her image in a round mirror, an object associated with the representation of Luxuria. The theme of the limitations of worldly chivalry is continued on the page proper in another historiated initial displaying male and female faces that in this case marks the episode in which Gauvain arrives at the Chastel aux Pucelles, an episode in which he declares himself powerless to expiate his many sins. In the bottom margin, a figure mounted on an ass and carrying a heavy burden watches two apish-looking creatures parading by on stilts. This is yet another instance of a grotesque inversion of human activities, which reinforces the opposition between sacred and profane quests pursued by humans seen elsewhere on the manuscript page.

The most striking juxtaposition of these two types of quests occurs on the last folio of the tenth quire of the codex. The imagery found there is anticipated by the upper marginalia on f. 81 (the first folio of the quire; fig. 11.5), which portray a burlesque religious procession. On the left two apes carrying a boar (an image of Christ, used here with parodic intent) on a litter follow an ape-headed clerical figure wearing white vestments and carrying a cross. Another ape playing musical bells heads the procession. Also a symbol of feigned piety, the ape was often employed to mock Church rituals (Janson, p. 168). The culmination of the juxtaposition of the sacred and profane quests in Ars. 5218 occurs on f. 88 (fig. 11.6). In the bottom margin, an ape makes a large dog with porcine attributes dance to the rhythm of his waved baton. On each side appear animal musicians. The boar on the right playing the tambourine recalls in particular the boar in the burlesque procession on f. 81. The image of the sacred liturgy on f. 88 receives its ironic counterpoint in the marginal depictions found in the last quire illustrating the *Queste* in Ars. 5218.

The figure of the ape, which characteristically "apes" human activities, dominates the marginalia. The ape was traditionally seen as the embodiment of erotic passion and impure love (Janson, p. 261). In his *Image on the Edge: The Margins of Medieval Art*, Michael Camille cites a specific example (Manchester, John Rylands Library, fr. 2, f. 212) in which the marginal image of an ape is used in a Lancelot romance to register a protest against lax monastic celibacy (pp. 30–31). Camille contends that the ape, here in its general sense, represents the danger of mimesis or illusion in God's created scheme of things. By envisioning the manuscript page with its images "on the edge" as the product of a unified conception of existence, Camille makes the claim that profane images found in the margins parody their sacred models only to reinstate them all the better (p. 10, p. 30).[39] In Ars. 5218 the marginal images of erotic quests and bestial countermodels of human activities serve to reinforce the emphasis accorded the sacred in the pictorial cycle. Yet beyond the general significance of the series of miniatures of which Camille speaks, meanings particular to Ars. 5218 are likewise present. In his evocation of the themes of erotic love as Luxuria and the world upside-down in the marginalia, the planner takes a stand against clerical incontinence, thereby reinforcing the theoretical positions assumed in the pictorial cycle regarding the notions of transubstantiation and the supremacy of the quest for the divine.

THE HISTORICAL ANNALS

Historical annals (fig. 11.7) occupy ff. 95–106 of Ars. 5218. Since the annals begin a separate gathering, it is not sure that the *Queste* and the annals were conceived of from the outset as two essential parts of the same book. On the other hand, both codicological evidence and thematic concerns establish connections between the texts. Almost assuredly copied in Pierart's hand, the annals are prepared and decorated in a manner closely resembling that of the *Queste*; for example, the ornamental letter on f. 95 is of a design similar to the one on f. 10 of the *Queste*; furthermore, the border design of the two texts is the same.[40] Since the two texts evidence a similar deliberate design and they are the only two texts known to have been copied by Pierart, it is logical to pair them (if Pierart did not pair them himself, someone else apparently had reasons for doing so!). Roger Middleton has noted that there is more than an accidental similarity between the way in which the vellum was prepared and ruled in the two works. He believes that the same hand probably did the ruling in both cases in accordance with a plan to produce a book of uniform appearance.[41] Middleton further notes that the illustration has left an offset between the first page of the annals (f. 95) and the blank leaf belonging to the last page of the *Queste* (f. 94v.) that resembles that found on the bifolium used as a flyleaf on f. 1, a similarity suggesting that the two works were originally bound together. Since Pierart states that he bound the manuscript book,[42] a possible inference is that he bound the annals with the *Queste* as a post scriptum to the latter.

Since the annals are of a type associated with a monastic milieu, the contention that Ars. 5218 was produced in or around St.-Martin de Tournai receives additional support. Most of the surviving annals were abridged translations into the vernacular made in the course of the thirteenth century.[43] Pierart could have copied them directly (I do not think the annals were of his own invention for reasons I shall specify below) or translated them from a Latin text preserved in the monastery library.

The annals document events from the beginning of time to the year 1281 with their main focus being on church history. Beginning with the ordination of Saint Peter in the year 45, the chronicler lists all the popes of the Western Church. After a brief introductory section that includes mention of Abraham (whose willingness, albeit reluctant, to sacrifice his son, Isaac, qualified him as a precursor of Christ in his role as celebrant of the mass), many of the initial entries of the annals are devoted to the life of Christ, beginning with his birth in A.D. 1 to the 14–year-old Virgin Mary. The entry for A.D. 33 detailing Christ's crucifixion and resurrection is followed by a mention of Pentecost, reminiscent of the *Queste*, which opens on the eve of this same feast and ends with a vision of the risen Christ in his manifestation as consecrated host. The annalist, who alternates dates concerning Christian martyrs, Roman emperors, French royalty, and Flemish nobility (Flanders was then was governed by France), adds incidents from local history when he approaches contemporary times. The entry for the year 1277 notes that construction was begun on a new wall in Tournai that would extend from the portal of Kokriel to that of Bordiel on the banks of the Escaut. Information on the building of this wall also figures in a chronicle authored by Gilles le Muisit, who praises the fact that it will extend and concentrate the jurisdiction of the city's legal and administrative powers (Guenée, p. 103).

The entry for year 1277 further states that 26 people were crushed to death in the procession held annually to commemorate the intercession of the Virgin Mary on behalf of the people of Tournai during the Great Plague of 1092. This disturbing event, which recalls the burlesque procession figured in the margins of the *Queste*, puts the very notion of the miraculous into question.[44] The naturalistic occurrence of people crushing others to death while in the throes of religious frenzy (all the more disturbing because the same thing had happened as recently as 1229)[45] recounted in the annals casts a doubtful light on the miraculous events pictured in the *Queste*. The theme of the questionable veracity of miracles, evident in the annals as well as in the pictorial cycle of the *Queste*, was a favorite of Gilles Le Muisit who in his chronicles recounts four pseudo-miracles as a warning to the reader not to judge by appearances (Guenée, p. 115).

Although breaking off about 30 years prior to the transfer of the papacy to Avignon, the annals would seem to anticipate the *translatio ecclesiae,* the displacement of the locus of Church power from its original seat in Rome to Avignon, a displacement that lasted from approximately 1309 to 1377. In 1351, the year when Pierart finished Ars. 5218, Christendom was ruled from Avignon; the pope himself, for example, confirmed the nomination of the abbots of St.-Martin. At first situating the papacy in its original seat in Rome, the annals end up by placing it in the context of the policies of the French monarchy that controlled francophone Flanders at the moment when the annals break off. Ties between the papacy and France were strengthened during the second half of the thirteenth century. The promotion of Charles d'Anjou as king of Naples was the primary event that solidified French influence on the papacy.[46] The last entry in the annals, for the year 1281, documents the ascent of Martin IV to the Holy See. Martin, whose given name was Simon de Brion, was favored by the French party that eventually had the seat of the papacy relocated to Avignon. An avid partisan of the policies of Charles d'Anjou and his brother, Louis IX, Martin IV was responsible for the decision to canonize the latter.[47]

The author of the annals (probably not Pierart, for reasons that will become clear) seems to favor the policies of Philippe II Auguste, Charles d'Anjou, and his brother, Louis IX, policies that were by and large continued by Philippe le Bel, the French monarch who made several visits to St.-Martin de Tournai in the years directly preceding Pierart's birth and who was instrumental in having the seat of the papacy relocated to Avignon. A municipal republic, Tournai had received a charter establishing it as a commune from Philippe II Auguste in 1188. Tournai's bishops were firm supporters of French royal policies (Guenée, pp. 71–72).[48] Gilles Le Muisit, abbot of St.-Martin, had a personal interest in the exploits of Charles d'Anjou since his uncle, Baudouin Le Muisit, had accompanied Charles in his campaign across the Alps and upon his return to Tournai had recounted the story to his young nephew (Guenée, p. 75).

Several examples should suffice to demonstrate the pro-French bias of the annals. The French king Philippe II Auguste, friend of the papacy and victor over the count of Flanders, Ferdinand of Portugal, at Bouvines, compared himself to the Romans by having his propagandists add the epithet "Augustus" to his name. The entry for

789 notes that in that year Charlemagne became emperor and king and received the designation "Augustus." The year 789 was an important date in the history of the papacy for it was only with Pope Gregory at the beginning of the seventh century that the supremacy of the the pope (as bishop of Rome) over other bishops had been recognized. In the same year Charlemagne confirmed the pope in his temporal sovereignty over Rome and its surrounding territories and in return, the pope consecrated Charlemagne and crowned him Holy Roman Emperor.[49] It is easy to see how Charlemagne's role in the strengthening of papal power could be used to legitimize the *translatio ecclesiae* to French soil at a later date.

The series of entries from the year 1212 to 1248 (the entries are chronological, although some years are completely omitted) provides convincing evidence that the author of the annals was a Tournaisian who supported the French party:

1212	The count of Boulogne was chased out of France.
1213	Louis, Louis's son, was born.
1214	Philippe, the king of France, won the Battle of Bouvines against Ferrand, the count of Flanders, and afterward he had Ferrand taken and put in prison.
1223	King Philippe died. His son Louis became king of France.
1226	Louis died. His son Louis became king of France.
1244	Jeanne, the countess of Flanders, died. Marguerite, her sister, became countess.
1248	King Louis of France and his two brothers left to cross the sea.

The entry for 1214 is clearly written from the point of view of a supporter of Philippe Auguste's victory at Bouvines. The sisters Jeanne and Marguerite de Flandre mentioned in the entry for 1244 were the Flemish countesses who received considerable support from Philippe le Bel.[50] The entry for 1248, which makes note of Louis IX's departure for his first Crusade, contains an oblique reference to Charles d'Anjou, one of Louis's two brothers.

The hypothesis that the annals in Ars. 5218 anticipate (and even express tacit approval of) the *translatio ecclesiae* to Avignon receives support from Brussels, KB 13076–77, Gilles Le Muisit's *Tractatus quartus* illuminated by Pierart dou Tielt (Caullet, pp. 200–22). The opening miniature, which portrays Clément VI, Benoît XII, and Jean XXII, all popes born in what is now French territory who governed Western Christendom from Avignon during the period from 1316 to 1352, heads a chapter of the chronicle comprising extended passages on each of these popes (the heading reads "Chest des papes . . . qui ont esté de mon temps" [This is about the popes who were of my time]).[51] The preceding section of Gilles's chronicles, the *Tractatus tertius*, contains annals combining sacred, ecclesiastical, and local history reminiscent of those found in the annals in Ars. 5218. By mentioning Poitiers, Albi, and the anti-pope, Gilles, who drew his power as abbot directly from the pope,[52] showed a lively interest in church politics in the south of France.

Perhaps prompted by Gilles's own desires in the matter, the planner evokes Gilles through his representation of Josephé in the miniature of the Grail liturgy on f. 88. The viewer (especially a monastic one) would naturally associate Josephé with Gilles, head of the monastic community for which Ars. 5218 was undoubtedly produced. Like Gilles, Josephé is an ecclesiastical dignitary presiding over a group of Christian men who participate in the eucharistic ceremony and embrace a celibate ideal. Pauphilet makes the argument that the *Queste* stresses the role of monastics, especially abbots, their leaders, in the church (p. 54). The similarity between Josephé and Gilles is heightened because the former, supposedly the first Christian bishop, holds a crozier that resembles the one Gilles is carrying in several miniatures in Brussels, KB IV 119 (Gilles's *Lamentations*) likewise illustrated by Pierart.[53] The representation of Josephé on f. 88 pays tribute to Gilles's varied roles as head of the monastery of St.-Martin, celebrant of the divine liturgy, and supporter of the Avignon papacy.

The analogies implied between Josephé and Gilles extend to earlier illustrious ecclesiastical figures. Thematic meanings are multiplied through a network of analogies in a very sophisticated use of *figura*. A monastic audience well versed in ecclesiastical history would be predisposed to discern analogies between Josephé, Gilles, and Saint

Benoît, founder of the Benedictine order, especially since the analogy between Gilles and Saint Benoît had been drawn in another manuscript illustrated by Pierart that was housed in the abbey library.[54] Shown kneeling in prayer in the historiated initial under the large miniature on f. 230 of the second volume of Brussels, KB IV 119, Gilles gives thanks for having been cured of blindness. In the upper register of the two-part miniature, the Virgin Mary is seated facing the Holy Trinity; on the left side of the group appears Saint Benoît, on the right, Saint Martin.[55] Analogies implied in the miniature on f. 88 between Josephé, Gilles, and Saint Benoît would be particularly suitable for emphasizing the importance of the abbot of a Benedictine monastery like Gilles.

The portrait of Josephé, the first Christian bishop, might have also called to mind Gregory the Great. The Benedictine abbot who as pope reformed papal administration and ecclesiastical life, Gregory was the author of works such as the *Moralia of Job,* the *Regula pastoris* (a treatise on ecclesiastical administration), and a commentary on the *Song of Songs*. All these texts, as well as at least four other volumes of his works, figured in the late-twelfth-century inventory of the library of St.-Martin (Delisle, vol. 2, p. 489). Gregory was one of the founders of the system of medieval monastic exegesis that led to later manifestations like those found in the *Queste* (and in the reading of the *Queste* evident in the pictorial cycle and marginal decoration of Ars. 5218). In his dual role as excellent administrator and writer, Gilles continued in a limited way the tradition represented by his Benedictine predecessor, Gregory the Great. The chain of analogies established between Gilles, Gregory the Great, and Saint Benoît would be especially fitting since Gregory was the major disseminator of information about the latter. The entire second book of Gregory's *Four Books of Dialogues on the Life and Miracles of the Italian Fathers* (written in 593–594) is the source of virtually all our knowlege of Saint Benoît (*New Catholic Encyclopedia,* vol. 6, p. 769). Like Gilles several centuries later, Gregory views miracles with a critical eye: for Gregory, saints like Benoît who had not worked miracles were just as great as those who had. Both Gregory the Great[56] and Saint Benoît would serve as legitimizing precursors for Gilles in his often difficult role as abbot of St.-Martin.

The implicit evocation of Gilles in the pictorial cycle of the *Queste*, a work that stresses the difficulties attendant upon those who occupy the "Siège périlleux," reinforces Gilles's legitimacy as abbot in relation to the papacy. The bishop of Tournai, Guillaume de Ventadour, a supporter of another candidate for the abbacy (Guillemain, pp. 520–21), had contested the unanimous election of Gilles as abbot that had taken place in St.-Martin on April 30, 1331 (Guenée, p. 72). Representatives of both sides succeeded in settling the affair in Gilles's favor only after a year and a half of negotiations in Avignon. The election in 1324 of Thierry de Parc, Gilles's predecessor, had also incited considerable controversy (Guillemain, p. 520). What was worse, Thierry was the third in a series of abbots whose poor management of St.-Martin had produced crisis conditions in the abbey during the period from 1290 to Jean XXII's confirmation of Gilles's election in 1332. Gilles made a considerable effort to put St.-Martin back on sure footing: he repaid its debts, reorganized the domain, and reconstructed the abbey.[57] Gilles's previously cited chapter on the popes that he had known during his lifetime contains statements designed to shore up his legitimacy as abbot with the papacy: claiming that the pope is answerable only to God, Gilles cautions the faithful that to question papal power is to fall into heresy (Guillemain, pp. 92–93).

The pictorial cycle of Ars. 5218 also reflects the bitter debates on the beatific vision that had taken place in Avignon during Gilles's time as abbot. Whereas Jean XXII (pope from 1316–1334) had affirmed that only on the Day of Judgment would the elect attain a full vision of the godhead, Benoît XII (pope from 1334–1342; formerly a Cistercian abbot) countered in his bull *Benedictus Deus* of 29 January 1336 that they would see God at the moment of their death (*New Catholic Encyclopedia,* vol. 2, pp. 275–76). Either of these two interpretations could be inferred by the story line of the *Queste* and the miniature on f. 88 of Ars. 5218 (fig. 11.3) in which both the Christian knights and Josephé, who according to the text has been brought back from death after more than three centuries, experience a *visio dei*.[58]

A manuscript made for the founder of the papal library in Avignon evidences intriguing parallels with Ars. 5218. An abundantly illustrated book containing only the *Queste,* this manuscript, Florence, Bibliotheca Medicea Laurenziana, Ashburnham 48 (121), was produced in 1319 in Avignon for Jean XXII (Jean's arms figure on the last folio of the manuscript directly before the colophon; Breillat, pp. 262–300). Besides figuring in the controversy over the nature of the beatific vision, Jean XXII was the pope who had confirmed Gilles's election as abbot (Guenée, p. 72). Transcribed in Franco-Provençal and obviously neither illuminated nor copied by Pierart, Laurenziana 48 appears to have had as one of its aims the legitimation of the housing of the papacy in Avignon.[59] Like Ars. 5218, it reinforces the concept of the real presence of Christ in the consecrated host, related to the institution of the feast of Corpus Christi in 1264, to which Jean XXII later lent his support by giving it an octave and by stipulating that the Eucharist could be carried in sacred processions.[60] The rubric describing the miniature on f. 86, "Coment les chevaliers sont devant le voisel et le vesque et vienent les iiii angles qui portent la lance et le cierges et la toalle" (How the knights are in front of the vessel and the bishop when the four angels arrive bearing the lance, the candles, and the piece of cloth) recalls the elements depicted on f. 88 of Ars. 5218. Other miniatures show a preoccupation with the eucharistic ceremony, such as the one on f. 86v, which depicts Christ distributing communion to kneeling knights, and the one on f. 22, which portrays a priest and two other figures kneeling before the altar. Like Ars. 5218, Laurenziana 48 reinforces the concept of transubstantiation and strengthens the legitimacy of the person for whom it was produced.

GUIBERT DE TOURNAI, AUTHOR OF THE ANNALS (?)

Whereas I accord Pierart a high degree of responsibility in the production of Ars. 5218, several facts cast doubt on his authorship of the annals. The bottom margin of folio 95 contains a Latin gloss[61] referring to the entry for the year 4 and noting the names of the three Herods; Pierart is evidently making a comment in Latin on a text he transcribed but did not compose. Middleton surmises that if he had composed the annals, he could have incorporated the gloss into the entry itself. The dates included in the chronology also cast doubt upon his authorship of the annals. The last entry is for the ascent of Martin to the papacy in 1281,[62] and Pierart, who was born around 1300 and who transcribed this copy of the chronicle in 1351, would not have lived through any of the events comprised by the time line.

The hypothesis that Gilles Le Muisit was the author of the annals, although more seductive than the one just discussed, is ultimately unconvincing. We have already seen that in several instances considerations expressed in the annals and in the illustrated, "commented" version of the *Queste* in Ars. 5218 are repeated in Gilles's writings. Although marked by similar concerns, the vernacular annals in Ars. 5218 and the Latin annals that form part of Gilles's chronicles neither look, feel, nor sound as if they were written by the same person. The historical annals in Ars. 5218 supplement rather than duplicate the annals that Gilles included in his *Tractatus tertius* (a text illustrated by Pierart). Extending from the creation to 1294, Gilles's annals serve as a type of prologue to his historical chronicle (which covers the period from 1294 to 1349).[63] Gilles's Latin annals have a flavor quite different from that of the vernacular annals in Ars. 5218.

Instead, a more likely candidate for the role of author of the annals found in Ars. 5218[64] is Guibert de Tournai (c. 1200–1284), the renowned Tournaisian theologican referred to in Gilles's Latin chronicles as "Brother Guibert de Moriel-Porte, doctor of theology in the Franciscan order."[65] Guibert was the author of several chronicles that have disappeared.[66] The annals in Ars. 5218 could be the copy or translation into the vernacular of all or part of a work called the *Chronica,* described as a "catalogue of historical events, perhaps taken from the works of Guibert."[67] Guibert occupied a Franciscan chair at the University of Paris following Bonaventure's resignation in 1257 and accompanied Louis IX on his first Crusade (1248–1254) (Moorman, p. 247). Guibert would have had a good reason for concluding his entries with the advent of Martin to the papacy in 1281: Martin IV remained in his seat until 1285, one year after the death of Guibert in October 1284.

There are other reasons for suspecting Guibert's hand in the composition of the annals. First, many entries deal with the Crusades, a fact that provides a strong link between the annals and the image of the Crusader shield found on f. 10 of the *Queste.* The entry for 1270, for instance, notes Louis IX's death at Tunis. Guibert was famous for his sermons in which he, like Louis IX (as reported in Jean de Joinville's *Vie de Saint Louis*), blamed the failure of the Crusades on the debauchery of pilgrims and Crusaders alike. In his *Eruditio regum et principum,* undertaken upon Louis's request, Guibert, writing as an eyewitness to Louis's first Crusade five years previously, tried (unsuccessfully) to dissuade the king from undertaking a second one (Gratien, p. 655). The *De viris illustribus* attributed to Henry of Ghent informs us that Guibert wrote another eyewitness account of Louis IX's first Crusade, entitled the *Hodoeporicon,* which disappeared subsequently from its home in the library of St.-Martin de Tournai (Curvis, p. 6).

Second, the entry for 1274, the only entry that mentions a papal council—the Second at Lyons—in the annals, states that over three hundred bishops, archbishops, and abbots were defrocked because they were "bigames la nuit,"[68] i.e., that they were married to a woman as well as to the church. One of the stated goals of the council was the reform of the morals of the clergy (Tanner, vol. 1, p. 309). At Bonaventure's request, Guibert composed his *Collectio de scandalis ecclesiae,* an attack on clerical abuses, for presentation to Gregory X before the Second Council, which Guibert attended in company of Bonaventure (who died during the course of the meeting). The annals entry for 1274 describes the concrete application of article 16 ("On Bigamists") of the council that mandated that bigamists were to be deprived of their clerical privileges and handed over to secular authorities. Bigamous clerics were forbidden furthermore to wear the tonsure or clerical dress. The close correspondence between the annal entry and the passage on bigamists found in the records of the papal council (Tanner, vol. l, p. 322) gives reason to believe that the person who wrote the former was familiar with the latter. Since Bonaventure had asked Guibert de Tournai to speak about clerical abuses at the council of 1274, it is not unlikely that Guibert's text influenced the written record of the proceedings or was even copied verbatim. Third, the entry for 1277 concerning the construction of new walls around the city may include references to Guibert's family history and to his status as a Franciscan.[69]

An additional connection exists between Guibert and Ars. 5218. Some of the major themes and techniques of Guibert's best-known works, his *Tractatus de pace*[70] and his *Tractatus de virginitate,* both heavily influenced by the *Song of Songs,* are recalled in the iconographically "glossed" version of the *Queste* appearing in Ars. 5218. Composed between 1273 and 1276 in the hope of reconciling the Cistercians with his own Franciscan order, Guibert's *Tractatus de pace* describes an allegorical journey of the soul towards peace. In the tracts written at a high level of abstraction, the closest the author comes to discussing a reconciliation between rival religious orders is in chapter 20, where he considers the notion that peace is not found in controversy. Guibert's narration of the soul's visionary voyage begins in heaven among the angels who had to regain their state of peacefulness after first losing it during the pitched battles that preceded the Fall. The ecstastic vision of the Grail witnessed by a procession of heavenly hosts as well as by illustrious Arthurian knights in Ars. 5218 (fig. 11.3), albeit very true to the text it illustrates, is also strangely reminiscent of Guibert's description of the final peace experienced by the angels in heaven.[71] In his *Tractatus de virginitate,* which also assumes the form of an allegorical quest for a state of inner tranquillity, Guibert counsels virginity as one of the ways to detach oneself from earthly goods and enter into a state of contemplation, prelude to the perfect possession of God in the beatific vision. Culminating in a virgin knight's transcendent visions, the *Queste,* especially in the form in which it appears in Ars. 5218, has obvious parallels with Guibert's treatise on virginity.

THE PRODUCTION OF ARS. 5218: SOME HYPOTHESES

What proceeds from the foregoing examination of historical and documentary evidence is that the close relationship between Pierart and the abbot of St.-Martin de Tournai, Gilles Le Muisit, was determinant in forming the character of Ars. 5218. Inspired in all likelihood by the memory of the renowned Tournaisian theologian, Guibert de Tournai, Pierart accomplished his work on Ars. 5218 under the guidance and direction of his employer, Gilles Le Muisit. Although evidently not the author of the chronicle, Pierart is what Alison Stones terms an "independent artistic personality" ("Sacred and Profane Art," p. 112), who took special interest in treating ecclesiastical matters in a manuscript intimately bound up with the intellectual and spiritual life of St.-Martin de Tournai.

Pierart, whose preoccupations in Ars. 5218 so often mirror Gilles's own, apparently had Gilles in mind when he produced the manuscript book. Since Gilles had commanded the production of at least one book himself in the past,[72] it is tempting to envision the abbot as having commissioned the fabrication of Ars. 5218. The question remains whether a person other than Pierart served as planner. To judge by the sophisticated treatment of church matters found in Ars. 5218, the planner most likely would have been someone associated with St.-Martin de Tournai as was Pierart. Yet additional evidence concerning Pierart's personal interest in the execution of Ars. 5218 given below strengthens my contention that he served as planner as well as exercising all the other functions of book production on Ars. 5218.

Besides supplying commentary on ecclesiastical issues and local events in the not too distant past, Ars. 5218 is an intensely moving document of Pierart's devotion to the abbot Gilles Le Muisit. Guibert de Tournai's doctrine of illumination, by which he attempted a reconciliation of the notion of God as divine light and human reason, applies well to a personal drama occuring in Gilles's life at the very time when Pierart was working on Ars. 5218. Gilles's literary activity starts up in earnest in 1346, when cataracts began claiming his eyesight (Guenée, p. 76). Even after becoming completely blind two years later, Gilles continued to compose and dictate works in Latin and the vernacular at a feverish pace, giving renewed meaning to the relationship between blindness and insight. Pierart had come into the direct employ of the monastery sometime after 1349, during the time of the now blind abbot's prodigious activity. Lovingly transcribed, illuminated, and bound by Pierart, Ars. 5218 was a fitting memorial to the abbot, a blind man fast approaching eighty years of age who had spent so much of his last years in book production.

The distinctive way that Pierart signs his work—by including his name at the end of the transcription of the *Queste* as if it were part of the text rather than a colophon—gives rise to the suspicion that he was preparing the book for inclusion in the abbey library in memory of Gilles. In taking particular care to delineate his contributions to the volume and to identify himself as the individual who completed his work on a specific date, Pierart gives testimony to his accomplishment.[73] The date recorded by Pierart, "le nuit notre dame en mi aoust" (f. 91v), evokes the date of the last mass celebrated by Gilles, August 15, 1348, the feast of the Assumption of the Blessed Virgin Mary (Guenée, p. 76). One of Gilles's greatest regrets (expressed in his *Lamentations*) was that because of his blindness he was unable to celebrate mass (Caullet, p. 223). As pointed out earlier, the miniature on f. 88 (fig.11-3) treats the mystery of transubstantiation celebrated by a priest during mass.

Pierart was not the only one to prepare a parting memorial for Gilles: Jacques Muevin, the monk who would succeed Gilles as abbot of St.-Martin, was at that time transcribing Gilles's chronicles in collections illuminated by Pierart. In the opening miniature on f. 1 of the *Tres Tractatus,* Kortrijk, SOB, fonds Goethals-Vercruysse 135 (fig. 11.8), begun in 1347 or 1348 and finished around Easter 1349 or 1350 (Caullet, pp. 208-09), Gilles (not yet completely blind) dictates his chronicles to Jacques. The depiction of the ailing abbot and his successor suggests that the two were close friends as well as collaborators on a common literary endeavor. (Pierart's rendering of the effect of the light shining through the monastery's leaded windows provides an uncanny reminder of Guibert de Tournai's doctrine of illumination.)

The story of Gilles's blindness was to have an unexpected twist. As Gilles recounts in his chronicle, the doctor Jean de Mayence appeared in Tournai in 1351 for the annual procession on behalf of the Virgin. Once at the monastery, he successfully performed a cataract operation on one of Gilles's eyes on 18 September 1351; on 22 September, he operated on the other. Gilles's cure forms the subject of a double miniature done by Pierart (found on f. 50v of Brussels, KB 13076–13077). On the left, the surgeon uses a lancet to operate on one of Gilles's eyes; on the right, the doctor announces Gilles's cure to his friends and relatives (Caullet, p. 215).[74] Still unable to read or write, Gilles could nonetheless recognize people and celebrate mass. Although he reassumed his charge as head of the monastery, Gilles composed no more verse or prose until his death on 15 October 1353 (Guenée, p. 101).

CONCLUSION: RESONANCE AND WONDER

The preceding observations lead to the conclusion that Ars. 5218 epitomizes Stephen Greenblatt's conception of a "cultural artifact," a collaborative effort accomplished by a manuscript producer or producers, the patrons or clients who commissioned the manuscript, and the authors of the several texts included on its folios, who all lived in particular times and places with links to a host of historical figures and discourses. Despite the utility of his term that applies so aptly to the illuminated medieval book, Greenblatt has discounted the visual appeal of the medieval manuscript, even an illuminated one:

> The experience of wonder was not initially regarded as essentially or even primarily visual. . . . The great medieval collections of marvels are almost entirely textual. . . . Some of the manuscripts, to be sure, were illuminated, but these illuminations were almost always ancillary to the textual record of wonders. . . . (p. 178)

In recent years critics of the Middle Ages have questioned the notion of a stable "text" of a work, pointing out that medieval textuality is characterized by *mouvance,* the shifting of textual parameters, and thus a work's meaning, within the context of different manuscripts. In its placement in Ars. 5218, a manuscript including annals concerning the city of Tournai, a pictorial cycle culminating in a vision of heavenly wonders, and irreverent marginalia, the *Queste* acquires doctrinal and historical meanings not duplicated elsewhere. In this study I have argued that Ars. 5218 in fact generates "resonance," which Greenblatt defines as "the power of the object displayed to reach out beyond its formal boundaries to a larger world, to evoke in the viewer the complex, dynamic cultural forces from which it has emerged and for which as metaphor or more simply as metonymy it may be taken by a viewer to stand" (p. 170).

Having been established as a cultural artifact full of resonance, Ars. 5218 speaks even more strongly to the sense of wonder that Greenblatt describes as "the power of the object displayed to stop the viewer in his tracks, to convey an arresting sense of uniqueness, to evoke an exalted attention" (p. 170). While ostensibly communicating the sense of amazement elicited by the vision of the sacred mysteries, the miniature of the Grail liturgy on f. 88 presents the dynamics of the wonder capable of being generated by the illuminated manuscript book.

A comprehensive view of a medieval book like Ars. 5218 necessitates an understanding of how Camille's so-called "images on the edge" provide a commentary on the major contents of manuscripts. My examination of Ars. 5218 indicates that the marginal images have a more subtle function than Camille allows for in his demonstration; in conjunction with other elements, they at once confirm and undermine the miraculous events ostensibly celebrated in the collection. At the very least, they caution that the true miracle must always be distinguished from its preternatural counterfeit, the mere marvel. The margins of Ars. 5218 stretch the limits of its apparently coherent world view, announcing, in subversive counterpoint to its strictly orthodox appearance, a naturalistic reality in which popes govern as princes and the miraculous can reveal itself to be a preposterous hoax or a scientific wonder. Not only is Ars. 5218 a precious example of a cultural artifact capable of evoking resonance and wonder, but the work of its executor, Pierart dou Tielt, when fully studied, will illuminate further the milieu of fourteenth-century Tournai as an important center of manuscript production, political activity, and theological debate in late medieval Europe.

NOTES

1. Unless stated otherwise, all the translations into English are my own. See Alison Stones's article in this volume for further discussion of manuscripts examined in my study. My thanks to Gloria Allaire, Maryann Brink, Cynthia Hahn, and Maureen Tilley for having read and commented on earlier versions of this article and to Richard Rouse and Roger Middleton for having shared their observations on the manuscript with me.

2. See Beat Brenk, "Le texte et l'image dans la *Vie de saints* au Moyen Age: rôle du concepteur et rôle du peintre," in *Texte et image: Actes du Colloque international de Chantilly* (13–15 October 1982) (Paris: Les Belles Lettres, 1984), pp. 31–40.

3. François Avril, *Les Fastes du Gothique: le Siècle de Charles V* (exhibition catalogue), ed. F. Baron, F. Avril, P. Chapu, and D. Gaborit-Chopin (Paris: Réunion des Musées Nationaux, 1981), p. 348.

4. Scholars are now redefining our understanding of manuscript production, including our conception of a workshop. See R. H. and M. A. Rouse, "The Commercial Production of Manuscript Books in Late-Thirteenth-Century and Early-Fourteenth-Century Paris," in *Medieval Book Production: Assessing the Evidence*, ed. Linda Brownrigg (Los Altos, Calif.: Los Altos Hills, 1990), pp. 103–15. See also François Avril and Nicole Reynaud's introduction to their exhibition catalogue, *Les Manuscrits à peinture en France: 1440–1520* (Paris: Bibliothèque Nationale, 1993).

5. There are other examples of manuscript illuminations that reflect opinions on church teachings. According to Jeffrey Hamburger, *The Rothschild Canticles: Art and Mysticism in Flanders and the Rhineland Circa 1300* (New Haven: Yale Univ. Press, 1990), p. 136, both the miniature on f. 16 and the accompanying text found in the manuscript of the *Omne bonum* (London, BL, Royal 6 E. vi) were intended as a declaration of orthodoxy regarding the beatific vision. See my discussion of this miniature in a note infra.

6. Stephen Greenblatt, *Learning to Curse: Essays in Early Modern Culture* (New York: Routledge, 1990).

7. Avril, Entry 301, "*La Queste du saint Graal*," *Les Fastes*, pp. 348–49.

8. Pierart no doubt was formed by the Master of the Ghent Ceremonial, an illuminator trained in Paris. See Avril, pp. 301–02, for a description of this manuscript, as well as my "Illuminating the Rose: Gui de Mori and the Illustrations of MS 101 of the Municipal Library, Tournai," in *Rethinking the 'Romance of the Rose'*, ed. Kevin Brownlee and Sylvia Huot (Philadelphia: Univ. of Pennsylvania Press, 1992), pp. 167–200. Pierart also collaborated with the Master of the Ghent Ceremonial on the Breviary of Sainte-Aldegonde, Maubeuge, Cambrai, BM 133.

9. Pierart illuminated two volumes of the *Speculum historiale* by Vincent de Beauvais, Brussels, KB 79 (part 2, books IX–XVI) and 118 (part 3, books XVII–XXIV); and the *Somme le Roi*, Lille, BM 366 (116), executed in 1358. See Alison Stones, "The Illustrated Chrétien Manuscripts and Their Artistic Context," in *The Manuscripts of Chrétien de Troyes*, ed. Keith Busby, Alison Stones, Terry Nixon, and Lori Walters, 2 vols. (Amsterdam: Rodopi, 1993), vol. 1, p. 259. According to information found in the manuscript catalogue of the Institut de Recherches et d'Histoire des Textes (Paris), Pierart also illuminated Brussels, KB II 1010 V.d.G. 1172, a manuscript of Jean Cassien's *Collationes*. Folio 92 bears the note, "Liber Martini Tornacensis. Servanti benedictis."

10. In a private consultation, François Avril identified the manuscript illuminations as being the work of Pierart.

11. A. D'Haenens, "Pierart dou Tielt, enlumineur des oeuvres de Gilles li Muisit, note sur son activité à Tournai vers 1350," *Scriptorium*, 23 (1969), 88–93.

12. Gilles is also known to have been the patron of the Gospel and Epistle Book, Brussels, KB 63, which Stones attributes to the painter of Fauveyn, Paris, BN, fr. 751/571.

13. His name is not found in the obituary list of St.-Martin. See Dom Ursmer Berlière, *Monasticon Belge*, vol. 1: Provinces de Namur et de Hainaut (Liège: Centre National d'Histoire Religieuse, 1973). Furthermore, it is likely that if he had been a monk, he would have indicated it in one of his colophons.

14. See Stones, "Prolegomena to a Corpus of Vincent de Beauvais Illustrations," *Vincent de Beauvais: intentions et réceptions d'une oeuvre encyclopédique au Moyen Age*, ed. Monique Paulmier-Foucart, Serge Lusignan and Alain Nadeau (Montreal: Bellarmin, 1990), pp. 301–02. On the abbey library, see also Bernard Guenée, *Entre l'église et l'état: Quatre vies de prélats français à la fin du Moyen Age (XIIIe-XVe siècle)* (Paris: Gallimard, 1987), p. 89.

15. Le Baron Etienne de Bethune-Sully, *Testaments Tournaisiens et Comptes d'Executions Testamentaires, XIIe–XVIIe siècle*, (Bruxelles: Anibel, 1967; Aalst, Chez l'auteur, 1970), p. 27.

16. Albert Pauphilet, ed. *La Queste del Saint Graal*. (Paris: Champion, 1984), p. xii.

17. See Michael Camille's discussion of this image, reproduced in Illustration 56, p. 107 of his *Image on the Edge: The Margins of Medieval Art*. (Cambridge: Harvard Univ. Press, 1992), p. 108.

18. Camille points out that medieval secular manuscripts often treat religious themes more seriously than liturgical books (p. 108).

19. Ars. 5218 illustrates precisely those scenes depicting transubstantiation in the *Queste*; see Albert Pauphilet, *Etudes sur la "Queste del saint Graal"* (Paris: Champion, 1968), pp. 28–29. Pauphilet, p. 57, contends that the views on transubstantiation set forth in the *Queste* reflect the official position at Cîteaux, the position that prevailed in the church as stated in the ecumenical councils of 1215 and 1274.

20. A collection of Cistercian tracts belonging to the abbey library takes up many of the same questions on the role of the priesthood, the meaning of the mass, and the relationship between divine and worldly love that Pierart examines in Ars. 5218. This manuscript book of 129 folios now identified as Brussels, KB II 1029, is largely devoted to the works of Saint Bernard, in particular to his sermons on the *Song of Songs,* in which he applies courtly love and marital imagery to the quest for religious truths. Folios 119v to 129 are occupied by a collection of other works, among which are found a long poem entitled *Pastoralis,* in which the author presents the portrait of the ideal prelate, a poem encouraging disdain for things of this world, and two pieces by Hildebert de Lavardin, one of which is, significantly, a poem on the sacrifice of the mass. See André Boutemy, "Analyse d'une Anthologie poétique de l'Abbaye de Saint-Martin de Tournai," *Revue belge de philologie et d'histoire* 17 (1938), 727–46. Hildebert, a prominent ecclesiastic, was among those who called for a entirely celibate priesthood. Although I am not arguing for the direct influence on Ars. 5218 of this manuscript miscellany, obviously only one of many that has been singled out in the literature, KB II 1029 is nonetheless representative of the books in the abbey library to which Pierart had access.

21. Nancy Freeman Regalado, "La Chevalerie Celestiel: Spiritual Transformation of Secular Romance in *La Queste del Saint Graal,"* in *Romance: Generic Transformation from Chrétien de Troyes to Cervantes,* ed. Kevin Brownlee and Marina S. Brownlee (Hanover and London: Univ. Press of New England, 1985), pp. 91–113, p. 108.

22. The three other manuscripts referred to by Regalado in which the *Queste* is taken out of its place in the *Lancelot–Graal* cycle are the following: (1) Paris, BN, fr. 25520, a thirteenth-century manuscript containing only the *Queste.* Unlike Ars. 5218, it was not very carefully copied, and has painted initials rather than a pictorial cycle. (2) Paris, BN, fr. 12581. The *Queste* occupies ff. 1–82 of this large thirteenth-century compendium. It is followed by a treatise on falconry; *chansons,* almost all by Thibaut de Navarre; *Li Livre dou Tresor;* a miscellany including some fabliaux and moral and religious works. Each work begins with an often damaged historiated initial. The sole initial in the *Queste* (f. 1), shows someone on foot carrying a javelin who approaches three knights on horseback, a standard type of illustration found in romance texts. (3) Ravenna, Biblioteca Comunale Classense 454. See Pierre Breillat, "*La Quête du Saint Graal* en Italie," *Mélanges d'Archéologie et d'Histoire de l'Ecole Française de Rome,* 54 (1937), p. 279. According to Breillat, this manuscript is "sans peinture et inachevé; on a laissé en blanc la place de toutes les initiales." A fifth manuscript devoted entirely to the *Queste,* (Florence, Laurenziana, Ashburnham 48), a manuscript with a pictorial cycle that orients an ideological reading of the type seen in Ars. 5218, will be discussed further on in the body of my essay.

23. According to Fanni Bogdanow, Frappier and Baumgartner believe that the author of the *Queste* condemns the errors of chivalry rather than chivalry per se. See "An Interpretation of the Meaning and Purpose of the Vulgate *Queste del Saint Graal* in light of the Mystical Theology of St.

Bernard," in *The Changing Face of Arthurian Romance: Essays on Arthurian Prose Romances in Memory of Cedric E. Pickford*, ed. A. Adams, A. Diverres, K. Stern, and K. Varty (Cambridge, 1986), pp. 23–46.

24. In "The *Song of Songs* and Courtly Literature," *Court and Poet*, ed. Glyn S. Burgess (Liverpool: Cairns, 1980), pp. 189–96, Tony Hunt characterizes the three traditions of Songs commentary operative in the Middle Ages: ecclesiological, Mariological, and tropological (the relationship between Christ and the individual soul).

25. Léopold Delisle, *Le Cabinet des manuscrits de la Bibliothèque nationale*, 3 vols. (Paris: Imprimerie Nationale, 1874), vol. 2, pp. 487–92.

26. Entry 62 has a Songs commentary whose author goes unnamed. Entry 2 contains the Biblical text of the *Song of Songs* grouped with two other "libri Salomonis" followed by several other books of the Bible.

27. See Matter's introduction for an explanation of the secondary genre of *Songs* commentary.

28. Norman P. Tanner, *Decrees of the Ecumenical Councils* (text est. by G. Alberigo et al.), 2 vols. (Georgetown: Georgetown Univ. Press, 1990), vol. 1, p. 230.

29. *New Catholic Encyclopedia* (New York: McGraw-Hill, 1967), vol. 14, p. 259.

30. The question of clerical incontinence was taken up in article 14 at the Second Council at Lyons (Tanner, vol. 1, p. 242).

31. (New York: AMS Press, 1966).

32. Anne Llewellyn Barstow, *Married Priests and the Reforming Papacy: The Eleventh-Century Debates* (New York: Mellen Press, 1982), p. 104.

33. See also James A. Brundage, *Law, Sex, and Christian Society in Medieval Europe* (Chicago: Univ. of Chicago Press, 1987) esp. pp. 213–14, 217, 402, 474.

34. Reproduced in Figure 719 of Lilian M.C. Randall, *Images in the Margins of Gothic Manuscripts* (Berkeley: Univ. of California Press, 1966).

35. H.W. Janson, *Apes and Ape Lore in the Middle Ages and the Renaissance* (London: Warburg Institute, 1952). See Janson and Randall for depictions of apes in manuscripts of this period.

36. The imagery of sexual combat appears throughout the marginalia with depictions of butting rams, parodic jousts, and dogs chasing and attacking stags.

37. Madeline H. Caviness, "Patron or Matron? A Capetian Bride and a Vade Mecum for Her Marriage Bed," *Speculum*, 68 (1993) 342. See her n. 46 for references to the negative connotations of riding a ram.

38. On f. 15 the marginalia again depict apes hunting. On the right, a fantastic creature has wings that will be recalled in the angel wings in the miniature on f. 88. On f. 18v an ape pushes a barrow filled with turds that is drawn by another ape.

39. See Jeffrey Hamburger's review of Camille's study in the *Art Bulletin*, 75 (1993), 319–27.

40. My thanks to M. Garetta, Conservateur en Chef de la Bibliothèque de l'Arsenal, for having examined this manuscript with me. The fact that Pierart copied both the *Queste* and the annals, and only these two works could be interpreted as an indication that he planned to bind them together sometime after having started the transcription of the *Queste*. According to Garetta, it is likely that Pierart began the annals before the *Queste* was finished; Pierart probably worked on the two texts concurrently.

41. The following are Middleton's findings on the ruling of the Arsenal manuscript. As for the horizontal ruling in the *Queste*, a pair of lines is found between the top of the page and the beginning of the text. 36 single lines are ruled to carry the text that begins above the top line. Of these, lines 1 (the top line) and 2, 18 and 19, and 35 and 36 are extended to the front edge of page on the recto and verso, although this extension is frequently not visible on the recto. Since the extension is never put to any use in either the *Queste* or the annals, it seems likely that it was either intended to be decorative or the result of a practice designed for some other text. A pair of lines occurs between the bottom of the text and the bottom of the page, which is used for catchwords (found on f. 16v, f. 24v, f. 32v, f. 40v, f. 48v, f. 56v, f. 64v, f. 72v, f. 80v, f. 88v; catchwords are lacking in the annals) and the occasional gloss (found only on f. 95). The vertical ruling is the same on recto and verso but in mirror image. The recto page is ruled vertically with a pair of lines to mark the left-hand edge of the first column, a single line to mark the right-hand edge of column 1, a single line for the left-hand column 2, a pair of lines for the right-hand column 2, a second pair of lines between the edge of column 2 and the edge of the page. The ruling is the same in the annals, except that an additional pair of lines for each column has been added to indicate the year. The unusual (and unnecessary) layout seen in both texts increases the likelihood that both texts were ruled by the same hand. Moreover, in both cases more parchment was prepared than needed; wasted parchment is found at the end of both texts (in the *Queste*, on ff. 92r and v, 93r and v, 94r and v; in the annals, f. 106v, 107r and v, 108r and v).

42. The term *livres* in the colophon probably refers to the entire manuscript book rather than to only the *Queste*. Citing Pierre Gallais, David Hult, *Self-Fulfilling Prophecies: Readership and Authority in the First 'Roman de la Rose'* (Cambridge: Cambridge Univ. Press, 1986), p. 53, maintains: " *livre* refers specifically to the material volume that results from the scribe's work." Pierart's statement that he bound the book should be understood as referring to his *intention* to do so since it is unlikely that he would have copied the *Queste* in an already bound volume.

43. Leopold Delisle, "Chroniques et Annales diverses," *Histoire Littéraire de la France*, 32 (1898), pp. 205–11. I thank Gillette Labory of the Institut de Recherche et d'Histoire des Textes for having indicated this reference to me.

44. The event could also be an indication that the Tournaisians were being punished for their sins, which could have included clerics' departure from

vows of celibacy. The question of clerical marriage is taken up in the entry for 1274, which I shall consider further on in this study.

45. A.J. Bozière, *Tournai, ancien et moderne* (Tournai: Delmée, 1864), p. 387: "Pendant la procession de l'an 1229, 40 personnes moururent étouffées aux abords de la porte Prime."

46. See pp. 177–80 of Bernhard Schimmelpfennig, *The Papacy*, trans. James Sievert (New York: Columbia Univ. Press, 1992), for a description of the deepening French influence on the papacy.

47. One can speculate about possible relationships between the *translatio ecclesiae* evident in the annals and the *translatio* implied by the story of Joseph d'Arimathie and his successors Josephé and Galaad.

48. See also G. Caullet, "Les Manuscrits de Gilles Le Muisit et l'Art de la Miniature au XIVe Siècle. Le Relieur Tournaisien Janvier," *Bulletin du Centre Historique et Archéologique de Courtrai* (1907–1908), 210.

49. Jean-Guy Vaillancourt, *Papal Power: A Study of Vatican Control over Lay Catholic Elites* (Berkeley: Univ. of California Press, 1980), pp. 26–27.

50. Some historians say they were controlled by the French monarchy. For further information on Jeanne de Flandre, see my "Jeanne and Marguerite de Flandre as Female Patrons," *Dalhousie French Studies,* 28 (1994), 15–29.

51. See Kervyn de Lettenhove, *Poésies de Gilles li Muisit,* 2 vols. (Louvain: Lefever, 1882), vol. 1, pp. 299–342.

52. Albert d'Haenens, *L'Abbaye Saint-Martin de Tournai de 1290 à 1350: Origines, Evolution et Dénouement d'une Crise* (Louvain: Publications Universitaires de Louvain, 1961), p. 168, notes that the pope in Avignon designated Jacques Muevin as Gilles's successor in 1353.

53. M. Garetta contends that during this period in Tournai the bishop's crozier was indistinguishable from an abbot's. Whereas the abbot's crozier was usually turned inward to signify that his jurisdiction was limited to his abbey, the bishop or archbishop's crozier was turned outward to imply the greater extent of his power. In Brussels, KB IV 119 Gilles's crozier is turned inward in the miniature on f. 1 of vol. l, but outward in the ones on f. 243 of vol. l and f. 230 of vol. 2.

54. See p. 128 of Antonius Sanderus's seventeenth-century inventory of the monastery library found in the *Bibliotheca Belgica Manuscripta* (1641; Brussels, 1972).

55. For a description of this miniature, see Caullet, p. 223; Caullet reproduces the miniature in plate XII. A similar technique is used to depict Saint Benoît in the miniature illustrating Benoît XII's papal bull on the beatific vision on f. 16 of the *Omne bonum* (London, BL, Royal 6 E.vi), an encyclopedic compendium of canon law compiled in London between 1360 and 1375. The evocation of Saint Benoît in the middle register in the company of Saint Paul shores up the legitimacy of Benoît XII, who with this bull overturned the pronouncements on the beatific vision made by his papal predecessor, Jean XXII (Hamburger, p. 136).

56. The viewer of the manuscript might also be reminded of the analogies between Gilles and another Gregory, Gregory VII, responsible for the institution of the monastic ideal with its emphasis on chastity.

57. D'Haenens, A. "La crise des abbayes bénédictines au Bas Moyen Age: Saint-Martin de Tournai de 1290 à 1350," *Le Moyen Age*, 65 (1959), 75–95.

58. See Decima Douie, "John XXII and the Beatific Vision," *Dominican Studies*, 3 (1950), 154–74, esp. p. 159, in which the author states that different passages of the same church father could be used to support contrary views on the beatific vision.

59. See Breillat, p. 266, for another example in which the story of Joseph d'Arimathie was used to support a historical *translatio*.

60. François Avril, "Une Curieuse Illustration de la Fête-Dieu: L'Iconographie du Christ Prêtre Elevant l'Hostie et sa Diffusion," *Rituels: Mélanges Père Gy*, ed. Paul De Clerck and Eric Palazzo (Paris: Les Editions du Cerf, 1990), p. 39.

61. Although the hand which wrote the gloss is slightly different from that which transcribed the annals, Middleton believes it could be Pierart's. Middleton advances two hypotheses to explain the difference in hand: Pierart added the glosses at a later time or he tried to produce a "gloss hand" that could be distinguished from his "transcription hand" and his "catchword hand."

62. How pertinent that this manuscript, created in the shadow of St.-Martin de Tournai, should end with an entry referring to another Martin who was a generous supporter of the Benedictines! See *The Lives of the Popes in the Middle Ages*, ed. Rev. Horace K. Mann and Johannes Hollnsteiner (St. Louis: Herder, 1932), vol. 16, p. 316.

63. Geneviève Hasenohr, "Gilles le Muisit," *Dictionnaire des Lettres Françaises*, ed. Geneviève Hasenohr and Michel Zink (1964; Paris: Fayard, 1992), p. 541.

64. The following comment, found in the introduction to the annals on f. 95, would seem to indicate that the annalist died in the late thirteenth century when the annals come to an end: "Chi conmencent li an dés le commencement del monde tres chi qu'en *nos temps*" (my emphasis).

65. Cited in Lucien Fourez, "Connaît-on le troisième auteur du *Roman de la Rose* de Tournai?" *Tournay: Reconstruction et Avenir*, 55–56 (1950), 4.

66. See M. Kervyn de Lettenhove, *Guibert de Tournay, Sa Biographie et ses Travaux Historiques* (Bruxelles: Librairie Polytechnique, 1860), pp. 12–13. For descriptions of the life and works of Guibert de Tournai, see Jean Longère, "Guibert de Tournai," *Dictionnaire des Lettres Françaises*, p. 590, J.F. Mullin, "Guibert de Tournai," *New Catholic Encyclopedia*, vol. 6, p. 837, and Pierre Gratien, *Histoire de la Fondation et de l'Evolution de l'Ordre des Frères Mineurs au Treizième Siècle* (Gembloux, Duculot, 1928), pp. 648 and 655.

67. *Dictionnaire de Spiritualité*, 16 vols. (Paris: Beauchesne: 1932–1993), vol. 6 (1967), p. 1141. The English translation is my own.

68. See Jean Dufournet, *Adam de la Halle à la recherche de lui-même ou le jeu dramatique de la Feuillée* (Paris: SEDES, 1974), esp. pp. 266–67, on the problem of bigamy in the nearby town of Arras in the late thirteenth century.

69. Guibert's given name, "de Moriel-Porte," recalls one of the seven gates of Tournai. Bozière mentions the seven French names, omitting the appellations "Kokriel" and "Bordiel" used by the chronicler. "Moriel" may well be the Flemish name for one of the other five portals. In addition to the seven main gates, there were little gates, "wiquettes," and the "portelette des Frères mineurs," Guibert's order.

70. Even though Sanderus does not specifically mention this title, since so many of Guibert's other works appear in his seventeenth-century inventory, we can entertain two possibilities concerning the presence of Guibert's *Tractatus de pace* in St.-Martin's fourteenth-century collection: that the title was unintentionally omitted within the listing of a long compendium, and that the work disappeared from the library between the Middle Ages and the seventeenth century.

71. The prominent motif of the candles held by the two angels enabling the onlookers to witness the Grail liturgy in the miniature on f. 88 recalls Guibert de Tournai's doctrine of illumination. See C. Berubé and S. Gieben, "Guibert de Tournai et Robert Grosseteste, sources inconnues de la doctrine de l'illumination, suivi de l'édition critique de trois chapitres du *Rudimentum doctrinae* de Guibert de Tournai," *S. Bonaventura*, 1274–1974, (Rome: Grottaferrata, 1973), vol. 2, pp. 627–54.

72. In the colophon to Brussels, KB 456–57, Gilles mentions that he commissioned this Latin Bible.

73. My thanks to Richard Rouse for this insight.

74. After having recovered his sight, Gilles refers to himself as having been "illuminé." Kervyn de Lettenhove, ed. *Poésies de Gilles Li Muisis*, 2 vols. (Louvain: Lefever, 1882), vol 2, p. 259.

Fig. 11.1. Paris, Ars. 5218, f. 1.
Reproduced by permission.

Fig. 11.2. Paris, Ars. 5218, f. 10.
Reproduced by permission.

Fig. 11.3. Paris, Ars. 5218, f. 88.
Reproduced by permission.

Fig. 11.4. Paris, Ars. 5218, f. 20.
Reproduced by permission.

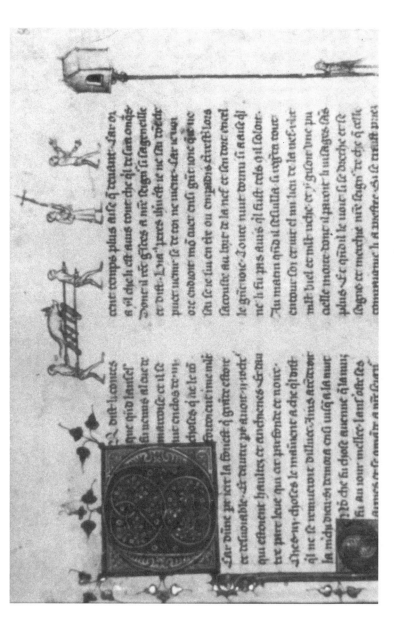

Fig. 11.5. Paris, Ars. 5218, f. 81.
Reproduced by permission.

Fig. 11.6. Paris, Ars. 5218, f. 88.
Reproduced by permission.

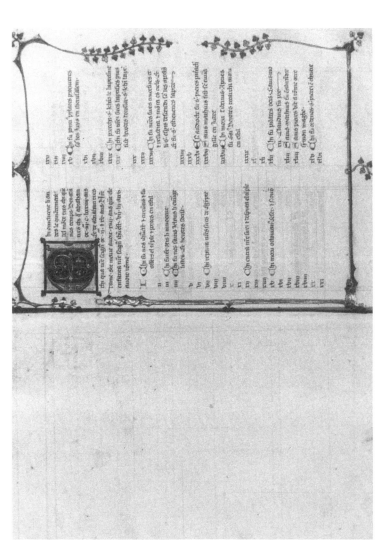

Fig. 11.7. Paris, Ars. 5218, f. 95.
Reproduced by permission.

Fig. 11.8. Kortrijk, Stedelijke Openbare Bibliotheek, Goethals-Vercruysse 135, f. 1. Reproduced by permission.

DATE DUE

Demco, Inc. 38-293